# PAGES FROM
# THE GONCOURT JOURNAL

PAGES FROM

# THE
# GONCOURT
JOURNAL

*Edited, Translated, and Introduced by*
ROBERT BALDICK

Oxford New York
OXFORD UNIVERSITY PRESS
1988

Oxford University Press, Walton Street, Oxford OX2 6DP
Oxford New York Toronto
Delhi Bombay Calcutta Madras Karachi
Petaling Jaya Singapore Hong Kong Tokyo
Nairobi Dar es Salaam Cape Town
Melbourne Auckland
and associated companies in
Berlin Ibadan

Oxford is a trade mark of Oxford University Press

English translation, Introduction, and Selection © Robert Baldick 1962

This English translation is made with the approval of the
copyright owners and of Librairie Flammarion

First published in 1962
First issued as an Oxford University Press paperback 1978
Reprinted 1988

British Library Cataloguing in Publication Data
Goncourt, Edmond de, 1822–1896
Pages from the Goncourt journal.—
(Oxford letters & memoirs).
1. Fiction in French. Goncourt, Edmond de &
Goncourt, Jules de – Correspondence, diaries, etc.
I. Title  II. Goncourt, Jules de, 1830–1870  III. Baldick, Robert
843'.8'09
ISBN 0-19-282192-X

Library of Congress Cataloging in Publication Data

Data available

Printed in Great Britain by
The Guernsey Press Co. Ltd.
Guernsey, Channel Islands

# INTRODUCTION

A diary is the most individual of all forms of literature, and it may seem surprising at first that one of the greatest and most celebrated diaries in the world, the Goncourt *Journal*, should be in part the work of two men. But Edmond and Jules de Goncourt formed a literary partnership which, if not unique in character—in France alone there have been the Rosnys and the Tharauds since—was remarkable for its closeness and intimacy. It was all the more remarkable in that the Goncourt brothers differed in both age and temperament. Edmond, born at Nancy in May 1822, was slow, serious, phlegmatic, very much the responsible elder brother; while Jules, born in Paris in December 1830, was volatile, quick-witted, mischievous, very much the spoilt younger brother. Yet from the point of view of instinct, taste, and sensibility the two men were one. In company Jules would find himself involuntarily smiling and nodding when Edmond smiled and nodded; and in conversation either brother could, at a moment's notice and without the slightest hesitation, pick up and develop the arguments advanced by the other. The two men shared the same likes and dislikes; they shared the same irrational impulses; for a time they even shared the same mistress. And in their work, although Jules was the more expert at composing dialogue—Edmond described him as 'a poet with an extraordinary ear, an eccentric who would spend hours in the Tuileries listening to the babies talking, just for the pleasure of studying the syntax of their childish phrases'—they achieved such a close integration of style that it is impossible to attribute with certainty any particular passage in their writings to one brother.

This astonishing partnership owed its cohesion and duration—for the Goncourts lived and worked together for over twenty years with never more than a few hours apart—not only to the brothers' affection and regard for each other but also to their fear, suspicion, and dislike of the outside world. They were sick men, tortured by their stomachs, their livers, and their nerves; sick men with high ideals, living in a world where everything and everyone wounded their delicate sensibilities or outraged their sense of values. They were also even more convinced than most writers that the critics and the public did not recognize their real worth; and it is true that they were regarded in their lifetime with a certain hostility—partly because of their arrogance and egocentricity, partly because of their loud and irritating complaints of unjust treatment, and also because they possessed the advantages of a noble name, financial independence, and numerical superiority. They might have sought comfort and reassurance in marriage—neither, after all, was insensitive to the charms of the opposite sex, and it was not for nothing that most of their novels and historical works were studies of women—but they were pathetically afraid of women in real life, and refused to sacrifice their tried and trusted partnership to the problematic joys of union with some uncomprehending, philistine female. 'In any marriage', they declared, 'the wife is nearly always the solvent of the husband's honour, using honour in the loftiest, purest sense of the word. She is the adviser who, in the name of material interest, urges the advantages of weakness, of insipidity, of cowardice, of all the miserable little compromises with one's conscience.' As for physical love, they derived little happiness from it. Their earliest sexual experiences had been unfortunate, not to say disastrous—Edmond had been initiated in the sexual rites by a hideous creature 'with a rhomboidal torso fitted with two little arms and two little legs, which, in bed, made her look like a crab on its back'; while Jules, at the age of nineteen, had contracted the syphilis which was to kill him twenty years later—and they once admitted that 'one week of love disgusts us for three months'. Their fear and mistrust of woman was confirmed in 1862, when they discovered that their devoted housekeeper Rose Malingre, who had just died after serving them and their mother for a quarter of a century, had been lying to them, robbing them, and indulging in wild erotic and alcoholic orgies for many years. 'Suspicion of the entire female sex', they wrote, 'has entered into our minds for the rest of our lives: a horror of the duplicity of woman's soul, of her prodigious gift, her consummate genius for mendacity.' Unappreciated by the public, attacked by the press, and plagued by the opposite sex, the two brothers drew closer together in an association which was to be interrupted only by death.

The amount of work which they produced in partnership was impressive, but it may be doubted whether it was the result of a compelling urge to write: Jules once declared that he would have been content to publish one slim volume in the whole of his life, and Edmond often grew weary of their self-imposed task. It was vanity which drove them on: the desire to prove to the whole world that they, the despised aristocratic dilettanti, could work harder and better than their envious Bohemian critics. No doubt it was vanity too which impelled them to try their hands at such a wide variety of genres: drama, art criticism, history, the novel. In each genre they made their mark, but in none did they ever obtain the popular acclaim or the financial reward which they needed to clear them of the stigma of being 'amateurs'. Thus in the theatre, their realistic modern play *Henriette Maréchal* provoked what has been called 'the Battle of *Hernani* of Realism' when it was produced at the Théâtre-Français on 5 December 1865; but it was taken off after a few days for political reasons, and nothing that the Goncourts wrote or had adapted for the stage after that had any great success. In the field of art criticism, they rescued Watteau and other masters of eighteenth-century French art from oblivion in *L'Art du dix-huitième siècle*, a pioneer work which has since become a classic; but published piece-meal as it was in their lifetime, it failed to impress the public, while its authors remained blind to the merits of Impressionism despite the fact that they were trying to achieve the same effects in literature as the Impressionists in painting. Their historical studies, such as *Histoire de la Société française pendant la Révolution* and *La Femme au dix-huitième siècle*, were inspired by a new and fruitful concept of history, using the trivia of everyday life, from dinner menus to dress patterns, to create a vivid picture of the period under examination; but the political historians of their time dismissed these valu-able works as amusing trifles. As for their novels, which they described as 'history which might have taken place' and which were as carefully documented as their historical works, they covered a vast range of social milieux, from the world of journalism in *Charles Demailly* to the artist world in *Manette Salomon*, from the hospital ward in *Sœur Philomène* to the bourgeois drawing-room in *Renée Mauperin*, and by their frank presentation of the various classes and their wealth of clinical detail pointed the way to the modern social novel; but the Goncourts' mannered style, the notorious *écriture artiste*, with its tortured syntax and countless neologisms, alienated the public, and it was their admiring disciple Zola who reaped a

fortune, won a world-wide reputation, and became the leader of the
Naturalist movement in French literature, by copying the methods
exemplified in their *Germinie Lacerteux*, the first realistic novel of
French working-class life. Small wonder, then, that the work which
gave them the greatest pleasure to write was the *Journal* which they
kept from the evening of 2 December 1851 to within a few months
or a few days of their respective deaths.

It is impossible to tell what decided them to embark on this work:
perhaps the temptation to record their impressions of a day which,
by an unfortunate coincidence, was fateful for both themselves and
their country, the day which saw the publication of their first novel,
*En 18 . .*, and the *coup d'état* by which Louis Napoleon seized
power. This first entry set the tone for the entire work, with its two-
fold interest in the authors' own affairs and the affairs of the outside
world; for the impression given by the first edition of the *Journal*—
that the brothers' only reaction to the *coup d'état* was one of annoyance that it should have interfered with their literary début—is a
misleading one, due to the suppression of notes and observations
on the day's events which Edmond apparently thought it ungentle-
manly to publish after the fall of the Second Empire. Starting with
this momentous date in their personal and France's national history,
the Goncourts continued, at first sporadically, then almost every
day, to keep a detailed record of their doings and feelings, their plans
for the future and their memories of the past, tales which had been
told to them and thoughts which had occurred to them, sights they
had seen and people they had met. 'In my *Journal*,' wrote Jules,
speaking for them both, 'I have tried to collect all the interesting
things which are lost in conversation'—a task which the younger
brother, with his sensitive ear and excellent memory, found easy
enough, and which the elder brother, so Flaubert tells us, carried out
with the aid of notes jotted down on his cuff. It has been said that
they wished to imitate Saint-Simon, but that is not strictly true;
they intended to surpass him, for to their gallery of portraits they
meant to add pictures of things and places. Night after night, then,
year after year, coming home to their Rue Saint-Georges flat or to
the Auteuil house they bought in 1868, from dinner at Saint-Gratien
with Princess Mathilde or at the Restaurant Magny with Gautier,
Sainte-Beuve, and Flaubert, they settled down to consign to paper
the harvest of anecdotes, conversations, or impressions which they

had gathered during the day. Jules usually acted as the scribe, with Edmond standing behind him and leaning over his shoulder, so that, as with their novels, it is impossible to attribute any entry to one or the other: even when an anecdote clearly refers to the experiences of one brother, the recording of it may well have been modified by the other, in the process of what Edmond called their 'dual dictation'.

When Jules died, on 20 June 1870, Edmond decided to stop keeping the *Journal*, in which the last entry was dated 19 January 1870; but the compulsion to describe his brother's long death-agony, partly to derive comfort from the memory, partly to pay tribute to the dead man, and partly no doubt out of habit, proved too strong for him. Then came the Franco-Prussian War, the Siege of Paris, and the Commune, and the fascination of recording his impressions of these events enslaved Edmond once more to the *Journal*.

Apart from certain inoffensive extracts which had appeared in 1866 under the title of *Idées et Sensations*, Edmond intended that no part of the *Journal* was to be made public until twenty years after his death, and he did his best to keep the very existence of the work a secret. But in July 1883 he could not resist letting Daudet and his wife into his confidence. 'The Daudets came to lunch today with their children', he wrote. 'I read them a few extracts from my Memoirs; they seemed to be truly amazed by the life of these pages which spoke of the dead past.' Encouraged by their interest, he eventually decided to publish that part of the *Journal* covering the years with Jules, shorn of any passage which might cause offence or lead to litigation. Some extracts were printed in the *Figaro* in 1886, eliciting few compliments but on the contrary some querulous criticism from Princess Mathilde. Nor was the publication of the first volume, in March 1887, a success. The *Figaro* attacked the *Journal* as a masterpiece of conceit; Taine wrote to the author begging him 'not to quote any of his opinions or observations on anything whatever, "earnestly requesting silence on his score" as he does not wish to be compromised by anything that he may have said in the frank expression of his ideas'; and three weeks after publication only two thousand copies had been sold. 'Really,' complained Edmond, 'for a result like that it is not worth risking duels, arousing so much anger, quarrelling with all your remaining relatives, and offending all your acquaintances. . . . But patience! I put my trust in the future.'

The second volume, appearing in October 1887, aroused fresh protests.

> How difficult it is [Edmond wrote] to tell even a millionth part of the truth, and how harshly one is punished for doing so. Never mind, I love the truth, and I am trying to tell it as far as one can in one's lifetime, that is in homeopathic doses. For this truth I could die if need be, as other men die for their country. Do our famous men, our academicians, our members of the Institut really imagine that they are going to be depicted to posterity as little tin gods, without any admixture of humanity whatever? Come now! All these conventional lies and subterfuges will be laid bare one day, sooner or later. . . .

There was little criticism of the third volume, which was published in the spring of 1888, possibly on account of the moving description of Jules's death which it contained; but there was little praise either. Nor was much interest expressed when, after an interval of two years, the fourth volume was serialized in the *Écho de Paris* in the spring and summer of 1890. 'Now and then,' complained Edmond, 'I feel tired of going on with this diary, but on faint-hearted days, when this weariness comes over me, I tell myself that I must have the energy of those who continue writing even in the frozen wastes or in the tropics, for this history of nineteenth-century life, as I am writing it, will really be of considerable interest for later centuries.'

When the fourth volume appeared in book form, however, in October 1890, there was a violent protest from Renan at the revelation of his pro-German remarks at the Café Brébant during the Siege of Paris. Through Jules Huret, whom the *Écho de Paris* sent to interview him, Edmond accepted the accusation that he was 'an indiscreet individual', maintaining that his indiscretions were not about his contemporaries' private lives but about their thoughts and ideas. 'I repeat,' he said, 'that I am not ashamed of what he calls me. For ever since the world began, the only memoirs of any interest have been written by "indiscreet individuals", and my only crime is to be still alive twenty years after these were written—something for which, humanly speaking, I cannot feel any remorse.' And as a parting shot he remarked that 'Monsieur Renan has been so indiscreet about Christ that he really ought to allow a little indiscreetness about himself'.

The fifth volume was published in February 1891, to be greeted by a savage article in the *Figaro* by Robert de Bonnières, an *habitué* of the literary salon, the so-called Grenier, which Edmond had opened in 1885 in two rooms in his house at Auteuil. 'Let him beware,' wrote Bonnières of his sometime host.

For the most part he listens and thinks he can hear, he looks and thinks he can see, and then he imagines he can think, and takes the sort of literary trepidation in which he has been indulging these past fifty years for the free flight of ideas. He has the eyes of a fly, eyes with facets, and, like a fly, he alights on everything but penetrates nothing. . . . Of the literary élite of his age, men such as Gautier, Sainte-Beuve, Taine, Flaubert, the best of their kind, all that he has managed to give us most of the time is a grotesque and often repulsive picture.

Not surprisingly, the sixth volume appeared in February 1892 with a valedictory preface:

For forty years now I have been endeavouring to tell the truth in novels, historical studies, and elsewhere. This misguided passion has stirred up so much hatred and so much anger against me and given rise to such libellous interpretations of my writings, that now that I am old and ailing and anxious for peace of mind, I hand on the task of telling this truth to the younger writers, who have rich blood in their veins and whose limbs are still supple. . . . This volume of the *Journal des Goncourt* is the last that will appear in my lifetime.

Inevitably, however, Edmond soon changed his mind, and in April 1894 the *Écho de Paris* started serializing the seventh volume. This volume called forth immediate criticism from an unexpected quarter: the Daudet family. First Ernest Daudet, Alphonse's brother, protested in a violent letter to Edmond at a reference to their mother; then Alphonse himself, in an embarrassed conversation recorded by Edmond in the *Journal*, 'began by describing the indignation of his fellow southerner Bonnet at my physical portrait of Mistral, told me of hostile articles in the *Débats* and the *Courrier français*, gave me the opinions of our friends, of Geffroy saying that it was "too topical as literature", and mentioned two or three little references to himself which had not hurt him but which he would have preferred not to see in print'. There were cruder, more direct reactions. In June 1894 the *Écho de Paris* forwarded to Edmond a reader's wordless protest: 'an envelope full of soiled rags, anonymous excrement'. And in January 1895 two personal attacks were made on him by the *Figaro* and *La Plume*, the one referring to a Funeral Committee being set up to organize his obsequies and the other criticizing him—for reasons best known to the author of the article—for using the personal pronoun *I* to refer to himself in his memoirs.

Although Edmond took the precaution of showing the Daudets the eighth volume before it was published in May 1895, they remained unsatisfied, regarding their old friend with growing suspicion and lending a credulous ear to Jean Lorrain's assurances that the unpublished part of the *Journal* contained spiteful criticism of them. Saddened by their lack of trust in his loyalty, discouraged by the difficulty he had experienced in finding an editor willing to serialize the ninth volume, and sickened by the fresh attacks which this volume occasioned when it was published on 26 May 1896, his seventy-fourth birthday, Edmond told the Daudets in the course of his annual summer holiday at their Champrosay home that he intended to cease publication of the *Journal*. They expressed delight and relief, telling him that the knowledge that their private conversations would be made public within a matter of months was placing an intolerable strain on their friendship with the old diarist, and attributing his decision to consideration for their feelings. In fact, however, it seems likely that Edmond, having brought the published *Journal* up to the end of 1895, suspected that he would not live long enough to record sufficient material for another volume, let alone another series of three. And indeed, only a few days after telling the Daudets that he was suspending publication of the *Journal*, he died at Champrosay, on 16 July 1896.

In his valedictory preface to the sixth volume of the *Journal*, Edmond had written:

In a diary such as the one I am publishing, the *absolute truth* about the men and women encountered in the course of my long life consists of an *agreeable truth*—to which people have no objection—but one which is nearly always tempered by a *disagreeable truth*—which people will not tolerate under any circumstances. Well, in this last volume, I have tried to the best of my ability to serve up to people, captured in my snapshot photographs, the agreeable truth: the other truth, which will be the absolute truth, will come twenty years after my death. . . .

He entrusted the task of publishing this 'absolute truth' to the Académie Goncourt, a literary academy endowed with his entire fortune and intended to consist of ten writers, who would each receive an annual stipend of six thousand francs and who would award a prize of five thousand francs every year to the author of an outstanding work of fiction. Attacked by a whole succession of journalists who had seen nothing in this project but a desire to rival the Académie française, buy the support of impoverished young writers, and perpetuate the name of Goncourt, and warned by his solicitor that the scheme was legally impracticable, Edmond wrote in March 1893: 'These last few days I have been haunted by the idea of death combined with anxiety as to the fate of my will, which may be annulled like my Academy, and anxiety as to the preservation of the manuscript of my *Journal*. I shall die not knowing what is to become of the two great projects of my life intended to ensure my survival.' His anxiety was justified. First of all there was prolonged litigation over the proposed academy, Edmond's natural heirs maintaining that money could not be bequeathed to a body which had no existence, and it was not until 1903 that the Académie Goncourt was officially constituted. Then, in 1916, when the eleven volumes of the manuscript *Journal* preserved in the Bibliothèque Nationale might legally have been made public, the Académie Goncourt, alarmed at the thought of the libel actions which would have been the certain consequence of publication at that early date, prudently decided that they should not. Only after the Second World War did the *Journal*'s guardians judge that the time was ripe for publication, commissioning Robert Burnand to edit the integral work. Robert Burnand died while still copying out the manuscript, and it was M. Robert Ricatte who took over and completed the arduous task of deciphering the unpublished passages in the manuscript, collating them with the published work, and editing the entire text. Even then the Académie Goncourt's troubles were not over, for Alphonse Daudet's heirs, learning that various unedifying episodes in their ancestor's life were about to come to light, went to law in an attempt to make certain cuts in the manuscript, asserting that the literary ownership of the *Journal* belonged to them, since Alphonse Daudet had been Goncourt's executor: a curious contention in itself, and one weakened by the fact that Goncourt had appointed two executors—Alphonse Daudet and Léon Hennique—and that Hennique's daughter dissociated herself from the cause of Daudet's heirs. The Académie Goncourt finally won their case, and publication of the integral *Journal*—from which the following selection has been made —began in 1956, ending three years later.

It is a fascinating work, in which every reader will have his favourite passages, whether the thumbnail sketches of the humble, the full-length portraits—usually *en pantoufles*—of the great, the conversations with Gautier, Sainte-Beuve, Flaubert, Zola, Degas, Rodin, and a host of other writers and artists, the moving account of Jules's last illness and death, the eye-witness record of life in Paris during the Siege and the Commune, the descriptions of slums, palaces, brothels, drawing-rooms, and studios, the critical judgements on works of art and literature, or the amusing and often scabrous anecdotes about men and women in every class of society. The very defects of the Goncourts' novels—their episodic composition, their gratuitous descriptions, their isolated snippets of dialogue—become virtues in the *Journal*. As for the much criticized *écriture artiste*, it is inconspicuous if not entirely absent, for the Goncourts' *Journal*, like Flaubert's *Correspondance*, was for the most part written late at night, with none of the laborious care and effort which is so evident in the same authors' novels. The criticism most frequently made of the *Journal*, during Edmond's lifetime and since, is that it is inaccurate: it was and is suggested that either the authors deliberately distorted other people's sayings or that with their inability to understand abstract ideas they unwittingly debased the arguments of their intellectual superiors. But Ludovic Halévy has testified that Edmond's record of the discussions at which he was present was extremely accurate, and it should be remembered that the table-talk of intellectuals is not invariably on a high intellectual level. As for the suggestion that the Goncourts practised deliberate distortion, there is no reason to doubt Edmond's emphatic declaration to Jules Huret in 1891, in reply to Renan's complaints of misrepresentation:

I assure you on my honour—and those who know me can testify that they have never heard me tell a lie—that the conversations I have quoted in the four volumes which have so far appeared are as it were shorthand transcripts, reproducing not only the speakers' ideas but more often than not their actual expressions. And I feel certain that every disinterested and perceptive reader will recognize that my desire and ambition have been to depict exactly the men I was portraying, and that not for anything in the world would I have wished to attribute remarks to them which they did not make.

Again, it is sometimes argued that the *Journal* contains an excessive number of malicious anecdotes which the brothers, and Edmond in particular, did not trouble to verify; but it is difficult to see how they could have checked these stories, which in any event are often entertaining and always enlightening—about either their subjects or their authors. For on every page of the *Journal* the authors stand revealed with their many qualities and their still more numerous defects—honest, upright, and independent, arrogant, envious, and spiteful—against a meticulously observed and brilliantly depicted background of the leading events and personalities of their age. Whether it is considered as a monumental autobiography or as a history of social and literary life in Paris in the second half of the nineteenth century, the Goncourt *Journal* is a document of absorbing interest and outstanding importance.

ROBERT BALDICK

# CONTENTS

# PREFACE

This journal is our nightly confession, the confession of two lives never separated in pleasure, in work or in pain, the confession of two twin spirits, two minds receiving from the contact of men and things impressions so alike, so identical, so homogeneous, that this confession may be considered as the effusion of a single ego, of a single *I*.

In this day-to-day autobiography there appear those people whom the accidents of life cast into the path of our existence. We have portrayed these men and women as we saw them on a given day and at a given hour, reverting to them in the course of our journal, displaying them later in a different light, according to the changes and modifications they had undergone, and doing our best not to emulate those compilers of memoirs who present their historic figures all of a piece or paint them in colours grown chill and damp with the recession into the past of their meeting. In a word, our ambition has been to show changing humanity in its *momentary reality*.

Sometimes, I must admit, I wonder whether the changes indicated in people close to us or dear to us were not really due to changes that took place in ourselves. That is certainly possible. We are well aware that we were temperamental, neurotic, unhealthily impressionable creatures, and therefore occasionally unjust. Nevertheless we are sure that, although we may sometimes have expressed ourselves with the injustice of prejudice or the blindness of unreasoning antipathy, we have never consciously lied about those of whom we speak.

What we have tried to do, then, is to bring our contemporaries to life for posterity in a speaking likeness, by means of the vivid stenography of a conversation, the physiological spontaneity of a gesture, those little signs of emotion that reveal a personality, those *imponderabilia* that render the intensity of existence, and, last of all, a touch of that fever which is the mark of the heady life of Paris.

And if, in our constant endeavour to be *true to life* in the recording of every still-warm recollection, hastily set down on paper and not always re-read, our syntax is sometimes happy-go-lucky and not all our words have passports, that is because we have invariably chosen those phrases and expressions which least blunted and *academized* the sharpness of our sensations and the independence of our ideas.

This journal was begun on 2 December 1851, the day on which our first book was put on sale, and the day of Louis-Napoleon's *coup d'état*. The whole manuscript was, so to speak, written by my brother at the dictation of us both, for this was the method we used in writing these memoirs. When my brother died, I considered that our literary work was ended and I decided to seal the journal at the date of 20 January 1870, after the last lines penned by his hand. But then I was seized with the bitter desire to recount to myself the last months and the death of the dear man, and almost immediately afterwards the tragic events of the Siege of Paris and the Commune impelled me to continue this journal, which is still from time to time the confidant of my thoughts.

                                                        EDMOND DE GONCOURT

*Schliersee, August 1872*

# 1851

On the Day of the Last Judgement, when men's souls are led to the Bar by great angels who, during the proceedings, will stand dozing like gendarmes with their chins resting on their white gloves folded on the pommels of their swords, and when God the Father with his long white beard, looking the way members of the Institut paint him in church cupolas, after questioning me about what I have done, questions me about everything to which I have lent the complicity of my eyes, he will doubtless ask me: 'Creature whom I made human and good, have you by any chance seen the bullfight at the Barrière du Combat, with five great famished bulldogs tearing to pieces some poor, thin old donkey incapable of defending itself?' To which I will reply: 'Alas, no, Lord, I have seen something worse than that: I have seen a *coup d'état*.'[1]

'Well, the revolution's happened!'

So spoke our cousin Villedeuil's friend, M. de Blamont—Cousin Blamont, an ex-guardsman who had become a dyed-in-the-wool conservative, asthmatic and apoplectic—as he swept into our bedrooms. With a characteristic gesture he pulled his frock-coat across his belly, as if he were tightening a belt, and took his leave of us to carry the triumphant news from the Notre-Dame-de-Lorette district to the Faubourg Saint-Germain, into the homes of all his half-awake acquaintances.

We jumped out of bed. Trousers, shoes and the rest, and then down to the street! The posters at the corner of the street announced the order and the march. In the middle of our Rue Saint-Georges, troops were occupying the *National* building.

To get to our uncle's house, we went along the Quai de la Cour

---

[1] On 2 December 1851, the anniversary of the Battle of Austerlitz, Louis-Napoleón Bonaparte, who had been elected President of the Second Republic in December 1848, ordered the arrest of the leaders of the Republican and Royalist parties, dissolved the National Assembly, and made himself dictator of France.

des Comptes and the Quai de la Légion d'honneur. A whole regiment was encamped on the embankment, with their arms piled and sausages and flasks of wine littering the benches, feasting in a public and praetorian fashion, drunk from the morning and the night before, and in high spirits. One pile of arms, badly set up by these tipsy warriors, collapsed on the pavement just as we were passing. Fortunately the muskets had not been drinking: they had not been included in the party and did not go off.

I feel sure that *coups d'état* would go much better if there were seats, boxes, and stalls so that one could see what was happening and not miss anything. But this *coup d'état* nearly fell flat; it dared to offend Paris in one of its chief predilections: it annoyed the public. It was played quietly, without any drums or trumpets; it was played quickly, as if it were a curtain-raiser. The audience scarcely had time to take their seats. We spectators were treated in a very offhand manner, and no mistake. Indeed, at the most interesting moments, the supernumeraries actually fired at people at their windows, I mean in the audience; and the worst of it was that they had forgotten to forget to load their muskets. I can assure you that this nearly spoilt everything. Even I, who found the play bad and yet watched patiently, like a well-trained critic, the police kicking men in the chest, the cuirassiers making terrifying charges, pistol in hand, at any cry of 'The Republic for ever!', the poor little wooden barricades that had often been set up single-handed on the boulevard, and the deputies beaten up as they were arrested; even I, I repeat, fearfully watching all this with anger in my heart, swallowing a little anger with a lot of shame, but remaining as silent as a carp, even I came close to booing when, at the end of the Rue Notre-Dame-de-Lorette, a woman walking past me had a bullet put through her dress by the Chasseurs de Vincennes, who were picking off passers-by from the Rue Laffitte.

Among all the posters which, on the Second of December and the following days, covered the walls, announcing the new company, its repertory, its functions, the leading men and the new address of the manager, who had moved from the Élysée to the Tuileries, there was one poster which failed to appear and yet which should have appeared—a fact of which Paris was completely unaware.

Nothing was disturbed by the absence of this poster, neither the order of the elements nor the order of things. Nonetheless it was no ordinary poster, this bill which was to have told the world, in two letters and two figures, of *En 18 . .*, and told France of two more men of letters: Edmond and Jules de Goncourt.

But Republics which want to become Empires, or rather men who have a heap of debts and a star of destiny, care nothing for things like that!

Gerdès's printing-house was surrounded by troops, and he himself was terrified, seeing a resemblance between the title of our novel, *En 18 . .*, and 18 Brumaire.[1] So Gerdès, who happened to be the printer of both the *Revue des Deux Mondes* and *En 18 . .*, threw the bundle of our posters into the fire. The result was that we came out on 5 December without posters—and with cuts in a political chapter: according to our printer, we had made the most dangerous allusions, six months before, to the events which had just taken place.

*En 18 . .* came out, then: that *En 18 . .* which was our first child, and which we had pampered and fondled so much, revising it over and over again for a whole year, an incomplete work, spoilt by certain imitations of Gautier, but original to the point of peculiarity for a first book; a first product of which we have no cause to be ashamed, because it contains in embryo every aspect of our talent and every colour on our palette, still a little too crude and bright. The first word of our sceptical Credo had been spoken, and what is more, spoken as befitted us, with a smile.

Poor *En 18 . .*! What a time it chose to appear! A symphony of words and ideas in the midst of that scramble for office.

One morning, however, Rose[2] happened to bring the *Débats* up for us. Edmond called out to me: Janin, in his eagerly awaited article, his first article after the Second of December, spoke of us, spoke of nothing but us, and spoke to us in every kind of way, with honey and thorns, lashing us with irony and forgiving us with esteem and serious advice, presenting our youthfulness as an excuse and a cause for congratulation. A fantastic hotchpotch of our book and the vaudevilles of the day, of M. de Varin's *Dinde truffée* and the

---

[1] 18 Brumaire (9 November 1799) was the date of the first Napoleon's *coup d'état*.

[2] Rose Malingre, the Goncourts' housekeeper.

*Crapauds immortels* of MM. Clairville and Dumanoir, an article in which he spoke of everything with reference to us and of us with reference to everything. We experienced a joy that filled our breasts; one of those joys that overflow from the moral to the physical, which infuse even the body with gladness; those first literary joys which one never feels again any more than one rediscovers the joys of first love. The joy of one's literary first communion, something which carries you away, which lends wings to your spirit, which keeps your eyes fixed, fascinated but not reading, upon the ugly newsprint in which your name seems to be written in letters of fire and which caresses your gaze as nothing—not even the loveliest *objet d'art*—will ever caress it again.

All that day we did not walk, we ran. We went to thank Janin, who gave us a bluff welcome, saying with a broad smile: 'Well, I'm damned! You look just as I thought you would!'

We dreamt dreams. We built castles in Spain. We already saw ourselves as great men, knighted by Janin with the flat of his pen. Bending over our illusions and pricking up our ears, we waited for the drum-roll of the newspapers. And along came an article in the *Revue des Deux Mondes*, fierce, ferocious, well-nigh ill-mannered, signed Pontmartin, which angrily rejected us out of hand, put dunces' caps on our heads, and dismissed us as 'smoke-room pedants'. 'At least,' we told each other, 'we aren't going to have any lukewarm enemies.'

In the end, when we settled our accounts with Dumineray, the only publisher in Paris who had dared to stock our poor book with the city under martial law, we found that we had sold sixty copies.

# 1852

*L'Éclair*, 'a Weekly Review of Literature, the Theatre, and the Arts', made its first appearance on 12 January 1852.[1]

And here we are, playing at publishing. Our review has an office on the ground floor of a building in the Rue d'Aumale, a street which has scarcely been finished. It has a manager, who is paid five francs for every signature: Pouthier, a Bohemian painter and a school friend of Edmond's. It carries free advertisements and even promises free gifts: Villedeuil, who brings to his business methods something of his extravagant style of dress, something of those watch-chains and velvet waistcoats which make him look like a boarding-house prince, thought up the idea of offering a ball as a free gift to his subscribers. In short, it is a review that wants for nothing—except subscribers.

We spend two or three hours a week in that office, waiting, every time we hear footsteps in that new street where there are few passers-by, for a subscription, the public, some colleagues. Nothing comes in, not even any copy, which is incredible, and not even a poet, which is even more of a miracle.

We bravely go on publishing our review in a vacuum, with an apostle's faith and a shareholder's illusions. Villedeuil was obliged to sell a collection of the *Decrees of the Kings of France* to eke out its existence; then he dug up a money-lender whom he persuaded to fork out five or six thousand francs. It made no difference. The world went on ignoring us. Our painter-manager was followed by a manager called Cahu, a fellow as fantastic as his name, who has a bookshop near the Sorbonne and is a member of the Academy of Avranches; then by another manager who looks like a pair of nut-crackers, an old army man with a nervous tic which makes him glance constantly at the place where his epaulettes should be and

---

[1] Founded by Pierre-Charles, Comte de Villedeuil, a young cousin of the Goncourts, *L'Éclair* disappeared on 15 March 1853 after 61 issues.

spit over his shoulder. I mentioned Gavarni's name to Villedeuil; he caught fire, and now the review is illustrated with Gavarni lithographs.

Thinking of his subscribers' ball, Villedeuil had accepted a job-lot of two hundred bottles of champagne as part of the loan from his money-lender: the wine started going bad, and so it was decided to turn the ball into a private party at the office. All the *Éclair's* acquaintances were invited: this added up to Pouthier, an architect, a picture-dealer, a few other nondescript individuals asked along on the spur of the moment, a couple of tarts picked up in a dance-hall—and Nadar, who had just begun a series of caricatures for our review, and who took it into his head to open the ground-floor shutters and invite the passers-by in to help get rid of the champagne.

When Gavarni and Balzac travelled to Bourg together, the latter, in order to make the postilions drive faster—his special mania—said to them at every posting-house: 'Hurry up, now. This gentleman earns fifty francs a day and I earn a hundred, so you can see that every minute you make us lose . . .', and the figure went up at every halt.

At Bourg, Gavarni had to keep a close watch on Balzac. 'Now look here,' he said to him, 'this is a serious business. You really must behave yourself during the few days we are here.' He had to tie Balzac's cravats and tidy him up. Once Gavarni had to go out, and Balzac escaped for an hour or two. Gavarni found him in the square. He had button-holed the Prefect and was telling him how little girls amuse themselves in boarding-schools.

One day Gavarni told him: 'My dear Balzac, what you need is a friend to wash you, clean you up, and dress you.' To which Balzac replied: 'If I had a friend like that, I'd pass him on to posterity.'

'Gentlemen,' Nodier said one day, getting rather heated at the end of a dinner, 'to give you some idea of the corruption of the Government, Monsieur Lainé, who is said to be the most virtuous of all the Ministers, sent us a five-hundred-franc note on New Year's Day to get a favourable article in our papers.'

'Did you send it back?' asked M. Leprévost.
'No,' replied Nodier, 'but I wrote an article against him.'


Argument between Mme Sand and Clésinger:[1]
Mme Sand: 'I'll publish an account of your behaviour.'
Clésinger: 'Then I'll do a carving of your backside. And every-body'll recognize it.'

*August*

I found Janin as gay and cheerful as ever, in spite of his gout. 'When they came to take my grandfather to the guillotine', he said, 'he had the gout in both feet. In any case, I'm not complaining: they say it gives you another ten years of life. I've never been ill, and', he added with a smile, 'I still have what it takes to be a man.'

A little actress from the Français, whose name I do not know, having asked him if he had seen a certain play, 'What!' he shouted, sitting up with a jerk, 'you mean to say you haven't read my notice?' Whereupon he terrified her with the assurance that she would never 'arrive' unless she read everything he wrote, unless she kept abreast of literature, unless she followed the example of Talma and Mlle Mars and never missed an important notice. The poor little actress made a big act of contrition.


De Lurde and Siméon, another important government official, were talking together very seriously. Somebody who had inter-rupted them said: 'You are busy, I'll leave you.' 'Yes', he was told. 'We were discussing whether one should wear one's decorations on a visit to a brothel or not. I say one shouldn't; Siméon says one should. He says that if you do, they give you women who haven't got the pox.'

*November*

We are supping out a great deal this year: mad suppers where they serve mulled wine made from Léoville and peaches *à la Condé*

[1] George Sand and her son-in-law, the sculptor Auguste Clésinger.

costing 72 francs the dish, in the company of trollops picked up at
Mabille and shopsoiled sluts who nibble at these feasts with a bit of
the sausage they had for dinner stuck in their teeth. One of them
once exclaimed naïvely: 'Why, it's four o'clock. . . . Ma's just peeling
her carrots.' We make them drunk, and strip the animal that lives
inside a silk dress. Villedeuil, with his bills forever falling due the
next day, spends nearly every night drowning his banknotes in an
orgy.

Mournful festivities, always haunted by ill-luck.

The other day, or rather the other night—it was four o'clock in
the morning—we were in Room No. 7 at the Maison d'Or, a room
with the wall-panels edged with strips of gilded wood, and decorated
with big flowers in bright red and white and broad leaves in relief
imitating Coromandel lacquer. On the red velvet sofa a red-haired
woman was sprawled on her belly, a street-walker called Sabine
with something of the she-wolf, the lioness, and the cow about her,
wearing neither a corset nor a dress, her breasts bare and her chemise
hitched up above her knees. There was a basket of fruit standing
untouched on the mantelpiece.

Now and then she uttered the cries of a drunken woman, her eyes
red, her lips feverish. Then she would swear, grind her teeth, and
try to bite; I raised her head whenever she let it fall. She vomited,
swearing all the while.

In the meantime Charles was weeping on Edmond's shoulder,
saying: 'Louise! I love her! I love her!' He was talking about La
Rouvroy. There was some sort of coolness between them at this
time. She was giving him the cold shoulder to get some more money
out of him. The tart kept sitting up to watch him crying and in between hiccoughs she said to him: 'Cry, that's right, cry, Monsieur le
Comte, I like to see a good cry! She doesn't love you! She'll never
love you! Go on, Charles, you can cry better than that. And then,
with a thousand-franc note . . . Or take her two thousand-franc
notes!' As for myself, I kept pouring the names of all her lovers over
his head, like so much cold water.

'Come now,' said Edmond, 'dammit all, forget about that bitch
and let's go to the brothel. La Rouvroy doesn't love you, it's time
somebody told you that to your face. She's making a fool of you.
Why, the other day I felt positively indignant: you send her your
carriage to cart her family to the theatre, you go to see her in the

box you have taken for her, and she fobs you off with a few words. . . . You are a laughing-stock at her theatre. They know she can do what she likes with you.'

'I've bought her twelve hundred francs' worth of jewels', said Charles, and great tears trickled down one by one on to his big black beard.

'Oh, get along with you! You're young, you've got a review, a carriage and a theatre, and one day you'll have an income of eighty thousand francs a year. Why, with all that, I'd walk on a woman as if she were a pavement!'

The tart started vomiting again. Edmond, sitting opposite with his chin in his hands, seemed to be looking into Villedeuil's future. Villedeuil, his long hair falling into his red eyes, was sobbing and kissing a miniature of La Rouvroy. I threw some iced water over the tart's head.

And the crossing-sweepers on the boulevard below, raising their eyes, envied all the pleasure which seemed to shine in the fading light of the candles in Room No. 7.

# 1853

Céleste Laveneur told me that when she threw herself into the Gironde, she had spent the whole night until four o'clock in the morning walking along the river-bank, wanting to go home; but her *amour-propre* prevented her, and the fear of being laughed at. The river-bed sloped: she went in step by step and when she was up to her knees in water, she was carried away: she did not lose consciousness, and she was perfectly aware of her head bumping against a cable and her hair spreading out around her. And when she heard a dog jump into the water, the only thing that worried her was that it might get hold of her in a tender spot.

She also told me that one day, leaving the house of a lover who had thrown her out and whom she adored, she said to the cab-driver who had brought her: 'Take me to a brothel.' And he retorted coldly: 'Which one?'

*Sunday, 20 February*

One day towards the end of December Villedeuil came in from the Ministry of Police and said in a fifth-act voice:

'The paper is being prosecuted. Two articles are concerned. One is by Karr. The other is an article with some verse in it. Who put some verse into an article this month?'

'We did', we said.

'So it's you? That's just wonderful!'

This was the pretext for the prosecution which was going to land us in police court, where we should be accused and doubtless convicted of an offence against public morality by an authority whose judgement alone would be published, mentioning the category of our offence in terms barely sufficient to distinguish us from a homosexual or an Ignorantine friar guilty of playing with little boys.

In the issue of 15 December we had published an article entitled: 'Journey from No. 43, Rue Saint-Georges to No. 1, Rue Laffitte', a journey in the Sterne manner from our street to the offices of the paper, in which we described in whimsical fashion the workshops, the dispensaries of weird products, the picture-dealers and the curiosity shops that lay along the route, and among others the shop of a woman who had once been well known as a painters' model. Into our account of this journey we had inserted—without giving the names—the story of a Diaz nude sent by Nathalie to Rachel and returned by her to Nathalie, who had taken her revenge on Rachel's assumed modesty with a letter. The two letters involved now belonged to Janin, who kept them in a copy of *Gabrielle*. And in connexion with the Diaz we had quoted these lines by Tahureau:

> Croisant ses beaux membres nus
> Sur son Adonis, qu'elle baise,
> Et lui pressant le doux flanc,
> Son cou douillettement blanc
> Mordille de trop grand aise.

It was for the quotation of these five lines that the law of our country was calling us to account and was going to punish us.

But behind this incredible, puerile pretext for the prosecution there were hidden reasons. There were underhand intrigues, secret instructions from the powers-that-be to the judges, the hand of the Ministry of Police, the spite of civil servants, the suspicion of departmental heads, the literary opinions of a ministry, perhaps even the vengeance of an actress: all the things which, in a Byzantine Empire, bring the storm-clouds down on a decent man's head.

We were summoned to appear in the police court on 2 February, before the Sixth Chamber. It was the chamber for this sort of affair, a chamber known for its loyalty and which had proved itself. Its complaisance had won it the honour of specializing in press trials and political convictions.

The Saturday of our trial arrived. Villedeuil took us to the Palace of Justice in his yellow barouche, a barouche which was part Louis XIV state-coach and part hospital trolley. Never had such a splendid carriage borne men to a police court. Villedeuil himself, for whom this trial was a wonderful opportunity for theatrical exhibitionism had had a prodigious box-coat made for the occasion, a dark box-coat with five capes, such as you see emigrant aristocrats wearing as they step down from their coaches in melodramas at the Ambigu. It was a fantastic sight, the arrival at the iron gates of that bearded man in his box-coat stepping out of that golden carriage: like a melodrama stepping out of a fairy-story. The usher at the courtroom door tried to prevent him from entering. 'But', exclaimed Villedeuil, 'I am the proprietor of the paper!' At that moment he would have given a great deal to be prosecuted himself.

Finally our case came up. The presiding judge said: 'Take your places on the bench', thus producing a certain impression on the public. For the bench was the bench for thieves and gendarmes. Never in any press trial, even at the Assizes, had a journalist been required to sit on the bench: he remained beside his lawyer. But we were to be spared nothing. 'I gather from a lawyer that there was a rehearsal yesterday', Karr said to me as he sat down with us between the gendarmes. 'We haven't a hope. I know the presiding judge too: I've had the misfortune to sleep with his wife. He was specially picked.'

My lawyer behaved just as we had expected: he represented us as a couple of decent young men, citing as a commendable trait of character the fact that we had had an old housekeeper for twenty years: a patriarchal speech which however, for just a moment, in the face of that fantastic accusation, rose to the occasion like a goose taking wing. We could feel that the public was impressed; we could sense that murmur of a case won in the body of the court, that conspiracy of the spectators' opinions which sets itself against a conviction. A conviction was impossible after those speeches. The court postponed the case for a week. 'That's it', we said. 'They want to pass sentence on us at the beginning of the hearing. Today they didn't dare.'

However, this postponement of the case was our salvation. In the intervening week there was a change of Public Prosecutor. Royer was succeeded by Rouland, who still had Orleanist connexions at the time. He was a relative of Janin's wife, who spoke to him on our behalf. And there were still links between him and the Passy family, who also argued our case warmly to him.

We returned a week later. The verdict in our case was postponed to the end of the hearing. We went to lunch with Karr, resigned and hopeless, in the Place du Palais-de-Justice. We came back to the courtroom. We stood up to hear the verdict and were uncommonly surprised to hear Legonidec announce that we were acquitted but admonished.

# 1854

All this winter we have been slaving away at our *Histoire de la Société française pendant la Révolution*. We carried off four hundred pamphlets at one fell swoop from the home of M. Perrot, a poor little man who lives in the Rue des Martyrs and who collects rare pamphlets, sometimes pawning his watch—a silver watch—to pay for them. We go through these pamphlets all day long and write our book at night. We have given away our old evening clothes and have had no new ones made, so as to be unable to go anywhere. No women, no pleasures, no amusements; just unceasing toil and brain-fag. To get a little exercise and avoid falling ill, we allow ourselves just a stroll after dinner, a stroll in the dark along the outer boulevards, where nothing can distract us from our work and our spiritual absorption in our labours.

*Undated*

Prayer of my cousin Villedeuil:
'O Lord, let my urine be less cloudy, let the little flies stop stinging me in the backside, let me live long enough to make another hundred thousand francs, let the Emperor stay in power so that my dividends may increase, and let the rise in Anzin Coal shares be maintained.'

His housekeeper used to read this out to him every night, and he would repeat it with his hands clasped together.

Grotesque and sinister, isn't it? And yet, fundamentally, what is it but Prayer, crude and simple?

M. Hiltbrunner, the manager of the Théâtre des Délassements, said one day to the architect Chabouillet:
'Monsieur, my theatre is a brothel!'

'Oh, come now, Monsieur!'

'No, I mean it. It's all very simple. I pay my actresses only fifty or sixty francs a month. My rent is thirty thousand francs a year, so I can't give them any more. My actors don't get much more than that, and they're all pimps and fairies. Often one of the women comes to see me and tells me that fifty francs isn't enough, and that she'll have to start picking men up in the audience at five sous a time. . . . But there's nothing I can do about it: my rent is thirty thousand francs a year.'

*End of August*

We went to spend a month sea-bathing at Sainte-Adresse, near Le Havre, staying at the Château-Vert. There, Asseline, a journalist on the *Mousquetaire*, introduced me to a young man called Turcas, a grandson of Cherubini, who gambled and won on the Stock Exchange. This Turcas was cordiality itself. He was chubby, gay, and charming. His mania was hospitality. Two days after meeting us he had practically forced us to take all our meals with him. It was a sweet, charming, lazy life, as calm as the sea, the life that he led and that we led with him. He had a little house, a little garden, a mistress who was none other than the tall, beautiful Brassine of the Théâtre du Palais-Royal, two or three rowing-boats which we would take out to sea, and a wooden bathing-hut on the beach where we played all sorts of games and smoked and chatted. Delicious hours of idleness. The sea beside us shone brightly and lulled us to sleep. Lunch led to dinner. There was no end to the nightcaps we drank. Turcas offered us a comfortable sort of hospitality; generous but uncomplicated, with something English about it. He had got rid of all the trimmings, without sacrificing anything in the way of quality.

A friend on the Stock Exchange had asked him to look after his mistress while he was away: an actress like Brassine, an actress at the Folies-Dramatiques called Dubuisson. She was what they call in a certain slang a vamp. She was a little thing that nibbled you like a kitten and teased you like a street-arab: a pretty, exasperating little animal. We had both of us got caught up in this game, and we were engaged in a teasing war when, one evening, as I was on my way home from Turcas's—it was eleven o'clock and her hotel was shut —she appeared on her balcony in a white dressing-gown. I was with Asseline, who was paying strenuous court to her: laughing, we started climbing the trellis which went up to her window. Asseline gave up before long: the trellis was not very safe. But I, once I had started, went on very earnestly. There was in me a desire for that woman up there which had come upon me in a flash. She stood there laughing and pretending to scold me. This went on for a few seconds—a few seconds during which someone inside me loved that woman, wanted her, aspired to her as one would long for a star in the sky. I climbed up as nimbly and feverishly as a madman and as automatically as a sleepwalker, drawn into the orbit of that white dressing-gown. Finally I got to the top and jumped on to the balcony: I had been in love for a distance of fifteen feet. I am convinced that I shall never be in love in all my life except in fits and starts like that. It rises, takes you by the throat and delights you: a paradise that comes and goes.

I spent the night with that woman, who said to me: 'You are funny! You look like a little boy staring at a jam sandwich.' But I had already sobered up: I was afraid that she might ask me, the next morning, for a little marmoset I had bought during the day at Le Havre. It seemed to me that she was bound to like monkeys.

That night was like the stripping of a soul. There were tears mingled with her lewdness. She told me the story of her life, a thousand sad, sinister things which she would suddenly interrupt with a ʒut! that seemed to drink up her tears. She asked me whether I knew her lover. 'When you meet him, you'll feel sorry for me!' In that little urchin's skin, I seemed to see a sad, thoughtful, dreamy figure drawn on the back of a theatre poster. After each bout of love-making, her heart went tick-tock like a clock in a village inn: a grim sound, the sound of pleasure tolling the death-knell. 'Oh, I know perfectly well', she told me, 'that if I lived a fast life for six months, it would be the death of me. With a chest like mine I'm bound to die young. If I started going out to supper every night, it wouldn't take long.'

# 1855

From the heights of pleasure we have fallen back into the depths of boredom. We are badly organized and easily tired. One week of love disgusts us for three months, and we come out of it spiritually sick and physically weary, dead to desire and filled with a vague, ineffable, infinite sadness. Our minds and bodies have mornings-after of an indescribable greyness, when life seems as flat as bad wine. After a little ardour and enthusiasm, an immense satiety comes over us. Nothing but ash is left to us of the fruit we have squeezed. We despair of ever feeling desire again, suffering from a moral indigestion brought on by debauchery. Everything stinks in our hearts and we are cured for a long time to come of any inclination to lead an active life. Sated and surfeited with things physical, we come away from those beds after those sleepless nights as if they were so many museums of anatomical specimens, and heaven knows what ghastly surgical memories we retain of those lovely bodies.

*2 September*
Between the Belvedere Apollo and a legless cripple there is not half the distance there is between two minds, at one end of the ladder and the other.

*3 September*
Savagery is necessary every four or five hundred years in order to bring the world back to life. Otherwise the world would. die of civilization. When bellies were full and men had lost the power of making love, hordes of barbarians six foot tall would sweep down upon them from the north. Now that there are no savages left, it is the workers who will be doing the job in fifty years or so. And they will call it the social revolution.

A conversation about woman, after a couple of tankards of beer at Binding's. Woman is an evil, stupid animal unless she is educated and civilized to a high degree. She is incapable of dreaming, thinking, or loving. Poetry in a woman is never natural but always a product of education. Only the woman of the world is a woman; the rest are females.

Inferiority of the feminine mind to the masculine mind. All the physical beauty, all the strength, and all the development of a woman is concentrated in and as it were directed towards the central and lower parts of the body: the pelvis, the buttocks, the thighs; the beauty of a man is to be found in the upper, nobler parts, the pectoral muscles, the broad shoulders, the high forehead. Venus has a narrow forehead. Dürer's *Three Graces* have flat heads at the back and little shoulders; only their hips are big and beautiful. As regards the inferiority of the feminine mind, consider the self-assurance of a woman, even when she is only a girl, which allows her to be extremely witty with nothing but a little vivacity and a touch of spontaneity. Only man is endowed with the modesty and timidity which woman lacks and which she uses only as weapons.

Woman: the most beautiful and most admirable of laying machines.

# 1856

When Murger wrote *La Vie de Bohème*, he had no idea that he was writing the history of something which was to become a power within five or six years—and yet this is what has happened. At the present moment, the world of petty journalism, the freemasonry of publicity, reigns and governs and bars the way to any gentleman. He is called an *amateur*, and with that word he is killed. He may have the learning of a Benedictine or the imagination of a Heine behind him, it makes no difference; he is still called an amateur by the dreary, untalented hacks in Villemessant's pay. Nobody realizes it, but this is socialism dominating literature and firing broadsides at the literary capital. And yet the Romantic movement of 1830 was led by men such as Hugo who were nearly all comfortably off.

*1 July*

Coming back from the country during the day, we dined this evening at the Restaurant de la Terrasse, a pot-house decorated with gilt trelliswork. The setting sun shed a golden light on the big, gilded placards over the Passage des Panoramas. Never were my heart and eyes gladdened more than by the sight of that slice of plaster covered with huge letters, scribbled on and dirtied and reeking wonderfully of Paris. Everything is man-made here, except for a stunted tree growing out of a crack in the asphalt—and these ugly walls appeal to me as Nature never does. The modern generations are too civilized, too advanced, too corrupt, too learned, and too sophisticated to find happiness in a little green and blue.

*16 July*

After reading Edgar Allan Poe. Something the critics have not noticed: a new literary world, pointing to the literature of the

twentieth century. Scientific miracles, fables on the pattern A + B;
a clear-sighted, sickly literature. No more poetry, but analytic
fantasy. Something monomaniacal. Things playing a more important part than people; love giving way to deductions and other
sources of ideas, style, subject, and interest; the basis of the novel
transferred from the heart to the head, from the passion to the
idea, from the drama to the denouement.


*A Saturday in July*

Just past the École Militaire, a shop-front with white curtains.
Another storey upstairs and a large number over the door. The Big
9. A large room lighted from above by the wan daylight. Some
tables and a bar lined with bottles of liquor. There are Zouaves,
soldiers, and workmen in smocks and grey hats sitting at the tables
with tarts perched on their knees. The girls wear white or coloured
blouses and dark skirts. They are young and pretty, with pink
fingernails and their hair carefully dressed with little ornaments in
it. Smoking cigarettes and drawing on a friend's Maryland, they walk
up and down in pairs between the tables, playfully jostling each
other, or else they sit playing draughts. Singers turn up now and
then to sing some filthy ditty in a bass voice. The waiters have
big black moustaches. The girls call the pimp who runs the establishment 'the old marquis'. A negress goes by in a sleeveless
dress.

On the first floor, there is a long corridor with a lot of tiny cells
just big enough to contain a little window with broken blinds, a bed,
a chest of drawers, and, on the floor, the inevitable basin and jug of
water. On the wall there is one of those coloured pictures entitled
*Spring* or *Summer* that you win at a fair, and, hanging from a mirror,
a little Zouave doll.

These twenty-sou women are not at all like the terrifying creatures drawn by Constantin Guys, but poor little things trying to ape
the language and dress of the higher-class prostitutes.


*1 August*

Pouthier's mother, reproaching her son for having neither a job
nor a career nor a means of earning his living, finished her maternal

sermon with this admirable comment: 'Why, at your age I was already a mother!'

How Musset came to write *Louison*:

Meeting him one day in the foyer at the Théâtre-Français, Augustine Brohan said to him:

'Monsieur de Musset, why don't you write any more of those delightful little plays of yours?'

'My rooms are too filthy. Brushes everywhere. Impossible to work. Too dirty.'

'But what if you were installed in a pretty, tidy apartment?'

'Oh, that would be splendid! No combs lying around. One room, two rooms, three rooms. . . .'

Brohan offered him her home. As soon as Musset arrived, he said:

'I haven't any cigars! You know, if I go out now . . . I'd rather start straight away.'

Brohan sent out for a couple of boxes of cigars. At lunch-time Musset said:

'I must go and have lunch now. And then I shall have a few drinks with friends of mine. Oh, it's impossible! A whole day wasted!'

'No, you'll eat here', said Brohan.

'If you insist.'

Evening came.

'Look, if I go home now, I shall go to bed late and get up heaven knows when.'

'Well then, I'll have a bed made up for you.'

'A bed? Oh no, please don't. You see, I'd rather sleep with you.'

'Oh!'

'Really I would!'

'Very well, then.'

The play was written in a few days and copied out. Whereupon Musset said to Brohan:

'A ribbon! I must have a ribbon, one of your ribbons, look, that one! You see, I've a habit of tying up my manuscripts with a silk favour. It's a stupid fancy, but there it is. . . .'

Brohan gave him the ribbon . . . and Musset rushed off to give the play to her rival Anaïs.

'What are you acting in now?' Banville asked Laferrière one day. 'Oh, my dear fellow, an impossible play. A play in which there are two suitors, one called Tisserant and the other Laferrière, and a girl who can't decide between them. Now can you imagine a girl being unable to decide between Tisserant—an old man—and Laferrière? My dear chap,' putting his hands on Banville's shoulders, 'there's no interest in it. The public knows whom she's going to choose: Laferrière, dammit. No, there's no interest in it. . . .'

*14 October*

Time cures one of everything—even of living.

# 1857

The offices of *L'Artiste*. Gautier, heavy of face, with all his features sagging, his lines thickening, a sleepy countenance, a mind drowned in a barrel of matter, the lassitude of a hippopotamus with intermittent flashes of understanding: a man deaf to new ideas, with aural hallucinations which make him listen over his shoulder when someone speaks to him face to face.

Today he kept repeating something which Flaubert had said to him this morning, the supreme formula of his School, which he said he longed to write on every wall: *The idea springs from the form.*

His toady, a stockbroker who is mad about Egypt and always turning up with some plaster cast of Egyptian basalt under his arm, a serious fellow full of serious talk, was explaining to all and sundry his working schedule: he goes to bed at eight in the evening, gets up at three in the morning, drinks two cups of black coffee and works till eleven.

Gautier, coming to life like a ruminant emerging from its digestion, and interrupting Feydeau, said:

'Oh, that would drive me mad! What wakes me up in the morning is dreaming that I'm hungry. I see red meat, tables groaning with food, whole wedding banquets. The meat gets me out of bed. When I've had breakfast, I smoke. I get up at half-past seven, and all this takes me to eleven. Then I drag up an armchair and put paper, pen, and ink on my table—or rather, my rack, because writing bores me. It has always bored me, and then it's so futile! . . . Well, I set to work and write at a steady rate like a public scribe. I don't go fast—he's seen me write—but I keep going because, you see, I don't aim at perfection. Whether it's an article or a page, I write it as it comes. It's like a child: either you've made it or you haven't. I never think about what I'm going to write. I pick up my pen and I write. I'm a man of letters and I'm supposed to know my job. So there I am in front of my paper, like an acrobat in front of his springboard. And then, I've got my syntax very tidily arranged in my head. I throw my sentences into the air, like so many cats, and I know that they'll fall on their feet. It's all very simple: all you need is a good grasp of syntax. I could guarantee to teach anybody how to write. I could start a course in article-writing in twenty-five lessons. Why, look at my copy: not a single word crossed out. . . . Hullo, Gaiffe! What, no copy?'

'My dear fellow, it's a queer thing, but I've lost all my talent. I know it by the fact that the silliest things amuse me nowadays. It's ridiculous, I know, but I can't help it: it makes me laugh.'

'Yet you used to be so *talentuous*.'

'All I want to do now is roll about with women.'

'Gaiffe, why don't you take to drink?'

'Oh, if he started drinking . . .'

'Have you got blue fibrils in your nose yet?'

'No, thank you. And if I drank, I should have rubies in my nose, let alone blue fibrils. The ladies wouldn't love me any more and I should have to fall back on twenty-sou women. I should become abject and repugnant . . . and then I should catch the pox.'

*7 January*

There has never been an age so full of humbug. Humbug everywhere, even in science. For years now the scientists have been promising us every morning a new miracle, a new element, a new metal, guaranteeing to warm us with copper discs immersed in water, to feed us with nothing, to kill us at no expense whatever and on a grand scale, to keep us alive indefinitely, to make iron out of heaven knows what. And all this fantastic, scientific humbugging leads to membership of the Institut, to decorations, to influence, to stipends, to the respect of serious people. In the meantime the cost of living rises, doubles, trebles; there is a shortage of raw materials; even death makes no progress—as we saw at Sebastopol, where men cut each other to ribbons—and the cheapest goods are still the worst goods in the world.

*20 January*

As we were talking in the offices of *L'Artiste* about Flaubert, who, like ourselves, is being dragged into the police court,[1] and I was explaining that the powers that be wanted to kill off Romanticism, which had become high treason, Gautier broke in:

'You know, I really blush for my profession. For the paltry sums which I have to earn because otherwise I should starve to death, I say only half or a quarter of what I think—and even then I risk being hauled into court with every sentence that I write.'

*8 February*

Louis said to me today:
'I think I can get hold of some documents on Boucher for you.'
'Ah! How?'
'Through his granddaughter.'
'You know her, then?'
'No, but at Mme Dailly's I met a doctor who's treating her for a disease, you know . . . and she has given him two pastels by Boucher which had been found in the house where he died, at Château-Thierry. . . . She's a prostitute.'

Boucher's granddaughter a whore! It must have been in his blood!

*6 April*

Why did we not write, day by day, at the beginning of our career, an account of that hard and horrible struggle against anonymity, that Passion with abuse at every station of the cross, that public sought after and forever slipping through our fingers, that future towards which we marched with resignation but often also in despair, that fight of impatient and feverish will against time and seniority, one of the great privileges of literature. No friends, no connexions, every door shut in our face, and our money all spent on books. That conspiracy of silence so well organized against all those beginners who want to eat of the cake of publicity; that sadness and weariness that comes from rolling the rock of Sisyphus for years on end. That monotonous, uneventful spiritual agony, written down while it was happening, would have made an interesting and

[1] Flaubert had been charged with offending public morals with the publication of *Madame Bovary* in the *Revue de Paris*, and summoned to appear before the same court which had tried the Goncourt brothers in February 1853.

instructive page of our lives; a page which nobody can write from memory because a little success, the discovery of a publisher, the earning of a few hundred francs and the smell of a little incense cure one so quickly of the past and banish it so far away. A ray of sunshine today is enough to heal the sores and wounds of yesterday. A little climb wipes out the memory of that dreadful, drawn-out Golgotha, those choked-back tears, those mute and hidden sorrows.

*7 April*

Rose has just seen in the concierge's lodge the night-clothes—or morning-clothes if you prefer—that our neighbour La Deslions sends by her maid to the house of the man to whom she is giving a night. It seems that she has a different outfit for each of her lovers in the colour that he prefers. This one consists of a white satin dressing-gown, quilted and pinked, with gold-embroidered slippers in the same colour—a dressing-gown costing between twelve and fifteen hundred francs—a nightdress in batiste trimmed with Valenciennes lace, with embroidered insertions costing three hundred francs, and a petticoat trimmed with three lace flounces at three or four hundred francs each, a total of some three thousand francs taken to any house whose master can afford her.

*11 April*

At five o'clock at *L'Artiste* we met Gautier, Feydeau, and Flaubert. Feydeau is still the child whose first article has just been printed; an infatuated admiration for himself, a self-satisfied pride so honest and artlessly insolent that it is quite disarming. He asked Gautier, referring to the first of his *Seasons*, one of which is to appear at each solstice: 'Do you think it's a gem? Because I want to dedicate a gem to you.'

There followed a great argument about metaphors. Massillon's 'His opinions had no cause to blush for his conduct' was acquitted by Flaubert and Gautier, but Lamartine's 'He practised equitation, that pedestal of princes' was condemned out of hand.

After that a tremendous argument about assonance, which Flaubert said had to be avoided even if it took a week to eliminate a single example. Then Flaubert and Feydeau started discussing a thousand different recipes for style and form, pompously and earnestly explaining little mechanical tricks of the trade, and expounding with childish gravity and ridiculous solemnity ways of writing and rules for producing good prose. They attached so much importance to the clothing of an idea, to its colour and material, that the idea became nothing but a peg on which to hang sound and light. We felt as if we were listening to an argument between grammarians of the Byzantine Empire.

*19 May*

Baudelaire, coming out of a tart's rooms, meets Sainte-Beuve on the stairs. Baudelaire: 'Ah! I know where you're going!' Sainte-Beuve: 'And I know where you've been. But look, I'd rather go and have a chat with you.' They go to a café. Sainte-Beuve: 'You know, what disgusts me about the philosophers, Cousin and the rest, what makes me positively loathe them, is that they talk of nothing but God and the immortality of the soul. They know perfectly well that the immortality of the soul doesn't exist any more than God does. It's disgusting!' There follows a tirade on atheism in comparison with which the most blasphemous eighteenth-century pamphlet would read like the Gospel according to St. John, with Sainte-Beuve—the same Sainte-Beuve who described Cardinal de Bernis as a sort of Father of the Church—getting angry and excited and attacking God so fiercely as to bring every game of dominoes in the café to a stop.

*21 May*

Men like ourselves need a woman of little breeding and education who is nothing but gaiety and natural wit, because a woman of that sort can charm and please us like an agreeable animal to which we may become quite attached. But if a mistress has acquired a veneer of breeding, art, or literature, and tries to talk to us on an equal footing about our thoughts and our feeling for beauty; if she wants to be a companion and partner in the cultivation of our tastes or the writing of our books, then she becomes for us as unbearable as a piano out of tune—and very soon an object of dislike.

*4 June*

Marie[1] came this morning dressed in mourning, her eyes swollen, her voice choking, to read us a black-edged letter: her sister was dead. Women, garrulous by nature, become eloquent under the stress of passion or emotion. All of them, whether illiterate or well educated, prostitutes or marchionesses, find words and phrases and gestures which are the ideal, the envy, and the despair of those who try to write works of true-to-life emotion. There is an overwhelming case against tragedy contained in those unrehearsed sorrows, those spontaneous tears and words, and that speech springing straight from grief.

Marie told us what she was doing about mourning clothes. I doubt if there is any woman's grief, and I am speaking of the most sincere and poignant grief, into which there does not enter, right at the beginning, a preoccupation with her mourning clothes. There are very few cases of bereavement in which the woman does not say to you: 'It's a good thing I didn't buy a summer dress.'

*7 June*

Dinner at Asseline's with Anna Deslions, Adèle Courtois, a certain Juliette,[2] and her sister.

Anna Deslions, Bianchi's former mistress and the woman who ruined Lauriston: thick black hair, magnificently untidy; velvety eyes with a glance like a warm caress; a big nose but sharply defined; thin lips and a full face—the superb head of an Italian youth, touched with gold by Rembrandt.

Adèle Courtois, an old, nondescript tart boosted by the *Figaro*.

Juliette, a little blonde pastel-portrait, with her rumpled, frizzled hair worn low on the forehead—she is mad about low foreheads—a slightly crazy La Tour, a little blonde with something of the Rosalba picture in the Louvre, *Woman with Monkey*, partaking of the monkey as well as the woman. And her sister, a dried-up little thing with flared nostrils and pregnant into the bargain: looking like a big-bellied spider.

And to provide a piano accompaniment to the evening's festivities, Quidant, a bordello jester with a thoroughly Parisian sense of

---

[1] Jules's mistress.          [2] Juliette Beau.

humour, a ferocious irony: hoarse-voiced, mealy-mouthed, red-faced, and slit-eyed.

The ladies were all wearing long white dresses, with hundreds of frills and furbelows, cut very low at the back in the shape of a triangle. Their conversation at first turned on the Emperor's mistresses. Juliette said:

'Giraud is doing my portrait, and this year he's painting Mme de Castiglione.'

'No, she's finished', said Adèle. 'I have that on good authority. It's La Serrano now. La Castiglione and the Empress have quarrelled. . . . You know the witty thing Constance said? "If I had resisted the Emperor, I should have been Empress." '

Juliette was in a crazy mood, bursting into nervous laughter without rhyme or reason, and talking with the spirited irony of a professional actress. Some name was mentioned, and Deslions said to Juliette:

'You know, that man you were madly in love with and for whom you committed suicide.'

'Oh, I've committed suicide three times.'

'You know whom I mean. What's-his-name. . . .'

Juliette put her hand over her eyes like someone peering into the distance, and screwed up her eyes to see if she could not recognize the gentleman in question coming along the highroad of her memories. Then she burst out laughing and said:

'It reminds me of the Scala at Milan. There was a gentleman there who kept bowing to me over and over again. And I said to myself: "I know that mouth." All I could remember was the mouth!'

'Do you remember', asked Deslions, 'when we went out in that filthy weather to see the place where Gérard de Nerval hanged himself?'

'Yes, and I even believe it was you who paid for the cab. I touched the bar; it was that that brought me luck. You know, Adèle, it was the week after that . . .'

After dinner Quidant did an imitation on the piano of that trill of a cuckoo with one note missing. The ladies started waltzing, the blonde and the brunette, Juliette and Anna, dancing together, all white in a room lined in red rep. With a playful air, Juliette caught Anna's necklace between her teeth and bit a magnificent black pearl hanging from the end of it. But the pearl was genuine and did not break.

In the midst of all this merriment, there was an icy chill, an instinctive hostility, between the women, who would draw in their claws as soon as someone bared her teeth. Now and then all the women would start talking Javanese, following every syllable with a *va*. Prisons have got slang: brothels have got Javanese. They talk it very fast and it is unintelligible to a man.

*October*

The Café Riche seems to be on the way to becoming the headquarters of those men of letters who wear gloves. It is strange how places make the people who frequent them. Beneath that white and gold, on that red plush, none of the guttersnipes of literature would dare to venture. Murger, with whom we had dinner, made his profession of faith to us. He is rejecting Bohemia and passing over bag and baggage to the side of the gentlemen of letters: a new Mirabeau.

It is at the far end of the Café Riche, in the room overlooking the Rue Le Peletier, that between eleven o'clock and half-past twelve at night, after the theatre or their work, you will find Saint-Victor, Uchard, About with his ape-like mask fixed in a bogus smile, Aubryet nervously drawing on the tables or insulting all and sundry from the waiters to M. Scribe, Albéric Second, Fiorentino, Villemot, the publisher Lévy, Beauvoir, the last of the Regency drunks, etc.

At the entrance, in the room separated from ours by two pillars, you can see here and there a few ears pricked up and drinking in the talk of our circle. They belong either to dandies frittering away the last of their little fortunes, or to young men from the Stock Exchange, Rothschild's clerks, who have brought along some high-grade tarts from the Cirque or Mabille to offer their little appetites the satisfaction of some fruit or a cup of tea and to point out from a distance the leading players in our company.

Baudelaire had supper at the next table to ours. He was without a cravat, his shirt open at the neck and his head shaved, just as if he were going to be guillotined. A single affectation: his little hands washed and cared for, the nails kept scrupulously clean. The face of a maniac, a voice that cuts like a knife, and a precise elocution that tries to copy Saint-Just and succeeds. He denies, with some obstinacy and a certain harsh anger, that he has offended morality with his verse.[1]

[1] On 20 August 1857 Baudelaire had been fined 300 francs for offending public morals, and six poems in his *Fleurs du Mal* had been suppressed.

# 1858

Went to see Alphonse, whom we found sitting by the fire, suffering from influenza. On the mantelpiece there was a pamphlet prospectus issued by a M. Vafilard, undertaker, with particulars and prices of every class of funeral, from the first down to the tenth. Nothing was overlooked in this menu of death: the number of priests, fringes, tapers, etc. There was even a wood-cut at the head of each class, offering a faithful picture of what you would get for your money.

Looking through it, I came across a sum in pencil and a total of four thousand and a few hundred francs. Alphonse's father was there: he had understood, but smiled and laughed with us. We teased Alphonse about his foresight, his tidy mind, his careful calculations. We went out, Alphonse walking ahead of his father, with me.

'Look,' I said, 'it isn't . . .'

'Yes,' he replied with a smile, 'it's for my father.'

The greatest comic writers have never invented anything so horrible. Even a parricide would not think of it. To sit by the fire, calmly working out, in the margin of an undertaker's prospectus, the expenses of one's father's funeral! And note that he had linked everything together in his estimate: decency with economy, respect for his father's position with contempt for needless extravagance; he had combined two classes: a first-class Mass with a second-class funeral procession. Like that, everything was saved, honour and money alike.

*20 February*

A few days ago I came across an old mistress of mine, who has grown plumper and more beautiful over the years: Maria the midwife.[1] Her conversation is as interesting as one of Dr. Baudelocque's

[1] The identity of this woman, who was Jules's mistress and perhaps the only woman he ever really loved, has never been discovered. We know only the initial of her surname—M—from a manuscript note on Jules's portrait of Maria, the etching entitled *Après Souper*.

books and her buttocks are as dimpled as one of Boucher's drawings. She tells me that she once aborted the mistress of the judge
who tried us for offending public morals, M. Legonidec. He was a
magistrate at the time and married, and he himself brought her the
woman, who was his wife's chambermaid.

*5 March*

It is all very strange. We see love everywhere, in books, on the
stage, in other people's lives. Everybody talks about it all the time.
It is something which seems to be extremely important and extremely absorbing. Yet here we are, both of us perfectly healthy, fit
for service in affairs of the heart, rich enough to wear clean socks
and buy a bouquet of flowers, and with our noses more or less in
the middle of our faces—and hanged if we can remember ever having been in love for more than a week at a time.

Overheard at the next table at Broggi's:
'I've met his mistress.'
'But that's his wife!'
'He introduced her to me as his mistress, to rehabilitate her. . . .'

*14 March*

The talk this evening at Uchard's was of 1830. To give us the
taste and notion of the period, with its fraternal spirit, its childish
and generous follies, its combination of the sublime and the ridiculous, and its feverish atmosphere which affected every heart, De
Belloy told us this story. Some time before the production of
*Marion Delorme* he wrote to a friend who was studying medicine
somewhere in the provinces. The friend found the letter sad,
thought De Belloy must be short of money, collected all that he
could lay his hands on, and brought it to him. De Belloy did not
need it, but thanked his friend and introduced him that evening to
the woman he loved. The three of them became inseparable. A few
days later, going to see his friend, De Belloy found in bed . . . a
monster. He thought the man must have gone mad, for he had
shaved off his hair, his eyebrows, his beard and his moustache
Pressed for an explanation, he admitted that he had fallen in love

with De Belloy's mistress and had wanted to make it impossible for himself to see her again. De Belloy took him to dine with her that same evening and then took him as he was to see *Marion Delorme*. The friend was very nearly the ruin of the play. Every time he turned round to impose silence on the opposition, the sight of the face of that enthusiastic, hairless monster brought the house down.

*31 March*

'You will never be decorated!' That is how our good friend Louis began the following story:

'At Biarritz there is a library of twenty-five volumes, including your *Histoire du Directoire*. Damas-Hinard said to the Empress: "Here is a new book which will interest you: the *Histoire de la Société française pendant le Directoire*." The Empress started reading it, but soon found the style a little tiring; then, all of a sudden, she burst out laughing. The Emperor came up and asked what she was laughing at; the Empress showed him the word *tétonnières*, applied to the big-bosomed women of the Directoire. The Emperor looked at the word, read it again, made sure of the epithet—and shut the book with an expression of stern disapproval on his face.'

*23 April*

Between the chocolate soufflé and the chartreuse Maria loosened her bodice and launched out on the story of her life.

It begins in a little village on the banks of the Marne, one of those cool, shady places landscape painters love. She is a bargee's daughter, thirteen-and-a-half years old, with fair hair and a white skin which the sun has not yet burnt. A young man comes to see her, disguised as an architect. As in the storybooks, this young man is really the Comte de Saint-Maurice, the owner of one of the neighbouring châteaux, a handsome, sophisticated young man of twenty-seven who entertains members of the Orléans family and is in the process of squandering his fortune.

Now the little village girl is installed in the château; and the young man loves her, for all that he locks her in her room whenever he brings down girls from Paris, whom he chases round his park, naked beneath gauze nightdresses with bows of ribbon which two little dogs from Havana tear with their teeth. And it all ends with the young man, completely ruined and hunted by the bailiffs, putting up the sort of resistance that belongs to more heroic times, and finally taking refuge on the roof of his château, where he blows out his brains. The girl is thrown out with her watch set in pearls and her diamond earrings. She is pregnant. She goes to a midwife to bear her child; the midwife sells her to a building contractor whom she hates at sight; and in order to earn a living she comes back to serve an apprenticeship to the midwife who delivered her child. And at that point Maria's story becomes the story of all women, with the difference that not many women learn how to be midwives.

### Sunday, 2 May

It is a strange thing—and nobody has noticed it so far—that the only monument of Atticism, of the delightful manners and the subtle, delicate wit of the great city of wit, Athens, namely Aristophanes, is the grossest, most scatalogical monument in the whole of literature. I'll be hanged if I believe in the delicacy of mind of the audience which applauded *The Clouds*, *Lysistrata*, and *The Frogs*. A delicate wit is a corruption which a nation takes a long time to acquire. It is only worn-out nations that possess it, nations which have no need to go to bed with women every night, nations which are not content with iron chairs and marble baths; nations whose constitution has become fragile and weary, nations whose physique has become anaemic; and finally, nations afflicted with those moral diseases which visit them as if they were fruit-trees that had grown too old and borne too abundantly. There is not a single madman, not a single melancholic in the whole of this picture of antiquity.

### 6 May

Javanese, the slang used by all the prostitutes of Paris, had a curious origin: it was invented at Saint-Denis by the schoolgirls there to keep their secrets from the mistresses. But theirs was a more complicated Javanese than the *va* after every syllable; it consisted of the repetition, after every syllable, of two syllables taking the same vowel. For example, 'How are you?' becomes 'How *dow gow* are *dar gar* you *doo goo*?' An impossible, incomprehensible language, bristling with diphthongs, which creates the effect of a stiff brush scouring one's ears.

Maria told us all this, and this too. There exist—this is a fact, she has seen one herself, taken along by another midwife—there exist imitation women, complete in every detail, with all the charms and uses of real women: manikins with flesh which you can push in and which comes out again, a tongue which darts in and out for five minutes, eyes which roll, hair which you would swear was the real thing, and moistness and warmth where you would expect to find them, on sale at the manufacturer's for 15,000 francs, for the use of religious communities or rich sailors. This one was for a ship whose name Maria has forgotten; but there are others to suit all pockets, down to male and female parts in gilded boxes which cost only 300 francs. Maria told us that the one she saw was a wonderful sight. It was nearly finished; there were only the toe-nails which still had to be stuck on.

The artist who makes these things—this public benefactor, this moralist endeavouring to avoid so many evils, to spare man, for instance, apart from anything else, that tempestuous age of woman, that unbearable period, the change of life—this rare artist was prosecuted six months ago and sent to prison, no doubt on a charge of immorality.

*27 May*

Maria's arrival is a burst of laughter, her face a holiday; and she brings into the bedroom a robust gaiety and country-style embraces. A plump woman; fair, frizzled hair worn back from the forehead; blue eyes of an extraordinary sweetness and tenderness; good thick lips; a kindly, full-fleshed face; the features, in fact, of a young Louis XVI. And then the bodice bursting under the strain of the bosom, the opulence and majesty of a Rubens goddess. She fills the whole bedroom. And this makes a delightful change after so many skinny graces, those spiteful, chlorotic little whores; after those sad, beggarly priestesses of the Venus Pandemos, always as melancholy and careworn as alms-collectors, with clouds of eviction on their foreheads, forever worried and, beneath the mask of laughter and caress, preoccupied with the parturition of their due; after all those shopworn chatterboxes, those mercenary parrots with their miserable, unhealthy slang picked up in the popular press, the brothel, and the workshop; after those touchy, peevish little things, this peasant health, this peasant good humour, this peasant language, with all its strength and vivacity, all its cordial exuberance, all its lusty, expansive contentment, and the heart inside with its coarse ways and rough tenderness—everything about this kindly, common woman delights me as if I were eating a solid, healthy farmhouse meal after a succession of cheap dinners in filthy Paris pothouses.

And then, to carry this Michelangelo torso, she has the slender legs of an Allegrain *Diana*, the feet of an antique statue, and beautifully shaped knees.

A man needs to expend every day certain crudities of thought and speech, especially a man of letters, a man of ideas, who lives up in the clouds and in whom matter, oppressed by the brain, seems to take its revenge by turning him into the coarsest of talkers. This is his way of coming to earth like Antaeus; this is his way of coming down from the basket in which Socrates meditates in Aristophanes' *Clouds*. . . . And this woman helps me to attain this end.

*July*

Criticism is the enemy and the negation of the genius of an age: Fréron with Voltaire, Chénier with Chateaubriand. Journalism is the triumph of criticism. That ephemeral sheet of paper, the newspaper, is the natural enemy of the book, as the whore is of the decent woman.

*October*

Nobody has noticed, although it is self-evident, that Napoleon's language, that language of brief, peremptory phrases which seems to be talking to itself, the language recorded by Las Cases in his *Mémorial de Sainte-Hélène* and even better in Roederer's conversations with the Emperor, was taken over by Balzac and put into the mouths of his military, governmental, and humanitarian characters, from the tirades of the Council of State to those of Vautrin.

Overheard a landowner saying to his son: 'You've got money behind you: speak up!'

*28 October*

One man only, a M. de Wailly in *L'Illustration*, has come to know us well enough through our books to state that if we fell in love we should fall in love with the same person, and that law and custom ought to make an exception in favour of our phenomenal duality.

David and Robespierre in the Revolution: two icy geniuses in a volcano.

*Sunday, November*

Saint-Victor, Charles-Edmond, and Mario dined with us. Flaubert's mind haunted by the Marquis de Sade, to whom he constantly returns as to a mystery that fascinates him. He is a glutton for depravity and looks for it everywhere, rejoicing, as he puts it, to see a scavenger eating cess, and exclaiming on the subject of Sade: 'It's the most entertaining nonsense I've ever come across.'

The next moment he was directing his coarse, Rabelaisian irony against God's opponents. He told the story of a man who was taken fishing by an atheist friend. They fished up a stone on which was carved: 'I do not exist. *Signed:* God.' 'What did I tell you?' said the friend.

For the setting of his next novel he has chosen Carthage as the most corrupt place and civilization in the world. In six months he has written only two chapters, on a brothel staffed by little boys and a meal eaten by mercenaries.[1]

*10 December*

The sadness and melancholy of modern times spring from the accumulation of books, in other words from the growth of ideas. The idea is the old age of the spirit and the disease of the mind.

[1] The first chapter mentioned was eventually omitted from *Salammbô*, but the mercenaries' feast was used for the opening chapter of the novel.

# 1859

What makes me think that people who practically starve to death or who have no security to look forward to, do not suffer as much as they are said to suffer, is that there is no bitterness in their works. It is in the works of rich men that you have to look for bitterness, in Byron, Musset, and Chateaubriand.

*Sunday, 16 January*

We went to the Musée today to see the restoration of the old pictures, begun under M. Villot's supervision. It is incredible that this should be allowed. It is the sort of restoration done by a picture-dealer who wants to sell some daubs to Americans. The Le Sueurs and the Rubens have already been done. In the case of the Le Sueurs, the loss, in my opinion, is not very great, but the Rubens! It is like a piece of music in which the semitones have been suppressed: everything screams and howls, like crockery gone mad. This must delight the hearts of the bourgeois. But not a single voice has been raised to protest at this vandalism, the most insolent and conscientious vandalism that I have ever seen. M. Villot belongs to M. Nieuwerkerke, who belongs to the Princess Mathilde, who belongs, etc. . . . A protest would be an attack on the Government!

Truth to tell, these pictures, stripped of their golden patina, have thrown us into considerable perplexity. Time is a great healer: could it be that it is also a great painter? For in front of those Rubens which are now nothing but mural decorations, we began to wonder whether it was not age that produced those soft, warm hues, the colouring of the masters.

*27 January*

Scholl came to lunch with me. He said something amusing about Barrière: 'Yes, yes, he has talent, but he doesn't know how to make people forgive him for it.'

*28 January*

Our novel is finished; nothing remains but to copy it out.[1] It is strange how, once a thing is done, it no longer grips your emotions; this thing which you are no longer carrying and feeding loses its ties and becomes as it were dead to you. It is a feeling similar to that which follows coition; your work arouses nothing in you but boredom, indifference, and disgust. All these last few days, we have felt something like that.

*17 February*

There have been many definitions of beauty in art. What is it? Beauty is what untrained eyes consider abominable. Beauty is what my mistress and my housekeeper instinctively regard as appalling.

*11 May*

A ring at the door. It was Flaubert, who had been told by Saint-Victor that we had seen somewhere a vaguely Carthaginian battle-mace, and had come to ask us where. He said that he was having trouble with his Carthaginian novel: there was nothing to work on, and he was having to invent what seemed probable.

He started looking out our portfolios, our books, our bric-à-brac, like an inquisitive, excited child. He looks extraordinarily like portraits of the actor Frédérick Lemaître as a young man, very big, very powerfully built, with large protuberant eyes under puffy lids, full cheeks, heavy drooping moustaches, and a complexion speckled with red patches.

He spends four or five months a year in Paris, going nowhere, seeing only a few friends and leading the bearish life we all lead—Saint-Victor just as much as he, and we just as much as Saint-Victor. This forced bearishness of the nineteenth-century man of letters is a

[1] *Les Hommes de lettres*, later entitled *Charles Demailly*.

strange phenomenon compared with the worldly life of the eighteenth-century man of letters, a life spent in the midst of society, and riddled with approaches, invitations, and connexions, the life of a Diderot or a Voltaire, whom the society of his time went to see at Ferney, or of lesser men, fashionable authors such as Crébillon *fils* or Marmontel. Approaches to the writer and interest in him ceased to exist with the rise of the bourgeoisie and the proclamation of equality. The man of letters no longer forms part of society, no longer reigns over it, no longer even enters into it. Of all the men of letters I know, not a single one goes into what is called society.

There are various reasons for this change. When society had a hierarchy of orders, the nobleman, deeply conscious and proud of his rank, did not feel jealous of the man of letters; he conversed with him on familiar terms, because talent did not encroach on his rank or offend his vanity. Then too, in that century of spleen, that century in the image of Louis XV, a century in which the aristocracy found life ready-made for them and exhausted it all too quickly, the emptiness and nothingness of the mind were incalculable, and the distraction offered by an intelligent man, the pleasure provided by conversation, were highly prized. A man of letters was a rare bird, whose intelligence and verve tickled delicate, sophisticated minds. Easy-going hospitality, a friendly welcome, flattering attentions did not strike eighteenth-century society as too high a price to pay for the pleasure of a writer's company.

But the bourgeoisie stopped all that. The grand passion of the bourgeoisie is equality. The man of letters offends it because a man of letters is better known than a bourgeois. He arouses a hidden rancour, a secret jealousy. Moreover, the bourgeoisie, an enormous family of active people, doing business and making children, has no need of intellectual intercourse: it is satisfied with the newspaper. The result is that in this century, the only men of letters accepted by the great bourgeois families are a Weiss and an Ampère, a jester and a guide.

*Château de Croissy, 12–26 August*

Yesterday I was at one end of the table and Edmond, at the other end, was chatting with Thérèse. I could not hear what he was saying, but when he smiled I smiled in spite of myself, with my head in the same attitude as his. Never has there been such a case of one soul placed in two bodies.

My mistress was lying there beside me, dead drunk with absinthe. I had made her drunk and she was sleeping. Sleeping and talking. Holding my breath, I listened. . . . It was a strange voice which aroused a peculiar emotion akin to fear, that involuntary voice bursting forth in uncontrolled speech, that voice of sleep—a slow voice with the tone, the accent, the poignancy of the voices in boulevard drama. To begin with, little by little, word by word and recollection by recollection, as if with the eyes of memory, she looked back into her youth, seeing things and faces emerge, under her fixed gaze, from the darkness in which the past lay sleeping: 'Oh, yes, he loved me all right! . . . Yes, they used to say that his mother had a *look*. . . . He had fair hair. . . . But it wouldn't work. . . . We'd be rich now, wouldn't we? . . . If only my father hadn't done that. . . . But what's done is done. . . . I don't like to say so. . . .'

There was something terrifying about bending over that body, in which everything seemed to be extinct and only an animal life lingered on, and hearing the past come back like a ghost returning to a deserted house. And then, those secrets about to emerge which were suddenly held back, that mystery of unconscious thought, that voice in a darkened bedroom, all that was as frightening as a corpse possessed by a dream. . . .

Then came impressions of the same day, a return to words uttered a few hours before and warm in her memory: a scene with a gentleman to make him recognize his child, the child of a woman she had delivered. And the strange thing is that this woman, so common in language and accent, told her story not only in perfectly correct French but also with the diction of an admirable actress. Sometimes she appealed to the man's feelings, but most of the time it was irony that she threw at him, a veiled, vibrant irony which nearly always ended in a nervous laugh. She had a verve, a logic, an eloquence, a marvellous skill in argument which I found quite amazing, and which captivated me as much as the most astonishing scene in a play. Rachel is the only person I have ever heard say certain words and throw out certain phrases as she threw them out. At moments, too, she had something of the consumptive voice of Mlle Thuillier, for her voice was changed and transmuted in some strange way, becoming sad and bitter.

When I woke her, her eyes were still full of tears, from the memories she had summoned up first of all; and soon, without any encouragement on my part, she started off by herself, consciously following the course of her dream and travelling to her childhood, her youth, her father, her lover.

*Rouen, Hôtel de Normandie, Tuesday, 15 November*

For the first time in our lives, a woman has separated us. That woman is Mme de Châteauroux who has persuaded one of us to come here to Rouen by himself to copy out a bundle of intimate letters written by her to Richelieu which are now in the Leber Collection. I am staying at a hotel, in one of those rooms where people inadvertently die on their travels, a room with an icy tiled floor and a greyish light filtering in from a well-like yard. And on the other side of the wall the voice of a thirty-year-old commercial traveller keeps on singing alternately the *Miserere* from *Il Trovatore* and the *King of Boeotia* from Offenbach's *Orpheus*.

Today I begin to understand what love must be, if it exists. Take away the carnal side of it, the mingling of the sexes, and you have what exists between the two of us—what produces a feeling of incompleteness when one of us is without the other, as in a couple of birds who can only live together. When we are parted, we each feel the lack of the other half of ourselves. We are left with nothing but half-sensations, a half-life; we are incomplete like a book in two volumes of which the first has been lost. That is what I imagine love to be: incompleteness in absence.

And yet, is that what love is? Should one not add to the fusion of two hearts the fusion of two minds, that complete and possibly unique marriage of the whole personality which is peculiar to ourselves? I flattered love when I compared it to our brotherhood.

# 1860

We are in our dining-room, and that pretty rep box, lined and canopied in tapestry and covered with drawings, among which we have hung Moreau's magnificent *Revue du Roi*, is lighted and enlivened by the soft glow and gay sparkle of the Bohemian crystal chandelier.

At our table are Flaubert, Saint-Victor, Scholl, Charles-Edmond, Julie, and Mme Doche, the latter with a red net over her lightly powdered hair. The talk is of Mme Colet's novel *Lui*, in which Flaubert is portrayed under the name of Léonce, and now and then Scholl, to draw attention to himself, pokes fun at something or criticizes somebody not in the present company. He ends up by solemnly swearing to break Lurine. At dessert, Doche goes off to the dress rehearsal of *La Pénélope normande*, which opens tomorrow night, and Saint-Victor, lacking copy for his column, also leaves for the rehearsal with Scholl.

The rest of us start talking about the stage, and Flaubert promptly gets astride this pretty hobby-horse. 'Being a dramatist isn't an art,' he said, 'it's a knack, and I've got hold of the knack from one of the people who possess it. This is it. First of all you have a few glasses of absinthe at the Café du Cirque. Then you say of whatever play is being discussed: "It's not bad, but it needs cutting", or "Yes . . . but there's no play there." Above all, you must always sketch out plots but never write a play. Once you've written a play, indeed once you've written an article in the *Figaro*, you're done for! I learnt all this from a fool, La Rounat, but a fool who knows his business. It was he who made that wonderful remark: "Beaumarchais is a prejudice." Beaumarchais!' shouts Flaubert; 'hell and damnation! Why, a fellow like La Rounat couldn't even create the character of Chérubin!'

He has always refused to allow *Madame Bovary* to be adapted for the stage, maintaining that an idea is made for a single mould and

cannot be used for two ends, and not wanting to entrust it to someone like Dennery. 'You know what you must do to make sure of a
success on the boulevards? You must let the audience guess what is
going to happen. I once found myself sitting next to two women
who, during every scene, worked out the next. They wrote the play
as they went along!'

Then the conversation passes on to this person or that in our
circle, and the difficulty of finding people one can get along with,
people who are neither vicious, nor unbearable, nor bourgeois, nor
ill-bred. And everyone starts expressing regret that Saint-Victor
lacks certain qualities: he could make such a delightful friend. But
he is a man whom one can never really make out; a man whom one
can never persuade to open his heart, even when he opens his mind
freely; a man who, after three years of friendship, can turn suddenly
chilly and give one a cold handshake as if one were a stranger.
Flaubert puts it all down to his upbringing, saying that the three
institutions which educated him—the church school, the army, and
the École Normale—always mark a man and his character with an
indelible stamp.

Then we go on to talk about all the actresses we know, and the
odd ways of those strange creatures. Flaubert gives us his recipe for
possessing them: you have to be sentimental and take them seriously. Then we discuss the question whether they make love as
often as men say they do, or whether care for their health and
the strain and fatigue of acting force them to confine themselves to
skirmishes. We talk about the extraordinary influence they have on
the criticism written by their lovers: and when the conversation
turns from women of the theatre to women in general, Flaubert remarks: 'I've found a simple way of doing without them. I just lie
face down, and during the night . . . it's infallible.'

Then we are left alone with him in the drawing-room all fuggy
with cigar-smoke, he pacing up and down the carpet, bumping his
head against the chandelier, opening himself up to us as to his
brothers in intellect. He tells us about the quiet, unsociable life he
leads, even in Paris, shut up and shut in. He hates the theatre, and
his only distraction is dinner every Sunday at Mme Sabatier's, or
the 'Présidente' as Gautier and his friends call her. He loathes the
country. He works ten hours a day but wastes a lot of time, forgetting himself in the books he starts reading and playing truant

from the book he is supposed to be writing. He scarcely ever warms to his work before five in the afternoon, although he starts at noon. He finds it impossible to write straight away on a blank sheet of paper, and needs first of all to cover it with ideas which he puts down as a painter puts down his first colours on his canvas.

Then we remark how few people there are who can appreciate something well done and beautiful in itself, like the rhythm of a sentence. 'Can you imagine anything more stupid', Flaubert asked, 'than struggling to eliminate the assonances from a sentence or the repetitions from a page? For whom? And then, even when the book succeeds, the success you obtain is never the kind you wanted. It was the farcical bits in *Madame Bovary* that made it a success. Success is always off the mark. As for style, how many readers enjoy and appreciate it? And remember that style is what makes us suspect in the eyes of the law, for the courts are all for the classics. . . . But in reality nobody has read the classics! There aren't eight men of letters who have read Voltaire, and I mean really *read* him. And there aren't five who could tell you the titles of Thomas Corneille's plays. Art for art's sake? It received its greatest consecration in the address delivered to the Academy by a classical writer, Buffon, when he said: "The manner in which a truth is enunciated is more useful to humanity than the truth itself." If that isn't art for art's sake, what is? And how about La Bruyère, who says: "The art of writing is the art of defining and depicting." '

He goes on to tell us that his three stylistic breviaries are La Bruyère, certain pages of Montesquieu, and certain chapters of Chateaubriand. And then, with his eyes popping out of his head, his face flushed, and his arms stretched out in a dramatic embrace to the full span of an Antaeus, he draws forth from his chest and his throat fragments of Montesquieu's *Dialogue de Sylla et d'Eucrate*, whose brassy sound he throws at us like the roaring of a lion.

Flaubert reels off for our benefit Limayrac's sublime review of *Madame Bovary*, the last sentence of which is: 'How can anyone allow himself to write in such an ignoble style when the throne is occupied by the greatest master of the French language, the Emperor?'

We talk about his Carthaginian novel, which he is in the midst of writing. He tells us of his research, his studies, the reading he has done, the piles of notes he has made, and the incomprehensibility of the words involved, which is forcing him to paraphrase all his terms. 'Do you know the full extent of my ambition?' he asks. 'I just want an intelligent man to shut himself up for four hours with my book, so that I can give him a feast of historical hashish. That's all I ask. . . . After all, work is still the best means of whiling away one's life.'

*25 January*

We are in the grip of that first performance feeling, that sort of vague expectation of some fashionable act of violence, a slap in the face or a blow with a cane, which drives you out of your house and into the street as out of a dull refuge which might make a coward of you.[1]

First of all we found ourselves on the Boulevard du Temple, in Flaubert's study, which looks out on the boulevard and has a gilded Indian idol in the middle of the mantelpiece. His writing-table was covered with pages of his novel, pages which were nothing but crossed-out lines. He paid us some warm, enthusiastic, and sincere compliments on our book which did our hearts good; his is a friendship we are proud of, a friendship which he demonstrates in a frank and open fashion, with a sort of robust familiarity and a generous lack of reserve.

During the evening we wandered along the boulevards, calculating our chances of a duel and our chances of success, and looking at the bookshop displays like a couple of provincials, with a certain nervous excitement we were unable to control. We ran into Scholl in the Passage des Panoramas. He took us along for a toddy at the Café des Variétés, the headquarters of vaudeville. He told us that he was going to slap somebody's face, that he felt the need of a duel. He insisted on taking us to see Lafontaine, and the next moment there we were with the wretched actor, who was in the hands of his hairdresser. He was quite overwhelmed by our call, piling up the furniture to make room for us. Everybody uses the familiar form of address in the theatre, and he looked positively moved when he shook hands with us. Scholl teased him about the Imperial visit to the theatre.

'Oh!' said Lafontaine. 'The Empress was charming. When my

[1] The Goncourts' novel *Les Hommes de lettres* had been published on 24 January.

manager told her that I was very hoarse, she said: "We shall come back another time."'

'That's just like the Bonapartes!' said Scholl. 'They always imagine they're going to come back!'

*Sunday, 29 January*

Saw Barrière who told us this striking anecdote. On the Place de Grève he had seen a condemned man whose hair had visibly stood on end when he had been turned to face the scaffold. Yet this was the man who, when Dr. Pariset had asked him what he wanted before he died, had answered: 'A leg of mutton and a woman.'

Spent the evening at Flaubert's. Bouilhet was there, a fellow with the physique of a good-looking workman. We heard some wonderful stories about provincial avarice and the masters at Rouen College. Then we talked about Sade, to whom Flaubert, as if fascinated, constantly reverts. 'He is the last word in Catholicism', he said. 'Let me explain: he is the spirit of the Inquisition, the spirit of torture, the spirit of the medieval Church, the horror of Nature. There isn't a single tree in Sade, or a single animal.' We talked about Romanticism. At school he slept with a dagger under his pillow, and once he stopped his tilbury outside Casimir Delavigne's country house, stood up on the seat and shouted 'guttersnipe abuse' at the man.

*Sunday, 5 February*

Lunch at Flaubert's. Bouilhet told us this delightful story of a sister at Rouen Hospital, where he had been a medical student.[1] She had apparently felt a platonic love for one of his student friends. Bouilhet found this friend hanged one morning. The sisters were enclosed and only came into the hospital yard on the Feast of Corpus Christi. But this sister came into the dead man's room, went down on her knees and prayed in silence for a quarter of an hour. Without saying a word, he put a lock of the dead man's hair into her hand. She never referred to what had happened, but from then on she always went out of her way to be of service to him.

---

[1] This was the anecdote which the Goncourts made the basis of their novel *Sœur Philomène*.

*Sunday, 19 February*

Sitting by his fireside, Flaubert told us the story of his first love. He was on his way to Corsica. Till then he had done no more than lose his innocence with his mother's chambermaid. He happened on a little hotel in Marseilles where some women from Lima had arrived with sixteenth-century ebony furniture inlaid with mother-of-pearl at which everyone who saw it marvelled. Three women in silk dressing-gowns falling in a straight line from the back to the heels, together with a little Negro dressed in nankeen and wearing Turkish slippers: for a young Norman who had hitherto travelled only from Normandy to Champagne and from Champagne to Normandy, all this was very tempting and exotic. It conjured up visions of a patio full of tropical flowers, with a fountain singing in the middle.

One day, coming back from a bathe in the Mediterranean and bringing with him all the life of that Fountain of Youth, he was invited into her bedroom by one of the women, a magnificent woman of thirty-five. He gave her one of those kisses into which one puts all one's soul. The woman came to his room that night and started making love with him straight away. There followed an orgy of delight, then tears, then letters, then silence.

He has gone back to Marseilles several times since then, but nobody has ever been able to tell him what became of those women. The last time he went through, on his way to Tunis to collect material for his Carthaginian novel, he went as usual to have a look at the house, but could not find it. He looked for it, hunted for it, and finally noticed that it had been turned into a toyshop, with a barber's on the first floor. He went upstairs, had himself shaved, and recognized the wallpaper of the bedroom.

*Saturday, 25 February*

Molière is the accession of the bourgeoisie, a solemn affirmation of the soul of the Third Estate. He is the inauguration of common sense and practical reasoning, the end of chivalry and poetry in everything. Woman, love, all the gallant and noble follies of life, are reduced in him to the mean yardstick of home and dowry. Everything spontaneous and impulsive is condemned and corrected. Corneille is the last herald of the aristocracy; Molière is the first poet of the middle classes.

*4 March*

We talked with Flaubert about Hugo's *Légende des siècles*. What strikes him most of all in Hugo, who wants to be regarded as a thinker, is the absence of thought. And that is why Flaubert likes him. 'Hugo isn't a thinker', he said; 'he's a naturalist. He is waist-deep in Nature. He has got the sap of trees in his blood.'

Then the conversation turned to the vengeful comedy which our age calls for but which our public would never stand for: something in the nature of a play entitled *Humbug*. And all three of us agreed that the most appalling kind of prostitution was the present-day prostitution of the family, the constant refrain of *My Mother* sung by all and sundry, the dedications *To my mother*, and so on. We admitted frankly to one another our hate and contempt for the works of writers such as Feuillet. 'A eunuch!' shouted Flaubert. 'The family Musset', as we were the first to call him. And referring to the base court he pays to women in his novels and all the profit it has brought him, Flaubert said: 'That proves he doesn't love women. . . . Men who love women write books in which they say what they have suffered through women, because we only love what makes us suffer.' 'Yes,' we said, 'that explains maternal love.'

Just then three fat quarto volumes printed at the Imperial Press were brought in: books about the mines of Algeria in which he hopes to find a word he needs about the mines near Tunis.

When we mentioned *Madame Bovary* to him, he told us there was only one character in the book drawn from life, and that very freely: old Bovary. He was based on a certain Esnault, a former paymaster in Napoleon's armies, a swaggering, loose-living scoundrel who would threaten his mother with a sabre to get money out of her, went about wearing leather breeches, high boots, and a police cap, and was a pillar of the Lalanne Circus at Sotteville, treating them to mulled wine warmed in basins on a stove and letting their bareback riders give birth in his house.

Then Flaubert changed to go to one of the famous Sunday dinners given by Mme Sabatier, the 'Présidente', and attended by Gautier, Royer, Feydeau, Du Camp, and himself. On the way, he told us the splendid reply made by La Lagier to a man who wanted to sleep with her again: 'You remember my belly in the old days? It was as firm as a rock. Well, now it's an accordion.'

*15 July*

I was told the other day how the Government buys scholars. It is easily done. I had always imagined that to corrupt a man tentative efforts were necessary, tactful approaches, negotiations conducted by a third party, a little time and tact at least.

The Emperor sent for M. Renan, told him that he had been following his work with interest, and asked him if he would not like to see the peoples and places of which he spoke in his books— Syria and Palestine. Renan replied that he would, but that he had no money for a journey of that sort. 'How much do you want?' asked the Emperor. Renan answered, like an attendant in a theatre: 'I don't know, whatever you like.' 'But I want you to fix the sum', said the Emperor. 'You must have some idea. . . .' To which Renan replied: 'Oh, well, I imagine that twenty-five thousand francs . . .'

And that makes one! The other is a certain M. Léon Renier, a confirmed Republican, whom the Emperor sent on a journey to Italy, under the pretext of helping him to study the life of Caesar, who he claimed was generally misrepresented. . . . And that makes two!

*24 August*

On Sunday, at Charles-Edmond's, Aubryet invited everybody to dinner at his house today. So there we were: Flaubert, Saint-Victor, Charles-Edmond, Halévy, Claudin, Gautier, and ourselves.

Somehow or other, we got on to the subject of immortality.

'It's absolutely unthinkable', said Gautier, coming over to us. 'Can you imagine my soul remaining conscious of my ego in the after-life, remembering that I wrote for the *Moniteur* at No. 13, Quai Voltaire, and that the owners of my paper were Turgan and Dalloz? I can't!'

'Or can you imagine', asked Saint-Victor, 'the soul of M. Prud-homme turning up before God wearing gold-rimmed spectacles and launching out into a speech beginning: "Architect of the universe"?'

'We all accept the idea of unconsciousness before life', Gautier went on. 'It's no more difficult to imagine it after life. The fable of the ancients, the cup of water from the river Lethe—that's what it must be like. All I'm afraid of is the actual transition, the moment

when my ego will enter into darkness and I shall lose the consciousness of having lived.'

'But in that case, what are we here for?' asked Claudin. 'I can't
understand. . . .'

'Look, Claudin, there are infusoria in hay for whom a ray of
sunshine is an aurora borealis.'

'No, you can't convince me . . . There is a great Clockmaker. . . .'

'Oh, if we are going to start on clockmaking. . . . Claudin, do
you know that matter is infinite?'

'Yes, I know, I know. . . .'

'But it's a very recent discovery!'

'Remember what Heine said', observed Saint-Victor. 'We ask
what the stars are, what God is, what life is; "our mouths are stopped
with a lump of clay, but is that an answer?"'

'Listen, Claudin', Gautier went on calmly and imperturbably.
'Supposing that the sun was inhabited, a man five foot tall on earth
would be two thousand miles tall on the sun. In other words,
the soles of your shoes, assuming that you wore heels, would be
five miles thick, a thickness equal to the depth of the sea at its
deepest. Or to take another example, and mark this well, Claudin,
you would have two hundred miles of virility in its natural, pendant
state!'

'That's all very well, but Catholicism . . . I'm a Catholic, you
know!'

'Claudin,' shouted Saint-Victor, '*Catholicism and Markowski*,
that's your motto.'

'You know,' said Gautier, coming over to us again, 'the immortality of the soul, free will and all that—it's all very amusing to talk
about up to the age of twenty-two, but not after that. Then one
ought to be giving one's mind to having fun without catching the
pox, arranging one's life as comfortably as possible, having a few
decent drawings on the wall, and above all writing well. That's the
important thing: well-made sentences . . . and then a few metaphors.
Yes, a few metaphors. They embellish a man's existence.'

'Markowski? What's that?' asked Flaubert.

'My dear fellow,' said Saint-Victor, 'Markowski was a bootmaker.
He taught himself to play the violin, and then he taught himself to
dance, and then he started organizing balls with tarts laid on whose
addresses he would provide on request. The good Lord blessed his

efforts, Adèle Courtois had him beaten up, and now he's the owner of the house where he lives.'

Coming downstairs, I asked Gautier if he did not find it a bore not living in Paris any more.

'Oh,' he said, 'it makes no difference to me. This is no longer the Paris I used to know. It's Philadelphia, St. Petersburg, anything you like, but not Paris.'

*Sunday, 18 November*

Our Paris, the Paris in which we were born, the Paris of the manners of 1830 to 1848, is disappearing. And it is not disappearing materially but morally. Social life is beginning to undergo a great change. I can see women, children, husbands and wives, whole families in this café. The home is dying. Life is threatening to become public. The club for the upper classes, the café for the lower—this is what society and the common people are coming to. All this makes me feel like a traveller in this my spiritual homeland. I am a stranger to what is coming and to what is here, as for example to these new boulevards which have nothing of Balzac's world about them but make one think of London or some Babylon of the future. It is silly to come into the world in a time of change; the soul feels as uncomfortable as a man who moves into a new house before the plaster is dry.

*7 December*

As a general truth, it is safe to say that any picture that produces a moral impression is a bad picture.

*10 December*

Coming out of the Odéon after *L'Oncle Million*,[1] I saw Flaubert and Bouilhet surrounded by men in cloth caps with whom they were shaking hands; and Bouilhet left us saying that he was going to the café next door. It seems that to keep a play going at the Odéon, one has to supply it with drinks and handshakes.

Flaubert told us that while writing the description of the poisoning

---

[1] A play by Flaubert's friend Bouilhet.

of Mme Bovary, he had felt a pain as if he had a copper plate in his
stomach, a pain which had made him vomit twice over. He said that
one of his most agreeable moments was when, working on the end
of his novel, he had been obliged to get up and look for another
handkerchief, because he had soaked the one he had! ... And all
that in order to amuse the bourgeois!


*Tuesday, 18 December*
We decided that this morning we should take the letter which
Dr. Follin, on Flaubert's recommendation, had given us to M.
Edmond Simon, a student in M. Velpeau's ward at the Hôpital
de la Charité. For, in order to write our novel *Sœur Philomène*,
we need to take notes in hospital, studies from life made on the
spot.

We had slept badly. We got up at seven. It was cold and damp;
and although we said nothing about it to each other, we both felt a
certain apprehension, a certain fear in our nerves. When we went
into the women's ward, passing a table loaded with a bundle of lint,
rolls of bandages, and a pyramid of sponges, something happened
inside us which made our hearts uneasy.

The tour of the ward began. We pulled ourselves together and
followed M. Velpeau with his students; but our legs were as weak
as if we had been drunk, and we were conscious of the knee-caps in
our legs and of a kind of chill in the marrow of our shin-bones. ...
When you see all that, and the card at the head of every bed, with
nothing on it but the words *Operated on* ... you feel tempted to
consider Providence an abomination and to see an executioner in
that God who is the reason for the existence of surgeons.

This evening we are left with a distant vision of all that, something which we seem to have dreamt rather than seen. And the
strange thing is that the horror of it all is so well covered with white
sheets, cleanliness, neatness, and silence that our recollection of it
is well-nigh pleasurable, curiously irritating. Those pale women's
faces, glimpsed on their pillows, almost bluish in colour and transformed by suffering and immobility, have left us with an impression which haunts our souls and fascinates us like something veiled
and frightening. Stranger still, we who hate pain in others as in
ourselves, we who find Sade and any incitement to bloodshed

nauseating, we feel more than usually in the mood for love and more than usually deprived of our mistress, who has written to say that she cannot come today. I once read somewhere that people who look after the sick are more given to making love than others. How disgusting it all is!

*26 December*

We went back to the hospital at four o'clock to hear the evening prayers; and at the sound of the thin, virginal, sharp yet melodious voice of the kneeling novice, offering up to God the thanks of all that suffering and agony, lifting itself up in its bed or crawling up to the altar, tears came twice to our eyes and we felt that we had not the strength to go on with our documentation from life, that for the time being we had had enough.

We made our escape, and suddenly we noticed that our nervous system, of which we had become unaware in the concentration of all our faculties of physical and moral observation, stirred and shaken on all sides without our knowing it, had been shattered by all that we had seen. We walked along the street, as dazed and exhausted as if we had spent a night at a masked ball or at the gaming tables, deep in a preoccupied mood in which ideas played no part but only pictures. Melancholy floated within us, a breath of hospital air which we had absorbed. This evening our nerves are in such a state that the sound of a dropped fork sends a shudder through our bodies and fills us with an almost angry impatience. We sink into silence beside our fire, sitting snug and still, with the same dread of moving as tired old men.

*27 December*

It is horrible, that hospital smell that follows you around. I do not know if it is real or imaginary, but you constantly feel the need to wash your hands. And the very scents that you put on your hands take on the same vague, insipid smell of ointment.

We must tear ourselves away from all that, tomorrow if possible, by means of some violent distraction which will throw us back into our old world of ideas and preoccupations. Ah, when you are caught up in a thing like that, when you feel all the drama of it throbbing in your head and the material for your work giving you that strange feeling of fear, how paltry the little success of the present day seems to you! And how keenly you realize that that is not what you are aiming at, but rather at rendering what you feel, what you have seen with your eyes and spirit!

# 1861

Saint-Victor, who came to see us today, brought us the news that Murger is dying of an illness in which one rots alive, a senile gangrene complicated by carbuncles, something horrible in which one falls to pieces. When they tried to trim his moustache the other day, the lip came away with the hairs. Ricord says that if they amputated both his legs, they might be able to keep him alive another week.

Death sometimes strikes me as a cruel jest, a joke played by some pitiless deity. The last time I saw Murger, a month ago at the Café Riche, he was looking wonderfully fit. He was gay and happy. He had just had a success with a one-act play produced at the Palais-Royal. All the papers had talked more about this trifle than about all his novels put together; and he told us that it was just too stupid to slave away at writing books for which nobody thanked you and which brought nothing in, and that he was going to go on writing for the stage and make money the easy way. This is the end of that future.

A death, when you come to think of it, which has something Biblical about it. It strikes me as the death of Bohemia, this death by decomposition, in which everything in Murger's life and the world which he depicted is combined: the orgies of work at night, the periods of poverty followed by periods of junketing, the neglected cases of pox, the ups and downs of an existence without a home, the suppers instead of dinners, and the glasses of absinthe bringing consolation after a visit to the pawnshop; everything which wears a man out, burns him up, and finally kills him; a life opposed to all the principles of physical and spiritual hygiene, which results in a man dying in shreds at the age of forty-two, without enough strength left in him to suffer, and complaining of only one thing, the smell of rotten meat in his bedroom—the smell of his own body.

Charles-Edmond and Julie dined with us this evening. Charles-Edmond had just met Dumas, who had told him about all that he had seen in Italy. Asked for news of his son, he had replied: 'Oh, Alexandre has everything I haven't, and I have everything he hasn't. If you locked me in my bedroom with five women, pens, paper, ink and a play to be written, by the end of an hour I'd have written the five acts and had the five women.'

*Sunday, 17 March*

Flaubert said to us today: 'The story, the plot of a novel is of no interest to me. When I write a novel I aim at rendering a colour, a shade. For instance, in my Carthaginian novel, I want to do something purple. The rest, the characters and the plot, is a mere detail. In *Madame Bovary*, all I wanted to do was to render a grey colour, the mouldy colour of a wood-louse's existence. The story of the novel mattered so little to me that a few days before starting on it I still had in mind a very different Madame Bovary from the one I created: the setting and the overall tone were the same, but she was to have been a chaste and devout old maid. And then I realized that she would have been an impossible character.'

*Sunday, 31 March*

Lunched at Flaubert's with that curious couple Sari and Lagier. Sari is a dark-skinned, crinkly-haired fellow, of the same race as Dumas *père*; intelligent, quick-witted, with sparkling eyes, a ready tongue, and a gift for repartee. He spoke about his Théâtre des Délassements, where the supernumeraries are paid twenty sous a night and the members of the chorus thirty sous. He spoke too about the incurable disease of the theatre which, once you have caught it, always brings you back to the stage—a disease like prostitution or beggary. He told us about workers, nearly all of them very good at their trade, who leave jobs bringing in ten francs a day in order to earn just enough to pay for a four-sou bowl of onion soup in a filthy tavern in the Rue Basse, fascinated as they are by the feverish, bustling life of the theatre; the gossip, comradeship, and love-making of the women; the satisfaction that comes of picking up a chair properly and taking in a letter properly; the interest they feel in the success or failure of a play; the electrifying applause of the audience. The female supernumeraries are often ordinary working-girls, complete with tartan shawls, who take on walking-on parts to fill out a fifty-sou day.

Talk about perfumes led to a mention of the scent of vanilla that hangs around Frédérick Lemaître, who has pods of it sewn into his coat-collars, and who was once nearly poisoned as a result of his habit of kissing the hair of the actresses he plays with, for he kissed Mlle Defodon, who used to put gold dust in her hair, and breathed in that powdered copper.

Still on the subject of smells, we talked about the odour of the theatre, that intoxicating odour composed of a basis of gas mixed with the smell of the wooden flats, the smell of the dust in the wings, and the smell of gluey paint. Then we discussed the scent that rises from the stage when the curtain goes up, that heady atmosphere created by all the elements of an artificial world which, behind the curtain, makes an actress flare her nostrils and neigh with delight as soon as she comes on stage.

*Monday, 6 May*

At four o'clock we were at Flaubert's, who had invited us to a reading of *Salammbô*, together with a painter called Gleyre whom we found already there. From four till six, Flaubert read to us in his booming, sonorous voice, which cradles you in a sound like a bronze murmur. At seven we dined, and after dinner and a pipe, the reading was resumed, taking us by way of readings and summaries of what was omitted, to the end of the last chapter, the copulation of Salammbô and Mathô. It was then two in the morning.

I am now going to write what I think, in my heart of hearts, of this work by a man I like—and there are not many such men—and whose first book I greatly admired. *Salammbô* is less than what I expected from Flaubert. His personality, so well dissembled, so completely absent from that impersonal work, *Madame Bovary*, comes through here, blown up, melodramatic, declamatory, resorting to bombastic writing and crude colouring, one might almost say illumination. Flaubert sees the Orient, and what is more the Orient of antiquity, in the guise of an Algerian bazaar. Some of his effects are childish, others ridiculous. The attempt to rival Chateaubriand is the great defect of the book, robbing it of originality: *Les Martyrs* keeps coming through. Then there is nothing more wearisome than the everlasting descriptions, the button-by-button portrayal of the characters, the miniature-like representation of every costume. The crowd scenes suffer as a result. The effects are narrowed down and concentrated on a single point; faces are eclipsed by clothes, feelings by landscapes. The effort is undoubtedly immense, the patience infinite, and the talent rare in this attempt to reconstruct in every detail a vanished civilization. But for this task, a hopeless task in my opinion, Flaubert had none of those inspirations, none of those revelations by analogy, which bring to light a bit of the soul of a nation which has disappeared. He believes that he has performed a 'moral reconstruction', and it is the 'moral colouring' that he prides himself on having rendered. But this moral colouring is the weakest part of his book. His characters' sentiments are not the product of a certain conscience, lost with a certain civilization: they are the commonplace, universal sentiments of all humanity and not of Carthaginian humanity; and his Mathô is at bottom no more than an opera tenor in a barbaric poem.

*26 May*

At dinner at Grosse-Tête's, the vaudeville-writer Martin told us that when he was chatting today with a tart, she complained that the business was being ruined by the railways. 'You see,' she said, 'imagine a poor girl who's bored and unhappy in the country. She saves up to buy a ticket on the railway. She arrives in Paris and gets a job as a maid with an old gentleman. The old gentleman does her up. He gives her twenty francs and she buys herself a silk dress. She goes for a walk along the boulevard in her silk dress. She picks up a twenty-franc man. And on her way home, she says to herself she's a fool to earn twenty francs a month when she can earn twenty francs any evening. She saves up to take a room in a hotel for a week. She takes the room and finds a dressmaker who rigs her out on tick. Off she goes to Mabille . . . and there's another one in circulation!'

*12 June*

The old age of certain old men is like the childhood of immortality.

*22 July*

I dined with Charles-Edmond, after spending the day delivering copies of *Sœur Philomène* to the critics. Charles-Edmond has just come back from a few days with Hugo in Brussels. The day he arrived there, Hugo had just written *finis* to *Les Misérables*. 'Dante', he said, 'made an Inferno out of poetry; I have tried to make one out of reality.'

It seems that he finds living in exile perfectly tolerable, refusing to acknowledge that a man's homeland is just a piece of earth. 'What is France?' he says. 'An idea. Paris? I have no need of Paris. Paris is the Rue de Rivoli, and I have always loathed the Rue de Rivoli.'

*30 July*

I have drunk my fill, I have had my mistress. I am in that condition in which the monstrosities one has committed seem like children's games. I am left with a craving which, in drunkenness, outlasts love and copulation, a craving which shows all over a man's face, in his mouth and in his flaring nostrils. How utterly futile debauchery seems once it has been accomplished, and what ashes of disgust it leaves in the soul! The pity of it is that the soul outlives the body, or in other words that impression judges sensation and that one thinks about and finds fault with the pleasure one has taken.

And these are the thoughts which occur to me.

The facts: nothing matters but the facts: worship of the facts leads to everything, to happiness first of all and then to wealth.

Touch this or that switch in a woman and out comes either pleasure or truth: you can make her admit at will that she is having an orgasm or that she loves you. This is appalling. Bonald's maxim needs to be reversed: man is a mind betrayed, not served, by his organs.

There are moments when, faced with our lack of success, I wonder whether we are failures, proud but impotent. One thing reassures me as to our value: the boredom that afflicts us. It is the hall-mark of quality in modern men. Chateaubriand died of it, long before his death. Byron was stillborn with it. The essence of bourgeois talent is to be gay. Voltaire spent his life taking an interest in something: himself.

There are moments of discouragement when glory seems as insignificant as the office of mayor of a little market-town.

Debauchery is perhaps an act of despair in the face of infinity.

Any man who does not see everything in terms of self, that is to say who wants to be something in respect of other men, to do good to them or simply give them something to do, is unhappy, disconsolate, and accursed.

*10 October*

Dining at home with Saint-Victor and Charles-Edmond, we talked about that great little theatre, the *Figaro* of theatres, the Bouffes: the place it occupies, the curiosity it arouses, the various worlds it touches upon, from the Jockey Club to the *demi-monde*. A high-class place of ill repute, the home of the short skirt, the naughty song and the dirty joke, a sweetmeat box of ditties and bidets, with photographs of the actresses in their low-cut dresses at the door, the theatre of private rooms and little boxes, a circus of dandies where the reputations of such as Hector Crémieux are made—Hector Crémieux who goes up and up, minting money with plays he does not write, a humbug who is also a Jewish clown, a buffoon who cooks up showy couplets.

These people form a little world of their own, from Halévy to Crémieux, from Crémieux to Villemessant, from Villemessant to Offenbach, Chevalier of the Legion of Honour—all doing shady deals, selling something of everything, selling even their wives to some extent, throwing them into the company of actors and actresses; a world that starts at the bottom with Commerson and reaches the top with Morny, Offenbach's patron, the amateur musician, the typical man of the Empire, steeped in all the corruption of Paris, the representative of every petty grandeur, a collector who sells pictures, a dilettante minister, one of the authors of the Second of December and of *Monsieur Choufleury*, doing business as an auctioneer and composing music for brothels, a vulgar libertine, the brains of Paris, so taken with Crémieux's wit that he carries him off to the country as his jester.

This world, these people, this rising generation—which one would swear had been brought into the world after a vaudeville, between two deals on the Stock Exchange, and which had promptly

learnt all by itself just how much a couplet brought in—all the immorality in whatever pushes and climbs, scores a success and cap-
tivates the public, all the mud we stir up in talking of this person or
that, all this fills our hearts with sadness and disgust.

*Monday, 28 October*

Sainte-Beuve, who had written to ask if he might come to see us,
came here at two o'clock. He is a short, tubby little man, stockily
built with a peasant's neck and shoulders, dressed in a simple country manner, rather like Béranger, without any stylish touches. He
has a high forehead, a bald white head, large eyes, a long, inquisitive, sensual nose, a wide, crudely shaped mouth, a broad smile
which reveals a set of white teeth, prominent cheekbones like a pair
of wens: altogether a somewhat batrachian face with a pink, well-fed
complexion. To judge by his hale and hearty appearance, his white
forehead and his rosy cheeks, one might take him for an intelligent
provincial coming out of a library, a cloister of books, under which
there was a cellar of rich burgundy.

His conversation is a kind of fluent chatter made up of tiny
touches, like the style of a woman painter who has a little palette
covered with pretty images neatly laid out. It reminds one of a picture by Metzu, painted in a hesitating manner without any broad
sweep of the brush.

Talking to us about Flaubert, he said: 'One shouldn't take so
long over writing a book, or else one arrives too late for one's own
time. For works like Virgil, of course, it's different. And then too,
he'll never give us anything but Chateaubriand's *Martyrs*. After
*Madame Bovary* he ought to have written something living; then
his name would have remained in the great battle of the novel,
whereas I have been forced to take the fight on to poorer ground,
with *Fanny*.[1]'

He said how frustrating it was to have to jump from one subject
to another, from one century to the next. 'A man has no time to fall
in love with a subject. You mustn't get attached. . . . It wears you
out: it's like tearing a horse's mouth by making it turn left and
right.' And he made the gesture of a man pulling on a rein.

Then he went on to the huge profits made in the theatre: 'Look,

[1] Feydeau's *Fanny* (1858) which Sainte-Beuve had acclaimed as a masterpiece.

barring accidents, I've got work on my hands for the next three years. Well, by the end of those three years I shall have earned about as much as a single unsuccessful play brings in. . . . Verse comedy seems to me to be finished; either you write verse which isn't comedy verse, or you write prose. . . . Everything will go to the novel in the future. It's so vast, it's a form that lends itself to everything. And there's a lot of talent in the novel these days.'

He left, giving us a priestly hand, soft, plump, and cold, and saying: ' Come to see me early in the week. After that I have my nose to the grindstone.'

*Sunday, 3 November*

Dinner at Peters' with Saint-Victor and Claudin. After dinner, Claudin took me off to the Délassements-Comiques. I had worked all week and felt the need, I don't know why, to breathe the air of a cheap theatre. Every now and then a man needs to let himself go. In a corridor I met the manager, Sari. He told me that Lagier had been to see Flaubert at Rouen and was afraid that work and solitude were going to send him off his head. He had talked to her about dancing dervishes and a brothel of birds in his bed and other incomprehensible things. On the subject of this fantastic, brain-fagging work of Flaubert's, somebody told me the other day—he had it from Mlle Bosquet, the governess of Flaubert's niece—that he had given instructions to his servant to speak to him only on Sundays, and then only in order to say: 'Sir, it is Sunday.'

*Thursday, 28 November*

Talking about Mme Swetchine and Sainte-Beuve's article on her, Saint-Victor said to us: 'You know, it was terribly embarrassing meeting her. When you were introduced to her, she would inquire after your soul in the way one inquires after somebody's health. She would ask if you were in a state of grace just as if she were asking whether you had a cold.'

He also told us Gautier's impressions of his visit to Compiègne:[1] 'Everybody behaves very awkwardly: the whole atmosphere is one

---

[1] As a guest in one of the house-parties held regularly by Napoleon III at Compiègne.

of embarrassment. They aren't used to it. They can't really believe that it has happened. The "Bourgeois" himself doesn't know quite how to behave. You can see that he's not sure whether he's playing his part correctly. The only people who are completely at their ease are the old servants, the remnants of the dynastic varletry, handed down from Charles X and Louis-Philippe. They are the only people who look as if they knew what a court was like.'

# 1862

New Year's Day, for us, is All Souls' Day. Our hearts grow chill and count those who are gone.

We climbed five flights of stairs to call on our cousin Cornélie in her poor little room. She was soon obliged to send us away, so many ladies, schoolboys, and relatives came to see her. She had not enough chairs to seat us nor enough space to accommodate us. It is one of the admirable things about the aristocracy that it does not shun poverty. It closes its ranks against it. In middle-class families there are no relatives below a certain degree of wealth or above the fourth floor of a house.

It was in France's bookshop on the Quai Voltaire.[1] A man came in, haggled over the price of a book, haggled for a long time, went out, came back, haggled some more, and finally bought the book. He was a big man with a square head and the gangling gait of a horse-trader. He gave his address so that the book might be sent to him: M. Claye, at Maintenon, near Rambouillet.

'Ah!' said France, writing it down, 'I was there in 1830 with Charles X.'

'So was I', said the big man. 'I was there too. I obtained his last signature, twenty minutes before the deputation from the Provisional Government arrived. I was there with my gig. Oh, he needed money badly just then! He was selling his plate and selling it cheap: I had twenty-five thousand francs' worth for twenty-three thousand. If only I had got there sooner! He sold two hundred thousand francs' worth in all. I had fifteen thousand men to feed— his Guard. I was an army contractor.'

[1] Edmond lived long enough to see the bookseller's son, Anatole France, win fame as a novelist and critic.

'In that case,' said France, 'you fed us very badly! I remember that we had to kill a poor cow in a field. . . .'

'What can you expect at times like that?'

Chance had brought them face to face: the old soldier of Charles X's Guard and the contractor who had taken advantage of royal misfortune to swindle a king at bay out of his plate. The soldier was now a bookseller, the contractor a bloated bourgeois basking in wealth and comfort. I wanted to see the book he had bought: it was a *History of the Crimes of the Papacy*.

*Friday, 21 February*

We dined with Flaubert at the Charles-Edmonds'. The conversation turned at one point to his love affair with Mme Colet and her novel about it, *Lui*. He showed no bitterness or resentment as he spoke about this woman who had apparently intoxicated him with her insane, dramatic love, full of thrills and shocks and emotions. There is a natural coarseness in Flaubert that takes pleasure in that sort of sensual, excitable woman who wears love out with her passionate transports, her outbursts of anger, her physical or spiritual frenzies. Once she went so far as to travel to his home to see him and made his mother stay and listen to their quarrel. His mother has never forgotten her son's harsh treatment of his mistress, which she regards as an injury done to the whole of her sex. 'It is the only point of discord between my mother and me', Flaubert said. He too had been madly in love with Mme Colet. One day he nearly killed her. 'I could hear the chair in the dock at the Assize Court creaking beneath me.' One of his grandfathers, he told us, had married a native woman in Canada, and one can indeed see something of the redskin in his appearance, his character, his very tastes—a certain violence, health, and vulgarity.

Claudin told me this story. He was having supper with Roger de Beauvoir at the Maison d'Or. They decided they wanted some tarts to amuse them, rang for the commissionaire, and sent him to fetch some from La Farcy's brothel. The tarts failed to arrive. Roger leant over the banister and saw the commissionaire deep in a book. He called him and asked him what he was reading.

'I'm reading what His Grace told me to read', said the man, a fair-haired booby of a German.

'Whose Grace?'

'His Grace the Bishop of Nancy, where I come from. He said to me: "You are going to Paris. It is a place of perdition. Read Tertullian." So I am reading Tertullian.'

He was reading Tertullian on the staircase of the Maison d'Or, in between running errands to La Farcy's. The imagination of man can never hope to match the improbabilities and contrasts of life.

*1 March*

Went to the opening night of *Rothomago* at the Cirque. A dazzling audience. It is becoming the fashion to go to premières. The balcony was resplendent with demi-mondaines and the corridors were crowded with those handsome men wearing foreign decorations who fill the corridors of the Opéra on ball nights. In the boxes there was quite a pretty array of prostitutes. It is wonderful what a centre of debauchery the theatre is. From the stage to the auditorium, from the wings to the stage, from the auditorium to the stage and from one side of the auditorium to the other, invisible threads criss-cross between dancers' legs, actresses' smiles and spectators' opera-glasses, presenting an overall picture of Pleasure, Orgy, and Intrigue. It would be impossible to gather together in a smaller space a greater number of sexual stimulants, of invitations to copulation. It is like a Stock Exchange dealing in women's nights.

I went and sat in Gisette Dennery's box. In the next box were her friends, the mistresses of Champs-Élysées horse-dealers called Tony, one of whom was a famous sometime bare-back rider at the Hippodrome, Rosalie. These women have horrifying heads, half antique cameo, half animal, sculpturally, implacably bestial in appearance— typical gladiators' women, beast-fighters' mistresses.

Into their box came a pale, brown-haired woman with velvety eyes like black diamonds, who said as she entered: 'He made a magnificent speech . . . and so moderate!' It was Jeanne de Tourbey, Prince Napoleon's latest mistress.

During one of the intervals I went out on to the boulevard.

Gautier hooked his arm through mine and we stood smoking and chatting.

'This is how I like the theatre', he said, '—outside! I've got three women in my box (his wife and his two daughters) who will tell me what has been happening on the stage.' Then, worried about the way things are shaping, the atmosphere of anxiety and uneasiness in the air, he went on: 'The trouble nowadays is that you've no sooner come to an arrangement with the powers that be. . . . Because after all, you can't withdraw from your time. There's a power and a morality imposed by the bourgeois of your age to which you have to submit. You have to be on good terms with your local police inspector. All I ask is to be left quietly in my corner.'

'You want the Government to guarantee your security.'

'That's it. You see, I got on very well with the Orléans family. Then '48 came along and the Republic put me on the shelf for a while. I came to terms with the Republic, and got on to the *Moniteur* . . . and now this business starts, and the man [Napoleon III] wobbles from right to left, so that nobody knows what he wants to do. And then, nowadays you aren't allowed to say anything at all. What can you do when they won't have any sex in a novel? I used to have a sculptural, plastic side to my talent which I've had to repress. Now I'm reduced to writing a conscientious description of a wall; and even so, I'm not allowed to describe what may be drawn on it, a phallus for instance.'

I went back into the theatre. The door of the next box was opened and a big sealed envelope was handed to Jeanne de Tourbey, who promptly hid it as ostentatiously as possible, so that all around her people whispered: 'It's from the Prince!' A quarter of an hour later another envelope arrived and the same thing happened. Perhaps they were the proofs of the Prince's speech. What a farce! This prince's mistress, chatting with circus artistes in a box full of whores, arranging for sealed envelopes to be delivered to her in public, for policemen with despatches to knock at her door! This sometime whore from a Reims brothel, still tied to a theatre manager by the bonds which join people who have prostituted themselves together, and procured for the Prince by Girardin! Come now! These are princely amours of a very petty, paltry sort. And I enjoy witnessing them from such close quarters in all their despicable absurdity.

*11 March*

I went today to see the famous *Spring* of M. Ingres. It is a reconstruction of a girl's body in antiquity, a polished, painstaking, ridicu-
lously naïve reconstruction. Woman's body is not immutable. It
changes with each civilization, age and way of life. Her body in the
time of Phidias was quite unlike her body in our own time. Other
days, other ways, other lines. The elongated, slender grace of
Goujon and Mazzola is simply the woman of their time depicted
in her essential elegance. Similarly all that Boucher does is portray
the typical eighteenth-century courtesan, all plump and dimpled. The
painter who does not paint the woman of his time will not endure.

*15 March*

This morning a doctor gave me this astonishing information
about the Emperor's amours.[1] Each new woman is brought to the
Tuileries in a cab, undressed in an ante-room, and taken naked into
the room where the Emperor, likewise naked, is waiting for her, by
Bacciochi, who gives her this warning and permission: 'You may
kiss His Majesty anywhere except on the face.' In the whole history
of deification, I cannot remember another instance of a man's face
being made a Holy of holies that would be profaned by a kiss!

*29 March*

Flaubert, sitting on his big divan with his legs crossed Turkish
fashion and talking of his dreams and plans for future novels, confided in us the desire which he had conceived long ago and which
he had never given up, to write a novel about the modern Orient,
the Orient in Western clothes. He became excited at the idea of all
the antitheses which his talent would find in the subject: scenes
taking place in Paris, scenes taking place in Constantinople and on
the Nile, scenes of European hypocrisy, scenes of secret savagery
in the East—the whole thing reminiscent of one of those boats
which have a Turk dressed by Dusautoy standing on the deck, forward, and below decks, aft, the same Turk's harem. He spoke of
heads cut off for a mere suspicion or in a sudden temper, and re-

---

[1] As a necessary precaution under the Second Empire, the Goncourts wrote only
the initials of the words *Emperor*, *Tuileries*, and *His Majesty*.

joiced at the thought of painting the scum of the earth—Europeans, Jews, Muscovites, Greeks. He dwelt at length on the strange contrasts he would show here and there between the Oriental becoming civilized and the European reverting to a state of savagery, like that French chemist who settled on the confines of the Libyan desert and abandoned all the habits and manners of his native land.

From this book which was just sketched out in his mind, he went on to another which he said he had been thinking about for a long time: an immense novel, a great picture of life, held together by a plot in which the characters would murder each other in a society based on Balzac's Thirteen, and where the penultimate survivor, a politician, would be sent to the guillotine by the last of them all, a judge, and that for a good deed.[1] He said that he would also like to write two or three short novels, very simple and uneventful, which would deal with the husband, the wife, and the lover.

In the evening, after dinner, we went to see Gautier at Neuilly, and found him still at table, though it was nine o'clock, doing honour to Prince Radziwill, who was dining with him, and to a little Pouilly wine which he declared to be very pleasant. He has the gaiety of a child: it is one of the delightful things about him.

Getting up from table, we all moved into the drawing-room, where Flaubert was asked to dance The Drawing-room Idiot. He borrowed Gautier's tail-coat, turned the collar up, and did something with his hair, his face, his physiognomy, which transformed him all of a sudden into a fantastic caricature of imbecility. In a spirit of emulation, Gautier took off his frock-coat and, dripping with sweat, his great bottom bulging out over his legs, danced The Creditor's Dance for us. And the evening ended with gypsy songs, wild melodies, whose strident notes Prince Radziwill rendered with wonderful gusto.

*30 March*

The fourth floor at No. 2, Rue Racine. We rang the bell and a very ordinary-looking little gentleman opened the door, said with

---

[1] The first novel mentioned, provisionally entitled *Harel-Bey*, came to nothing. The second, which was to have been called *Le Serment des amis*, was also never written, but the ironical ending was transferred to *L'Éducation sentimentale*, where Dussardier is killed in the *coup d'état* of 1851 by Sénécal, a former friend who has become a policeman.

a smile: 'Messieurs de Goncourt?', pushed open another door, and showed us into a very large room, a big studio. Sitting with its back to the window at the far end, through which the cold light of early evening was falling, was a sort of grey shadow silhouetted against that pale light: a woman who did not rise or make any movement in response to the greeting expressed in our bow and our words. This shadow, sitting there apparently asleep, was Mme George Sand, and the man who had shown us in was her lover, the engraver Manceau.

Mme Sand looks like a ghostly automaton. She talks in a mechanical, monotonous voice which neither rises nor falls but maintains a dead level. In her attitude there is an almost elephantine gravity and dignity, the placidity of a ruminant. She recalls those cold, calm women in Mierevelt's portraits, or perhaps the mother superior of a Magdalen hospital. Her gestures are the slow gestures of a somnambulist; every now and then a wax match is struck, a little flame appears and her cigarette lights up, always with the same methodical movements. There is not a gleam of light either in the sound of her voice or in the colour of her speech.

She was very nice to us and extremely complimentary, but with such commonplace kindliness, such platitudinous expressions, and such childish ideas that the overall effect was as chilling as a bare wall. This was banality in the highest degree.

Manceau introduced a little life into the conversation. We talked about her theatre at Nohant, where plays are put on for her and her maid, lasting until four in the morning: she seems to suffer from a mania for marionettes, putting on gala performances for her friends and their children during the three summer months she calls her holidays. Then we spoke of her prodigious faculty for work. She told us that there was no merit in her work, that there were people whose work was meritorious but that she had always found it easy. She works every night from one o'clock until four, and gets up at eleven; then she works for another two hours during the day. 'It doesn't matter if she's disturbed', Manceau told us, as if he were a guide explaining a natural phenomenon. 'It's as if you had a tap running. Somebody comes in and you turn it off. . . .' And she said: 'Yes, I don't mind being interrupted by people I like, by peasants who come to talk to me. . . .' Here the humanitarian note was struck.

When we got up to go, she rose, gave us her hand and showed

us to the door. At that point we were able to catch a glimpse of her face, which is sweet, gentle, and serene; the colour has gone out of it but the features are still delicately defined in a pallid, matt complexion of a pale amber hue. There is a serenity and a subtlety in these features which her latest portrait, coarsening her and over-emphasizing the line of her nose, entirely fails to reveal.

*Tuesday, 8 April*

Dined with Charles, who told me that Hugo always has a note-book in his pocket and that if, in conversation with you, he happens to express the tiniest thought, to put forward the smallest idea, he promptly turns away from you, takes out his note-book and writes down what he has just said. He turns everything into copy or munitions. Nothing is ever lost: it all goes into some book or other. He has brought this system to such a pitch of perfection that his sons, who live in hopes of using what they hear him say, are always beaten to it: whenever one of their father's books comes out, they see all the notes they have been taking in print.

*22 July*

Little by little, disease is accomplishing its frightful work in our poor Rose. It is like a slow, gradual death of the almost immaterial things which emanated from her body. She no longer has the same looks. Her face has completely altered, and she seems to be ridding herself and as it were stripping herself of all that surrounds a human being, of that something by which one can recognize a personality. A human being sheds its leaves like a tree. Sickness prunes it down; and it no longer offers the same silhouette to the eyes which loved it, to the people to whom it afforded shade and comfort. Those who are dear to us fade from our sight before they die. The unknown takes possession of them: something strange and new and stiff in their appearance.

*31 July*

I am waiting, this morning, for Dr. Simon, who is going to tell me whether Rose is to live or die. I am waiting for the dreadful sound of the doorbell as if it were the sound of the bell that marks the return of the jury to the courtroom. . . .

It is all over. There is no hope: it is only a question of time. The disease has made swift progress. One lung is done for and the other is affected.

And now we have to go back to the sick woman, to pour serenity over her with our smiles and to suggest the idea of convalescence with everything in our bearing. We feel impatient to escape from the apartment and this poor woman.

*16 August*

At ten o'clock this morning there was a ring at the door. I heard the maid and the porter exchanging a few words. The door opened and the porter came in with a letter. 'Gentlemen,' he said, 'I bring you sad news.' I took the letter; it bore the stamp of Lariboisière. Rose had died this morning at seven o'clock.

Poor woman! So it was all over! I had known that she was doomed, but after seeing her on Thursday, still looking very much alive, almost happy and gay. . . . The two of us stood there in the drawing-room with the thought which the news of somebody's death always inspires: 'We shall never see her again!'—a mechanical thought which recurs again and again.

What a loss, what a gap in our lives! A habit, an affection, a devotion of twenty-five years' duration: a servant who knew all about our lives, who opened our letters when we were away, to whom we told everything. I rolled a hoop with her when I was a boy, and she bought me apple turnovers on the bridges. She used to wait up for Edmond until the morning when he went to the Opéra ball in my mother's time. It was this woman, this admirable nurse, whose hands our dying mother put into ours. She had the keys to everything; she decided and did everything for us. For as long as we could remember we had made the same old jokes about her ugliness and her ungainly body, and for twenty-five years she had given us a kiss every night. She shared everything with us, our sorrows and our joys. Hers was one of those devotions which one hopes will be there to close one's eyes when death comes. Our bodies, in sickness or pain, were accustomed to her attentions. She knew all our habits, and she had known all our mistresses. She was a portion of our life, part of the furniture in our apartment, a piece of flotsam from our youth; something tender and devoted, gruff and solicitous, like a watchdog; something which was always beside us and around us and which we expected to disappear only when we did.

And now we shall never, never see her again! It is not Rose whom we can hear moving about in the kitchen; it will not be Rose who will open the door for us; it will not be Rose who will come into our bedrooms in the morning and bid us good day! This is a great rent in our lives, a great change which somehow seems to us one of those solemn ruptures in existence when, as Byron puts it, the Fates change horses.

At the end of all this journeying into the past, peace came to our grief. Recollection gave it comfort; and then too, we had something like an impression of deliverance for her and for ourselves.

The chance or irony of things! This evening, exactly twelve hours after the poor woman breathed her last, we have to go and dine with Princess Mathilde, who for some reason or other wants to make our acquaintance.

*Thursday, 21 August*

Yesterday I learnt things about poor Rose, only lately dead and practically still warm, which astonished me more than anything else in the whole of my life; things which completely took away my appetite, filling me with a stupefaction from which I have not yet recovered and which has left me positively dazed. All of a sudden, within a matter of minutes, I was brought face to face with an unknown, dreadful, horrible side of the poor woman's life.[1]

Those bills she signed, those debts she left with all the tradesmen, all had an unbelievable, horrifying explanation. She had lovers whom she paid. One of them was the son of our dairywoman, who fleeced her and for whom she furnished a room. Another was given our wine and chickens. A secret life of dreadful orgies, nights out, sensual frenzies that prompted one of her lovers to say: 'It's going to kill one of us, me or her!' A passion, a sum of passions, of head, heart, and senses, in which all the unfortunate woman's ailments

[1] Altering this entry in 1887, Edmond explained that it was the midwife Maria who, in the course of a lunch saddened by reminiscences of the dead woman, had suddenly lost patience with the two brothers and told them the story of Rose's secret life.

played their part: consumption, making her desperate for satisfaction, hysteria, and madness. She had two children by the dairywoman's son, one of which lived six months. When, a few years ago, she told us she was going into hospital, it was to have a child. And her love for all these men was so sickly, excessive, and overwhelming that she, who was the very soul of honesty, robbed us, yes, robbed us of a twenty-franc piece out of every hundred francs, and all in order to keep her lovers and pay for their sprees.

Then, after these involuntary offences, committed in violent contradiction to her upright nature, she would sink into such despondency, such remorse, such self-reproach, that in this inferno in which she went from one lapse to another without ever finding satisfaction, she started drinking in order to escape from herself, to postpone the future, to flee the present, to sink and drown for a few hours in one of those slumbers, those torpors which used to lay her out for a whole day on a bed on to which she had collapsed while making it.

And what did the unfortunate woman die of? Of having gone to Montmartre one night eight months ago, during the winter, unable to repress her curiosity, in order to spy on the dairywoman's son, who had thrown her out; a night spent standing at a ground-floor window, trying to see who the woman was who had replaced her; a night from which she had returned soaked to the skin and mortally sick with pleurisy.

Poor woman! We forgive her. Indeed, seeing something of what she must have suffered at the hands of those working-class pimps, we pity her. We are filled with a deep commiseration for her, but also with a great bitterness at this astounding revelation. Remembering our mother, who was so pure and to whom we were everything, and then thinking of Rose's heart, which we believed belonged to us, we feel something of a disappointment at the discovery that there was a great part of it which we did not occupy. Suspicion of the entire female sex has entered into our minds for the rest of our lives: a horror of the duplicity of woman's soul, of her prodigious gift, her consummate genius for mendacity.

*Sunday, 26 October*

It was Chapuys-Montlaville, the senator, who, after the Emperor had taken a bath at the Prefecture in the course of his tour of the south of France, had the bath-water drawn off and bottled. He decanted it as if it were Jordan water. And this happened in the middle of the nineteenth century—which does not prevent us from laughing at a nation which worships a Grand Lama's excrement. There are two infinites in this world: God up above, and down below, human baseness.

*15 November*

Every now and then, at Compiègne, a writer or artist is included at the end of a batch of guests: tradition has to be respected! Here is an instance of the sort of gracious welcome which is accorded to them. It was given to us by the very person who had the honour of attracting the Emperor's kindly notice. The Emperor was complaining that his sight was failing: 'The queer thing is that I can't tell the difference between black and blue any more. Who is that over there?' 'Sire, it is Monsieur Berlioz.' He raised his voice.

'Monsieur Berlioz, is your tail-coat blue or black?'

'Sire,' Berlioz hastened to reply, 'I should never take the liberty of appearing before Your Majesty in a blue tail-coat; it is black.'

'Good', said the Emperor.

And that was all the Emperor said to him in four days.

*Saturday, 22 November*

Gavarni, together with Veyne, the accredited doctor of Bohemia, Sainte-Beuve, and ourselves, has organized a dinner which is to take place twice a month and which is to be enlarged to include other guests. The first was held this evening at Magny's, where Sainte-Beuve usually dines. We had an exquisite meal, perfect in every respect, a meal such as I had thought impossible to obtain in a Paris restaurant.

*Sunday, 23 November*

Flaubert's immense, secret pride can be seen in *Salammbô*: he uses the same format, the same posters as Hugo, even the same type as in the title of *Les Contemplations*.

There is still a slight chill between us: we are guilty in his eyes of leading Sainte-Beuve astray. I begin to see all manner of hidden sides to him. He quietly pushes himself forward, establishes relations with important people, creates a network of useful acquaintances, all the time pretending to be independent, lazy, and fond of solitude. The other day, he showed me a letter from Jeanne de Tourbey inviting him to dinner and saying: 'Somebody would like to see you.' He told me that he was not going, that he had no desire to see that *somebody* who was the Prince. I learnt from Sainte-Beuve yesterday that he went after all.

Saint-Victor, with whom I dined this evening, dined at Jeanne de Tourbey's yesterday with the Prince. That tart considers it incumbent on her to play the Pompadour: she has taken to inviting writers to her table. Somebody has persuaded her that she can read: she apparently believes it and talks about literature. She complained bitterly yesterday about a slang expression used in Feydeau's current serial, like a delicate creature wounded and offended in the purity of her taste. It seems that wealth teaches those women everything, even to blush at their mother-tongue.

*6 December*

Flaubert came to see me yesterday during the day. I told him more or less what Sainte-Beuve had said to me about *Salammbô*. He could not conceal his anger and humiliation. The word *tragedy* and the epithet *classical* had cut him to the quick, and showing his real feelings in his anger, he said two minutes later: 'Oh, he's a proper blackguard, our friend Sainte-Beuve! He's a lickspittle of Prince Napoleon's, and a filthy pig too.'

This evening there was the dinner of our society, which we have decided to call the Gavarni Society, at Magny's. As I went in I saw Flaubert getting hold of Sainte-Beuve and, with a wealth of gestures, trying to convince him of the excellence of his work.

After dinner, in a private aside, Sainte-Beuve let out the reason for his profound but hidden melancholy, his buried but nonetheless real despair: he would like to be handsome, to possess what he calls a physique, to have an irresistible attraction for women—his temptation, his supreme preoccupation, the object to which he constantly reverts, his ideal, his inclination, his fancy, his fascination, the humiliating desire of an old man. There is a melancholy, disappointed satyr at the bottom of that little old man, who is conscious of his ugliness, his repulsiveness, and above all his age. 'Ah,' he said, 'I'm all for the ordinary, commonplace ideas: it is better to be young than old, rich than poor. Not that I should like to live my life over again: I wouldn't want to live three days of it a second time.'

The first thing Flaubert said as we came out was: 'He has come round quite a lot, old Sainte-Beuve. He is going to give me three articles and apologize to me in the last.' And almost immediately afterwards he said: 'He's a charming man.'

His pride has grown to such proportions that he is almost bursting with it. He told us that he had made a great many alterations to Feydeau's *Fanny*, and that since Feydeau had asked his advice less and less after that, it was not surprising that the quality of his work had deteriorated so considerably!

He is full of paradoxes which, like his vanity, have something provincial about them. They are coarse, heavy, clumsy, laboured, and graceless. He has a dirty wit. On the subject of love, which he often talks about, he has all manner of complicated, fanciful theories, affected theories designed to impress. At bottom, there is a great deal of the rhetor and the sophist in him. He is at once coarse and precious in his obscenity. On the excitement that women give him, he will establish a thousand subdivisions, saying that one woman arouses in him only the desire to kiss her eyebrows, another to kiss her hand, a third to stroke her hair, bringing studied affectation and an expert lover's elaborate technique to such simple things as these. For instance, describing his first attempt at making love to Colet, while taking her home one day in a cab, he told us that he had played the part of a pessimist, a melancholic with suicidal tendencies, a part which had amused him so much that he had been obliged to look out of the window every now and then, so as to be able to laugh freely.

# 1863

There is no straight line in Nature. It is a human invention, perhaps the only one which is entirely due to man. Greek architecture, the principle of which is the straight line, is absolutely contrary to Nature.

*21 January*

This week we received an invitation to spend this evening at Princess Mathilde's. Flaubert was there too. The three of us formed an odd-looking group: we were almost the only three people there without decorations. And looking at the three of us, I reflected that the government of that man sitting near us, the justice of that Emperor whom we could almost touch with our elbows, had dragged all three of us through the police courts for outraging public morality. The irony of it all!

*14 February*

Our Saturday dinners are delightful. The conversation touches upon everything under the sun.

Nogent-Saint-Laurent, who is a member of the Committee on Literary Copyright, said that he favoured perpetuity of rights. Sainte-Beuve protested violently: 'You are paid by the smoke and noise you stir up. You ought to say, every writer ought to say: "Take it all: you're welcome to it!"' Flaubert, going to the opposite extreme, exclaimed: 'If I had invented the railways I shouldn't want anybody to travel on them without my permission!' Thoroughly roused, Sainte-Beuve retorted: 'No more literary property than any other property! There should be no property at all. Everything should be regularly renewed, so that everybody can take his turn.'

In these few words, sprung from the most secret and sincere

depths of his soul, I saw the fanatical revolutionary bachelor in Sainte-Beuve, and he seemed at that moment to have the character and almost the appearance of one of the levellers of the Convention. I saw the basic destructive urge in that man who, rubbing shoulders with society, money, and power, had conceived a secret hatred for them, a bitter jealousy which extended to everything, to youth, to the conquest of women, to the good looks of his neighbour at dinner, Nieuwerkerke, who had slept with real society women without having to pay.

We talked about love and women. 'For my part,' said Sainte-Beuve, 'my ideal is eyes, hair, teeth, shoulders and the rest. A little dirt doesn't upset me: I like dirt.' An argument started as to whether a woman could be satisfied only at a certain age. Sainte-Beuve maintained the wrong-headed theory that any man can satisfy a woman and that it is up to him. After that we talked about women at night and the nightcaps which ladies wear in bed. 'Then I've never slept with a lady', said Sainte-Beuve. 'My women don't wear nightcaps. I've never seen anything more than a net. Come to that, I've never in my life spent a whole night with a woman, on account of my work.' He displayed tremendous indignation against the depilation of oriental women. 'It must look like a priest's chin', said Saint-Victor, backing him up. And the incident ended with a violent diatribe by Sainte-Beuve against the Orient for mutilating everything.

The conversation went back to literature. Somebody mentioned Hugo, and Sainte-Beuve jumped as if he had been bitten, declaring: 'He's a charlatan, a fake, the first writer to speculate in literature!' And when Flaubert said that he would rather be Hugo than anybody else, Sainte-Beuve rightly retorted: 'No, in literature one would not wish to be anybody but oneself; one would like to appropriate some of another writer's qualities, but remaining oneself.' He agreed too that Hugo had a wonderful gift of initiation:

'He taught me to write poetry. And one day, at the Louvre, looking at the pictures, he taught me about painting, although I have forgotten it all since. He's got an amazing constitution, that man. His barber told me once that his beard was three times as stiff as anybody else's and that it nicked all his razors. He had the teeth of a shark and he could crack peach stones with them. And his eyes! When he was writing his *Feuilles d'automne* we went up to the top of the towers of Notre-Dame nearly every evening to see the sun-sets—which, incidentally, didn't amuse me very much. Well, from up there, he could tell the colour of the dress Mademoiselle Nodier was wearing on the balcony of the Arsenal.'

A constitution like that may be the strength of a man of genius. But all our fellow diners forgot that this strength has a complementary defect, which is coarseness. The coarseness of the health of men of genius enters into their genius. If a writer is to produce a work of delicacy and exquisite melancholy, if he is to play rare and delicious variations on the vibrant strings of the heart and the soul, then he must have a sickly side to his nature. Like Heine, the Christ of his art, he must be somewhat crucified physically.

*28 February*

Dinner at Magny's. Charles-Edmond brought along Turgenev, that exquisitely gifted Russian, the author of *Memoirs of a Russian Noble*, *Anteor*, and *A Russian Hamlet*. He is a delightful colossus, a gentle, white-haired giant, who looks like a druid or the kindly old monk in *Romeo and Juliet*. He is handsome, but in an awe-inspiring, impressive way, like Nieuwerkerke. But Nieuwerkerke's eyes are a silky blue, and there is the blue of the heavens in Turgenev's eyes. With the kindliness of his gaze goes the gentle caress of the Russian accent, something like the singing of a child or a Negro. A modest man, touched by the ovation we gave him, he spoke to us about Russian literature, saying that it was tending towards realism in every field from the theatre to the novel. He said that the public in Russia were great readers of periodical literature and blushed to confess that he and a dozen others whom we did not know were paid 600 francs a sheet. On the other hand, a book brought in very little, 4,000 francs at the most.

Somebody mentioned Heine, and we seized the opportunity to express our enthusiastic admiration for him. Sainte-Beuve, who had known him well, said that the man was a frightful rogue, and then, interrupted by a chorus of protest, stopped short and covered his face with his hands while the rest of us praised Heine.

Baudry told us this delightful remark made by Heine on his death-bed. His wife was praying beside him that God might forgive him. 'Have no fear, darling', he said. 'He will forgive me; that's His job.'

*Saturday, 14 March*

Dinner at Magny's. Taine dined with us this evening, with his pleasant, friendly glance under his spectacles, his almost affectionate consideration for others, his rather puny but distinguished appearance, his smooth, flowing, picturesque conversation, full of historical and scientific ideas, and the overall impression he creates of a young, intelligent, even witty professor, in deadly fear of being pedantic.

We talked about the absence of intellectual life in the French provinces, compared with all the active literary societies in the English counties and second or third-class German towns; about the way Paris absorbed everything, attracted everything, and did everything; and about the future of France which, in the circumstances, seemed destined to die of a cerebral haemorrhage. 'Paris', said Taine, 'makes me think of Alexandria in its hey-day. Below Alexandria there dangled the valley of the Nile, but it was a dead valley.'

Apropos of England, I heard Sainte-Beuve confide in Taine his disgust with being a Frenchman. 'But a Parisian isn't a Frenchman,' Taine replied; 'he's a Parisian.' To which Sainte-Beuve retorted: 'Oh, yes, he's still a Frenchman, that is to say he's nothing, he counts for nothing. . . . A country swarming with policemen. . . . I should like to be an Englishman; at least an Englishman is somebody. As a matter of fact, I have some English blood in me. I was born in Boulogne, you know, and my grandmother was English.'

*5 May*

Aubryet told us the other day that a little girl in the street had offered him her sister, a child of fourteen. Her job was to breathe on the windows of the carriage so that the police could not see inside.

*11 May*

The Magny dinner today, with everybody present and two new members, Théophile Gautier and Nefftzer.

The conversation came round to Balzac and stopped there. Sainte-Beuve attacked him: 'It isn't true to life, Balzac isn't true to life. He's a genius if you like, but a monstrosity!'

'But we are all monstrosities', said Gautier.

'And who painted our age?' asked somebody else. 'In what book can we find our society, if not in Balzac?'

'It's all imagination, invention!' cried Sainte-Beuve. 'I knew that Rue Langlade he describes: it wasn't a bit like that.'

'Then in what novels do you find reality?' I asked. 'In Madame Sand's?'

'I must say,' remarked Renan, who was sitting beside me, 'I find Madame Sand more realistic than Balzac.'

'Do you now?'

'Yes. The passions she depicts are universal.'

'But the passions are always universal!'

'And then there's Balzac's style!' exclaimed Sainte-Beuve. 'It's all twisted: it's a *corded* style.'

'Three hundred years from now,' Renan went on, 'people will still be reading Madame Sand.'

'As much as Madame de Genlis! She won't last any more than Madame de Genlis.'

'Balzac is already old-fashioned', said Saint-Victor. 'And what is more, he's too complicated.'

'But look at Hulot!' exclaimed Nefftzer. 'There's a wonderful human character for you!'

'Beauty is always simple', Saint-Victor declared. 'There is nothing more beautiful than the feelings of Homer's characters. They are still fresh and youthful. And you must admit that Andromache is more interesting than Madame Marneffe.'

'Not to me!' said Edmond.

'You can't mean that! Homer . . .'

'Homer', said Gautier, 'is just a poem by Bitaubé for most Frenchmen. It was Bitaubé who made him acceptable. But Homer isn't like that at all. You've only to read him in the Greek to see that. It's really very barbaric, all about people who *paint* themselves!'

'And then,' said Edmond, 'Homer depicts nothing but physical suffering. Depicting moral suffering is quite another matter. Why, any little psychological novel moves me more than Homer.'

'What's that you say?' exclaimed Saint-Victor.

'Yes, *Adolphe* for instance moves me more than Homer.'

'It's enough to make a man throw himself out of the window, to hear things like that!' shouted Saint-Victor, his eyes popping out of his head. Edmond had trampled on his god, and spat upon his host. He stamped and roared, as red in the face as if somebody had insulted his father. 'There's no arguing about the Greeks. . . . Crazy . . . How on earth . . . Homer is absolutely divine. . . .'

There was a general uproar, with everybody talking at once. A voice could be heard saying: 'But Ulysses' dog. . . .'

'Homer, Homer', murmured Sainte-Beuve, with the piety of an Oratorian.

'We are the future!' I shouted at him.

'I am afraid so', he replied sadly.

'Isn't it strange', I said to Renan. 'You may argue about the Pope, deny God, question anything, attack Heaven, the Church, the Holy Sacrament, anything except Homer! Literary religions are peculiar things.'

Finally calm was restored. We gently covered up again the myth called Homer with the three thousand years that have passed over his ashes. And Saint-Victor shook hands with Edmond.

*8 June*

Coming away from a violent discussion at Magny's, my heart pounding in my breast, my throat and tongue parched, I feel convinced that every political argument boils down to this: 'I am better than you are', every literary argument to this: 'I have more taste than you', every argument about art to this: 'I have better eyes than you', every argument about music to this: 'I have a finer ear than you'. It is alarming to see how, in every discussion, we are always alone and never make converts. Perhaps that is why God made us two.

*12 July*

There was a ring at the door. It was a messenger with a note from Sainte-Beuve saying that he was indisposed and asking if we would go and see him to discuss his article on Gavarni.

After a few words about the artist's life, we went on to his lithographs. And we were amazed to hear Sainte-Beuve mangling the captions as he read them out, showing a total ignorance of every Parisian idiom. In the drawings themselves he saw nothing, perceived nothing, failed to see the point of the picture, and could not make out which of the characters in the dialogue was which. He went so far as to take the shadow of one of them for a third character, and for a moment he was comically angry in his insistence that there were three people involved.

And on every point he wanted explanations which he drank in and noted down. He grasped at the slightest remark we let drop and jotted it down on a sheet of paper on which he was building his article with the help of notes scattered here and there, so that it looked like a drawing of a centipede. He asked us for the names of some other genre painters.

'Abraham Bosse', we said.

'What period?' he asked.

'Freudeberg.'

'What was that?'

'Freudeberg.'

'How do you spell it?'

And so it went on. He snatches at your ideas, your remarks, your knowledge, catching it on the wing and gulping it down, without understanding or digesting any of it. We were horrified and embarrassed at the depths of latent stupidity in that man, who can never feel anything himself but has to trust to others, picking their brains and manufacturing articles with the aid of experts, friends, and relatives.

*Monday, 20 July*

Dinner at Magny's. Apropos of Mme Hugo's book about her husband, Gautier said that it was not a red waistcoat he had worn at the opening night of *Hernani*, but a pink doublet. When everybody laughed, he protested: 'But it's a very important point. A red waistcoat would have had a political signification, indicating that I was a republican, when in fact politics didn't come in to it. We were simply *medievalists*. All of us, Hugo included. We didn't know what a republican was. Pétrus Borel was the only republican we knew. We were all against the bourgeois and for Marchangy. We were the portcullis party, that's all. And when, later on, I eulogized antiquity in the preface to *Mademoiselle de Maupin*, the party broke up. Portcullises and nothing but portcullises. I admit that Uncle Beuve has always been a liberal. But in those days Hugo was for Louis XVII.'

'Oh, come now!'

'Yes, Louis XVII. Nobody can tell me that Hugo was a liberal and believed in all that nonsense in 1828. He didn't get mixed up in that filthy business till later. It was on 30 July 1830 that he started to change sides. At bottom, Hugo is absolutely medieval. His house at Jersey is littered with his coats of arms. He was always the Vicomte Hugo. I've got two hundred letters from Madame Hugo, all signed *the Vicomtesse Hugo.*'

'Gautier,' said Sainte-Beuve, 'do you know how we spent the day of the first night of *Hernani*? At two in the afternoon we went with Hugo, whose *fidus Achates* I then was, to the Théâtre-Français. We climbed right up into a lantern-turret and looked down at the queue of people going into the theatre, all of them Hugo's troops. He took fright for a moment when he saw Lassailly going in, because he hadn't given him a ticket. But I reassured him, saying that I could vouch for Lassailly. And then we went and had dinner at Véfour's, downstairs, I think, because Hugo's face was not as famous then as it later became.'

*Wednesday, 19 August*

The conversation this evening at the Princess's turned to Mme Sand. We discussed the question of Mme Sand's love affairs and everybody agreed that she had a very unfeminine nature, with a basic coldness which allowed her to write about her lovers when practically in bed with them. When Mérimée got out of her bed one day and picked up a sheet of paper lying on the table, she snatched it out of his hand: it was a pen-portrait she had done of him.

She hardly ever dressed as a man except at the time of her liaison with Sandeau, and then only to go to the pit at the theatre and to a little restaurant kept by a man called Pinson, who used to say naïvely: 'It's a funny thing, but when she's dressed as a man I call her Madame, and when she's dressed as a woman I call her Monsieur.'

Sainte-Beuve saw her in men's clothes on only one occasion. He was asked to go to the *entresol* where Buloz, who was a bachelor then, was living. As he went in, a young man jumped up from

a divan to greet him: 'Hullo, my dear, Musset knows everything. . . . Will you take me to see the Abbé de Lamennais?' It was
Mme Sand in the throes of breaking with Musset on her return
from Venice. 'Just think of it,' said Sainte-Beuve, 'Lamennais was
still a priest at that time. It was in the winter. And what's more, he
was living in Brittany just then.' Instead of taking her to see Lamennais, he ended up by taking her to see Musset, whom he had urged
to make it up with her. And at the door, when he asked her whether
he should stay, she drew the sword from her swordstick and said:
'No, thank you.' He bowed and left her.

In all these stories of Sainte-Beuve's, one can see the part he
played at that time, the part of an eavesdropper, father-confessor,
and conciliator, constantly entrusted with women's secrets; and
perhaps, already, the curiosity of a man who lies under beds taking
notes for his memoirs.

*14 September*

Dinner at Magny's. Afterwards, Sainte-Beuve left us drinking
the mixture of rum and curaçao he always prepares for us at dessert.

'By the way, Gautier, you are just back from Madame Sand's at
Nohant, aren't you? Is it amusing?'

'As amusing as a Moravian monastery! I arrived in the evening.
It's a long way from the station. They left my box in a bush. I
reached the house by way of the farm, with the most frightening
dogs following me. They gave me dinner. The food's good, but
there's too much game and chicken, and that doesn't suit me. There
was Marchal, the painter, there and Alexandre Dumas *fils* and
Madame Calamatta.'

'And how's Dumas *fils*? Still ill?'

'Oh, terribly unhappy. You know what he does these days? He
sits down in front of a sheet of paper and stays there for four hours.
He writes three lines. He goes off to have a cold bath or do some
exercises, because he's full of ideas on hygiene.   Then he comes
back and decides that his three lines are damn stupid.'

'Well, that shows some sense!' said somebody.

'And he crosses out everything except three words. Every now
and then his father arrives from Naples and says: 'Get me a cutlet
and I'll finish your play for you', writes the scenario, brings in a

whore, borrows some money and goes off again. Dumas *fils* reads the scenario, likes it, goes and has a bath, reads the scenario again, decides that it's stupid, and spends a year revising it. And when his father comes back, he finds the same three words from the same three lines as the year before!'

'And what sort of life do they lead at Nohant?'

'You breakfast at ten. On the last stroke, when the hand is exactly at ten o'clock, everybody sits down without waiting for Mme Sand, who arrives looking like a sleepwalker and stays asleep throughout the meal. After breakfast, you go into the garden and play bowls; that wakes her up. She sits down and begins to talk. The conversation at that hour of the day is usually about pronunciation, for instance how to pronounce *ailleurs* and *meilleur*. But the chief conversational pleasure in that company is the scatological joke.'

'Get along with you!'

'Yes, all their fun comes from farting. Marchal was wildly popular with his wind. But never a word about relations between the sexes. I do believe they would throw you out of the house if you made the slightest allusion to the subject. . . . At three o'clock Madame Sand goes back upstairs to churn out copy till six. Then you have dinner, but in rather a hurry, to give Marie Caillot time to eat. She's the housemaid, a *petite Fadette* Madame Sand found near Nohant to play in her private theatre, and who comes to the sitting-room in the evening after her meal. After dinner Madame Sand plays patience until midnight without uttering a single word. On the second day I said that if there was no talk about literature I was going to leave. The word *literature* seemed to bring them back from another world. I forgot to tell you that the only thing that interests them at the moment is mineralogy. Everybody has his little hammer and never goes out of doors without it. So in the end I declared that Rousseau was the worst writer in all French literature, and that started an argument with Madame Sand that lasted until one in the morning.

'I must say that Manceau has got Nohant splendidly organized so far as copy goes. Madame Sand can't sit down in a room without pens appearing in front of her, together with blue ink, cigarette paper, Turkish tobacco, and striped note-paper. And it simply pours out of her! Because she starts again at midnight and works until four in the morning. You know what happened to her once? Something absolutely monstrous! One day she finished a novel at one o'clock in the morning. "Good heavens," she said, "I've finished!" And she promptly started another. Turning out copy is a natural function for her.

'All in all, though, she does you very well. The service, for instance, is absolutely silent. There's a box in the hall with two compartments, one for letters intended for the post and the other for internal correspondence. If you need anything, you write for it, giving your name and room, and put the letter in this second compartment. I needed a comb. I wrote: "M. Théophile Gautier, such-and-such a room" and what I wanted. The next morning at six o'clock, I had thirty combs to choose from.'


*28 September*

We returned to Paris today for the Magny dinner. The conversation was about Vigny, the corpse of the day, with Sainte-Beuve throwing anecdotes on his grave. When I hear Sainte-Beuve, with his little phrases, talk about a dead man, it seems to me that I can see a colony of ants attacking a corpse; he will pick a reputation clean for you and leave you nothing of the person concerned but the bare bones of a little skeleton neatly laid out.

'The fact is,' he said with an oily gesture, 'nobody can be sure that he was a nobleman, since nobody has ever seen his family. He was a nobleman of 1814; in those days, people didn't look too closely into those matters. In Garrick's correspondence there's a letter from a Vigny asking him for money, but doing it very *nobly*, and explaining that he was doing Garrick an honour by picking on him. It would be interesting to know whether our Vigny was a descendant. He was an angel, Vigny was, and no mistake. Nobody ever saw a beefsteak in his house. When you left him at seven o'clock to go and dine, he would say: "What, are you going already?" He understood nothing of reality: it didn't exist for him. He could say the most amazingly naïve things. After he had delivered his speech to the Academy, a friend remarked to him that it had struck him as rather long. "But I'm not in the least tired!" replied Vigny. He still had something of the soldier about him too. That same day, the day he was admitted to the Academy, he was wearing a black cravat. Meeting Spontini, who in accordance with etiquette was wearing the imperial uniform, he exclaimed: "Uniform becomes second nature to one, doesn't it, Spontini!" Gaspard de Pons, who had served in the same regiment as Vigny, used to say of him: "There goes a man who doesn't look any of the three things he is—a soldier, a poet, and a wit." He was terribly clumsy and tactless. He never understood the first thing about the arrangement that got him into the Academy. When he recommended somebody for one of our prizes, he always bungled the job. He used to bring along extracts from the book he was championing and read them aloud, putting everybody out of patience. Take Taine's book on Livy for instance: everybody had agreed to give it the prize. Then Vigny came along, said that it was excellent, that he had just read it, and that he would be grateful for the Academy's permission to read out a few passages. The first passage he quoted was an unhappy choice; Saint-Marc-Girardin said: "Is it no better than that? In that case I'm not giving it the prize!" And so it went on. . . . He put that prize back a year.'

*29–30 October, at Croisset, near Rouen*

We were met at the station by Flaubert and his brother, chief surgeon at Rouen hospital, a very tall, thin, mephistophelian fellow with a big black beard, a profile as sharply defined as the shadow of a face, and a swaying body as supple as a tropical creeper. We were then brought in a carriage to Croisset, a pretty house with a Louis Seize façade built at the foot of a hill on the banks of the Seine, which at this point looks like one end of a lake, though the water has something of the swell of the sea. Flaubert lives here with a niece, the daughter of the dead sister whose bust he keeps in his study, and his mother. The latter, born in 1793, retains the vitality of the people of that period and also, beneath her wrinkled features, the dignity of what was once great beauty. The house is run in an austere, bourgeois, rather close-fisted fashion. The fires are small and the carpets stop when they come to the tiles. There is Norman thrift in even the most extravagant aspect of provincial life, the food. There is no other metal than silver-plate, which creates a rather chilly effect when you remember that you are in a surgeon's house and that the soup-tureen may represent the fee for the amputation of a leg, the serving-dish for the removal of a breast. With that reservation, which I imagine to be characteristic of the race rather than the household, the hospitality here is warm, friendly, and unaffected. The poor little girl, caught between the studiousness of her uncle and the old age of her grandmother, chatters gaily to you, looks at you with pretty blue eyes, and makes a delightful grimace of regret when, at seven o'clock, after Flaubert has bid his mother 'good night, old dear', her grandmother takes her off to bed.

*1 November*

We stayed indoors all day. This pleased Flaubert, who seems to loathe taking exercise and who has to be badgered by his mother before he will set foot in the garden. She told us that often, when she came back from Rouen, she would find her son in the same place and the same posture as when she had left him, and would be almost frightened by his immobility. He never stirs, but lives in his writing and his study. He never goes riding; he never goes out in a boat. All day long, without a single pause, in a stentorian voice and with the bellowing of an actor in a boulevard theatre, he read us his first novel, written in the third form at school, and whose only title as given on the cover was *Fragments of Unremarkable Style*. The subject is a youth's loss of his virginity with an *ideal whore*. There is a great deal of Flaubert himself in the youth: his hopes, his aspirations, his melancholy, his misanthropy, his hatred of the masses. Except for the dialogue, which is not worth considering, it is all amazingly powerful for a writer of his age. Already, in the details of landscape, there is the same skilful and delightful observation as in *Madame Bovary*. The beginning of the novel, an evocation of autumnal sadness, is something which he could sign today, without shame. In a word, despite its imperfections, it is a most impressive work.

By way of recreation, after dinner, he went and rummaged among all the old clothes and souvenirs he had brought back from his travels. He was delighted to come across his oriental trappings and promptly got all three of us into fancy dress, looking magnificently Turkish himself, with a tarboosh on his head, his handsome, fleshy features, his sanguine complexion, and his drooping moustache. And he ended up by digging out with a sigh the old leather breeches he had worn on his long travels, looking at them with the tenderness of a snake contemplating the skin it has shed.

Hunting for his novel, he had discovered an untidy collection of papers which he read out to us this evening. There was the manuscript confession of the homosexual Chollet, who killed his lover out of jealousy and was guillotined at Le Havre, a confession describing his passion in detail. There was a letter from a prostitute to a customer, offering him all her filthy services. There was a horrifying, sinister letter written by an unfortunate creature who had grown a hump in front and behind at the age of three; had contracted an agonizing skin disease and been burnt with nitric acid and cantharides by quacks; had gone lame and then lost both legs; and who had finally written this account, all the more terrifying in that it contained no word of complaint, of his martyrdom to fate. This scrap of paper remains the greatest objection I have ever encountered to the idea of Providence and the goodness of God.

# 1864

We took the Princess a Japanese album which she had asked us for. She spoke to us about Sainte-Beuve, who, at Compiègne, had been unable to restrain himself.

'Just imagine, he had to go and see the young ladies of the town. He didn't think very highly of them. . . . The whole Court knew about it!'

'And did he make a good impression?'

'At Compiègne? Nobody understood him. The Emperor understands only practical matters. If Sainte-Beuve had asked him for something, an official position. . . . But you know that he doesn't want to be in charge of anything, so that he can criticize other people more freely. But don't you find his behaviour at Compiègne astonishing?'

And she started pressing us on the question of his taste in women which she refused to take seriously, so as to get more out of us: 'What, in the street? Now, if he were a young man. . . . With a young man, it would be amusing. But Sainte-Beuve, with his little pot-belly. . . .'

Dinner at Magny's. We talked about filthy tricks in the literary profession. Gautier denied their very existence. Sainte-Beuve thumped the table with his fist and shouted: 'Get along with you! Every day, I get the most infamous letters! One, for instance, said: "Everybody hopes that you are going to write something about Monsieur de Vigny, who said that you were a toad that poisoned the water where you swam." I'm sure that was written by a university professor. They are the only people capable of such a cowardly trick.'

We went on to woman, the usual subject of conversation. Gautier said that the only woman that really attracted him was the asexual woman, that is to say the woman so young that she banishes all ideas of childbearing and obstetrics; and he added that since he was unable to satisfy this penchant, on account of the police, all other women, whether they were twenty or fifty years old, were the same age to him.

Thereupon Flaubert, with his face flushed and his eyes rolling, proclaimed in his booming voice that beauty was not erotic, that beautiful women were not meant to be bedded, that the only useful purpose they served was inspiring statuary, and that love was born of that mysterious element which was produced by excitement and only very rarely by beauty. He expatiated on his ideal, which turned out to be the ideal of an ignoble Turk. Chaffed about it, he went on to say that he had never really possessed a woman, that he was a virgin, and that he had used all the women he had had as the mattress for another woman, the woman of his dreams.

Meanwhile, Nefftzer and Taine were arguing about the word *concrete*, expressing their astonishment at all the ideas it contained, and constantly firing off words like *idiosyncrasy*.

Flaubert, who was even more than usually verbose this evening and kept throwing out paradoxes, not with the ease of an Indian juggler like Gautier but with the clumsiness of a professional strongman or rather just an egregious provincial, declared that copulation was in no way necessary to the health of the organism and that it was a necessity created by our imagination. Taine pointed out that even so, when he who was no debauchee indulged in sexual intercourse every two or three weeks, he was relieved of a certain anxiety, a certain obsession, and felt his mind freer for work. Flaubert retorted that he was mistaken, that what a man needed was not a seminal discharge but a nervous discharge; that since Taine went to a brothel for his love-making, he could not possibly experience any relief; and that he needed love, emotion, the thrill of squeezing a hand. Whereupon we pointed out to him that very few of us were in that happy position, seeing that those who did not go to a brothel for satisfaction had an old mistress, a passing fancy, or a legitimate wife, with whom there could be no question of an emotion or a thrill; the result was that three-quarters of the human race never had a nervous discharge, and that a man was lucky if he experienced it three times in a lifetime of copulation.

From copulation we went on to spleen. Taine deplored this ailment peculiar to our profession. We who consider that genius is a
form of neurosis declared that we considered it perfectly natural.
But Gautier maintained on the contrary that genius was the luxury
of good health, the perfect equilibrium of the vital forces. 'Then
what about talent?' I asked. 'Oh, yes,' he replied, 'I grant you that
talent may be a sickly disposition.'

In the meantime Taine had climbed on to his hobby-horse like a
Scottish preacher on to his portable wooden pulpit. He wanted
spleen to be fought with all the weapons of medicine, hygiene, and
morality, and above all methodically. Insist as we might that this
neurosis was probably a necessary condition of our talent, he went
on calling for a reaction against those moods of flabbiness and lazi-
ness which struck him as symptomatic of the decline of a civilization. And like an English Protestant, he told us to look for the cure
for spleen, the salvation and renovation of our decadent society, in
a childish imitation of English manners, in a life of civic activity
modelled on theirs, in emulation of English patriotism and patrol-
ism. 'Yes,' one of us shouted, 'an alliance of talent and the National
Guard!'

Everybody laughed, and the company broke up.

*15 February*

One of the sad things in life is that one is put off the things one
obtains by the people who obtain them, the women one has by the
men who have had them, the houses where one is received by those
who are received there.

*28 February*

The Emperor spoke for a long time yesterday to Houssaye.
Claudin, that omniscient cockchafer, gave us the explanation of this
favour. It originated in the course of the Prince-President's tour of
France. At his last halting-place, Blois, he wanted to sleep with
little Fix of the Théâtre-Français, but he needed a pretext for spending a day and above all a night in that one-horse town. Houssaye
sent Fix off to Blois, and to provide the Emperor with a pretext for
staying the night he arranged for him to open an art gallery which

the town had asked for and which he improvised with a couple of dozen daubs. The Emperor never forgot this ingenious bit of pimping, which he rewarded with a diamond tie-pin bearing the monogram N, a tie-pin that Houssaye wears on great occasions.

*21 March*

Levallois told us about that mistress of Sainte-Beuve's, Mme de Vaquez, whom he firmly believed to be Spanish and consulted about all the Spanish literature that came his way, Calderon and so forth. She had persuaded him that she was Spanish, first by telling him so, and then by going to bed with a dagger. But she happened to die in his house, of consumption; and her papers showed that she was a native of Picardy.

*Monday, 11 April*

Dinner at Magny's. The conversation turned to Pasquier.

'A little man mixed up in great affairs,' we said.

'Really, you are being hard on the man,' said Sainte-Beuve, with his little ecclesiastical gesture of appeasement, and promptly began pawing the dead man's memory and turning it over and over:

'I shan't exactly talk to you about him as a writer. In Chateaubriand's circle he was barely tolerated. When Joubert's letters were published, the editors cut out all the jokes in which Joubert covered him with ridicule. And nobody could say anything worse about him than Rémusat did in my hearing at Madame So-and-so's: "Pasquier doesn't know anything about anything"—after which he enumerated all the things of which Pasquier was ignorant and ended up by saying: "All he's capable of doing is being Minister of all that!" And as for the academic eulogies, the venerable priest, you know, the story told by Dufaure, the truth of the matter is that two hours before he died he had Voltaire's *Contes philosophiques* read out to him. What's more, he spent his life quoting lines from the same author's *Pucelle*, though admittedly he always got them wrong.'

'Ah,' I said to Sainte-Beuve, 'if I should die, God forbid that I should be mourned by you!'

That, in fact, is Sainte-Beuve's greatest and perhaps only conversational skill—savage criticism in the guise of support. He is a master of the art of poisoning with praise.

He spent the rest of the dinner confiding his little personal secrets to me. Boredom is his principal enemy and he lives in terror of it. He has fallen back upon the philosophy of Sénac de Meilhan. The pleasures of the senses are the only ones for him. He has practically no social life now. There are only three women he sees regularly: the Princess, La Païva, and Jeanne de Tourbey. He works from eight o'clock until five, then goes for a walk until six in order to *deserve* an appetite. On Tuesdays he invites his secretary Troubat and a *little lady* to dinner. On Saturdays he takes another *little lady* to dinner at a tavern where he has ordered the meal in advance. He prefers the exhaustion of hard work to boredom and emptiness. But he admits that he overworks because he needs the money.

*16 April*

Spent the evening with the famous 'Présidente', Mme Sabatier, whose body was modelled by Clésinger in his *Bacchante*. A biggish woman with a coarse, hearty manner; a courtesan with something common about her. This rather vulgar creature endowed with classical beauty left me with the impression of a camp-follower for fauns.

*8 May*

Went to the Clignancourt gate to find a landscape for our *Germinie Lacerteux*. Near the fortifications, in the midst of a group of wretched huts, the hovels of rag-pickers and gypsies, I suddenly saw a rush of people towards a young man whom three women in faded rags were holding fast, slapping him and punching his hat in. It all happened in a moment: a swarm of people appearing as if they had come up from under the ground; laughing children running up to see what was going on; and gypsy women appearing in the doorways with women so old that there was a kind of mushroom-white mould on their faces.

Then, in the midst of all this, a powerfully built man in a smock ran up to the frail, weak, fair-haired young man, planted himself in front of him, and started raining blows on to his eyes with the full force of his huge fists, going on without meeting any resistance until the young man fell to the ground, and even then wanting to continue his assault. The onlookers stood around, feasting their eyes upon the sight with cruel pleasure as if they were at a show, and obviously feeling none of the revulsion which overwhelmed us at this onslaught of the strong against the weak.

Then everything disappeared as it had come, like a nightmare coming to an end. . . .

A quarter of an hour later, out beyond the fortifications, I met the young man who had been beaten up, stumbling along in the plaster-filled ruts, wandering at random and waving his arms, hatless and coatless, his shirt hanging in ribbons, dazed and bemused as if he were drunk, and every now and then automatically wiping with his sleeve a bleeding eye that hung half-way out of its socket.

And on the way home I asked myself: 'Why do we feel that a man who is beaten up is our neighbour, and a man who is killed, our brother?'

*29 May*

Our little cousin Labille came to see us this morning. He had a rendezvous with a cocotte who was going to take him out to Asnières in her carriage. There exists a peculiar type of high-class prostitute nowadays who finds her custom among boys still at school, emptying their pocket-books and building up a reserve of men who will keep her in later years.

When the boy had gone, we reflected on the course taken by love in our three generations. The elder of us, at our cousin's age, had a girl who stitched shoes for a living. I had a tart who always had a few sous in her chest of drawers. And this youngster has a woman who keeps her own carriage and horses. The world progresses. Here we have the three periods: Louis-Philippe, 1848, and the Second Empire.

*30 May*

It is strange indeed that it should be we, living in the midst of all that was prettiest in the eighteenth century, who give ourselves up to the most austere and possibly the most repugnant study of the lower classes; and that it should be we, in whose lives women play so small a part, who have undertaken the most serious, profound, and intimate examination of the sex.

*23 July*

A book is never a masterpiece: it becomes one. Genius is the talent of a dead man.


*12 September*

When Sainte-Beuve is tired and decides to take a nap during the day, he tells Mme Dufour: 'If the Pope comes, say I am not at home; and if my poor mother returns from the grave, ask her to wait.'

He told us this story about Musset. Véron asked Musset for a serial for the *Constitutionnel*. Musset said that he had a story in mind, and that he wanted four thousand francs for it. Véron agreed, sent him the money one morning. That evening he went to Véry's to dine, saw the staircase beautifully decorated with flowers, and asked who was responsible. 'It's Monsieur de Musset', said the waiter with a meaning smile. Véron asked if he could have a look. There was a whole brothel upstairs, on which Musset was spending his four thousand francs. By the time the women arrived he was already so drunk that he could not enjoy his own orgy. 'Silly, isn't it!' said Sainte-Beuve.

Coming out, we sat down with Bouilhet at a café opposite the Théâtre-Français. A young man prowled round us, decided to speak to Bouilhet, and sat down to have a glass of beer with us. He was a typical literary Bohemian or unknown poet. His hair, which was parted in the middle, kept falling in stringy locks over his eyes, and he would push it back with the gestures of a maniac or an illuminee. He had the feverish eyes of a victim of hallucinations, the face of an opium addict or a masturbator, and a crazy, mechanical laugh which came and went in his throat. Altogether, something unhealthy and spectral after the fashion of Philoxène Boyer.

After a discussion about fantasy, about Hoffmann, and about Poe, whom I nicknamed Hoffmann-Barnum, Bouilhet said to him: 'What about your Greek throne?' To which the young man replied: 'Oh, don't talk to me about it!' And he launched out into one of his stories, which are the weirdest fantasies of our time.

He decided to become King of Greece when the position was vacant, to jump from a beer-hall to a Parthenon. He planned to announce his candidature by a telegram to *The Times* which would be reported in Paris. He obtained the support of two of his cousins, one in London, Lord Buckingham, the other in Russia, a certain M. de Villiers, governor of Siberia. He went to see Pereire and suggested raising a loan of ten million francs in Greece. He hoped to impress the Emperor with his telegram to London. 'After all,' he said, 'the Emperor believes what he sees in print like anybody else!' In short, he bustled about so much that he achieved something at least: he spoke to the Emperor. He went up to him heavily made up, bent double, and plastered with foreign decorations, looking like a broken-down old King of Greece. The Emperor was most impressed. 'Monsieur le Comte,' he said, 'I'll think about it. . . .'

For I forgot to say that the little fellow is called the Comte Villiers de l'Isle-Adam. He looks as if he were descended from the Templars by way of the Funambules.

### 22 September

The passion in our books is most certainly the product of our brains, of the excitement of our minds. One of us was once in love for eight days with a woman of fairly easy virtue, and the other for three days with a ten-franc whore. Altogether, eleven days of love between the two of us.

### 23 October

The reason for the sadness of this modern age and the men who live in it is that it looks for the truth in everything and finds it.

### 24 October

The movement, the gestures, and the life of the drama appeared in the novel only with Diderot. Until then, there were dialogues but no novels.

Since Balzac, the novel has had nothing in common with what our fathers understood by the word. The novel of today is based on documents related verbally or taken from nature, just as history is based on written documents.

Historians tell the story of the past; novelists tell the story of the present.

*25 October*

Charpentier told me today that according to Constant Napoleon was in the habit of rolling his excrement into balls between his fingers: a habit which bears a curious and horrifying resemblance to the similar cases, symptomatic of insanity, noted by Dr. Trélat.

Genius is undoubtedly a form of insanity, a kind of neurosis. Musing upon the two greatest minds of the nineteenth century, the two brains best fitted to serve as moulds for a world, Napoleon and Balzac, I remember Chateaubriand's remark: 'Napoleon wrote . . . he wrote . . . why, he wrote like Balzac!'

# 1865

Sainte-Beuve saw the first Emperor once: it was at Boulogne and he was urinating. It is, so to speak, in that posture that he has seen and judged all great men ever since.

*Wednesday, 1 February*

This evening at the Princess's there was a tableful of men of letters, including Dumas *père*. He is a sort of giant with grey negroid hair, the tiny eyes of a hippopotamus, bright, shrewd, and watchful even when veiled, and features set in the middle of an enormous face dribbling at the bottom. There is something about him of a fairground showman or a bagman in the *Arabian Nights*. He is the sober artisan, as it were the athlete of the serial story, who drinks no wine, takes no coffee, and does not smoke.

He talks fluently but without sparkle, colour, or wit: all he does is fish facts with a hoarse voice from the depths of an immense memory. He talks nearly all the time about himself, with a childish vanity which is quite disarming. He told us for instance that an article he had written about Mount Carmel had brought the Carmelites seven hundred thousand francs.

Lesseps, the piercer of isthmuses, with his eyes dark and handsome beneath his grey hair, dined with us this evening on his return from Egypt. This man of iron will confessed to us that he had been dissuaded from doing a great many things in his life by a fortune-teller in the Rue de Tournon, Mlle Lenormand's successor.

After dinner, while we were smoking, Nieuwerkerke told us that Bénédict Masson, having been engaged to paint the history of France round the courtyard of the Invalides, had been unable to think of anything better to symbolize the reign of Louis-Philippe than a barricade. 'It wasn't in the best of taste,' said Nieuwerkerke.

After all, there were other possibilities. . . . In the end, instead of the barricade, I persuaded him to paint the Return of the Emperor's Ashes.'

*27 March*

Yes, it is true that there is an element of sickness in our talent, and a considerable element at that. But this, which at the moment causes displeasure and irritation, will one day be regarded as our charm and our strength. Sickness sensitizes man for observation, like a photographic plate.

*11 April*

I wrote recently to the manager of the Vaudeville, asking him to fix a time when I might come and read him our play *Henriette Maréchal*. This morning I received a letter from Banville saying that Thierry of the Théâtre-Français, whom we do not know and have seen only once in our lives, would very much like to read our play, not as a theatre manager but as a colleague, a man of letters. But the play is absolutely impossible for his theatre—we have no illusions on that score—with a first act so unconventional as to take place at an Opéra ball and a climax so monstrous as to consist of a pistol shot actually fired on the stage.

*Wednesday, 26 April*

The Princess received us this evening as coldly as she knows how. She scarcely looked at us. If we spoke, she contradicted us. She had eyes, a place beside her, attention and interest for nobody but Flaubert, who told me as we came away that she made him walk her twice round the garden in the dark.

It is good that princes and especially princesses should have these chilly moods, these excessive ups and downs, so that liking for them should not become devotion.

Would she like to take Flaubert for her lover? I think not. I imagine, judging by the affectation of her behaviour this evening, that she is using him as a blind against the slanderous rumour, which must have reached her ears, that she had granted us her favours.

*Thursday, 27 April*

We left our play at the Théâtre-Français on Saturday without the slightest hope or suspicion that it might be accepted. Thierry was to have sent it back yesterday. In response to a letter from us, he returned it this morning with a note asking why we did not offer it to his theatre. We went to see him this evening. He spoke of the play as if it had a chance of being performed, and dazzled us with the cast he had in mind: all the great names of the Théâtre-Français —Mme Plessy, Victoria, Got, Bressant, Delaunay.

We came away crazy with excitement, going down the stairs looking at each other like thieves who have just committed a burglary. Two hours of frenzied joy such as we have rarely experienced.

*8 May*

We were sitting on a red plush sofa, at a table covered with a green baize cloth on which there stood a reading desk and something to drink. There were ten people there, silent and solemn, and on the wall facing us hung a picture representing the death of Talma.

Thierry started reading. He read the first act, the Opéra ball, to the accompaniment of laughter and friendly glances thrown in our direction. Then he read the second and went on to the third. There were few ideas in us during this time, but an anxiety deep down which we tried to suppress and dispel by listening attentively to our play, to the words, to the sound of Thierry's voice as he read. The audience had fallen into a serious mood, that mute, secret seriousness which makes one want to question it, penetrate it, catch it off its guard. Then it was all over.

Thierry led us into his office. We sat down. The window was hung with twisted muslin curtains which let in a discreet white light as in a bathroom. We looked at the ceiling, with its mythological scenes depicted on a white ground, as if we were sending up a prayer to our beloved eighteenth century. Then, as happens in moments of great emotion, we found ourselves gazing with profound, mechanical application at a terra-cotta bust, our eyes travelling from the tip of its nose down the pedestal to the gilded edge at the bottom. Through one of the double doors, which alone was shut, we could hear the sound of voices, dominated by the voice of Got, of whom we were afraid. Then there was a succession of little metallic noises as the balls were dropped into the lead box.

We heard the door open. Our eyes were on the hands of the clock, which stood at three thirty-five. I did not see Thierry come in, but I felt somebody take hold of my hands and heard a soothing voice say: 'Your play has been accepted, and enthusiastically accepted.' It was Thierry. He wanted to talk to us, but after a couple of minutes we begged to be excused and dashed out to go for a drive in an open carriage, cutting the air with our hatless heads.

*9 May*

Saint-Victor told us yesterday at Magny's that according to Montguyon, who had known Morny[1] very well, the dead man's friends were extremely worried over the disappearance of a little casket which Morny always kept on his bedside table, a casket containing portraits of all his conquests in all strata of society, photographed naked—usually with flowers decorating their privy parts. They are afraid that his personal valet has stolen it with the intention of blackmailing the women involved.

As we were leaving Magny's Flaubert said to us: 'When I was young my vanity was such that when I went to a brothel with my friends I always picked the ugliest girl and insisted on making love to her in front of them all without taking my cigar out of my mouth. It wasn't any fun for me: I just did it for the gallery.' Flaubert still has a little of this vanity left, which explains why, though perfectly frank by nature, he is never wholly sincere in what he says he feels or suffers or loves.

*22 May*

There is now only one consuming interest left in our life, the passion for the study of living reality. Apart from that there is nothing but boredom and emptiness. Admittedly we have galvanized history into reality, and done so with a truer truthfulness than other historians. But now the truth that is dead no longer holds any

[1] The Duc de Morny, Napoleon III's natural brother, President of the Legislative Body and architect of the *coup d'état* of 1851, had died on 10 March 1865.

interest for us. We are like a man accustomed to drawing from a wax dummy who has suddenly been presented with a living model, or rather life itself with its entrails warm and active, its guts palpitating.

*23 July*

In the novel as we understand it, the material description of things and places is not description for the sake of description. It is a means of installing the reader in a certain setting favourable to the moral emotion which should arise from those things and places.

*Saint-Gratien, 7 August*

The Princess, who had written to us that *Germinie* had made her sick, drew us into a corner. She was devoured with curiosity to find out why people like ourselves should write books like that. She swore by all the gods that that housekeeper of ours inspired no interest whatever in her and that what revolted her about the book was that she was condemned to make love in the same way as unfortunate women of that sort.

*29 August*

After dinner, while we were still at table, we talked about ourselves.

There is some nineteenth-century lymph in me, an exalted life of the mind. And I do not know whether if I had been born in another place and age, in sixteenth-century Germany for instance, I would not have found myself in an atmosphere better suited to my nature, an atmosphere of force and materialism, eating wild boar, drinking and making love. There is an animal strain in me which it seems to me has not reached its full development.

I have not the same aspirations as the other of us. He, if he had not been what he is, would have inclined towards home life, the bourgeois ideal of communion with a sentimental wife. I am a materialistic melancholic; he is an ardent and tender melancholic.

I can feel in myself something of an eighteenth-century abbé and also a little of the ironic perfidy of sixteenth-century Italy—for although I detest bloodshed and physical suffering, I rather enjoy practising mental cruelty. Edmond, on the other hand, is almost unbelievably good-natured. He was born in Lorraine and is Germanic in temperament. We have just noticed this for the first time. I am a Latin and a Parisian. Edmond can see himself perfectly well as a soldier in another age, with his Lorraine blood, no distaste for fighting, and a love of daydreaming. I for my part see myself involved in chapter-house negotiations, in monastic diplomacy, taking a vainglorious delight in tricking men and women for my own pleasure and the irony of it all. Could there be a natural predestination of elder brother and younger, just as there used to be a social predestination in the past?

The strange thing is that although we are absolutely different in temperament, taste, and character, we are absolutely identical in our ideas, our judgements, our likes and dislikes as regards other people, and our intellectual perspective. Our minds see alike and see with the same eyes.

*11 September*

The reading of our play to the cast. Now that Got has been persuaded to play Bressant's part and Mme Plessy to take the part of a mother; now that we have expended more solicitations, errands, diplomacy, words, and worry on these people than would be called for in the negotiation of a peace treaty, here is Delaunay—the character on whom the whole play is built—turning down his part! It is not that he considers the play a poor one or dislikes the part, quite the contrary; but he thinks the character is too young for him. Unfortunately, this very morning the *Constitutionnel* said that he looked too old in the part of Damis.[1] What is more, like all juvenile leads, with their perverse vanity, he aspires to older men's parts, to the part of Molière's misanthrope. At bottom, he seems to want to have his hand forced, to be covered by an order from the Ministry of Fine Arts compelling him to take the part.

*14 September*

Delaunay has definitely refused his part, and this refusal seems to render the production of the play impossible. The casting has gone

---

[1] Not the young man in Molière's *Tartuffe* but the poet in Piron's play *La Métromanie*. In fact, the *Constitutionnel* had nothing but praise for Delaunay.

all awry, for as Thierry puts it, with this thread snapping, the whole fabric falls apart. We spent the day wandering about in despair, dragging our feet through the dead leaves in the Tuileries Gardens, blind to things and people, with a bitter taste in our mouths and a void in our heads.

*1 November*

At the Princess's, after dinner, Sainte-Beuve spoke of his fits of temper at the Thursday sessions of the Academy, when his nerves are raw and his susceptibilities tender as a result of writing his article for the *Constitutionnel.* He admitted that one day he had got into such a state that after a brief altercation with Villemain he had shouted that he was as contemptible as the first syllable of his name and raised his umbrella against him—for there is always an umbrella in all Sainte-Beuve's great actions.

Mérimée arrived in the evening and for the first time we heard him talk. He talks listening to himself, slowly, with deadly silences, word by word, drop by drop, as if he were distilling his effects, creating around himself, little by little, a sort of icy chill. No wit, no bravura, but a studied affectation, the enunciation of an old actor taking his time, together with something of the impertinence of a spoiled conversationalist, a conceited contempt for all illusion, modesty, and social convention. There is something indescribably offensive to ordinary, healthy people in this dry, malicious irony, carefully elaborated in order to impress and subjugate women and weak men.

*5 November*

I am buried under the eiderdowns of the Provinces. A letter is tossed on to my bed. I open it. It is from Thierry, telling me that Delaunay has agreed to take the part, that I must come back to Paris, and that the play will open on 1 December. The theatre is really an amazing box of surprises, emotions, and changes.

*29 November*

Thierry showed us a letter from Doucet in which the Minister of State, Rouher, and the Minister of the Emperor's Household,

Marshal Vaillant, do us the honour of seeking, finding, and proposing a way to end our play. Rouher wants the daughter to be merely wounded, so that there remains the *hope of a marriage with her mother's lover*! Marshal Vaillant had found another ending in about the same taste which I cannot remember. Fortunately he does not insist on our adopting it, and being a soldier he has no great objection to the pistol shot at the end.

*5 December*

Had a good night. We left cards on the critics and called on Roqueplan, whom we found at lunch. He was all in red and wearing embroidered slippers or moccasins, so that he looked like a cross between a public executioner and an Ojibway Indian. He told us that in our profession a man had to fight against nervous waste, that he had just eaten two beefsteaks, and that there was an art of knocking one's stomach into shape. And when we complimented him on his health and stamina, he said: 'Oh, everybody has some ailment or other. I too have my dustbin. But every morning I hawk up my phlegm, and that cleans me out for the day.'

Then we went to see old Janin, who no longer stirs out of his house and is now, on account of his gout, a fireside critic. He said that his wife was dressing to go to our play. Despite ourselves, and despite his ferocious attack on our *Hommes de lettres*, we remembered our first call on him and his first article about us.

At last it was dinner-time. We went to dine at Bignon's, where we ate and drank to the tune of 26 francs, as if we had a hundred performances before us. We were not in the least nervous, but perfectly calm and easy in our minds, convinced that even if the audience did not consider our play perfect, the actors were so good that their performance would make it a success. We called for a copy of *L'Entr'acte* and read the names of the cast over and over again. Then we smoked a cigar, rubbing shoulders with that Paris which was already beginning to talk about us and which would be discussing nothing else the next day, and breathing in so to speak the first whiff of a great noise around us. The theatre! We had got into the theatre! And we thought about those little bits of parts we had glimpsed on the bedside tables of minor actresses and which had always filled us with excitement.

We reached the theatre. The street outside seemed to be full of bustling activity. We went like conquerors up that staircase which we had so often climbed with varying degrees of anxiety. We had agreed during the day that if, towards the end of the play, we saw the audience becoming too enthusiastic, we should slip out quickly so as not to be dragged in triumph on to the stage.

Nine o'clock. At the tobacconist's I heard a stage-hand say that they had booed *Horace et Lydie*.[1] Our ears were burning. No need of overcoats.

The corridors of the theatre were crowded. Everyone seemed to be chattering with excitement. We caught a few words in the general hubbub: 'The queue broke the railing in front of the box-office.' Guichard, still in Roman costume, came into the green-room looking rather upset: he had been booed in *Horace et Lydie*. Little by little we became conscious of a stormy atmosphere. We went downstairs and got hold of our actors. Got gave us a peculiar smile and said of the audience: 'They aren't very affectionate tonight.'

We went to the peephole in the curtain and tried to look at the house, but in the dazzling light all we could see was a sea of faces. Then, all of a sudden, we realized that the play had begun. The raising of the curtain, the three traditional knocks, those solemn moments which we had been waiting for, had completely escaped us. And then, to our astonishment, we heard a catcall, two catcalls, three catcalls, a tempest of hisses answered by a hurricane of cheers. We were standing there in the wings, among the masked dancers, with our backs to a flat. I was gazing mechanically at the blue silk sleeve of a woman in fancy dress beside me. It seemed to me that as the supernumeraries went by they threw us pitying glances. The hissing and applause went on.

The curtain came down and we went out without putting on our overcoats. We were hot. The second act began. The hissing started up again, accompanied by animal noises and imitations of the actors' intonations. They hissed everything, even Mme Plessy's silence. And so the battle went on, between the actors and nearly all the stalls and boxes, which were applauding, and the whole of the

---

[1] *Horace et Lydie*, a one-act play by the Goncourts' *bête noire*, Ponsard, was performed as a curtain-raiser before *Henriette Maréchal* and, by a stroke of irony, booed by the cabal in mistake for the Goncourts' play.

gallery, which was trying by means of shrieks, interruptions, angry shouts, and vulgar jokes to force down the curtain.

'It's a bit rough out there', Got said to us now and then. We stayed there all the time, leaning against a flat, taking it all full in the face, pale and nervous but erect and unflinching, forcing the actors by our angry presence to go through with it to the bitter end.

The pistol shot was fired. The curtain came down with the whole house in uproar. I saw Mme Plessy coming off stage as angry as a lioness, muttering abuse against the audience that had insulted her. And from behind the back-cloth we listened for a quarter of an hour to angry shouting that would not allow Got to observe the tradition of naming the authors of the play.

We made our way out through the noisy, gesticulating groups of people filling the lobbies of the theatre and went to have supper at the Maison d'Or with Flaubert, Bouilhet, Pouthier, and Osmoy. We put up a pretty good show, in spite of a nervousness which blocked our stomachs and made us want to vomit every time we picked up a piece of food. Flaubert could not help saying that he thought we were superb, and we returned home more infinitely weary than we had ever been in the whole of our lives, as weary as if we had spent ten nights on end at the gaming-table.[1]

6 December

The chief of the *claque* told me this morning that the theatre had not witnessed a tumult like that of last night since *Hernani* and *Les Burgraves*.

Dined with the Princess, who went home last night with her hands burning from having clapped so hard, and furious with the hissers, who she felt had been hissing her much more than the play.

Spent this evening with my mistress, who said that after attending last night's performance she had not dared to go out into the street this morning, for she felt as if she had it written all over her face.

[1] The attack on *Henriette Maréchal* was largely political in origin, the writers and students of the Latin Quarter imagining that the play had been accepted and passed by the censorship on account of the authors' friendship with Princess Mathilde. The police for their part did nothing to restore order, apparently on instructions from the Empress and her friends, who were jealous of Princess Mathilde's rival court.

*15 December*

Thierry came to see us this morning. He had received the first copy of our preface last night. I saw straight away that our preface had killed our play.[1]

Well, what does it matter? I am conscious of having spoken the truth and of having revealed the existence of that new socialism of the beer-halls and Bohemia directed against all decent writers, against all the men of talent who have never loafed around in pubs; that socialism which at the present moment, in the world of letters, is starting all over again the insurrection of 20 May 1795, with its war-cry of 'Down with the gloves!' Because that is what this cabal is after! And perhaps those who consider it amusing, because we are its only victims today, will not laugh so heartily later on.

Thierry showed us a copy of the *Gazette de France* containing an attack on us followed by a curious appeal to the taxpayers whose money was used to produce works such as *Henriette Maréchal*, and went on to ask us to withdraw our play. We refused, telling him that he knew as well as we did that it was not our play that was being hissed, and that we were determined to go on until the play was banned by the Government.

This evening, with a house that had paid four thousand francs for its seats and the warm support of anonymous friends which all these mad, senseless attacks had won us, the performance was a triumph. At the first catcall, the whole audience rose and demanded the expulsion of the culprit. After this success we asked Thierry to allow one more performance. He replied that he could make no promises.

Eugène Giraud told us this evening in the wings that the Princess had received some appalling anonymous letters about our play, saying that her house would be the first to be burned down and that 'all her lovers' would be hanged. All her lovers? We have been frequenting that salon of hers for three years now, and we are a fairly observant pair, but we cannot for the life of us think of a single person there who has been invited to deceive Nieuwerkerke! Oh, the slanderous legends that are invented about the loves of princesses

[1] In this preface to *Henriette Maréchal*, dated 12 December and published on 15 December, the Goncourts paid tribute to Princess Mathilde, though denying that she had imposed the play on the Théâtre-Français, and blamed the nightly attacks on their work on a cabal of envious, class-conscious Bohemians.

and queens! Our thoughts turned to Marie-Antoinette. . . . And to
think that all that nonsense goes down to history!

I notice that my birthday is always marked by some fateful event.
Ten years ago we were hauled before the courts on account of an
article published on 15 December. Today our play is taken off.

# 1866

*Le Havre, 1 January*

Printed discussion of the morality of a work of art ought to be forbidden. Criticism on this question is never anything but a denunciation of the work involved to public hypocrisy, law, and the police.

Travelling in France, it is a misfortune to be a Frenchman. The wing of the chicken at a *table d'hôte* always goes to the Englishman. He is the only person the waiter serves. Why is this? Because the Englishman does not look upon the waiter as a man, and any servant who feels that he is being regarded as a human being despises the person considering him in that light.

*15 January*

At Magny's, Taine declared that all men of talent were products of their environment. We and Gautier maintained that on the contrary they were exceptions. 'Where', we asked, 'will you find the roots of Chateaubriand's exoticism? It is a pineapple growing on a barrack-square!' In Gautier's opinion, an artist's brain was the same in the time of the Pharaohs as it is today. As for the bourgeois, whom he called *fluid nonentities*, it was possible that their brains had changed, but that was of no importance whatever.

*21 January*

Taine has the admirable ability to teach others today what he did not know himself yesterday.

In the reading-room of the Bibliothèque Impériale I saw, as I went by, a man reading a book while holding the hand of a young woman sitting beside him. I passed the same way two hours later: the man was still reading and he was still holding the young woman's hand. It was a German couple. Or rather, it was Germany.

*12 February*

Mme Sand dined today at Magny's. She sat beside me, with her beautiful, charming face, in which, as she grows older, the characteristics of the half-caste become daily more visible. She looked shyly at the assembled company and whispered into Flaubert's ear: 'You are the only person here who doesn't frighten me.' She listened, said nothing, and shed a tear over a piece of poetry by Hugo, just at the sentimental point. She has wonderfully delicate little hands, almost entirely hidden in lace cuffs.

*14 February*

At the Princess's, resplendent in white tie and white waistcoat, huge, out of breath, and as happy as a Negro's fortune, Dumas *père* made his appearance. He had just got back from Austria, Hungary, and Bohemia. He spoke about Pesth, where they had staged his plays in Hungarian; about Vienna, where the Emperor had lent him a room in his palace in which to give a lecture; about his novels, about his plays which the Théâtre-Français refused to put on, about his *Chevalier de Maison-Rouge* which had been banned; about a *reconstruction* which he wanted to do on the Champs-Élysées for the International Exhibition, and about a theatre licence which he had been unable to obtain.

An enormous, overflowing ego, but sparkling with wit and agreeably wrapped up in childish vanity: 'What can you expect,' he said, 'when the only way to make money in the theatre nowadays is with tights that split? Yes, Hostein made a fortune that way. He told his dancers to wear nothing but tights that split, and always in the same place! The audience loved it, but the censors interfered in the end, and now the trade in opera-glasses is in the doldrums. . . . Something spectacular, that's all you need. You have to make sure that the audience say as they go out: "What beautiful costumes! What beautiful scenery! But what stupid authors!" When you hear that, you've got a success on your hands!'

*25 February*

How little they live, people with lively minds! Taine going to bed at nine, getting up at seven, working till noon, dining at a positively provincial hour, paying calls, rushing round the libraries, and spending the evening, after supper, with his mother and his piano. Flaubert chained to his work like a convict in a mine. And we ourselves in our cloistered incubations, with no distractions or family affairs or social life, with the exception of a fortnightly dinner with the Princess and a few strolls along the embankments to satisfy the maniacal curiosity of a pair of bibliographical and icono-graphical fanatics.

*27 June*

Sickness, disease. That is the reproach which is constantly thrown at our books. But what is not sickness in this age of ours? Byron or Chateaubriand: is that not sickness? The great revolution of Christianity, Jesus Christ: is that not sickness and suffering? Jupiter was health. But what has health produced in our time? Ponsard!

*7 October*

Dinner at Magny's. More examples of Sainte-Beuve's amazing, gossipy memory. Pasquier had told him that he could never return to public life, that the Emperor would never forgive him for his remark when, Louis Napoleon having been brought into Pasquier's office after the Strasburg incident and having kept his cap on, Pasquier had said: 'Gendarmes, remove the prisoner's cap!'

Then Sainte-Beuve jumped from Pasquier to Louis XVIII and what he had once said to his ministers: 'Gentlemen, there will be no meeting of the Council on Tuesday: the King will be taking his pleasure.' Mme du Cayla had succeeded Mme de Mirbel, whom one encounter with the King had been sufficient to disgust. On the Tuesday in question, everybody fearing a fainting fit on the part of the King, the whole Court had collected in the anteroom to eaves-drop. Immediately afterwards Baron Portal had taken the King's pulse, and they had heard him say: 'Slow, very slow.'

When a warrant for Chateaubriand's arrest had been issued in

1817, the author of *Le Génie du Christianisme* had been found, at six o'clock in the morning, in bed with two prostitutes.[1]

*12 October*

The Princess occasionally comes out with a very subtle observation: for instance, she has noticed that many women have voices to match their dresses: a silk voice, a velvet voice, and so on.

*Monday, 22 October*

This evening at Magny's, the conversation started at an exalted level with the question of other worlds and hypotheses as to whether or not the planets were inhabited. Like a half-filled balloon, it touched upon infinity. From infinity, it was naturally led to God. Definitions of the Deity rained upon the table. Against us who, with our plastic imagination, could picture God, if He existed at all, only as a person, a figurative creature, a kindly bearded deity in the Michelangelo manner, Taine and Renan and Berthelot countered with Hegelian definitions, showing Him as a vast, vague diffusion whose worlds were just so many globules or crab-lice. And launching out into a respectful description of a living whole, Renan ended up by comparing God, his particular God, with all possible piety and seriousness, to an oyster. At this comparison, an enormous gust of laughter swept the table, in which Renan himself eventually joined.

I do not know whether it was on account of this Homeric laughter or not, but in any case we went on to talk about Homer. And straight away all these destroyers of faith, all these critics of God burst into the most disgusting song of praise: these partisans of progress proclaimed that there was a time and a country, at the beginning of humanity, when a work was written in which everything was divine, above all discussion and even all examination. They began to swoon with admiration over individual phrases.

'*The long-tailed birds!*' Taine cried out enthusiastically.

'*The unharvestable sea!*' exclaimed Sainte-Beuve, raising his

---

[1] Even if it is true, this anecdote is wrongly dated: the only time that Chateaubriand was arrested was on 16 June 1832, as a result of the support he had given the rebellious Duchesse de Berry.

little voice. 'A sea where there are no grapes! What could be more beautiful than that?'

'An *unharvestable sea* doesn't make sense', said Renan. 'But there's a German society which has found another meaning for the words.'

'And what is it?' asked Sainte-Beuve.

'I can't remember', replied Renan. 'But it's wonderful.'

'Well, what have you to say, you there,' Taine called out, addressing us; 'you who wrote that antiquity was created to be the daily bread of schoolmasters?'

So far we had let the hosanna go on without comment, but now we said: 'Oh, you know, we consider that Hugo has more talent than Homer.'

At this blasphemy Saint-Victor became positively wild with fury, shouting like a madman and shrieking in his tinny voice that this was impossible to stomach, that it was too much, that we were insulting the religion of all intelligent people, that everybody admired Homer and that without him Hugo would not exist. We retorted that we did not care what the majority thought in literary religions and that we could not allow him to forbid us to express our minority opinion on Homer at a table where everybody was free to discuss any subject under the sun. He shouted and flew into a passion. We shouted louder and flew into a greater passion, angered by his sneering tone and at the same time carried away by the contempt we felt for this talented man who has no opinions of his own and always toadies to consecrated opinion on all matters, for this ferocious critic who lowers his voice and begins to whine and whimper when faced with somebody who shows his teeth.

Sainte-Beuve, upset by this quarrel, persuaded me to sit down beside him and tried to calm me down by stroking my arms, at the same time attempting to bring about a general reconciliation by proposing the foundation of a Homer Club.

Little by little our anger died down. Saint-Victor, as he went out, shook hands with us. Frankly, I wished that he had not held out his hand. This is a friendship that weighs heavily upon us, with its painful conflict between our admiration for the man's work, our anger at his boorish intolerance, moments of sympathy with his personality, and the fundamental contempt inspired in us, despite ourselves, by what we know and what we suspect about him.

*Sunday, 28 October*

Today Flaubert brought Bouilhet along to present him to the Princess. I cannot imagine what unfortunate inspiration that poet had had at lunch, but he stank like an omnibus. Coming upstairs, Nieuwerkerke said with a shudder: 'There's a writer down there who reeks of garlic.' The Princess for her part scarcely noticed it, and then only after everybody else. It is amazing how imperceptive that woman is about so many subtle things, like the freshness of butter or fish. The best thing and the worst thing about her is that she is not entirely civilized.

*11 December*

Chesneau came to see us today. We talked about the veiled but obvious hostility between the Empress and the Princess and the trouble this causes Nieuwerkerke.

He told us that on the Empress's last visit to the Bank, noticing the bare panels between the windows, she had asked Rouland if there had not once been some paintings there, and Rouland had replied that they had been taken by the Louvre. No sooner had she got back to the Tuileries than the Empress had ordered Vaillant to return them to the Bank. Now if those paintings, removed to the Louvre before the Revolution and partly dispersed among provincial art-galleries, had been allowed to go back to the Bank, the way would have been opened to all manner of claims resulting in the breaking up of the Louvre collections. On receiving this particular order from the Empress, Nieuwerkerke had offered his resignation to Vaillant, declaring that after working to enrich the Louvre he could not agree to its despoliation. Whereupon Vaillant, realizing that it was against himself that the public's indignation would be directed, had gone to see the Emperor and spoken of joining his resignation to that of the Keeper. Faced with this double resignation, the Emperor had made Eugénie see reason, though not without difficulty, and ever since she had borne a grudge against Nieuwerkerke, whom she accused of thwarting all her wishes so that it made no difference whether she was Empress or not.

She bears him a grudge too on account of another incident. Having been put up at Windsor by the Queen of England in a suite of rooms full of old pictures, she decided, when the Queen visited

France, to decorate her suite in like manner. Nieuwerkerke raised no objection to a demand for some masterpieces from the Louvre, with which it seems that the sovereigns of France have always had the right to decorate their palaces. At three o'clock—the Queen was due to arrive at five—he sent over the Louvre's finest pictures. But the Empress had two embarrassing moments as a result. First of all, on her arrival, the Queen recognized the pictures from the Louvre and came out with: 'Ah, that picture comes from the Salon Carré, and that one over there. . . .' And then, the next day, she wanted to go to the Louvre, and the Empress, going with her, found notices hanging where the paintings had been, announcing in capital letters: *Removed by order and taken temporarily to the Tuileries*. Which struck her as a protest to the nation against her caprices.

# 1867

Dined at the Princess's with Gautier, Amédée Achard and Octave Feuillet. Achard is a wilted, faded man of the world, with an undistinguished mind and an expressionless voice: self-effacement in person. Feuillet is like his talent, vulgar with distinction.

Ponsard was pulled to pieces by Gautier and ourselves, with the Princess defending him. Afterwards Gautier was asked why he did not publish what he had just been saying. 'Let me tell you a little story', he said. 'One day, Monsieur Walewski told me to stop being so indulgent and to start in the next issue saying exactly what I thought about the plays I saw. "But," said I, "there's Doucet's play opening this week." "Oh, is there?" he exclaimed. "In that case, suppose you start next week?" Well, I'm still waiting for next week to arrive.'

A sign of the times: there are no longer any chairs in the bookshops along the embankments. France was the last bookseller who provided chairs where you could sit down and chat and waste a little time between sales. Nowadays books are bought standing. A request for a book and the naming of the price: that is the sort of transaction to which the all-devouring activity of modern trade has reduced bookselling, which used to be a matter for dawdling, idling, and chatty, friendly browsing.

3 February

It is said that in the course of one of Ollivier's conversations with the Emperor, the latter asked him to tell him frankly what people were saying about him, and to speak as if he were not addressing the Emperor. Ollivier having finally told him that people thought his faculties were declining, the Emperor remarked impassively: 'That is consistent with all the reports I have received.'

The remark is in character. In his impersonality he attains a certain grandeur.

16 March

The opening night of *Les Idées de Madame Aubray*, the first play by Dumas *fils* I have seen since *La Dame aux Camélias*. A special audience, of a kind which I have never come across anywhere else. It is not a play that is being performed, it is a kind of mass being celebrated before a pious congregation. There is a *claque* which seems to be officiating, while the audience writhes with ecstasy, swoons with pleasure, and utters cries of 'Adorable!' at every line. The author writes: 'Love is the springtime, it is not the whole year', and there is a salvo of applause. He goes on, working the idea to death: 'It is not the fruit, it is the flower', and the audience claps more than ever. And so it goes on. Nothing is judged, nothing is appreciated; everything is applauded with an enthusiasm brought along in advance and impatient to express itself.

Dumas has a great gift: he knows how to appeal to his public, this first-night public of whores, speculators, and depraved society-women. He is their poet, and he ladles out to them, in a language they can understand, the ideal of their commonplace emotions.

2 April

We are off to Rome.

6 April

Civita-Vecchia, ten in the morning.

At last we have found twisting streets, narrow alleys and filthy markets, alive and swarming with people; stained, gimcrack buildings; a picturesque town full of exotic charm and showing no sign of municipal activity; a colourful pile of refuse. I am conscious of a peculiar sensation: my eyes are breathing. I feel that I have escaped from the Americanized modern world and hidebound Paris.

Wandering along at random, I catch sight of a red grating, like an air-hole in a medieval leper-house. Out of one of the little squares of plaited iron comes a cloth bag on the end of a stick, together with a voice that says: '*Moussu!*' It is a prisoner. For this is the prison, and this window serves as a sort of visiting-room whereby the jailbird can enjoy all the pity and all the gossip passing along the street. I do not know why, but this kindly form of repression appeals to me.

These towns in the Papal States seem to me the last in which the poor are still to some extent at home. There is a compassion, a natural sympathy, almost a familiarity in the attitude of the middle classes towards the poor, the unfortunate, and the ragged that astonishes a man from a so-called philanthropic country. It is almost with a caress that a café-owner here gently propels a beggar into the street.

*8 April*

How can religion possibly be eradicated in a nation with a religious temperament, a religious character? After all, idolatry is a basic element of human nature. And truth to tell, between a monument such as the one I can see here beneath my window, a monument to a myth, the Immaculate Conception, and a monument to Voltaire, I do not know which of the two strikes me as the more degrading to the dignity of human reason.

*9 April*

The woman of the south speaks only to the senses. The impression she makes goes no further than that. She appeals exclusively to the appetite. And in the evening, after looking at all the types of wild and splendid beauty to be seen in the streets of Rome, in the Pincio or on the Corso, only an Englishwoman or a German woman at the *table d'hôte* can create an effect of femininity, of tender emotion.

*15 April*

Everything is unique, nothing happens more than once in a lifetime. The physical pleasure which a certain woman gave you at a certain moment, the exquisite dish which you ate on a certain day— you will never meet either again. Nothing is repeated, and everything is unparalleled.

The people of Rome are fortunate indeed, gay with the gaiety of the skies above, and blessed with inexpensive joys; sober as a judge, dining on little more than their sunshine, able to buy first-rate meat for a few coppers, with no blood-levy, no conscription, practically no taxes, no humiliation in poverty, no bitterness or despair in destitution, succoured by so many charitable institutions and the poor man's hand reaching into his pocket to help the poorer.

When I compare these people with the people of free, progressive countries, branded with the mark of the sinister industry of modern life, crippled by taxation, struggling with the daily budget, and saddled with constant revolutions, which cause an increase in taxation, even the tax on human life, over-excite all the fevers of ambition, and poison all the sores of poverty, discontent, and envy, I begin to think that we pay dearly for our catchwords.

*17 April*

For this show that is Holy Week in Rome, one could swear that the Papacy puts a sly ecclesiastical malice into humiliating and torturing the foreigner's curiosity, what with a wait lasting four hours, the brutality of the Swiss Guards, the women forced to remain standing, a staircase which you climb like a pack of hounds, with all the savagery of a cavalry charge, headlong rushes which break against the doors, and surveying all this, the smiles of Italian prelates who seem to have kept for the *forestiere* something of the contempt Rome felt for the Barbarian.

*20 April*

This evening there was an unforgettable scene at the Pellegrini hostel: rows of wild-looking, lice-ridden peasants seated on benches beneath a gas lamp which threw their heads into shadow and lit up their white, open-necked shirts; and, peeling off their stockings and washing their feet in buckets, friars of the Pilgrim Trinity, dressed in red with white bands and aprons, and carrying napkins over their arms like waiters, friars who were cardinals, princes, and young nobles, with varnished boots peeping out from under their robes and their emblazoned carriages waiting for them in the square. And when each pair of filthy feet had been washed and dried, the friar would take them in their hands, bend down and kiss them in two places.

In our heart of hearts, we felt a certain emotion at the sight of this impressive egalitarian ceremony. The Catholic religion is a beautiful thing and a great source of humanity, and it irritates us to see men of culture and intelligence go down on their knees before the iron and marble religion of antiquity. Everything that is gentle and sensitive and movingly beautiful in modernity comes from Christ.

*23 April*

I dined yesterday at our Embassy and sat beside the wife of the United States minister in Brussels, an American woman. Studying the free and confident grace of this spirited example of a young race, the potential coquetry that retains the charm and tyranny of flirtatiousness in these young girls who have become wives, and thinking meanwhile of the activity and *drive* of that American Harrisse whom I saw at work in Paris, I said to myself that these men and women were destined to be the future conquerors of the world. They will be the Barbarians of civilization, who will devour the Latin world as the Barbarians of barbarism devoured it in the past.

*3 May*

Everything that is beautiful in Rome, whether it is the women, the flowers, or the sky, is beautiful in a coarse, material way. The beauty of the Roman woman is the beauty of a splendid animal. The horizon is clearly defined, the landscape devoid of dreamy mistiness. The cloudy spirituality of all Northern things does not exist here.

*4 May*

Raphael's *Transfiguration*: the most disagreeable impression of wallpaper that a painting could possibly make on a painter's eye. It would be impossible to see—if one is capable of seeing—a cruder discord of blues, yellows, reds, and greens, including an abominable serge green, all associated in violent contrasts such as blue and yellow, and heightened by harsh lights which are invariably out of tune with the colour of the material, for instance yellow on violet or white on green.

But let us leave the man's wretched colouring and consider the composition of this masterpiece, this so-called *sursum corda* of Christianity. A Christ who is a vulgar lay-brother, all pink and red, painted—as has been justly observed—in colours intended for the light of another world, rising clumsily into the sky on the tips of a model's feet; a Moses and an Elijah going up with him, with their hands on their hips like dancers; and nothing here of the glory, the radiance, the magic which the poorest painters try at least to put into their pictures of Heaven. Underneath is Mount Tabor, a hill as round and smooth as the top of a patty, on which there lie flattened, and as it were filleted, three puppet apostles, real caricatures of amazement; and down at the bottom, an incomprehensible medley of academic studies, faces wearing expressions of the sort that are copied in art-school, arms waving like those of actors in a tragedy, and eyes which look as if they had been put in by a drawing-master.

In all this there is not an inkling, not so much as a suspicion of the feeling which in the least gifted of the Primitives, in all Raphael's predecessors, in Perugino, Pinturicchio, and the rest, lent these scenes an expression of devotion, almost of compunction, a saintly calm in the contemplation of the miracle, angelizing, so to speak, the eyes of the onlookers.

In Raphael, the Resurrection is purely academic, impregnated with a paganism which is particularly apparent in the foreground where a woman, a piece of antique statuary, is kneeling like a heathen to whom the Gospel has never spoken. This, Christian? I know no picture which inflicts on Catholicism a more alien style or disfigures it more by its materialism. This, a representation of a supernatural event, a divine legend? I know no canvas which depicts it in a commoner prose, a more vulgar beauty.

*Sunday, 19 May*

Italy ends up by giving one a nostalgia for grey. Rain, on one's return, seems like home. Back to Paris. . . .

*Friday, 24 May*

Gautier, who is at the moment *maestro di casa*, introduced us today to La Païva in her legendary house on the Champs-Élysées.

An old courtesan, painted and plastered, looking like a provincial actress with a false smile and false hair.

We were given tea in the dining-room which, with all its luxury and its extravagant Renaissance decoration in the worst possible taste, looks like nothing so much as a private room in an expensive restaurant, the Provençaux for instance, and this in spite of all the money spent on its marbles, its wainscoting, its enamels, its paintings, and its candelabra wrought in solid silver from the mines of the Prussian protector who was also present.

In this setting, an embarrassed, languishing conversation as in an artificial society. Gautier, for all his usual imperturbability, was ill at ease. Turgan, whom we were meeting here for the first time, tried to create an impression with his little effects. Saint-Victor crumpled his hat in his hands in an effort to find something to say. We could feel, falling on this magnificent table laden with crystal and lighted by flaming sconces, that chill, that horrible chill which characterizes the houses of tarts playing at being ladies, and that compound of boredom and uneasiness which, in the palaces of prostitution and the Louvres of whoredom, freezes the temperament and wit of all who enter.

*17 June*

Berthelot told us at Magny's today that not only is France at the moment the country in which the fewest children are born, but it is also the country with the highest number of old people, having four hundred of these for every fifty-eight in Prussia. He attributed our present stupidity to this fact.

*27 June*

Apropos of *Hernani*.[1] It is sad to think that an author has to live forty years, almost half a century, to be applauded as vigorously as he has been hissed.

*Vichy, 3 July*

In this place, one loses the illusion that sickness is a distinction.

[1] Hugo's play had been banned since 1852, and when the authorities, in one of the Second Empire's tardy displays of tolerance, gave permission for it to be revived, on 20 June 1867, it was given an enthusiastic reception by the public.

*9 July*

I read this morning that Ponsard was dead. He will remain the immortal example of France's admiration for mediocrity and her envy of genius. I can think of nothing else about him which is likely to save him from oblivion.

*12 July*

There are only two great currents in the history of mankind: the baseness which makes conservatives and the envy which makes revolutionaries.

*Trouville, 4 September*

At lunch today, at the Bras d'Or, we opened a letter from the Princess: the elder of us has been made a Chevalier of the Legion of Honour. Like all the joys of this life, this one is incomplete, and the brother who has been decorated derives more pain than pleasure from it. At bottom, however, we feel a certain pride in this decoration, which has that rare distinction of not having been asked for or solicited by so much as a single word or allusion, but obtained by a friend who thought of it by herself and by anonymous admirers.

*15 September*

We were talking this evening about heredity and the handing down of characteristics in the blood. Viollet-le-Duc spoke of certain gestures made by a child which betray the father and practically name him; and he maintained that an enlightened cuckold who made a study of the question could identify the father of his child among his friends and acquaintances without any possibility of a mistake. 'I can tell you a delightful story about that', said the Princess. 'A lady I know gave birth to a child with two of its toes webbed. The same evening I met a gentleman who I knew suffered from that infirmity but who did not move in the same circles as the lady. I jokingly congratulated him, pressed him a little . . . and, upon my word, he confessed!'

*18 September*

Nothing, nothing, nothing at all in this exhibition of Courbet's.[1]

[1] The one-man show which Courbet staged on the fringe of the Universal Exhibition of 1867, at the Rond-Point de l'Alma.

Two paintings of the sea and the sky at the very most. Apart from that, for all that he calls himself the master of realism, there is not a single study from nature. The body of his *Woman with a Parrot* is as far removed in its way from the real nude as any academic study done in the eighteenth century.

Ugliness, and more ugliness. And ugliness without any of its grandeur, ugliness without the beauty of ugliness.

*16 October*

Dined with Hébert at Philippe's. He comes from the Dauphiné, like Berlioz. They lived in two houses in the mountains, one a little higher than the other. He had seen Berlioz this morning and the composer had told him that at the age of twelve he had fallen in love with a local girl of twenty.[1] Since then he had been in love many times, madly, romantically, frantically in love, but deep down in his heart there had always remained the memory of that first love, which had recently revived in full force when he had come across the girl in Lyons, aged seventy-four. And now he wrote regularly to her, talking to her of nothing but memories of his twelve-year-old heart, and living for nothing but that bygone passion.

*21 October*

At the English buffets in the Exhibition, there is a fantastic quality about the women, with their splendid beauty, their crude pallor, their flaming hair; they are like whores of the Apocalypse, something terrifying, frightening, inhuman. Their eyes gaze unseeingly into the distance. A cross between clowns and cattle, they are magnificent, alarming animals.

*14 November*

This evening Sainte-Beuve gave a dinner for the Princess. His little cook, Marie, showed us into the dining-room, where the table was laid as if for a banquet arranged by a parish priest entertaining his bishop, and then into a ground-floor drawing-room, all bare and white and gold, with brand-new daffodil-yellow furniture looking like a suite chosen by an upholsterer for a tart.

[1] Estelle Gautier, the *Stella Montis* of Berlioz's *Memoirs*.

The guests arrived: the Princess, Nieuwerkerke, Mme Espinasse, Dr. Philips, and old Giraud of the Institut. The Princess looked gay and in high spirits: she was looking forward to the evening as if it were a bachelor party. At dinner she insisted upon serving everything and carving everything. Her father, she said, always carved. He had very pretty hands. He used to eat salad with his fingers, and when he was told that it was an unclean habit, he answered: 'In my day, if we had eaten it in any other way, we should have been scolded and told that our hands were dirty.'

Sitting at the head of the table, Sainte-Beuve looked like a butler. It was a gloomy meal, and anybody might have thought that it was the host's own funeral feast. He looked broken, old, and doddering, complaining of the agony of living with those senile grimaces of old men, that closing of the eyes that seems to say: 'There, I can feel it again', those gestures of miserable compunction and those empty words of self-pity. He ate nothing, got up two or three times during dinner, asking us to pay no attention to him, and came back like the ghost in his house, like the shade of an old man anxious not to disturb anybody.

All of us tried hard to whip up the conversation over the champagne, but the laughter was forced and icy. The Princess became serious, looked ill and went out. When she returned to the drawing-room, Sainte-Beuve, sitting at the end of the yellow sofa and bearing down on the silk with both fists, tried to smile and launched into an account of his friendless life with the people on the *Globe*—people like Cousin and Vitet who gave him nothing but their wit and amiability, nothing more, and often disconcerted him with their arguments, in which he was once astonished to hear Cousin call Louis XIV's Le Brun a country bumpkin.

He spoke of his days as a medical student at the Hospital of Saint-Louis in 1827, and of his room in the Rue de Lancry, 'on the eighteenth floor, where I lived in such isolation,' he said, 'that nobody came to see me for seven months, except my mother, and she came only once'. It was because of the sadness of those lonely days that he had always reacted in the opposite direction, constantly needing to have people around him, wanting women and cats in his dining-room. He cited the example of Saint-Évremond surrounding himself, as he grew older, with animals, 'and men too,' he added with a smile, 'in order to create a little more life around him'.

And he went on: 'Oh, if only I had had a real teacher at the hospital! But I was under Richerand, a charlatan. . . .'

Thereupon, Dr. Philips, with his great sunken head, his protuberant eyes, and his stiff-jointed body, started talking surgery and operations, speaking of Roux, that artist in bandaging who killed his patients with the prettiness of his dressings. The Princess interrupted him to reproach him with the cruelty of surgeons, their insensitivity, their obvious lack of feeling. 'That isn't true,' said Philips. 'I feel deeply, but only for children. One can't make the poor little things understand that it is all for their own good. That's really horrible! . . . You see, in our trade, you get to the point where nothing matters but the operation you are performing, the science you are practising. It's so beautiful. I sometimes think that I should stop living if I couldn't operate. It's my absinthe.'

This unfortunate conversation, the atmosphere of the house, and the approaching death of the old bachelor who was entertaining us made us look sadly at the assembled company. Sainte-Beuve first of all; Giraud, that satyr who would die one day from his failure to become a senator; Nieuwerkerke, who had arrived dragging one leg, like a Hercules on whom Death was trying his grip; the Princess, whose face and speech so often revealed involuntary presentiments of exile and a lonely death in Italy; and ourselves, condemned to suffer with our bodies and fight with our minds for the rest of our lives.

*29 December*

At four o'clock we went to see how Sainte-Beuve was getting on. He sent word that he would like us to come up. We climbed the narrow stairs, crossed the little landing, and went into that bare yet crowded bedroom with its curtainless iron bed and its general appearance of a camp pitched in an untidy library.

From the bed two hands stretched out, warm and soft. We could just distinguish a head enveloped in coverings and a body which pain, doubling it up under the sheets, had practically robbed of its shape.

'Badly . . . it's going badly!' These were almost his first words. 'But the doctors . . .'

'What doctors?' he retorted, with a note of anger in his voice. 'I haven't any doctors left. They've all deserted me. Alton-Shee has given me Nelson. Philips has been very kind, but he's a surgeon. Perhaps I shall come to that tomorrow, because I can't go three hours now without being probed. And then I get on the chamber and spend ages twisting and turning, with awful spasms of the bladder. . . .'

And he entered into all the technical details of his horrible illness, talking about the pus he excreted as if by revealing the disgust he inspired in himself he hoped to disarm the disgust he aroused in others. He seemed to us to be despairingly resigned. He drew a deep breath and then said: 'I still have myself read to, but off and on, you understand. . . . I can't collect my ideas any more.' There was a pause, then: 'Good-bye', and he held out both his hands to us again and turned his face to the wall.

# 1868

In a snowstorm which made one shudder in sympathy for the poor of Paris, we rang the bell of the house on the Champs-Élysées, insolent in its dazzling light and ablaze with the chandeliers and red curtains that could be seen through the windows. In the huge drawing-room, there was no fire in the enormous grate: nothing but a stove that had just been lit. La Païva dislikes open fires. She came in soon afterwards, dripping with emeralds all over the flesh of her shoulders and arms. 'I'm still a little blue with cold', she said. 'It's because my maid has just done my hair with all the windows wide open.' This woman, with her Russian blood, is not built like other women. In this kind of weather, she lives in icy air and water like a sort of monster from a Scandinavian myth.

She is always the same, disagreeable, unpleasant, contradicting others in a cutting, wounding way. At table she expounded a frightening theory of will-power, saying that everything was the result of an effort of the will, that there were no such things as fortuitous circumstances, that one created one's own circumstances, and that unfortunate people were so only because they did not want to stop being unfortunate. And when Taine—a philosopher whom one runs into at all the great courtesans' houses, and who was dining here for the first time—provided her with an example, citing Newton who concentrated so hard on his experiments for years on end that he nearly went out of his mind, she spoke of a woman who, in order to attain some unspecified aim, shut herself up for three years, completely cut off from the world, scarcely eating anything and often forgetting about food, walled up within herself and entirely given over to the plan she was developing. And she concluded: 'I was that woman.'

*24 January*

If there is a God, atheism must strike Him as less of an insult than religion.

*8 February*

One of the proud joys of the man of letters—if that man of letters is an artist—is to feel within himself the power to immortalize at will anything he chooses to immortalize. Insignificant though he may be, he is conscious of possessing a creative divinity. God creates lives; the man of imagination creates fictional lives which may make a more profound and as it were a more living impression on the world's memory.

*14 February*

A fantastic remark which shows the effect of a slanderous rumour about a woman and what sort of idea of her it gives everybody. The first time the painter Frère was invited to dinner at the Princess's, he said to a friend as he set out: 'I've taken a bath just in case. ... You never know what might happen!' And the poor Princess talks ingenuously about all the things people have said of Marie-Antoinette!

*24 February*

Exactly twenty years ago today, about one o'clock, from the balcony of the flat where we lived in the Rue des Capucines, I saw the ironmonger across the street run up a ladder and, with hurried hammer strokes, knock down the words *to the King* which followed the word *Ironmonger* on the sign over his shop. After that we went to the Tuileries Gardens and saw a roebuck's head which had been cut off lying on the ground, and an equestrienne from the Hippodrome caracoling on her horse. The statue of Spartacus had a red bonnet on its head and a bunch of flowers in its hand. The palace clock had been stopped, and on the great balcony one of the victorious revolutionaries, wearing Louis-Philippe's dressing-gown and looking like a Daumier caricature, was mimicking the King's pet phrase: 'It is always with renewed pleasure. . . .'

Nowadays, when I go along the Rue des Capucines, I see the words *to the Emperor* on the ironmonger's sign, where it once read *to the King*.

*4 March*

This evening the Princess said: 'I enjoy only those novels of which I should have liked to be the heroine.' A perfect illustration of the standard by which women judge novels.

*4 May*

M. Marcellus, the Christian grandee, took communion at his château only with consecrated wafers stamped with his coat of arms. One day the priest noticed to his horror that the stock of stamped wafers was exhausted. He ventured to proffer to the noble, pious mouth a common, plebeian wafer, the wafer of ordinary folk, at the same time tendering this truly admirable apology: 'Potluck, Monsieur le Comte!'

*6 May*

Since, this time, it was two poets that stood as candidates for the Academy, one called Autran and the other Théophile Gautier, and since the Academy elected Autran, it is now my absolute and unalterable conviction that the Academy is largely composed of cretins or thoroughly dishonest men: I leave it to them to make the choice.

*14 May*

This is the home in which, this week, Maria delivered a woman of her child. At the upper end of the Boulevard Magenta, in a colony of huts—which are leased to the poorest of the poor of Paris by whom? Baron James de Rothschild—a room where the planks that form the walls are coming apart and the floor is full of holes, through which rats are constantly appearing, rats which also come in whenever the door is opened, impudent poor men's rats which climb on to the table, carrying away whole hunks of bread, and worry the feet of the sleeping occupants. In this room, six children: the four biggest in a bed; and at their feet, which they are unable to stretch out, the two smallest in a crate. The man, a costermonger who has known better days, dead-drunk during his wife's labour. The woman, as drunk as her husband, lying on a straw mattress and being plied with drink by a friend of hers, an old canteen attendant who developed a thirst in twenty-five years' campaigning and spends all her pension on liquor. And during the delivery in this shanty, the wretched shanty of civilization, an organ-grinder's monkey, imitating and parodying the cries and angry oaths of the shrew in the throes of childbirth, piddling through a crack in the roof on to the snoring husband's back.

*16 May*

The persistent fatality of books! Here we are—we whose sympathies of race and skin draw us towards the Pope, we who feel no hatred for the man who wears a priest's robes—here we are, impelled by some irresistible force which is in the air, writing a book which is cruel to the Church. Why? But who knows the why and wherefore of what he writes?

*Fontainebleau, 27 May*

There come moments of despair over our health when we say: 'Let us embrace one another; it will give us courage!' And we kiss without another word.

*31 May*

This evening, in the dining-room of a hotel at Fontainebleau, in the midst of horrible couples of starchy bourgeois, old stock-brokers, and affected nonentities, we dined next to an old English couple. The French lack this nobility in the evening of life, this breeding in old age, the distinction of this old lady with her womanly smile, the Franklin-like aristocratic beauty of this old gentleman with his crown still retaining a few white hairs, his happy eyes, his firm mouth, his fine, human expression—a perfect example of a full and honourable life, a limpid soul, an easy conscienc~

There is something in the Englishman of the aristocracy of the good English dog.

*1 June*

Dinner at Magny's. We heard some curious details about the German scholars Froehner and Oppert, a couple of pedants who are no more learned than anybody else but to whom the present-day cult of Germanism in the world of learning has brought ironic blessings—to the first a cosy sinecure in the Louvre, and to the other a prize of a hundred thousand francs for his work on cuneiforms, a language of which he alone knows the secrets and which nobody has ever been able to check.

One of our number had known Froehner when he was humble, poor, and wretched, and, like all Germans, played a piano in his garret. When he met him again, Froehner was wearing a cravat with pink spots and an astonishing suit, the sort of suit you can imagine a German scholar turned dandy would wear. 'I dare say you find me changed, my dear fellow,' he said. 'The fact is that I discovered that hard work, application, and all that was just nonsense. Hase told me that the only way to get to the top here was through women. Look at Longpérier: if he hadn't begun frequenting drawing-rooms. . . .'

On another occasion Froehner had got hold of our guest, taken him into a window recess and anxiously asked him if he thought that a German like himself, Froehner, would ever be able to talk smut to women as Frenchmen did, saying that he had tried but that what he said always became so coarse and filthy that he could never finish it properly.

What a comic sign of the times, erudition employing this method to achieve success! Erudition represented by these two Germans, these two vulgar natives of the land of artlessness, trying to succeed by means of the delicate corruption of France.

*18 July*

There is a fundamental antagonism between tobacco and woman. One diminishes the other. This is so true that sooner or later men in love with women stop smoking because they feel or imagine that tobacco has a deadening effect on sexual desire and the sexual act. The fact is that love is gross and material compared with the spirituality of a pipe.

20 July

The Princess spoke to us today about her father's sensual temperament, his constant need of women. She painted a strange picture of his life at home with his fanatically jealous wife, having leeches applied in her presence by a woman who had formerly been his mistress, and his feet rubbed by another woman who was still his mistress, at the same time taking an interest in a little maid who used to give him assignations in the latrines, while all the while he was living as man and wife with his lawful spouse.

She went on to talk about the Murats, the whole family sleeping together pell-mell. 'They were just like rabbits!' she said. 'Anna, at the age of ten, was always in her nightdress. I had all the trouble in the world preventing her from kissing one of the valets. Joachim, when he was a child, used to smoke the coachmen's pipes. As for the other girl, Caroline, Madame de Chassiron, it was impossible to wash her feet. Now she has what you two call attacks of hysteria.' And she turned to us and smiled. 'Yes, she bays at the moon. I have heard her several times.'

Whereupon a long discussion began between the three of us on hysteria, *globus hystericus*, on the physical characteristics of the hysterical woman, and all those questions of pathological love in which she shows an almost passionate interest.

At one o'clock she went off to preside over the prize-giving at Saint-Gratien. And at the door she turned round with a laugh and said: 'I hope a *globus hystericus* doesn't come over me during the ceremony! Think of the scandal if I kissed Théret!' He is the mayor.

4 August

There we stood on the steps of the house in Auteuil that we wanted to buy. The sun was shining through the trees in the garden, and the lawn and the leaves were glittering under the rain of a garden hose.

'Eighty-two thousand five hundred?' said my brother, and our hearts pounded in our breasts.

'I'll write to you tomorrow,' said the owner, 'and I shall probably accept your offer.'

'Eighty-three thousand and an immediate answer!'

He thought it over for five eternal minutes and then said sadly: 'Done.'

We went off intoxicated with happiness.

7 August

Yesterday the Princess gave Flaubert a terrible wigging on account of his visits to La Tourbey. Speaking with all the pride of a princess and a woman of society, she complained this morning, with a certain wittiness, that it was with women of that sort that she had to share the company and thoughts of her friends, of men like Taine, Renan, and Sainte-Beuve, who, when dining with her, would steal twenty minutes of her time to go and present them to that trollop.

She went on to protest at the dominion enjoyed by these women, honoured by the company of philosophers, men of letters, scientists, and thinkers; at the power wielded by these sluts, without so much as the excuse of an art, a talent, a name, the genius of a Rachel or even a Plessy-Arnould, and in whose houses the purest of men could be seen eating the truffles of the courtesan. This led to talk about the contagion of their corruption, the imitation of their fashions; and the names of society women who vied with them. At the name of Mme Mercy-Argenteau, the Princess said: 'She's another! She recommended a milliner to me and asked me to grant her my warrant. Well, do you know who it was? A woman in whose house she met her lovers!'

Mme Malvezzi's voice remarked: 'Oh, the example comes from high up!'

'That's true enough,' said the Princess. 'When the head . . . That woman . . . Why, she said to me one day: "I've made a wonderful find! Anna Murat has given me the name of the woman who dresses the courtesans." I was furious. Imagine wearing the same dresses as Mlle Coco!'

And getting to her feet, she went on:

'Oh, she'll go out of her mind one day! They'll have to give her a little house at Charenton! But I was forgetting that you haven't seen all that I've seen. I remember when she wanted to go to Africa, she had some military uniforms made specially for her. There were two of them: one black with gold brandenburgs and the other a spahi outfit. She looked lovely: she's very slim, you know. . . . And then, she had contrived to stick the Crown jewels all over. . . . She came in holding her riding-skirt in both hands and jumped on to the arm of an easy-chair. There was an icy silence. It was embarrassing, you understand. Luckily, she spoke to Vaillant and not to me. It was the only time that Vaillant ever showed a little wit. She asked him what he thought of her costume. He replied very politely: "Madame, I don't like women dressed like men any more than I like men dressed like women." And all this time the little prince was saying to his mother: "Maman, go and undress!" We never saw those costumes again. Perhaps she turned them into breeches for her son. . . .'

*Auteuil, 16 September*

We are not quite sure that this is not a dream. Is this really ours, this big tasteful plaything, these two drawing-rooms, that sunshine in the greenery, that clump of trees silhouetted against the sky, this little plot of earth and the birds flying overhead?

*17 September*

Yes, it is all ours; but unfortunately for us who came here to escape from the noise of Paris, we have the noise of a horse in the house on the right, the noise of children in the house on the left, and the noise of trains going by in front, rumbling and whistling and disturbing our insomnia.

*29 October*

The English are crooked as a nation and honest as individuals. The contrary is true of the French, who are honest as a nation and crooked as individuals.

*2 November*

This evening, coming down the Princess's staircase after having been appointed librarian to the Princess, Gautier asked us in all

sincerity: 'But tell me, has the Princess really got a library?' I replied: 'Take my advice, Gautier, and act as if she hadn't. . . .'

*5 November*

This is the story of Prince Napoleon's wedding night, as told by
the Abbé Doussot, chaplain to the Palais-Royal, to Charles-
Edmond.

On her arrival at the palace, the Princess sent a message to the
Abbé asking for some holy water. The Abbé sent her a small carafe;
less than an hour later, the Princess asked for more. This time the
Abbé sent a large carafe. The Princess was indefatigably sprinkling
her bedroom and the other rooms in her apartment in order to
cleanse them of the abominations which she suspected them of
having witnessed. The second carafe was emptied. A third request
for holy water. Another carafe.

But it was beginning to get late. It was time to dress for dinner.
The carafe, full of water for the next day's aspersions, was placed
on the mantelpiece in the Princess's bedroom. That night, the
Prince was in the nuptial chamber when he felt thirsty and poured
himself a glass of water. 'This water tastes beastly!' he remarked.
The Princess took care to say nothing, rejoicing in her pious heart
at this blessed purification, this holy cleansing of her husband. The
Prince went on talking—he talks a great deal—and mechanically
poured himself another glass; the Princess let him. The holy water
had a miraculous effect, with the result that that night Prince Napoleon was purged by his chaplain more thoroughly than he had ever
been by his pharmacist.

*2 December*

In front of me, in the Princess's drawing-room, I had the broad
back of Gautier, who was sitting on the carpet Turkish-fashion, with
his legs crossed, and supporting himself on his arms, and who, fore-
shortened in this way, looked like a humpbacked dwarf. He was
leaning against the armchair occupied by Sacy, who was talking
to him over his shoulder and whose genial contempt seemed

to be descending from a great height upon this weird Romantic candidate.

It pained me to see Gautier in this humble posture: it offended me like the combination of a noble talent and a base character. Oh, poor Théo's dreadful hunger and thirst for the Academy! And what natural, obsequious servility! And all enhanced by a melancholy, sickly grace, delicate paradoxes, and ironic pleasantries, an amalgam of Falstaff and Mercutio. A deep cough racked his chest every now and then, and a cruel remark went round the drawing-room to the effect that he was coughing to get into the Academy.

Then he sat down in a little armchair close to the Princess's skirts, like a poor, tired court jester. And his head fell forward, his great, heavy, wrinkled eyelids dropped down over his eyes, his hands dangled limply, and sleep, bending him forward, seemed to be pushing him towards one of those deaths which are found with their faces on the floor. We were seized with gloomy forebodings about this man, laden with honours at the moment and standing on the threshold of academic immortality, a threshold on which it seemed to us that the cruel irony of life's compensations was already nailing together his coffin.

Once, when he happened to find himself next to Saint-Victor, the latter said to him, with a sickly smile and that nervous grimace which he always gives in the Princess's drawing-room at the sight of our group of friends:

'Well, that was a fine article you wrote on Ponsard, and no mistake. It seems that he's a genius now. . . .'

'Oh,' said Gautier mildly, 'it's all so unimportant. . . . And then, you've read enough of my articles to know that with me you have to read between the lines.'

'All the same,' Saint-Victor went on in his driest voice, 'you did say that his work was taking on "the solidity of eternal things".'

'Oh, pooh!' said Gautier.

As we were leaving, the Princess, who, worried about Gautier's health, had sent him her doctor, Dr. Le Helloco, drew us to one side and said in a low voice: 'It seems that it isn't the chest but the heart. . . .' Taking us home in a cab, he was touching and moving with us, bringing tears to our eyes with the comic effects of a dying man in Rabelais or Shakespeare: 'I tell you, once a fellow starts looking after himself . . . Here I am, taking medicine; well, that's a bad sign.'

Our admirer and pupil Zola came to lunch today. It was the first time we had ever seen him. Our immediate impression was of a worn-out *Normalien*, at once sturdy and puny, with Sarcey's neck and shoulders and a waxy, anaemic complexion, a strapping young fellow with something of the delicate modelling of fine porcelain in his features, in the line of his eyes, in the angry planes of his nose, and in his hands. The whole of his person was built rather like his characters, which he constructs with two contrary types, mingling male and female in them; and in his temperament too he offered a certain resemblance to the natures he creates, with their ambiguous contrasts. The dominant side of him, the sickly, suffering, hypersensitive side, occasionally gives you the impression of being in the company of a gentle victim of some heart disease. In a word, an incomprehensible, deep, complex character; unhappy, worried, evasive, and disquieting.

He talked to us about how hard life was for him, and how much he wanted and needed to find a publisher who would give him thirty-six thousand francs for six years, so that he might be assured of six thousand francs a year, food for himself and his mother, and freedom to write the 'story of a family', a novel in ten volumes. For he would like to do 'something big' and not—as he said in a voice full of self-contempt—'those foul, ignoble articles I have to write these days for the *Tribune*, among people whose idiotic opinions I am forced to adopt. For there's no doubt about it, the Government, with its ignorance of talent and its indifference to literature, flings us poorer writers into the opposition press, because only there can we earn enough to eat. That's the truth; there's no alternative! . . . The trouble is, I have so many enemies! And it's so hard to make a name for oneself!'

And every now and then, in a mood of bitter recrimination in which he would repeat to us and to himself that he was only twenty-eight, there burst forth a vibrant note of pungent determination and furious energy:

'And then, I've a lot of research to do. . . . Yes, you are right, my

*Madeleine Férat* does go off the rails: I should have had only the three main characters. But I'll take your advice: I'll do my play that way. . . . But after all, we are the younger generation: we know that you are our masters, you and Flaubert. Why, even your enemies admit that you invented your art. They think that that's nothing, but it's everything!'

# 1869

At Magny's, Dr. Robin gave us details of fascinating, terrifying experiments on decapitated men, headless bodies which, after forty-five minutes of death, moved their hands as if they were alive to touch their chests at the place where they were being pinched; and many other proofs in support of the theory that heart and brain are independent.

There is no distraction better able to draw us out of our sickly melancholy and stifle our anxiety about our health than these exalted scientific revelations, these dreams of the scalpel, so to speak, which provide us with the forgetfulness, pleasure, excitement, and intoxication which other people find in a social gathering, a ball, or a play.

*Wednesday, 6 January*

I told the Princess that I had been to see Sainte-Beuve and had found him tired, preoccupied, and despondent. She did not reply but passed in front of me and took me into the first drawing-room, the setting of her intimate conversations and confidential chats. And there she burst forth:

'I shall never see Sainte-Beuve again! Never! He has behaved with me like . . . Why, it was because of him that I quarrelled with the Empress. . . . And to think of all I've done for him! The last time I went to Compiègne he asked me for three things, and I got two of them out of the Emperor. And what did I ask in return? I didn't ask him to give up one of his convictions. I just asked him not to sign a contract with the *Temps*, and offered him everything on Rouher's behalf. If he had gone to Girardin's *Liberté*, I could have understood, seeing that that is his circle. But the *Temps*! The family's personal enemy! Where every single day we are insulted! He has behaved . . .'

She stopped short, then went on: 'Oh, he's a wicked man. As long as six months ago, I wrote to Flaubert: "I am sure that some day soon Sainte-Beuve is going to play a dirty trick on us." ' And with almost a hiss of bitterness, she added: 'He wrote to me on New Year's Day to thank me for all the comfort and attention that surrounded him in his illness and to say that he owed it all to me. . . . No, nobody has a right to behave like that.'

She was choking and spluttering, beating her breast with the top of her dress which she was holding with both hands, while tears rose in her voice and emotion choked her from time to time. 'I'm not speaking as a princess,' she said, 'but as a woman, a woman!' She shook me by the lapels of my tail-coat as if to thrust her indignation into me and stir up my feelings. 'Come now, Goncourt, don't you think it's disgusting?' And her eyes, full of the anger of her heart, searched mine for a response.

Then she took a few steps across the carpet, waving behind her the long train of her white silk gown, and came back to me. 'As a woman!' she said again. 'I have dined at his table, I have sat in the same chair in which Madame Rattazzi had sat. As a matter of fact, I said to him there in his own house: "Your house is a house of trollops, a house of ill fame, and yet I have come here. I have come here for your sake." Oh, I didn't mince my words. I said to him: "Who are you, anyway? A feeble old man. You can't even attend to your own needs! What further ambitions can you possibly have? You know, I wish that you had died last year: at least you would have left me the memory of a friend." That scene upset me dreadfully', she added, still shuddering at the memory of it.

And as the Keeper of the Louvre passed by, with all his decorations, returning from some reception, she said: 'Don't repeat what I've just told you. I haven't said anything to Monsieur Nieuwerkerke. I just acted on the spur of the moment.'

*8 January*

Hydrotherapy, cold water: fear and terror. Mornings beginning in the apprehension of that rain of torture which makes you scream at the anguish of your every nerve and dance in the enamel bowl the St. Vitus's dance of the madman's shower. I could not stand it longer than three days: if I had gone on it would have killed me.

*11 January*

Brown, the painter of horses, told me this story about Pointel, the very Christian editor of an illustrated paper, the present power behind Dalloz and his *Moniteur*, and the man who forced Sainte-Beuve to go to the *Temps*. Pointel sent for Brown to do some wood-cuts for his paper, and asked him what he painted.

'Why, horses', said Brown.

'Horses!' Pointel strode feverishly twice round his office and came back to Brown.

'Horses!' he repeated. 'Horses lead to whores. Whores lead to the death of the family. There will be no horses in my paper.'

*Wednesday, 13 January*

After dinner the Princess gave vent to another outburst against Sainte-Beuve: 'I was suffocating: I had to leave his house or I should have burst into tears. But do you know what he said to me? That he didn't consider himself obliged to resign from the Senate; and that in any case he was determined not to serve the Prince Imperial.'

Then, all of a sudden, she came out with this remark which revealed the fundamental reason for the break: 'You know, the fact is that for a woman like me there can be no friendship with an incomplete man. . . .' A profound observation, a real find, which shows the physiological incompatibility of their two natures.

*15 January*

A life without a minute's rest; the ceaseless correction of proofs; errands to Paris; all the hard labour of alterations on the spot; the need for constant inspiration in order to improvise changes; days when we have not a quarter of an hour to ourselves and sigh for the time when we shall be able to smoke a cigar in peace. And all this while we are both of us ailing, casting inquiring glances at each other and measuring each other's sufferings, sharing our courage, the one tormented by constant headaches, the other by a continual queasiness of the stomach which makes him look as if he had risen from the dead when the gaslamps are lit in the evening.

Oh yes, we are certainly martyrs to our books, forever standing in the breach of work and thought, illness or no illness.

*10 February*

We have just escaped being killed together. We were going to our Wednesday dinner at the Princess's. A drunken cabby whom we had hired at Auteuil drove us hell-for-leather into the wheels of a waggon on the Passy embankment, and the collision was so violent that Edmond was thrown against the window in front of him and broke it with his face. We looked at each other: an awful, mutual glance in which each felt the other's bones. His face and one eye were covered with blood. We got out of the cab for a closer look. I examined him: the impact had been just below the eye, and the glass had cut open the upper and lower lids. That was all I could see; but a little later Edmond was blinded by the blood and, though he said nothing to me, was afraid that he had lost the sight of one eye.

From the embankment we went up to Passy, I supporting him under one arm and he walking steadily along with his handkerchief all red, like the victim of a bloody accident, a mason who had fallen off a roof. And until the eye had been cleaned up at a chemist's we felt anguish and emotion for seconds that lasted an eternity. A miracle: the eye was unharmed.

We went to a post office to send a telegram to the Rue de Courcelles, and Edmond told me a peculiar thing: that a split-second before the collision he had had a premonition of the accident; only, by a sort of transposition of his fraternal second sight, it had been I whom he had seen injured, and injured in the eye.

*19 February*

We went to see Sainte-Beuve. We found him despondent about the state of his health, the state of politics, and the state of literature. He talked about the degradation of the Academy, the gerrymandering, the cliques, and Guizot's wire-pulling. He retailed to us this dialogue between Mme de Galliera and Lebrun, which Lebrun had reported to him with all the indignation and bitterness of an old scholar:

'Well, Monsieur Lebrun, the first seat has been awarded. Yes, to Monsieur de Haussonville. That much is settled.'

'I didn't know', the academician said with a bow.

'As for the second, it will probably go to Monsieur de Champagny.'

'Ah!'

'And the third, in all probability, to Monsieur Barbier.'

After this, the melancholy of the hour of five o'clock, the dying day, and the threat of a lonely evening to come, brought to Sainte-Beuve's lips a complaint, uttered in low spirits and a low voice, about all the privations he was suffering and the impossibility of getting about and mixing with other people, an impossibility which produced a complete lack of interest in the rest of humanity.

He described to us, as in a conversation poking at a dead fire, his life during these days that followed one after another: waking in the morning with a little lucidity and a few illusions left, still interested towards the middle of the day in work and what friends had not forgotten him, but after that faced with nothing but the dreary prospect of the evening. 'You know, I don't call that existence', he said. 'Life is just a bare wall for me now. It could do with some paper and pictures. . . .' And a little wave of the hand sketched out in the air a nostalgia for things of the past.

Night fell gently and the old man's voice became more and more a chiaroscuro voice, a voice gradually approaching the great silence.

*22 February*

Since the publication of our *Madame Gervaisais*, we have had a painful time. Not a single letter, not a single word, not the slightest comment from anybody, with the exception of a hearty handshake from Flaubert.

*22 March*

We went to call on Sainte-Beuve, who through a common friend had offered to write a savage criticism of *Madame Gervaisais* and had politely asked us for a reply. And for a whole hour he treated us to a sort of bitter, repetitious sermon, interspersed with outbursts of senile anger.

After an hour of this cold douche, he accused us of having distorted the meaning of the *Imitation of Christ*, that sweet book of love and melancholy. He sent Troubat to find his copy, and showed it to us stuffed with pressed flowers like a herbal and full of marginal notes. Then, turning towards the failing light, he started reading the

Latin through his nose, spelling it out in a voice that had suddenly changed, a priestly voice. And he closed the book with the remark: 'Oh, there's real love there. . . . Enough sweetness for a lifetime.'

Meanwhile we were laughing inside ourselves at the idea that perhaps the 'bishop of the atheists' diocese' was going to undertake a hypocritical defence of Religion against our novel!

*1 April*

Sat in an omnibus next to a little peasant girl who looked as if she had just arrived in Paris to go into service. It was impossible for her to sit still. Try as she might to appear unconcerned, to keep her arms folded in perfect immobility, she seemed to feel a sort of restless embarrassment in this huge, overwhelming city, a shy, agitated disquiet mingled with a curiosity which made her turn her head time and again to look out of the window behind. A little dumpling in a white bonnet. Like a goat rubbing itself against a post, or as if she were still carrying some of the fleas of her native province, she kept straightening herself against the back of her seat, shifting haunches that were already soft and lascivious and ready to slip into the limp routine of a Parisian streetwalker. As nervous as an animal in a waggon, biting her nails, absent-minded, happy but a little frightened, she would mutter something to herself and then give a tired yawn.

*16 April*

We recently had an encounter with Sainte-Beuve that was peculiar from beginning to end.

After his bitter, hateful expectorations against our novel and his almost personal hostility to its heroine, he proposed, through Charles-Edmond, to give us a couple of articles in the *Temps*. He asked us to accept the pleasure and the pain which these would give us, adding that he expected us to reply in the same paper to his strictures. We promptly accepted this proposal and the courteous offer of a reply.

After this had all been agreed in the course of a visit we paid Sainte-Beuve, we met somebody who told us that he was not writing the articles and that he was saying it was all our fault. We wrote to him. He replied in a letter in which he substituted *Chers Messieurs* for the usual *Chers amis*, an embarrassed, involved letter in which he seemed to be hinting that his present position *vis-à-vis* the Princess prevented him from writing the articles he was supposed to be devoting to us. At the very first words of the letter I guessed that some enemy had been at work, some spy at the Wednesday dinner—a Taine perhaps, who knows?

Right to the end, on the very edge of the grave, Sainte-Beuve is the Sainte-Beuve he has always been, a man forever influenced in his criticism by tiny trivialities, minor considerations, personal matters, and the pressure of opinion around him: a critic who has never delivered an independent, personal judgement on a single book.

The fact of the matter is that at the moment he wants to break with the Princess's friends and to create the impression that the fault is theirs.


*Wednesday, 28 April*

At the Princess's. By way of providing a touching surprise for the Emperor, who is coming tomorrow, the Princess asked the court improviser, Théophile Gautier, to turn into verse a bit of prose written by the prisoner of Ham on the return of his uncle's ashes: a bit of first-rate prose at that. During the day Gautier galloped his Muse through ninety lines of verse—*O platitudo!*— which were applauded in the drawing-room. Then a discussion arose as to whether it was more fitting to call the Emperor a *dreamer* than a *thinker* or a *thinker* than a *dreamer*. I must admit that we slipped out to have a smoke with Chesneau.

When we came downstairs again we found Gautier in the midst of telling the Princess one of those fantastic dirty stories with which he seems to take an unconscious revenge for every contemptible action he commits. He was describing with absolute frankness his bestial relations with one of the women he had loved most in his life, a panther woman, as spotted as her name would suggest, who worked in a side-show. And to the Princess's 'oh's' and 'ah's' he replied in what he calls his *suave* voice: 'But I assure you, Princess, that a skin like that is very pretty indeed.'

Sacy came in. Tableau! A chill fell on the company. Gautier, excited by the sight of the academician, whose vote he will need at tomorrow's Academy election, pounced on the old puritan, who, out of deference to the Princess and her protégé, listened with apparent approval to the amazing and increasingly coarse account of that animal romance. Sitting on the divan, Gautier's son, the civil servant, said to me:

'My father's at it again!'

'But why don't you go and give him a nudge?'

'Oh, you don't know him. He's perfectly capable of turning to me as he does when I wake him up at the theatre and saying: "*Merde!*" '

*29 April*

We arrived at half-past eleven. The imperial ceremony was over. Gautier, who lost his election at the Academy today and with whom we shook hands commiseratingly, said: 'Bah! I've already got over it. My thing here went over very well. The Emperor actually cried.'

The poor innocent, made to compromise himself in such a public manner and with such exaggerated flattery, to receive scarcely a word of thanks from the august lips, the Emperor talking for the rest of the evening to Ricord about pineapple growing, and the Empress for a whole hour to Dumas *fils* about his repentant Magdalens.

*30 April*

Claude Bernard's reception at the Academy keeps being put off for the comical reason that Patin is incapable of replying to him with the customary eulogy. Every day the unfortunate Patin forgets at the bottom of Bernard's stairs the physiology which the physiologist has just taught him in his consulting-room.

*7 July*

This evening at Saint-Gratien, Dr. Philips talked about Lord Hertford. It is a cancer of the bladder that is killing, to the accompaniment of frightful torture, the English multi-millionaire, who for nine years has borne the pain inflicted by the disease with iron courage. There have never been more miserly millions than those of the noble lord. He has never invited anyone to dinner, though it is said that someone who dropped in on him at lunchtime was treated to a cutlet, and Philips was given a bowl of soup at the beginning of his illness. Even then, the Major, Lord Hertford's friend and so-called 'companion in debauchery', slapped the surgeon on the back as he was showing him out and said: 'You were lucky to be given that much in this house.'

A complete, absolute, unashamed monster, even more of a monster than his brother Seymour, who redeemed the black wickedness of his family with certain generous qualities. It is Lord Hertford who is given to making the dreadful remark: 'Men are evil, and when I die I shall at least have the consolation of knowing that I have never rendered anyone a service.'

*14 August*

This morning after breakfast, walking alone with us in her park after reading in the *Moniteur* of Baudry's promotion to the rank of Officer of the Legion of Honour, a promotion which he owes to the Empress's influence, the Princess returned to the subject of the Empress.

'What is amazing', she said, 'is that she hasn't acquired any maturity, poise, or respectability over the years. She is still as mad about clothes as she was on her wedding-day. Yes, she talks of nothing else. The last time I was at Saint-Cloud, she showed me all her dresses for the trip to Suez. And that was all! The whole journey is nothing to her but an opportunity to make eyes at some Eastern prince from her steamboat. Because she always needs men around her to pay court to her and talk smut to her without rumpling her dress. You see, she carries flirtation as far as it will go. Why, the other day she actually said to me that a woman could yield almost everything, except the *main thing*! And she's so dry in her coquetry. A trollop without any temperament.'

She let this judgement fall from her lips like the blade of the guillotine. She went on:

'And no modesty at all. You know, Spanish women don't know what modesty means. When she was ill—because she hasn't been any use to the Emperor for years, what with her corns: yes, she had corns there!—it was incredible how ready she was to show people, hitching up her skirts in front of everybody! And on top of that she has never been able to arouse anybody's affection. She never shows any sign of tenderness, never even kisses her son! The last time I saw her, she had just changed all her women. You ought to hear what her ladies-in-waiting say about her! One day she covers them with kisses and the next day she's positively rude to them. I had to ask Madame Espinasse to tell Madame de Lourmel that I could not allow her to speak about her again as she had spoken about her to me. . . . The woman isn't French; she doesn't like France or the French. The only times I have seen her being polite were when she was with foreign sovereigns. You should have seen her with the Emperor of Austria! And then she has a stupid passion for foreign fads, trying to introduce customs and etiquette from other countries into the Tuileries and teaching the Prince Imperial the Prussian salute! And there's her cult of Marie-Antoinette. . . . Have you ever heard of anything so stupid, ridiculous, indecent? Do you know what she has in her bedroom? First a portrait of her sister, whom she loathed and whom she used to insult by telegraph—so the Emperor told me—then a portrait of Mérimée, another of Madame Metternich, a Sèvres bust of Marie-Antoinette, a portrait of the little Dauphin, and on her table a copy of a life of Marie-Antoinette, which she hasn't read, because she doesn't read, doesn't take an interest in anything. . . . And nothing she does is ever decent or decorous. Do you know which were the two women she hunted out to present to the Prince of Wales when he came to the Tuileries? Madame de Gallifet and Madame de Canisy! Two women to spend the night with!'

*Wednesday, 25 August*

How erratic the Princess's head and heart can be! How she alternates between hot and cold, like the successive waves of a stormy sea! What rapid changes from brutal words which suggest that she is heartless to tender effusions which beg your forgiveness!

Yesterday, in the course of a discussion about that old Jew Franck, she said something unpleasant to me about my liver complaint. Today at lunch I was still smarting from her remark, and when she began eulogizing Franck and Jewry in general once more I blurted out, in a moment of sickly irascibility over which I had no control: 'Well then, Princess, why don't you turn Jew?' There was a silence, and every guest turned pale. The remark was impolite, and I regretted it as soon as I had made it, seeing that it had hurt her. When we got up from table I apologized to her, telling her how very fond of her I was, and in spite of myself, in my nervous condition, tears dropped from my eyes on her hands while I was kissing them. Affected by the contagion of my emotion, she took me in her arms and kissed me on both cheeks, saying: 'Come, now! You know very well how fond I am of you. I too have been in a nervous state for some time. . . .'

And the scene ended in the sweetness of an emotion, respected by a moment of silence, from which our friendship drew new strength.

*15 October*

We have just learnt at Trouville of Sainte-Beuve's death. The deceased has been ill paid for all his fawning flattery of the Press.

*18 October*

Left Trouville for Paris after spending twenty days there, the worst twenty days of our lives.

*1 November*

We really are hounded by bad luck. Today we moved into the lodge at Catinat which the Princess has lent us, to get away from the noise round our house; and today they started trying out the bells she has just presented to the local church. The priest is having them rung only ten minutes out of every fifteen!

The agony of being ill and unable to be ill at home, of having to drag one's pain and weakness from one place to another, from rented lodgings to borrowed lodgings!

# 1870

*1 January*

Today, the first day of the year, no calls, none of our friends, nobody: solitude and suffering.

*10 January*

Dizziness, uneasiness, a sort of terror: such is the effect that crowds have today on my poor nervous system.

*19 January*

How strange and peculiar nervous diseases are! Vaucorbeil, the composer, has a horror of velvet, and suffers absolute agony whenever he is invited somewhere for the first time, wondering whether the dining-room chairs are covered in velvet.

. . . . . .

*After an interval of many months, I am taking up the pen fallen from my brother's fingers. At first I felt inclined to close this journal at his last entry. 'Why continue this book?' I asked myself. 'My literary career is over, my literary ambition dead.' I feel now as I felt then, but I also find a certain consolation in recounting to myself the story of these months of despair, this death-agony. Perhaps too I am impelled by a vague desire to capture the poignancy of it all for friends of his memory. Why? I cannot tell, but it is a kind of obsession. I resume this journal, then, with the help of notes jotted down during my nights of distress, notes comparable to those cries by which we relieve the pain of great physical suffering.*

. . . . . .

*Undated*

We were walking at dusk in the Bois de Boulogne, neither of us speaking. He was sad that evening, sadder than ever. I said to him:

'Look here, old fellow, let's suppose that you need a year, or even two years, to get on your feet again. What of it? You are young; you are not yet forty. Doesn't that leave you plenty of time to turn out books?'

He looked at me with the astonished stare of a man who sees that his secret thoughts have been divined, and answered, stressing every word: 'I feel that I shall never be able to work again. Never again.' And the only effect of anything I said after that was to introduce a note of anger into the despairing phrase that he repeated over and over again.

That scene distressed me cruelly. All night long I could see the sombre, concentrated despair in his face, his voice, his attitude. Poor lad! I understood now why he had been possessed by that passion for work during October and November, and why I could never get him out of that chair in which he sat day and night, relentlessly driving his pen along and refusing all rest, slaving at the last book to which he was to put his name. The writer in him was hurrying, hastening, fighting stubbornly and obstinately against the clock, to use up every minute of the last hours of a mind and a talent about to go under.

I think of that last chapter of our book on Gavarni which, one morning at Trouville, he had read to me while I was still in bed. He had written it during the insomnia of that night. I cannot describe the profound sadness into which I fell when he declaimed with solemn concentration that brief passage which we had not worked on together and which was not to have been written then but later. I felt that in mourning Gavarni he was mourning himself, and the sentence '*He sleeps near us in the cemetery at Auteuil*' became, I cannot say why, fixed in my memory like a droning note. For the first time I had an idea which had never occurred to me before: I had an idea that he might die.

*March*

Tact was his very nature. No one had ever been more delicately organized for the exercise of that faculty in which instinct and reason both play their part. And now he is losing that faculty, which was so highly developed in him; he can no longer gauge the degrees of politeness befitting the rank of the people he meets; he can no longer gauge the degrees of intelligence suited to the minds with which he comes in contact.

For some time now—and it grows more noticeable every day—there have been certain letters that he pronounces badly, *r*'s that he elides, *c*'s that become *t*'s in his mouth. I remember, when he was a little boy, how sweet and charming it was to hear him stumbling over those two consonants. To hear the same childish pronunciation today, to hear his voice as I used to hear it in the distant and forgotten past, where my memories encounter nothing but things long dead, frightens me.

*8 April*

Over that beloved face, once so full of intelligence and irony, that shrewd and wonderfully malicious countenance of the mind, I can see the haggard mask of imbecility slipping minute by minute. Little by little he is stripping himself of his affectionate nature, *dehumanizing* himself; other people have begun to lose their reality for him, and he has started to return to the cruel egoism of childhood.

Hardly ever do you get an answer to the question you have asked him. If you ask him why he is so depressed, he will reply: 'All right, I'll read some Chateaubriand this evening.' Reading the *Mémoires d'outre-tombe* aloud is his obsession, his mania: he pesters me with it from morning to night, and my face has to look as if it were listening.

*18 April*

To witness, day by day, the destruction of everything that once went to mark out this young man—distinguished among all others —to see him emptying the salt-cellar over his fish, holding his fork in both hands, eating like a child, is too much for me to bear.

So it was not enough that this busy mind should stop producing, should cease creating, should be inhabited by nothingness. The human being had to be stricken in these qualities of grace and elegance which I imagined to be inaccessible to sickness, in these

gifts of the man who is well born, well bred, well brought up. And
finally, as in the old vengeances of the gods, all the aristocratic virtues in him, all the superior graces inherent so to speak in his skin,
had to be degraded to the level of animality.

*2 May*

This evening—I am ashamed to record this—on account of
something which I wanted him to do for the sake of his health and
which he refused to do, I felt so wretched, so angry and irritated,
that I could not control myself and went out, telling him not to wait
up for me because I did not know when I should be back. He let me
go with every sign of indifference.

I roamed through the Bois de Boulogne in the darkness, hacking
away at the weeds and the leaves with my stick, and running away
from my roof whenever I caught a glimpse of it through the trees.
Finally, very late at night, I came home.

I rang the bell, and when the door opened I saw at the head of the
stairs my beloved brother, who had got out of bed in his nightshirt,
and heard his voice gently asking all manner of affectionate questions. It is impossible to express the almost stupid joy I felt at this
revelation of a heart in whose existence I had ceased to believe.

*6 May*

In my unhappiness I have acquired an indifference to the unhappiness of others which I never possessed before. I answer a
beggar now with an 'I haven't any change' whose heartlessness
astonishes me.

*11 June*

This morning he found it impossible to remember the title of a
single one of his novels.

This evening I was painfully moved. We had nearly finished
dinner at a restaurant. The waiter brought him a bowl. He used
it clumsily. His clumsiness did not really matter very much, but
people started looking at us. I said to him rather impatiently: 'Be

careful, old fellow, please, or I shan't be able to take you out to dinner any more.' He promptly burst into tears, crying: 'It's not my fault, it's not my fault!' And his tense, trembling hand sought mine on the tablecloth. 'It's not my fault', he went on. 'I know how it upsets you, *but I often want to and I can't*' (*sic*). And his hand squeezed mine with a pitiful 'Forgive me'.

Then both of us started crying into our napkins in front of the astonished diners.

*The night of Saturday–Sunday, 18–19 June*

It is two in the morning. I have got up to take Pélagie's place at the bedside of my poor dear brother, who has not spoken a word nor recovered consciousness since two o'clock on Thursday afternoon.

I listen to his gasping breath. In the shadow of the curtains I have his fixed stare before me. Every now and then his arm comes out of the bedclothes and brushes against me, while unintelligible words are broken and aborted in his mouth. Over the tall, black trees and through the open window, the electric whiteness of a ballad-singer's moon falls across the floor. There are sinister silences, in which the only sound is the ticking of our father's repeater watch, with which, from time to time, I count the pulse-rate of his last-born. In spite of three spoonfuls of potassium bromide taken in a little water, he cannot sleep a minute and his head tosses incessantly on his pillow from side to side, noisy with all the stupid din of a paralysed brain, and sending out through the corners of his mouth embryonic phrases, truncated words, half-formulated syllables, which he begins by repeating angrily and which finally die away in a sigh. In the distance I can hear distinctly the eerie howling of a dog.

Now it is the hour when the blackbirds start singing in the growing light of the sky; and between the bed-curtains I can still see the white gleam of his eyelids, beneath which his eyes are wide awake despite their calm semblance of sleep.

The day before yesterday—Thursday, that is—he was still reading to me from Chateaubriand's *Mémoires d'outre-tombe*, which was the poor lad's sole interest and distraction. I noticed that he was tired and reading badly. I begged him to stop reading and come for a walk in the Bois de Boulogne. He resisted a little, then gave way. As he got up to leave the room with me, I saw him stagger and drop into an armchair. I picked him up and carried him to his bed, questioning him, asking him how he felt, trying to force him to reply to me in my anxiety to hear him speak. But just as in his first attack, he was unable to utter anything but sounds that were unrecognizable as words. Frantic with worry, I asked him if he could still recognize me. He answered with a burst of mocking laughter, as if to say: 'What a fool you are to ask a question like that!' Soon afterwards there followed a moment of calm, of tranquillity, when he gazed at me with a gentle smile. I was thinking that this was another attack like the one in May when suddenly, throwing back his head, he let out a raucous, guttural, terrifying scream which made me shut the window. Instantly his handsome face was seized with convulsions which completely transformed it, deforming all his features, while terrible spasms jerked his arms as if they were being twisted in their sockets and his ravaged mouth emitted a trickle of bloody foam. Sitting on the bolster behind him and holding his hands in mine, I pressed his head against my heart and into the hollow of my stomach, feeling the sweat of death wetting my shirt and running down the skin of my thighs.

This attack was followed by other, less violent convulsions in the course of which his face took on again the features I knew, and finally he fell into a delirious calm. He would raise his arms above his head, blowing kisses to a vision and appealing to it to come to him. He would throw himself about like a wounded bird trying to take wing, while over his calm face, into his bloodshot eyes, across his livid forehead and on to his half-open, pale violet lips, there spread an expression that was no longer human, the veiled, mysterious expression of a Leonardo da Vinci. More often still, he would be seized with panic, his body would shrink back in terror, and he would cower under the sheets, as if hiding from an apparition stubbornly lodged in the curtains of his bed and against which he would hurl incoherent words, pointing at it with a frightened finger and on one occasion distinctly crying out: 'Go away!' He would come out with a flood of truncated sentences, spoken with that haughty expression, that ironic tone, that lofty intellectual contempt, that sort of indignation characteristic of him when he heard someone make a stupid remark or praise an inferior article. Now and then, in the constant agitation of fever and delirium, he would repeat all the actions of his everyday life, going through the gestures of screwing in his monocle, lifting the dumb-bells which I had inflicted on him in the last few months, and plying his literary craft. There were brief moments when his roving, darting eyes would meet mine or Pélagie's, and would seem to recognize us as they stared at us for a second and a faint smile touched his lips. But all too soon they would wander off again in the direction of some horrible or pleasant vision.

Last night Béni-Barde told me that it was all over, that a disintegration of the brain had occurred at the base of the skull, at the back of his head, and that there was no hope left. After that—by which time I had stopped listening—I think he said something about nerves in the chest being affected by the damage to the brain and about an attack of galloping consumption which would follow. The first day that I had sensed that he was irrevocably stricken, my pride, the pride I felt in us both, had said to me: 'It would be best for him to die.' But now I ask to be allowed to keep him, however crippled in mind and body he may be as the result of this attack, and I ask that on my knees.

To think that it is finished, finished for ever! To think that this intimate, indissoluble partnership that has lasted twenty-two years, to think that these days and nights spent together ever since our mother's death in 1848, to think that this long period during which we have known only two separations of twenty-four hours, to think that all this is finished, finished for ever! Is it possible?

I shall no longer have him walking beside me when I go out. I shall no longer have him facing me when I eat. In my sleep, I shall no longer be aware of him sleeping in the next room. I shall no longer have his eyes joining with mine to see landscapes, pictures, modern life. I shall no longer have his twin mind to say before me what I was going to say or to repeat what I have just been saying. In a few days, in a few hours, there is going to enter into my life, so full of that affection which was my one and only happiness, the horrifying solitude of an old man left alone in the world.

What is this expiation of which we are the victims? This is what I ask myself as I look back over this life which has only a few hours left to it; this life which has derived nothing from existence but bitterness, nothing from literature and the laborious quest for fame but insults, contempt, and abuse; this life which for five years has been struggling daily with physical pain and is about to end in physical and mental agony; this life which seems to me to have been pursued everywhere and all the time by a murderous fate.

Ah, Divine Providence, Divine Providence! How right we were to doubt its existence!

*Sunday, 19 June, ten o'clock in the morning*

At the moment, I curse and abominate literature. Perhaps, but for me, he would have become a painter. Gifted as he was, he would have made his name without wearing out his brain . . . and he would have gone on living.

*The night of Sunday–Monday, 19–20 June*

Pélagie's clear-cut profile, bent over a little prayer-book whose black covers are reflected in the white pile of pillows in which his head has disappeared and from which his death-rattle emerges.

All night long, that rasping sound of breathing like the sound of a saw cutting through wet wood, punctuated every now and then by heart-rending groans and plaintive cries. All night long, that beating and heaving of his chest against the sheet.

God has not spared me the death-agony of my beloved brother: will He spare me the final convulsions?

The first light of day steals over his face, which has taken on the dull, holystoned yellow hue of death, and over his deep, dark, tear-filled eyes.

*Monday, 20 June, five o'clock in the morning*

In his eyes, an indescribable expression of suffering and misery.

To create a being like this, so gifted and intelligent, and then to break it at the age of thirty-nine! Why?

*Nine o'clock*

In his dim eyes, a sudden, smiling gleam of light, and a different glance that lingers upon me for a long time and seems to plunge slowly into the distance. . . . I touch his hands: they are like moist marble.

*Twenty minutes to ten*

He is dying, he has just died. God be praised, he died after two or three gentle, sighing breaths, like a little child falling asleep.

How frightful is the immobility of this body under the sheets, no longer rising and falling with the gentle movement of respiration, no longer living the life of sleep.

The Magny dinners were founded by Gavarni, Sainte-Beuve, and ourselves. Gavarni is dead. Sainte-Beuve is dead. My brother is dead. Will Death be content with one half of us, or will he be coming soon for me? I am ready to go.

The more I gaze at him, the more I study his features, the more I discover in his face a look of moral suffering such as I have never seen lingering on any face in death, the more struck I am by his heart-rending sadness. And it seems to me that I can discern in it, beyond the frontiers of life, regret for his interrupted work, regret for life, *regret for me.*

*Tuesday, 21 June*

At midday, through the crack of the dining-room door, I saw the hats of four men in black.

We went upstairs to the little bedroom. They pulled back the blanket, slid a sheet underneath him, and in a second or so had transformed his thin corpse, of which I caught scarcely a glimpse, into a long bundle with one end of the sheet turned back over the face.

'Gently', I said. 'I know he is dead, but all the same . . . go gently.'

Then they laid him in the coffin, on a bed of scented powder, and one of the men said: 'If it's going to upset this gentleman, he'd better go.' I stayed. . . . Another man said: 'If Monsieur has some souvenir he wants to put in the coffin, now's the moment.' I told the gardener: 'Go and cut all the roses in the garden, so that at least he can take with him something of this house he loved so much!' The roses were laid in the space around his body, and a white one was placed on the sheet, where it was raised a little by his mouth. Then

the form of his body disappeared under a heap of brown powder.
The lid was screwed down. It was all over. I went downstairs.

*22 June*

It is strange, but everything going on around me today had the
vagueness of things seen at the beginning of a swoon, and my ears
were filled with a sound like the roaring of great waters flowing
away in the distance. . . . Yet I saw Gautier and Saint-Victor weeping. . . . The singing got on my nerves, with its eternal, implacable
*Requiescat in pace.* But after all, that is right and proper: after a life of
toil and strife, a peaceful rest is the least that is due to him.

To reach the cemetery, we took the road which had so many
times led us to the Princess's; then we went along parts of the outer
boulevards where we had so often gone to gather material for
*Germinie Lacerteux* and *Manette Salomon.* Some rustic trelliswork outside the door of a tavern reminded me of a comparison in
one of our books. Then I fell into a sort of weary slumber, from
which I was roused by a sharp bend, the bend that led into the
cemetery.

I saw him disappear into the vault where my father and mother
lie and where there is still room for me. And that was all.

When I got home I went to bed. I covered my bedclothes
with portraits of him, and his image remained with me until night
fell.

*14 July*

I had put up for sale the house in which he died and to which I
had no desire to return. Today I received some perfectly acceptable
offers for a six-year lease. Well, unreasonable and illogical though
it may seem, these offers have plunged me into a profound melancholy. I find that I am attached to this house in which I have suffered
so much by bonds whose existence I never suspected.

*6 August*

From the Print Room of the Bibliothèque Impériale I saw people
running along the Rue Vivienne; I promptly ran after them.

The steps of the Stock Exchange, from top to bottom, were a sea of bare heads, with hats flung into the air and every voice raised in a tremendous *Marseillaise*, the roar of which drowned the buzz of noise from the stockbrokers' enclosure inside the building. I have never seen such an outburst of enthusiasm. One kept running into men pale with emotion, children hopping around in excitement and women making drunken gestures. Capoul was singing the *Marseillaise* from the top of an omnibus in the Place de la Bourse; on the Boulevard, Marie Sasse was singing it standing in her carriage, practically carried along by the delirium of the mob.

But the dispatch announcing the defeat of the Crown Prince of Prussia and the capture of twenty-five thousand prisoners, the dispatch which everybody claimed to have read with his own eyes, the dispatch which I was told had been posted up inside the Stock Exchange, the dispatch which, by some strange hallucination, people thought they could actually see, telling me: 'Look, there it is!' and pointing to a wall in the distance where there was nothing at all—this dispatch I was unable to find.[1]

*Saturday, 27 August*

Zola came to lunch today. He spoke to me about a series of novels which he wants to write, an epic in ten volumes called *The Natural and Social History of a Family* which he wants to attempt, depicting temperaments, characters, vices, and virtues developed by various environments and as sharply distinguished as the sunny and shady parts of a garden.

He said to me: 'After the analysis of the smallest subtleties of feeling, such as Flaubert did in *Madame Bovary*, after the analysis of things artistic, plastic, and neurotic, such as you have done, after these jewelled works, these chiselled volumes, there is no room for the young, nothing for them to do, no characters left for them to conceive and construct. It is only by the bulk of their work, the power of their creation that they can appeal to the public.'

[1] War had been declared on Prussia on 29 July. On 6 August a rumour was started at the Stock Exchange to the effect that the Crown Prince's army had been defeated, in an attempt to rig the market. In fact, the very same evening, the Government learnt of two major defeats suffered by MacMahon and Frossard in Alsace and Lorraine which left France open to invasion.

*31 August*

This morning, at the Point-du-Jour, the demolition of the houses in the military zone began, in the midst of a general move from the suburbs which resembles the migration of an ancient people. One catches unexpected glimpses of the interiors of half-demolished houses still containing a few odd pieces of furniture: for instance, a barber's shop whose gaping front reveals the forgotten curule chair in which the laundry workers used to have their beards trimmed on Sundays.

*1 September*

Yesterday the Princess asked me to come to dinner, saying that there would be nobody there. I arrived to find that the curtains had been taken down from the windows. The Princess seemed utterly dazed; she repeated several times: 'If anybody had told me on the first of August what was going to happen, I wouldn't have believed him.'

We had dinner. Around the table were old Giraud, Popelin, Soulié, Zeller, the new Rector of the University of Strasbourg, and his daughter. Everybody contributed his piece of news, which he had culled from the *Figaro* or the *Gaulois*. Nobody really knew anything. Concern was expressed over the citizens of Strasbourg, and more particularly over the manuscripts. Somebody said that the cathedral spire had collapsed. Whereupon the Princess, whose thoughts were elsewhere, said: 'But the church can't have been very well built, then?'

Nobody had the heart to smile at her naïvety.

*2 September*

Coming out of the Louvre, I met Chennevières, who told me that he was leaving for Brest tomorrow, to escort the third trainful of pictures from the Louvre, which are being taken out of their frames, rolled up and sent to the arsenal or the prison at Brest to save them from the Prussians. He described to me the melancholy, humiliating spectacle of this packing operation, with Reiset crying like a baby over *La Belle Jardinière* lying at the bottom of her crate, as if over a loved one about to be nailed into her coffin. This evening, after dinner, we went to the station at the Rue d'Enfer, and I saw the seventeen crates containing the *Antiope*, the finest Venetian paintings, and other treasures—pictures which one had imagined fixed to the walls of the Louvre for all eternity and which were now nothing but parcels, protected against the hazards of removal by the word *Fragile*.

*3 September*

What a sight, that of Paris this evening, with the news of Mac-Mahon's defeat and the capture of the Emperor spreading from group to group! Who can describe the consternation written on every face, the sound of aimless steps pacing the streets at random, the anxious conversations of shopkeepers and concierges on their doorsteps, the crowds collecting at street-corners and outside town-halls, the siege of the newspaper kiosks, the triple line of readers gathering around every gas-lamp, and on chairs at the back of shops the dejected figures of women whom one senses to be alone and deprived of their men?

Then there is the menacing roar of the crowd, in which stupe-faction has begun to give place to anger. Next there are great crowds moving along the boulevards, led by flags and shouting: 'Down with the Empire! Long live Trochu!' And finally there is the wild, tumultuous spectacle of a nation determined to perish or to save itself by an enormous effort, by one of those impossible feats of revolutionary times.

*4 September*

This was the scene outside the Chamber about four o'clock today. Against its grey façade, from which the sunlight had faded, around its columns and all the way down its steps, there was a crowd, a vast multitude of men, in which smocks formed blue and white patches among the black coats. Many were carrying branches in their hands and had green leaves fastened to their hats. There were a few soldiers with twigs tied to the barrels of their rifles.

A hand rose above the heads of the crowd and chalked the names of the members of the Provisional Government in big red letters on one of the columns. On another column somebody had already written: *The Republic has been proclaimed.* There was shouting and cheering; hats were thrown into the air; people clambered on to the pedestals of the statues, clustering together beneath the figure of Minerva; a man in a smock was calmly smoking his pipe on the knees of Chancellor de L'Hospital; bunches of women were hanging on the railing facing the Pont de la Concorde.

All around one could hear people greeting each other with the excited words: 'It's happened!' And right at the top of the façade, a man tore the blue and white stripes from the tricolour, leaving only the red waving in the air. On the terrace overlooking the Quai d'Orsay, infantrymen were stripping the shrubs and handing green branches over the parapet to women fighting to take them.

At the gate of the Tuileries, near the great pool, the gilt 'N's were hidden beneath old newspapers, and wreaths of immortelles hung in the place of the missing eagles.

*Tuesday, 6 September*

At the Café Brébant, Renan was sitting all by himself at the big table in the red drawing-room, reading a newspaper and making despairing gestures.

Saint-Victor came in, sat down heavily on a chair, and exclaimed: 'The Apocalypse! . . . Behold a pale horse, and his name that sat on him was Death. . . .'

Then Charles-Edmond, Du Mesnil, Nefftzer, and Berthelot arrived, and we sat down to dinner to the accompaniment of sad remarks on every side.

We spoke of the great defeat, of the impossibility of putting up an adequate defence, of the incompetence of the eleven men in the Government of National Defence, of the deplorable lack of weight they carry with the diplomatic corps and the neutral governments.

Somebody remarked: 'Precision weapons are contrary to the French temperament. Shooting fast and charging with a bayonet, that's what our soldier needs to do. If he can't do that, then he's paralysed. The mechanization of the individual is not for him. And that is where the Prussian soldier is superior at present.'

Renan looked up from his plate.

'In all the subjects I have studied, I have always been struck by the superiority of the German mind and German workmanship.

It is not surprising that in the art of war, which is an art after all, inferior but complicated, they should have achieved the superiority which, I repeat, I have observed in all the subjects I have studied and with which I am familiar. . . . Yes, gentlemen, the Germans are a superior race!'

'Oh, come now!' everyone shouted.

'Yes, very superior to us', Renan went on, warming to his theme. 'Catholicism cretinizes the individual; the education given by the Jesuits or the brothers of the Christian School arrests and constricts the mental faculties, whereas Protestantism develops them.'

Berthelot's soft, sickly voice brought our thoughts down from sophistical speculation to menacing reality.

'You may not be aware, gentlemen,' he said, 'that we are surrounded by enormous stocks of petroleum which are stored at the gates of Paris, and not allowed in because of the city toll. If the Prussians get hold of this petroleum and empty it into the Seine, they will turn it into a river of fire which will burn both banks. That was how the Greeks set fire to the Arab fleet.'

'But why not warn Trochu?'

'Has he got time?'

Berthelot went on: 'Unless they blow up the locks along the Marne canal, all the big Prussian siege artillery will come sailing up to the walls of Paris. The locks are mined, I believe, but will they remember to blow them up? . . . I could go on telling you about things like that until the cows come home.'

Renan, clinging stubbornly to his thesis of the superiority of the German people, was expounding it to his two neighbours when Du Mesnil interrupted him to say: 'As for the independent spirit of your German peasants, all I can say is that when I went shooting in Baden, we used to send them to pick up the game with a kick in the arse!'

'Well,' retorted Renan, dropping the main argument of his thesis, 'I would rather have peasants you kicked in the arse than peasants like ours, whom universal suffrage has made our masters, peasants— the very dregs of civilization—who were responsible for inflicting that government on us for twenty years!'

Berthelot went on with his dispiriting revelations, at the end of which I exclaimed:

'So it's all over? There's nothing left for us to do but rear a new generation to exact vengeance?'

'No, no,' cried Renan, standing up and going red in the face, 'no, not vengeance! Let France perish, let the Nation perish: there is a higher ideal of Duty and Reason!'

'No, no,' howled the whole company, 'there is nothing higher than the Nation!'

'No,' shouted Saint-Victor, louder and more angrily than the rest, 'let's have no quibbling and aestheticizing. There is nothing higher than the Nation!'

Renan had got up and begun walking round the table rather unsteadily, waving his little arms in the air, quoting Holy Writ, and saying that it was all there. Then he went over to the window, beneath which Paris life was going on in apparent unconcern, and said to me: 'That is what will save us: the flabbiness of that people.'

And the company broke up, with everyone thinking: 'Perhaps, a fortnight from now, it will be the Prussians who will be dining at this table and sitting in our places.'

*8 September*

Empire or Republic, nothing really changes. It is annoying to hear people saying all the time: 'It is the Emperor's fault.' If our generals have shown themselves to be inefficient, if our officers are ignorant, if our troops have had their moments of cowardice, that is not the Emperor's fault. Moreover, a single man cannot have so great an influence on a nation, and if the French nation had not been disintegrating, the Emperor's extraordinary mediocrity would not have robbed it of victory. Let us not forget that sovereigns always reflect the nation over which they rule, and that they would not remain on their thrones for three days if they were at variance with its soul.

*Friday, 16 September*

Today, I amused myself by travelling right round Paris on the ring railway. It is an amusing sight, that vision, swift as speed, afforded as one emerges from the darkness of a tunnel, of rows of white tents, of guns rolling along country lanes, of river banks lined with little crenellated parapets of olden times, of canteens with their tables and glasses set out in the sunshine and their girl attendants who have sewn braid along the hems of their jackets and skirts—a vision constantly interrupted and blocked by a high embankment, at the end of which there reappears the familiar horizon of the yellow ramparts dotted with the little silhouettes of National Guards.

*Thursday, 22 September*

On the heights of the Trocadéro, in the fresh breezes bearing along the incessant sound of drumming from the Champ-de-Mars, there are groups of sightseers, including some immaculate Englishmen holding enormous fieldglasses in glacé-kid gloves. There are also some girls clutching a long eyeglass with charming clumsiness in one skinny hand, while they cover one eye with the other hand in the way children do. Every few yards, the telescopes which in peacetime look at the sun and the moon are pointed at Vanves, Issy, Meudon; and in the midst of the citizens queuing up for a look, a soldier is perched on a little ladder, a rifle across his back and his eye glued to the magnifying lens. The horizon is just mist and dust, with a few puffs of white smoke which one assumes to come from the guns.

*24 September*

In the capital of fresh food and early vegetables, it is really ironical to come across Parisians consulting one another in front of the displays of tinned goods in the windows of delicatessen shops or cosmopolitan groceries. Finally they go in, and come out carrying tins of *Boiled Mutton*, *Boiled Beef*, etc., every possible and impossible variety of preserved meat and vegetable, things that nobody would ever have thought might one day become the food of the rich city of Paris.

*Tuesday, 27 September*

A serious expression comes over the faces of the people strolling along the street who go up to the white posters gleaming in the gaslight. I see them read carefully and then walk away slowly, silent and thoughtful. These posters are the statutes of the courts-martial set up at Vincennes and Saint-Denis. One stops short at these words: 'Sentence will be executed forthwith by the squad detailed to guard the courtroom.' And one realizes with a slight shudder that we are entering the summary, dramatic atmosphere of a siege.

*Saturday, 1 October*

Horse-meat is sneaking slyly into the diet of the people of Paris. The day before yesterday, Pélagie brought home a piece of fillet which, on account of its suspicious appearance, I did not eat. Today, at Peters' restaurant, I was served some roast beef that was watery, devoid of fat, and streaked with white sinews; and my painter's eye noticed that it was a dark red colour very different from the pinky red of beef. The waiter could give me only a feeble assurance that this horse was beef.

*Monday, 3 October*

Paris has never known an October like this. The clear, starry nights are like nights in the south of France. God loves the Prussians.

*Tuesday, 4 October*

The bombardment seems imminent. Yesterday somebody came to my house to ask if I had a stock of water on every floor. Today I noticed barrels of water in every alley-way, and in front of the church in the Rue de la Chaussée-d'Antin a huge iron cylinder, mounted on piles, which is apparently a municipal reservoir.

Next to the pavement, standing in the gutter, erect, immobile, seeing nothing, hearing nothing, heedless of the carriages brushing past her, there was an old countrywoman wearing a tile-shaped bonnet and wrapped, in her petrified rigidity, in folds which resembled the ledgerstones at Bruges. She carried within her such stupefied grief that I went up to her and spoke to her. Then this woman, slowly coming to, said to me in a voice like a groan: 'I thank you for your kindness. I am not in need. I am simply unhappy.'

*Monday, 10 October*

This morning I went to get a card for my meat ration. It seemed to me that I was looking at one of those queues in the great Revolution which my poor old cousin Cornélie used to describe to me, in that patient line of heterogeneous individuals, of ragged old women, of men in peaked caps, of small shopkeepers, cooped up in those improvised offices, those whitewashed rooms, where you recognized, sitting round a table, omnipotent in their uniforms of officers of the National Guard and supreme dispensers of your food, your far from honest tradesmen.

I came away with a piece of blue paper, a typographical curiosity for future Goncourts and times to come, which entitles me and my housekeeper to buy every day two rations of raw meat or two portions of food cooked in the municipal canteens. There are coupons up to 14 November: a good many things may happen between now and then.

*Friday, 14 October*

I went to meet Burty at the Tuileries. While I was waiting for him, I had a look round. There were some National Guards playing cards in the courtyard. Under the peristyle, next to a pile of camp-beds, a horrible-looking canteen attendant had set up her little table. The banisters of the staircase were covered with a dust-sheet on which a piece of paper had been pinned, bearing the words: 'Death to thieves.'

Burty did me the honours of the palace, looking happy and almost proud to tread these floors. You could sense in every step he took the victory of the shopkeeper's son who had moved into the home of royalty; and I distinguished a sort of base satisfaction in the bourgeois pleasure my friend derived from planting his buttocks on one of the chairs where the last of the emperors had sat.

Beneath those old ceilings blackened by the smoke of the receptions and suppers of the Empire, beneath that beautiful burnished gold which reminded me of the gold of the ceilings of Venice, in the midst of those bronzes and marbles in the process of being packed into crates, and in the glass of those splendid mirrors, could be seen ugly pen-pushers' faces, heads framed in long republican locks or crowned with greying red hair, the surly countenances of the pure and virtuous.

Deal cupboards had been arranged along the walls and went up as far as the ceiling, packed with files and bundles of documents. There were trestle-tables sagging under untidy heaps of letters, papers, bills, and receipts. On the end of a nail that had been hammered into the gilt frame of a mirror hung the *Instructions regarding the examination of the Correspondence.* I felt as if I had entered the secret chamber of the Revolutionary Inquisition, and this odious unsealing of History had something about it which I found repugnant.

It is in the Salle Louis XIV that the members of the Commission hold their sittings. It is there that the final sorting is done. Among the papers that were there I picked up one at random: it was a bill showing that the extravagant Napoleon III used to have his socks darned at a cost of 25 centimes a hole.

*Monday, 31 October*

On people's faces and in their attitudes one could read the effect of the great and terrible things that are in the air. Standing behind a group of people questioning a National Guard, I heard the words *revolver shots, rifle shots, wounded.* Outside the Théâtre-Français, Lafontaine told me the official news of Bazaine's capitulation.[1]

The Rue de Rivoli was packed with people, and the crowd, sheltering under umbrellas, grew thicker as one approached the Hôtel de Ville.[2] There, there was a throng, a multitude, a mêlée of people of all sorts and conditions, through which National Guards would force their way now and then, waving their rifles in the air and shouting: 'The Commune for ever!' The building was in darkness, with time moving heedlessly round the illuminated clock-face, the windows all wide open, and the workmen who had led the movement of 4 September sitting on the sills with their legs dangling

---

[1] On 27 October Marshal Bazaine, surrounded in Metz with the Army of the Rhine, had surrendered himself, 4,000 officers and 150,000 troops to the Prussians.

[2] Angered by the Government's refusal to hold fresh elections, by the latest Prussian success at Le Bourget, and by the news of Bazaine's capitulation, the working-class battalions of the National Guard stormed the Hôtel de Ville on 31 October and set up an Insurrectional Commune under Flourens and Blanqui. They were expelled by middle-class National Guards; municipal elections with a limited franchise were held on 3 and 4 November; and the Government then proceeded to take repressive measures which were partly responsible for the insurrection of the Commune of 1871.

outside. The square was a forest of rifle butts raised in the air, the metal plates gleaming in the rain.

On every face could be seen distress at Bazaine's capitulation, a sort of fury over yesterday's reverse at Le Bourget, and at the same time an angry and rashly heroic determination not to make peace. Some workmen in bowler hats were writing in pencil, on greasy pocket-books, a list a gentleman was dictating to them. Among the names I heard those of Blanqui, Flourens, Ledru-Rollin, and Mottu. 'Things are going to move now!' said one workman, in the midst of the eloquent silence of my neighbours; and I came across a group of women already talking fearfully of the division of property.

It seemed, as I had guessed from the workmen's legs dangling from the windows of the Hôtel de Ville, that the Government had been overthrown and the Commune established, and that the list of the gentleman in the square was due to be confirmed by universal suffrage within twenty-four hours. It was all over. Today one could write: *Finis Franciae.* . . .

Shouts of 'The Commune for ever!' went up all over the square, and fresh battalions went rushing off down the Rue de Rivoli, followed by a screaming, gesticulating riff-raff. . . . Poor France, to have fallen under the control of those stupid bayonets! Just then an old lady, seeing me buy the evening paper, asked me—oh, the irony of it!—whether the price of Government stock was quoted in my paper.

After dinner, I heard a man in a workman's smock say to the tobacconist whom I had asked for a light: 'They can't go on fooling us like that for ever! There'll be a '93 before long, with everybody hanging everybody else!'

The Boulevard was in darkness, the shops were all shut, and there were no passers-by. A few groups of people, each person holding a parcel of food tied with a string cutting into one finger, stood in the gaslight coming from stalls and cafés whose owners kept coming to the door, uncertain as to whether to close or not. The call to arms was sounded. An apoplectic old National Guard went by, cap in hand, shouting: 'The scum!' An officer of the National Guard appeared at the door of the Café Riche and called for the men in his battalion. The rumour went round that General Tamisier was a prisoner of the Commune. The call to arms went on sounding insistently. A young National Guard went running along the middle of the Boulevard, shouting at the top of his voice: 'To arms, damn you!'

Civil war, with starvation and bombardment, is that what tomorrow holds in store for us?

*Monday, 7 November*

I went to call on Hugo, to thank him for the sympathetic letter which the great master was kind enough to send me on the occasion of my brother's death.

It was an address on the Avenue Frochot: Meurice's apartment, I think. I was asked to wait in the dining-room, where the table was still littered with the remains of lunch in a jumble of glass and porcelain. Then I was shown into a little drawing-room whose ceiling and walls were lined with old tapestry. There were two women in black by the fireside, whose features I could just make out against the light. Around the poet, lounging on a sofa, were some of his friends, among whom I recognized Vacquerie. In one corner was Victor Hugo's portly son, dressed in the uniform of a National Guard; he and a few ladies were playing with a fair-haired child wearing a cherry-red sash and perched on a stool.

Hugo, after shaking hands with me, went back and stood in front of the fire. In that old-fashioned room, in the half-light of autumn dulled by the old colours of the walls and turning blue with the smoke from the cigars, in that setting of another age in which everything was a little vague and uncertain, things as well as people, Hugo's head, seen in the full light, looked right and imposing. In his hair there were some rebellious white locks reminiscent of Michelangelo's prophets, and on his face a strange, almost ecstatic tranquillity. Yes, a sort of ecstasy, but in which now and then his dark bright eyes, so it seemed to me, lit up with an indefinable expression of evil cunning.

When I asked him if he felt at home again in Paris, he replied roughly to this effect: 'Yes, I like Paris as it is today. I wouldn't have liked to see the Bois de Boulogne in the days when it was crowded with carriages, barouches, and landaus. But now that it's a quagmire, a ruin, it appeals to me . . . it's beautiful, it's grandiose! But don't imagine that I'm condemning everything that has been done in Paris in my absence: Notre-Dame and the Sainte-Chapelle have been beautifully restored, and there are undeniably some fine new houses.' When I said that the Parisian of the past felt lost here, that the city had been americanized, he replied: 'Yes, it's true that it's an anglicized Paris, but it has two things, thank heavens, to distinguish it from England: the comparative beauty of its climate and the absence of coal. . . . As a matter of personal taste, I prefer my old streets. . . .' And answering somebody who spoke of great arteries, he said: 'Yes, the Empire did nothing to provide a defence against foreigners; everything it did was designed to provide a defence against the population.'

*Monday, 5 December*

Saint-Victor, in his article yesterday, said in a striking fashion that France had to rid herself of the idea which she had entertained until now of Germany, of that country which she had been accustomed to consider, on the strength of its poetry, as the land of innocence and good nature, as the sentimental nest of platonic love. He recalled that the ideal, fictional world of Werther and Charlotte, of Hermann and Dorothea, had produced the toughest of soldiers, the wiliest of diplomats, the craftiest of bankers. He might have added the most mercenary of courtesans. We must be on our guard against that race, which arouses in us the idea of childlike innocence: their fair hair is the equivalent of the hypocrisy and sly determination of the Slav races.

*Saturday, 31 December*

In the streets of Paris, death passes death, the undertaker's waggon drives past the hearse. Outside the Madeleine today I saw three coffins, each covered with a soldier's greatcoat with a wreath of immortelles on top.

Out of curiosity I went into Roos's, the English butcher's shop on the Boulevard Haussmann, where I saw all sorts of weird remains. On the wall, hung in a place of honour, was the skinned trunk of young Pollux, the elephant at the Zoo; and in the midst of nameless meats and unusual horns, a boy was offering some camel's kidneys for sale.

The master-butcher was perorating to a group of women: 'It's forty francs a pound for the fillet and the trunk. . . . Yes, forty francs. . . . You think that's dear? But I assure you I don't know how I'm going to make anything out of it. I was counting on three thousand pounds of meat and he has only yielded two thousand, three hundred. . . . The feet, you want to know the price of the feet? It's twenty francs. . . . For the other pieces, it ranges from eight francs to forty. . . . But let me recommend the black pudding. As you know, the elephant's blood is the richest there is. His heart weighed twenty-five pounds. . . . And there's onion, ladies, in my black pudding.'

I fell back on a couple of larks which I carried off for my lunch tomorrow.

# 1871

The shells have begun falling in the Rue Boileau and the Rue La Fontaine. Tomorrow, no doubt, they will be falling here; and even if they do not kill me, they will destroy everything I still love in life, my house, my knick-knacks, my books.

On every doorstep, women and children stand, half frightened, half inquisitive, watching the medical orderlies going by, dressed in white smocks with red crosses on their arms, and carrying stretchers, mattresses, and pillows.

The sufferings of Paris during the siege? A joke for two months. In the third month the joke went sour. Now nobody finds it funny any more, and we are moving fast towards starvation or, for the moment at least, towards an epidemic of gastritis. Half a pound of horsemeat, including the bones, which is two people's ration for three days, is lunch for an ordinary appetite. The prices of edible chickens or pies put them out of reach. Failing meat, you cannot fall back on vegetables; a little turnip costs eight sous and you have to pay seven francs for a pound of onions. Nobody talks about butter any more, and every other sort of fat except candle-fat and axle-grease has disappeared too. As for the two staple items of the diet of the poorer classes—potatoes and cheese—cheese is just a memory, and you have to have friends in high places to obtain potatoes at twenty francs a bushel. The greater part of Paris is living on coffee, wine, and bread.

This evening, at the station, when I asked for my ticket to Auteuil, the clerk told me that as from today trains would not run beyond Passy. Auteuil is no longer part of Paris.

*Thursday, 12 January*

Today I went on a tour of the districts of Paris which have been shelled. There is no panic or alarm. Everybody seems to be leading his usual life, and the café proprietors, with admirable sang-froid, are replacing the mirrors shattered by the blast of exploding shells. Only, here and there among the crowds, you notice a gentleman carrying a clock under his arm; and the streets are full of handcarts trundling a few poor sticks of furniture towards the centre of the city, often with an old man incapable of walking perched in the middle of the jumble.

The cellar ventilators are blocked with bags of earth. One shop has devised an ingenious protective screen consisting of rows of planks lined with bags of earth and reaching up to the first floor. On the steps of Saint-Sulpice, angry voices can be heard accusing the generals of treason. The paving-stones in the Place du Panthéon are being taken up. A shell has taken off the Ionic capital of one of the columns of the Law School. In the Rue Saint-Jacques there are holes in the walls and dents from which small pieces of plaster keep falling. Huge blocks of freestone, part of the coping of the Sorbonne, have fallen in front of the old building to form a barricade. But where the shelling has left the most impressive traces is the Boulevard Saint-Michel, where all the houses on the corners of the streets running parallel to Julian's Baths have been damaged by shell splinters. On the corner of the Rue Soufflot, the whole first-floor balcony, torn away from the front, is hanging menacingly over the street.

From Passy to Auteuil, the snow-covered road is coloured pink by the glow of the fires at Saint-Cloud.

*Wednesday, 18 January*

It is no longer a case of a stray shell now and then as it has been these last few days, but a deluge of cast iron gradually closing in on me and hemming me in. All around me there are explosions fifty yards away, twenty yards away, at the railway station, in the Rue Poussin, where a woman has just had a foot blown off, and next door, where a shell had already fallen the day before yesterday. And while, standing at the window, I try to make out the Meudon batteries with the aid of a telescope, a shell-splinter flies past me and sends mud splashing against my front door.

At three o'clock I was going through the gate at the Étoile when I saw some troops marching past and stopped to look. The monument to our victories, lit by a ray of sunshine, the distant cannonade, the immense march-past, with the bayonets of the troops in the rear flashing beneath the obelisk, all this was something theatrical, lyrical, epic in nature. It was a grandiose, soul-stirring sight, that army marching towards the guns booming in the distance, an army with, in its midst, grey-bearded civilians who were fathers, beardless youngsters who were sons, and in its open ranks women carrying their husband's or their lover's rifle slung across their backs. And it is impossible to convey the picturesque touch brought to the war by this citizen multitude escorted by cabs, unpainted omnibuses, and removal vans converted into army provision waggons.

*Thursday, 26 January*

The shells are coming closer. New batteries seem to be opening fire. Shells are exploding every few minutes along the railway line, and people cross our boulevard on their hands and feet.

You can see everybody performing the painful mental operation of accustoming the mind to the shameful idea of capitulation. Yet there are some strong-minded men and women who go on resisting. I have been told of some poor women who, even this morning, were shouting in the queues outside the bakers' shops: 'Let them cut our ration again! We're ready to suffer anything! But don't let them surrender!'

*Monday, 30 January*

In a newspaper giving the news of the capitulation, I read the news of King William's enthronement as Emperor of Germany at Versailles, in the Hall of Mirrors, under the nose of the stone Louis XIV in the courtyard outside. That really marks the end of the greatness of France.

*Friday, 24 February*

Today something like a taste for literature came back to me. I was bitten this morning with the desire to write *La Fille Élisa*, the book

which we were going to write, he and I, after *Madame Gervaisais*.
I jotted down four or five lines on a piece of paper. Perhaps these
will one day grow into the first chapter.

*Sunday, 5 March*

The peace conditions strike me as so oppressive, so crushing,
so mortal for France, that I am afraid that war may break out again
before we are ready to wage it.

*Sunday, 19 March*

In the train, people around me were saying that the army was
retiring towards Versailles and that Paris was in the grip of
insurrection.[1]

The embankment and the two big streets leading to the Hôtel de
Ville were blocked by barricades, with cordons of National Guards
lined up in front. One was overcome with disgust at the sight of
their stupid, abject faces, in which triumph and intoxication created
a sort of dissolute radiance. Every now and then they could be seen,
their caps cocked over one ear, staggering out of the half-open door
of some wine-shop, the only sort of shop open today. Around these
barricades there was a pack of street-corner Diogenes and fat
bourgeois of dubious professions, with clay pipes in their mouths
and their wives on their arms.

Above the Hôtel de Ville, a red flag was flying; and down below,
the square was swarming with an armed mob behind three guns.

On the way home, I read on people's faces dazed indifference,
sometimes melancholy irony, most often sheer consternation, with
old gentlemen raising their hands in despair and whispering among
themselves after looking cautiously all around.

*Tuesday, 28 March*

The newspapers see nothing in what is going on but a question of
decentralization: as if it had anything to do with decentralization!

---

[1] In the afternoon of 18 March Thiers had ordered the Government and the Army
to leave Paris for Versailles, allowing a revolution to develop which he would crush
with merciless severity two months later, in the notorious 'Bloody Week'.

What is happening is nothing less than the conquest of France by the worker and the reduction to slavery under his rule of the noble, the bourgeois, and the peasant. Government is passing from the hands of the have's to those of the have-not's, from those who have a material interest in the preservation of society to those who have no interest whatever in order, stability, or preservation. Perhaps, in the great law of change that governs all earthly things, the workers are for modern society what the Barbarians were for ancient society, the convulsive agents of dissolution and destruction.

*Sunday, 2 April*

The sound of gunfire, about ten o'clock, in the direction of Courbevoie. Thank God, civil war has broken out! When things have reached this pass, civil war is preferable to hypocritical skull-duggery. The firing dies down. Has Versailles been beaten? Alas, if Versailles suffers the slightest reverse, Versailles is lost! Somebody calls to see me and says that from remarks he has overheard he fears a defeat.

I set out straight away for Paris, studying people's faces, which are a sort of barometer of events in revolutionary times; I see in them a hidden satisfaction, a sly joy. Finally a newspaper tells me that the Belleville troops have been beaten! I am filled with a jubilation which I savour at length. Let tomorrow bring what it will.

*Wednesday, 12 April*

On awaking this morning, I saw that the fort at Issy, which I thought had been taken, was still flying the red flag. So the Versailles troops have been thrown back again.

Why this stubborn resistance which the Prussians did not encounter? Because the idea of the motherland is dying. Because the formula: 'The nations are brothers' has done its work, even in this time of invasion and cruel defeat. Because the International's doctrines of indifference to nationality have penetrated the masses.

Why this stubborn resistance? Because in this war, the common people are waging their own war and are not under the Army's orders. This keeps the men amused and interested, with the result that nothing tires or discourages or dispirits them. One can get anything out of them, even heroism.

*Tuesday, 18 April*

In the Place Vendôme, the scaffolding has been put up in readiness for the demolition of the Column.[1] The square is the centre of a fantastic tumult and a medley of amazing uniforms. There are some extraordinary National Guards to be seen there, including one who looks like a Velasquez dwarf, dressed in a military greatcoat with his twisted feet poking out at the bottom.

From all I hear, the employees of the Louvre are extremely worried. The Venus de Milo is hidden—guess where—at the Prefecture of Police. She is even hidden very deep down, and concealed underneath another hiding-place filled with police dossiers and papers calculated to stop any searchers in their investigations. All the same, it is thought that Courbet is on her track, and the silly employees fear the worst if the fanatical modernist lays his hands on the classical masterpiece.

*Wednesday, 19 April*

Charles-Edmond told me yesterday that it was estimated that seven hundred thousand people had left Paris since the elections.

All day long, there was a great deal of movement on the part of the National Guards. I saw some battalions coming back wearing bunches of lilac, but looking rather sheepish. On the Quai Voltaire there was a smell of gunpowder carried up the Seine by the wind. For a long time I stood listening to the gunfire from the end of the waterside terrace, behind the figure of Fame riding side-saddle on her stone horse and standing out all white against a showery, smoky sky with great purple clouds scudding across it.

*Sunday, 21 May*

I spent the whole of the day dreading a defeat for Versailles, and remembering a remark which Burty had kept repeating: 'The Versailles troops have been thrown back seven times.'

Sad and worried, I set off this evening for my usual place of

---

[1] In the autumn of 1870, Courbet, on behalf of the Artists' Commission, and others had urged the demolition of the Vendôme Column, describing it as a symbol of Bonapartism and militarism. On 12 April 1871 the Commune decided to demolish it, and the operation was carried out on 16 May.

observation, the Place de la Concorde. When I got to the square I saw a huge crowd surrounding a cab with an escort of National Guards. 'What is it?' I asked. 'It's a gentleman they've just arrested', a woman replied. 'He was shouting out of the window that the Versailles troops had entered the city.' I remembered the little groups of National Guards I had just met in the Rue Saint-Florentin, running along as if in full retreat. But there have been so many mistakes and disappointments that I placed no confidence in the good news, though I was deeply stirred and agitated by that sickly condition which doctors call precordial anxiety.

I wandered around for a long time in search of information. . . . Nothing, nothing at all. The people who were still in the streets were like the people I saw yesterday. They were just as calm, just as dazed. Nobody seemed to have heard about that shout in the Place de la Concorde. Another rumour!

I returned home and went to bed in despair. I could not sleep. Through my hermetically closed curtains I seemed to be able to hear a confused murmur in the distance. I got up and opened the window. In a street some way off there was the usual noise of one company relieving another, as happened every night. I told myself I had been imagining things and went back to bed . . . but this time there was no mistaking the sound of drum and bugle! I rushed back to the window. The call to arms was sounding all over Paris, and soon, drowning the noise of the drums and the bugles and the shouting and the cries of 'To Arms!' came the great, tragic, booming notes of the tocsin being rung in all the churches—a sinister sound which filled me with joy and sounded the death-knell of the odious tyranny oppressing Paris.[1]

*Monday, 22 May*

I could not stay indoors today, I simply had to see and know.

Coming out, I found everybody standing in the carriage gateways in angry, excited groups, hoping for the best and already plucking up the courage to boo the mounted orderlies.

All of a sudden, a shell exploded on the Madeleine and all the

---

[1] On 21 May the Versailles troops entered Paris through the unguarded Porte de Saint-Cloud, slowly clearing the city of the Communards and killing twenty thousand men and women in savage reprisals.

tenants promptly went back indoors. Near the new Opéra I saw a
National Guard being carried along with his thigh broken. In the
square, in a few scattered groups, they were saying that the Versailles troops had reached the Palace of Industry. The National
Guards, coming back in small bands, and looking tired and shamefaced, were obviously demoralized and discouraged.

I came to call on Burty and found myself a prisoner in his apartment for I do not know how long. It was not safe to go out, as anybody seen in the streets by the National Guards was promptly
enrolled and forced to work on the barricades. Burty started copying
out extracts of the *Correspondence found at the Tuileries* while I
buried myself in his *Delacroix* to the sound of exploding shells
coming gradually nearer.

Soon they were falling very close. The house in the Rue Vivienne
on the other side of the street had its porch shattered. Another shell
smashed the street-lamp opposite. And a final shell, falling during
dinner, exploded right outside and shook us on our chairs.

A bed was made up for me and I threw myself on to it, fully
dressed. Under the windows I could hear the noise of drunken
National Guards and their hoarse voices challenging every passer-
by. At daybreak I fell into a sleep haunted by nightmares and
explosions.

*Tuesday, 23 May*

Today the sound of firing came nearer and nearer. We could distinctly hear rifle-shots in the Rue Drouot. Suddenly a squad of
workers appeared who had been ordered to block the boulevard on
a level with the Rue Vivienne and to build a barricade under our
windows. Their hearts were not in it. Some of them took up two
or three paving-stones from the roadway, and the others, as if for
form's sake, gave a few blows with a pick-axe at the asphalt pavement. But almost immediately bullets started raking the boulevard
and passing over their heads, and they downed tools. Burty and I
saw them disappear down the Rue Vivienne with a sigh of relief.
We were both thinking of the National Guards who would have
come into the house to fire from the windows, trampling our
collections under their feet.

Then a large band of National Guards appeared with their officers, falling back slowly and in good order. Others followed, marching faster. And finally some more came rushing along in a general stampede, in the midst of which we saw a dead man with his head covered in blood, whom four men were carrying by his arms and legs like a bundle of dirty washing, taking him from door to door without finding a single one open.

On the other side of the boulevard there was a man stretched out on the ground of whom I could see only the soles of his boots and a bit of gold braid. There were two men standing by the corpse, a National Guard and a lieutenant. The bullets were making the leaves rain down on them from a little tree spreading its branches over their heads. I was forgetting a dramatic detail: behind them, in front of the closed doors of a carriage entrance, a woman was lying flat on the ground, holding a peaked cap in one hand.

At last our boulevard was in the hands of the Versailles troops. We had ventured out on to our balcony to have a look at them when a bullet struck the wall just above us. It was a fool of a tenant who had taken it into his head to light his pipe at his window.

The shells started falling again—this time shells fired by the Federates at the positions captured by the Versailles troops. We camped in the anteroom. Renée's little iron bed was pulled into a safe corner. Madeleine lay down on a sofa near her father, her face lit up by the lamp and silhouetted against the white pillow, her thin little body lost in the folds and shadows of a shawl. Mme Burty sank into an armchair. As for myself, I kept listening to the heart-rending cries of a wounded infantryman who had dragged himself up to our door and whom the concierge, out of a cowardly fear of compromising herself, refused to let in.

Now and then I went to the windows overlooking the boulevard, to look out at that black night of Paris, unrelieved by a gleam of gaslight or lamplight, and whose deep, fearful darkness concealed those of the day's dead who had not been collected.

*Wednesday, 24 May*

When I awoke I looked for the corpse of the National Guard who had been killed yesterday. It had not been removed. It had simply been partly covered with the branches of the tree under which he had been killed.

The fires burning all over Paris were creating a light like the light of an eclipse.

There was a pause in the bombardment. I took advantage of it to leave Burty and go to the Rue de l'Arcade. There I found Pélagie, who had had the courage to cross the whole battlefield yesterday, holding a big bunch of roses from my *Gloire de Dijon* rose-tree, helped and protected by the Versailles officers, who in their admiration for this woman advancing fearlessly through the rifle-fire and grapeshot, had guided her through the breaches opened up by the engineers near the Expiatory Chapel.

We set off for Auteuil, trying to get a glimpse of the Tuileries on the way. A shell which exploded practically at our feet in the Place de la Madeleine forced us to fall back along the Faubourg Saint-Honoré, where we were followed by splinters striking the walls above our heads and to the left and right of us.

All evening, through a gap in the trees, I watched the fire of Paris, a fire which, against the night sky, looked like one of those Neapolitan gouaches of an eruption of Vesuvius on a sheet of black paper.

*Thursday, 25 May*

All day long, the guns and rifles have gone on firing. I spent the day walking round the ruins of Auteuil, where the damage and destruction is such as might have been caused by a whirlwind.

Carriages kept going by along the road from Saint-Denis to Versailles, taking back to Paris people whose stay in the country had made them positively archaic.

Paris is decidedly under a curse! After a drought lasting a whole month, there is now a wind of hurricane force blowing across the burning city.

*Friday, 26 May*

Today I was walking beside the railway line near Passy station when I saw some men and women surrounded by soldiers. I plunged through a gap in the fence and found myself at the edge of the road on which the prisoners were waiting to be taken to Versailles. There were a great many prisoners there, for I heard an officer say to the colonel, as he handed over a piece of paper: 'Four hundred and seven, including sixty-six women.'

The men had been split up into lines of seven or eight and tied to each other with string that cut into their wrists. They were just as they had been captured, most of them without hats or caps, and with their hair plastered down on their foreheads and faces by the fine rain that had been falling ever since this morning. There were men of the people there who had made themselves head coverings out of blue check handkerchiefs. Others, drenched to the skin by the rain, were holding thin overcoats tight across their chests, with a bulge where they were carrying a hunk of bread. They came from every class of society: hard-faced workmen, bourgeois in socialist hats, National Guards who had not had time to change out of their uniforms, and a couple of infantrymen with ghostly-white faces—stupid, fierce, indifferent, mute figures.

There was the same variety among the women. There were women wearing kerchiefs next to women in silk gowns. I noticed housewives, working-girls, and prostitutes, one of whom was wearing the uniform of a National Guard. And in the midst of them all there stood out the bestial head of a creature whose face was half-covered with an enormous bruise. Not one of these women showed the apathetic resignation of the men. There was anger and scorn on their faces, and many of them had a gleam of madness in their eyes.

Among these women, there was one who was singularly beautiful, with the implacable beauty of a young Fate. She was a girl with dark, curly hair, steely eyes, and cheekbones red with dried tears. She stood frozen as it were in a defiant posture, hurling insults at officers and men from a throat and lips so contracted by anger that they were unable to form sounds or words. Her mute, twisted mouth masticated abuse without being able to spit it out. 'She's just like the girl who stabbed Barbier!' a young officer said to one of his friends.

Everyone was ready to go when pity, which can never entirely abandon man, induced some of the soldiers to hold out their water-bottles to the women, who with graceful movements turned their heads and opened parched mouths to drink, at the same time keeping a wary eye on the scowling face of an old gendarme. The signal for departure was given and the pitiful column moved off on its journey to Versailles under a watery sky.

*Sunday, 28 May*

Driving along the Champs-Élysées in a cab, I saw, in the distance, legs running in the direction of the great avenue. I leaned out of the window. The whole avenue was filled by a huge crowd between two lines of troopers. I got out and joined the people running to see what it was. It was the prisoners who had just been taken at the Buttes-Chaumont, walking along in fives with a few women in their midst. 'There are six thousand of them', a trooper in the escort told me. 'Five hundred were shot on the spot.' At the head of this haggard multitude a nonagenarian was walking along on trembling legs.

Despite all the horror one felt for these men, one was saddened by the sight of this dismal procession, in the midst of which one could see some soldiers, army deserters, who had their tunics on inside out, with their grey cloth pockets hanging by their sides, and who seemed to be already half stripped for the firing-squad.

I met Burty in the Place de la Madeleine. We walked along the streets and boulevards, suddenly crowded with people who had emerged from their cellars and hiding-places, thirsting for light and sunshine, and wearing on their faces the joy of liberation. We went to collect Mme Burty, whom we persuaded to come out for a stroll. While Burty, who had suddenly been stopped in the street by Mme Verlaine, was discussing ways and means of concealing her husband, Mme Burty told me a secret which Burty had kept from me. One of his friends on the Public Committee, whose name she did not mention, had told Burty, four or five days ago, that the Government no longer had control over anything and that they were going to enter all the houses in Paris, confiscate the valuables they contained, and shoot all the householders.

I took leave of the Burtys and went to see how much of Paris had been burnt by the Federates. The Palais-Royal has been burnt down, but the pretty façade of the two wings-overlooking the square are intact; money will have to be spent on reconstructing the interior. The Tuileries need to be rebuilt along the garden and overlooking the Rue de Rivoli.

There is smoke everywhere, the air smells of burning and varnish, and on all sides one can hear the hissing of hose-pipes. In a good many places there are still horrible traces of the fighting: here a dead horse; there, beside the paving-stones from a half-demolished barricade, a peaked cap swimming in a pool of blood.

The large-scale destruction begins at the Châtelet and carries on from there. Behind the burnt-out theatre, the costumes have been spread out on the ground: carbonized silk in which, here and there, one catches sight of the gleam of golden spangles, the sparkle of silver.

On the other side of the embankment, the Palais de Justice has had the roof of its round tower decapitated. There is nothing left of the new buildings but the iron skeleton of the roof. The Prefecture of Police is a smouldering ruin, in whose bluish smoke the brand-new gold of the Sainte-Chapelle shines brightly.

By way of little paths made through barricades which have not yet been demolished, I eventually reached the Hôtel de Ville.

It is a splendid, a magnificent ruin. All pink and ash-green and the colour of white-hot steel, or turned to shining agate where the stonework has been burnt by paraffin, it looks like the ruin of an Italian palace, tinted by the sunshine of several centuries, or better still like the ruin of a magic palace, bathed in the theatrical glow of electric light. With its empty niches, its shattered or truncated statues, its broken clock, its tall window-frames and chimneys still standing in mid-air by some miracle of equilibrium, and its jagged silhouette outlined against the blue sky, it is a picturesque wonder which ought to be preserved if the country were not irrevocably condemned to the restorations of M. Viollet-le-Duc. The irony of chance! In the utter ruin of the whole building there shines, on a marble plaque intact in its new gilt frame, the lying inscription: *Liberty, Equality, Fraternity*.

*Monday, 29 May*

Posted up on all the walls I see MacMahon's proclamation announcing that it was all over at four o'clock yesterday afternoon.

This evening one can hear the movement of Parisian life starting up again, and its murmur like a distant tide: the hours no longer fall into the silence of the desert.

*Wednesday, 31 May*

There are tricolours in every window and on every carriage. The cellar ventilators of all the houses have been blocked up again. Across the paving-stones which are being replaced, the people of Paris, dressed in their travelling-clothes, are swarming in to take possession of their city once more.

All is well. There has been neither compromise nor conciliation. The solution has been brutal, imposed by sheer force of arms. The solution has saved everyone from the dangers of cowardly compromise. The solution has restored its self-confidence to the Army, which has learnt in the blood of the Communards that it was still capable of fighting. And finally, the bleeding has been done thoroughly, and a bleeding like that, by killing the rebellious part of a population, postpones the next revolution by a whole conscription. The old society has twenty years of peace before it, if the powers that be dare what they are free to dare at the moment.

*Saturday, 10 June*

Dined this evening with Flaubert, whom I had not seen since my brother's death. He has come to Paris to find some information for his *Tentation de Saint Antoine*. He is still the same, a writer above all else. This cataclysm seems to have passed over him without distracting him for one moment from the impassive making of books.

*Saturday, 1 July*

At the Gare du Nord, prisoners of war were arriving back from Germany. Pale faces, thin bodies in greatcoats too big for them, faded red cloth and worn grey cloth: this is the sight to which the trains from Germany are treating Paris every day.

They walked along with little sticks in their hands, bent under grey canvas kitbags. Some of them were dressed in German breeches, and others were wearing a cloth cap in the place of the peaked cap they had left on some battlefield. Poor fellows! When they were turned loose, it was a pleasure to see them straighten up, it was a pleasure to hear their worn soles tread the pavements of Paris with a brisk, eager step.

The Princess received me with that liveliness which is peculiar to her and which she puts into her handshake. She took me for a stroll in the park and started telling me about herself, about her stay in Belgium, about her sufferings in exile. She told me that for a long time she could not understand what was happening to her in Belgium, but that she knows now: she was present there in body but completely absent in mind, so completely indeed that she used to wake up in the morning thinking that she was in her Paris house. When I congratulated her on her good health, she said: 'Oh, it hasn't always been like that! There was a bad period, a peculiar period, during which my jaws set so hard, after all that I had been through, that sometimes I really had difficulty in eating anything.'

She spoke to me too of the Emperor, whom she had seen again, and whom she characterized as an *impersonal being*, a man whose fall did not seem to have affected him.

*Sunday, 9 November*

Flaubert told me today of the unexpected good fortune which had come to the 'Présidente', who had received a bond to the value of fifty thousand francs a year, two days before the Siege: a gift from Richard Wallace, who had slept with her in the past and had told her: 'You'll see, if ever I become a rich man, I'll remember you.'

He told me too about a Chinese envoy who had arrived in Paris during our Siege and our Commune, in the midst of our cataclysm, and to whom somebody had remarked:

'You must find all this extremely surprising.'

'No, not at all', he had replied. 'You are young, you Westerners, you have hardly any history to speak of. . . . It has always been like this. . . . The Siege and the Commune are everyday events for the human race. . . .'

Flaubert invited me to stay for dinner, and afterwards he read to me from his *Tentation de Saint Antoine*. My first impression: the Bible, the Christian past, brought up to date in the Horace Vernet manner, with the addition of Bedouin and Turkish bric-à-brac. My second impression: a huge book of notes on Antiquity forced into the stupid machinery of a spectacular play, with a good many sheets of the compilation refusing to go through the mill.

*25 November*

What seems to me to foreshadow the end of the bourgeoisie is the presidential apotheosis of M. Thiers, the most complete representative of the caste. For me, it is as if the bourgeoisie, before dying, were crowning itself with its own hands.

# 1872

Last night I sought in vain in the brutality of animal pleasure forgetfulness of the first hour of a new year.

*15 January*

A few days ago, seeing a block of private carriages in the Rue de la Paix like that outside the Théâtre-Français on a first night, I was wondering who was the great personage whose door was beset by so many important people when I looked up above the carriage entrance and saw the name: Worth. Paris has not changed.

*Saturday, 2 March*

The guests at dinner at Flaubert's today were Théo, Turgenev, and myself.

Turgenev, that gentle giant, that lovable barbarian, with his white hair falling into his eyes, with a deep line crossing his forehead from one temple to the other like a furrow, and with his childish language, enchanted us from the soup-course on, *wreathed* us, as the Russians put it, with his combination of innocence and shrewdness —the great charm of the Slav race, heightened in him by the originality of a superior intelligence and by an immense, cosmopolitan fund of knowledge.

He spoke to us of the month's imprisonment he had served after the publication of the *Memoirs of a Huntsman*, of that month in which his cell had been the room housing the police archives of a whole district, whose secret dossiers he had studied at leisure. And he depicted for us, with all the skill of a painter and a novelist, the chief of police who, one day, after Turgenev had made him drunk with champagne, had said to him, giving him a nudge and raising his glass in the air: 'To Robespierre!'

Then he paused and said: 'If I set any store by such things, all I would want to be carved on my tombstone would be a tribute to what my book had done for the emancipation of the serfs. The Tsar Alexander once sent word to me that my book had been one of the main factors governing his decision.'

After dinner Gautier sank on to a sofa, saying: 'The fact is, nothing interests me any more. I have a feeling that I have ceased to be a contemporary. I'm perfectly prepared to talk about myself in the third person, as if I were already dead!'

'I have a different feeling', said Turgenev. 'You know how sometimes in a room there's an imperceptible smell of musk that you can't get rid of? Well, in my case, all around me, all the time, there's a smell of death, dissolution, and decay.'

He went on after a pause: 'The explanation lies, I believe, in the fact that for various reasons—my white hair and so on—I cannot make love any more. I am quite incapable of it. And when that happens to a man, he is as good as dead.'

And when Flaubert and I denied that love was all-important for a writer, the Russian novelist let his hands fall to his sides and exclaimed: 'All I can say is that my life has always been saturated with femininity. There isn't a book or anything else which can take the place of a woman for me. How can I explain that to you? I believe that love produces a certain flowering of the whole personality which nothing else can achieve.'

His memory searched the past for a moment, and a flash of happiness lit up his face.

'Look, when I was a young man I had a mistress, a miller's daughter who lived near St. Petersburg and whom I used to see when I went hunting. She was a delightful girl, very pale, with a cast in one eye, something which is fairly common in our country. She would never accept anything from me. One day, however, she said to me: "You must bring me a present." "What do you want?" I asked. "Bring me some soap." I brought her a tablet of soap. She took it, disappeared, came back covered with blushes, and said, holding out her scented hands: "Now kiss my hands as you kiss the hands of the ladies in the drawing-rooms of St. Petersburg!" I threw myself on my knees before her ... Well, there isn't a moment in my life to equal that one!'

*Monday, 3 June*

Zola came to lunch with me today. I saw him take a glass of claret in both hands, saying to me: 'Look at the way my fingers tremble!' And he told me of an incipient heart disease, of a possible bladder ailment, of a threat of rheumatism in the joints.

Never have men of letters seemed more stillborn than in our day, and yet never have they worked harder or more incessantly. Sickly and neurotic as he is, Zola works every day from nine until half-past twelve and from three until eight. That is what is necessary nowadays, with talent and something of a reputation, in order to earn a living. 'I have to work like that', he told me. 'But don't imagine that I'm a man of strong will-power: by nature I'm the weakest of creatures and the least capable of determination. In me, the place of will-power is taken by an obsession—an obsession which would make me ill if I didn't obey it.'

*24 October*

Yesterday, reading a newspaper over dinner—this is the only way I can eat when dining alone—I came unexpectedly across the news of Théo's death.

This morning I went to the Rue Longchamp at Neuilly. Bergerat took me into the dead man's bedroom. His face, a pale orange colour, was sunk in the midst of his long black hair. On his chest there was a rosary whose white beads, arranged round a pink rose on the point of fading, looked like the berries from a branch of *symphoricarpos*. Seen thus, the poet had the fierce serenity of a barbarian who had fallen asleep in nothingness. There was nothing there to indicate a modern death. Memories of the stone figures outside Chartres Cathedral, mingled with recollections of stories of Merovingian times, came back to me, I cannot tell why.

*25 October*

For the father's funeral I went to the church at Neuilly where, only a few months ago, I attended the daughter's wedding.[1]

It was a stately funeral. The Army's bugles paid the final tribute to the Officer of the Legion of Honour. The most touching of the

[1] The wedding of Estelle Gautier and Émile Bergerat, on 15 May 1872.

Opéra's voices sang the Requiem of the author of *Gisèle*. We followed the hearse on foot to the Montmartre Cemetery. I caught sight of Dumas in a brougham, reading the funeral oration which lay in store for us to fat old Marchal, who was resting his huge bulk on a little folding seat opposite his famous friend. The cemetery was full of base admirers, anonymous colleagues, and scribblers in cheap rags, who were all escorting the journalist and not the poet, not the author of *Mademoiselle de Maupin*. For my part, it seems to me that my corpse would loathe having that pen-pushing rabble behind its coffin, and all I ask for when my turn comes is the company of the men of talent of the day and the six earnest cobblers who attended Heine's funeral.

# 1873

This week Thiers asked Édouard to dinner at his house, to give him his impressions of Germany. In the event, Thiers did not let him open his mouth, and all the time it was the President who told Édouard the story of his negotiations with Bismarck.

Bismarck, according to the profound study of him made by the historian of the Revolution, is *an ambitious man*, but *a man who did not feel any enmity towards France*. At bottom, what really made Thiers forgive Bismarck everything—he practically admitted as much—was that during the negotiations over Belfort, the Prussian Minister, knowing M. Thiers's habit of taking a nap during the day, had his feet wrapped in a greatcoat so that he would not catch cold. We can count ourselves lucky that this little attention did not cost us Belfort.

Édouard came away appalled by the senile, sententious ramblings of our great statesman.


*Sunday, 16 March*

Alphonse Daudet, whom I had seen only very briefly at the opening night of *Henriette Maréchal* and whom I met again today at Flaubert's, talked to us about Morny, for whom he had acted as a sort of secretary. While sparing him and disguising the man's nullity with words of gratitude, he depicted him as having had one eminent quality: a certain instinctive appreciation of human beings, the ability to distinguish at first sight between an incompetent and an intelligent man.

Daudet was very amusing and reached the heights of comedy when describing the writer, the manufacturer of operettas. He told us of one morning in particular, when he had brought along a comic negro song which Morny had asked him to write. In the enthusiasm of the first hearing, Persigny and Boittelle, who were waiting in the anteroom, were completely forgotten. With the result that while Daudet, the composer L'épine, and Morny himself, wearing the skull-cap and the long dressing-gown in which he aped Cardinal Richelieu, were all three of them jumping about on stools and singing: '*Zim boum, zim badaboum*' at the top of their voices, the Ministers of the Interior and Police sat twiddling their thumbs outside.

*18 March*

All the absence of virility in Sainte-Beuve, all the femininity of his talent, all the tortuous, shifty, despicable sides of his character can be explained in a few words. He was . . . No, he was not impotent, as Philips led the Princess to believe, but he found it so difficult, so uncomfortable, and so embarrassing to perform the gymnastics of love that it amounted to the same thing. Sainte-Beuve is one of the most interesting examples of the deficiency in character produced in a man by the imperfection of his genital organs.

*Saturday, 3 May*

The older Flaubert gets, the more provincial he becomes. The truth is that if you subtract from my good friend the ox in him, the hard-working animal, the manufacturer of books at the rate of a word an hour, you find yourself faced with a creature of very ordinary talent, of very little originality. And I am not talking here of the originality of ideas and concepts; I am talking of the originality of actions and taste; I am talking of that special originality which is the hallmark of the superior human being. Heaven knows he does his best to disguise the bourgeois resemblance of his brain to everybody else's—something which, I feel sure, must make him wild with fury—by means of truculent paradoxes, scarifying axioms, revolutionary tirades, and a brutal, even ill-bred, repudiation of all received and accepted ideas. Sometimes he even succeeds. But with whom? The violence of his exaggeration soon betrays and reveals to the perceptive observer the emptiness of what he has to say.

In a word, Flaubert makes himself out to be the most passionate man in the world; but in fact his friends have always known that woman plays a relatively minor part in his life. Flaubert makes himself out to be the most extravagant and careless of men when it comes to handling money; but in fact he has no tastes to indulge, never buys anything, and has never been known to allow a sudden whim to make a hole in his pocket. Flaubert makes himself out to be the most extraordinary of innovators in matters of interior decoration; but in fact the only idea he has had so far has been to use jam-jars as flower-vases, something of which he is inordinately proud. And so on and so forth. . . . The author of *Madame Bovary* has just the same ideas, tastes, habits, prejudices, qualities, and vices as the majority of men.

*Tuesday, 5 August*

Mme Charles Hugo invited me to dinner this evening on behalf of her father-in-law.

In the damp garden behind the little house, François Hugo was lying on a chaise-longue, his complexion waxy, his eyes at once vague and fixed, his arms folded across his body as if he were feeling cold. He was despondent, with all the despondency of anaemia. Standing beside his chair, as still and erect as an old Huguenot in a boulevard play, was his father. Bocher, a friend of the family, arrived, followed by Meurice, a man who looks like a church-mouse and walks without making a sound.

We sat down at table. And straight away, tumbling into everybody's plate, there appeared two children: the sad-faced little boy and sharp-eyed little Jeanne; and with little Jeanne, the happy laughter, the familiar pokes, the noisy movements, and the adorable coquetry of a four-year-old.

After the soup, Hugo, who had announced that he was suffering from cholerine, ate some melon and drank some iced water, saying that it would not do him any harm.

The night air grew chilly. François Hugo's pale face took on a greenish tinge. The great man, bare-headed and wearing a short alpaca jacket, did not feel cold: he was full of gaiety, energy, and vitality. And the unconsciousness of his robust health and strength, beside the death-agony of his son, was painful to see.

As we were leaving, Bocher said to me: 'That man is an absolute tiger. It was I who persuaded him to come back from Guernsey. . . . He doesn't give a thought to his son. He's busy making love just now to his tenant. It's the same with that girl walking in front of us.'

Left to myself, I started thinking about that family, about that father, that genius, that monster—about that first daughter who had been drowned, and that second daughter who had been carried off by an American and brought back to France raving mad—about those two sons, one dead and the other dying—about Mme Hugo, committing adultery with her son-in-law—about Vacquerie, marrying one daughter, sleeping with the mother, and practically raping his sister-in-law—and finally about that Juliette, that Pompadour of the poet's, still pursuing with her kisses, at this late date, the dying son. *A Tragic Family*, such is the title the dying man gave a novel he once wrote—and such is the title of the Hugo family.[1]

*Sunday, 28 December*

At François Hugo's funeral, Flaubert and I were stopped outside Père-Lachaise by Judith Gautier. In her fur and feathers, Théo's daughter looked beautiful, with a strange, almost terrifying beauty. Her pale complexion barely tinged with pink, her mouth standing out like the mouth of a Primitive against the ivory of her broad teeth, her clearly defined and as it were drowsy features, her big eyes, whose animal lashes, stiff lashes like little black pins, did not soften their gaze with a veil of shadow, all gave the lethargic creature the indefinable, mysterious air of a sphinx, of a flesh, a matter in which there were no modern nerves.

And to set off her dazzling youth, the young woman had on one side the flat-faced, slit-eyed Chinese Tsing, and on the other her mother, the aged Grisi, who, shrunk and shrivelled as she was, looked like an old consumptive monkey.

Finally, to make everything about this encounter weird, eccentric, and fantastic, Judith apologized to Flaubert for having missed him the day before: she had gone out to take her lesson in *magic*— yes, to take her lesson in magic!

[1] Léopoldine and Charles Vacquerie had been drowned at Villequier on 4 September 1843, six months after their marriage. Hugo's surviving daughter, Adèle, had followed an English officer called Pinson to America in 1863; brought back by François-Victor Hugo, she had been committed to a lunatic asylum where she died in 1915. The author of *Une Famille tragique* was not François-Victor but his elder brother Charles, who had died in 1871. François-Victor himself was to die soon afterwards, on 26 December 1873. No evidence has come to light to substantiate the accusation levelled by Goncourt at Mme Victor Hugo.

# 1874

*Tuesday, 6 January*

'*Post coitum omne animal triste.—Praeter asinum et sacerdotem*',
Renan added suavely, at the end of a long discussion on physical
love.[1]

*Wednesday, 28 January*

At the Princess's Flaubert exclaimed: 'There doesn't exist a caste
I despise more than that of the doctors, I who come from a family of
doctors, father, son, even cousins, for I'm the only Flaubert who
isn't a doctor. But when I speak of my contempt for the caste, I
don't count my father. I've seen him shake his fist at my brother,
behind his back, when he qualified as a doctor, and say: "If I'd been
in his place, at his age, with the money he has, what a man I'd have
been!" You can tell from that how he despised the practice of
medicine for money.'

And Flaubert went on, describing his father at the age of sixty, on
fine Sundays in the summer, telling his wife that he was going for a
walk in the country and slipping out by a back door to run to the
mortuary and start dissecting like a medical student. He told us too
how he once spent two hundred francs in fares to go and perform
an operation of scientific interest in some distant corner of the department, an operation on a fishmonger's wife, who paid him with a
dozen herrings.

Then we got on to the subject of how unobservant doctors were,
and somebody told the story of a writer who had been struck by
some madmen's drawings at Dr. Blanche's clinic showing flames
coming out of human heads, and who had asked the mental specialist
whether these flames had been drawn instinctively or copied from
another picture. Blanche had replied: 'It's amazing, the way you
writers complicate things! They are madmen's drawings, and that's
all there is to it!'

[1] 'Every animal is sad after copulation—except the ass and the priest.'

*Friday, 13 February*

Yesterday I spent the whole day in the studio of a strange painter called Degas. After a great many essays and experiments and trial shots in all directions, he has fallen in love with modern life, and out of all the subjects in modern life he has chosen washerwomen and ballet-dancers. When you come to think of it, it is not a bad choice.

It is a world of pink and white, of female flesh in lawn and gauze, the most delightful of pretexts for using pale, soft tints.

He showed me, in their various poses and their graceful fore-shortening, washerwomen and still more washerwomen . . . speaking their language and explaining the technicalities of the different movements in pressing and ironing.

Then it was the turn of the dancers. There was their green-room with, outlined against the light of a window, the curious silhouette of dancers' legs coming down a little staircase, with the bright red of a tartan in the midst of all those puffed-out white clouds, and a ridiculous ballet-master serving as a vulgar foil. And there before one, drawn from nature, was the graceful twisting and turning of the gestures of those little monkey-girls.

An original fellow, this Degas, sickly, neurotic, and so ophthal-mic that he is afraid of losing his sight; but for this very reason an eminently receptive creature and sensitive to the character of things. Among all the artists I have met so far, he is the one who has best been able, in representing modern life, to catch the spirit of that life.

*Thursday, 12 March*

It was dismal yesterday, the sort of ice that fell little by little, during the performance of *Le Candidat*, over that audience full of warm sympathy for the author, over that audience waiting in all good faith for sublime tirades, for superhuman witticisms, for world-shaking lines, and faced with nothingness, nothingness, nothingness. First of all an expression of pity and sadness appeared on every face; then, suppressed for a long time by respect for Flaubert's person and talent, the public's disappointment took its revenge in a sort of gentle hissing, a smiling mockery of the whole pathetic business.

After the performance I went backstage to shake hands with Flaubert. I found him on the already deserted stage, together with two or three dazed-looking Normans. There was not a single actor or a single actress left on the boards. Everybody was deserting the author. The stage-hands who had not finished their tour of duty could be seen hurrying through their work with fumbling gestures, their eyes fixed on the exit. The supernumeraries came running down the stairs in silence. It was both sad and slightly fantastic, like a rout, a stampede in a peep-show at twilight.

When he saw me, Flaubert gave a start as if he were waking up, as if he wanted to reassume his official strong-man pose. 'Well, there you are!' he said to me, with an angry wave of the hand and a contemptuous laugh which tried, unsuccessfully, to suggest lack of concern. And when I said that the play would pick up again at the second performance, he launched out into a tirade against the frivolous audiences at opening nights, and so on and so forth.

In this morning's press the critics seemed to be competing with one another in their eagerness to cushion Flaubert's fall. I reflected that if it had been I who had written that play, if it had been I who had had last night's reception, then what kicks, what insults, what screams of abuse I should have had to endure from the press. And why? We both lead the same life of work, toil, and devotion to art.

*Tuesday, 14 April*

Dinner at the Café Riche with Flaubert, Zola, Turgenev, and Alphonse Daudet. A dinner of men of talent who have a high opinion of each other's work, and one which we hope to make a monthly occasion in the winters to come.

We began with a long discussion on the special aptitudes of writers suffering from constipation and diarrhoea; and we went on to talk about the mechanics of the French language. On this subject Turgenev said something to this effect: 'Your language, gentlemen, strikes me as an instrument from which its inventors expected only clarity, logic, crude and approximate definition, whereas today it so happens that this instrument is being handled by the most highly strung and sensitive of writers, and the least likely to be satisfied with approximations.'

*Sunday, 31 May*

Nowadays it is like a reproach when the post brings me a book published by a colleague. Today I threw into a corner Zola's *La*

*Conquête de Plassans*, suffering at the sight of that pretty yellow volume lying on my table, with its new cover and its fresh print, which seemed to be saying to me: 'Are you completely finished then?'

*Wednesday, 8 July*

I spent the day at Alphonse Daudet's house at Champrosay, Delacroix's favourite retreat. He lives in a bourgeois house with a pretty little garden. A gay note is struck by a handsome, intelligent child, in whose face the features of father and mother are prettily combined. The house is full too of the charm of the wife, a cultured woman who lives a life of discreet and devoted self-effacement. One might suppose that there was everything there to create within those four walls the blissful bourgeois calm of the bourgeois, yet the place is as gloomy as a workshop of the mind, only rarely visited by a factitious gaiety, the sort of gaiety that is whipped up by champagne and intoxicated after-dinner paradoxes.

I should add that those delightful people, like their home, appeared to me in a melancholy light on account of the absence of any elegant or artistic refinement, any fanciful or amusing touches. It is the most disastrously bourgeois establishment imaginable, where there is not a picture nor a print nor a knick-knack nor even a mildly exotic straw hat to be seen. There is nothing, absolutely nothing, there that is not utterly ordinary, commonplace, and banal. I cannot reconcile myself to that in the homes of people belonging to the liberal professions, and houses like that which are so completely out of character with the arts practised by their owners eventually plunge me—silly though it may seem—into a profound melancholy.

*Sunday, 12 July*

For the past two or three days and two or three nights the horse that killed my brother off has had a successor in the stable of the house next door. Oh, the irony of life and the murderous little things it invents to kill you with pinpricks! This artistic treasure-house, on whose decoration so much care, imagination, and money has been lavished, no longer contains a single room where I can sleep or work, and I am forced to take my meals in the kitchen. Everywhere there is that irritating, exasperating, hostile noise, a noise that has become the unique preoccupation of my mind, rendering it incapable of application and absorption. And faced with this persecution by Fate, which seems to pick out those who try to do things better and in more individual fashion than the common herd, I am overwhelmed by weariness, discouragement, and disgust: I feel something like that supreme detachment which comes to those about to die.

*Monday, 24 August*

This evening Mme de Béhaine produced an admirable definition of the taste in clothes of the Parisienne of old: 'She insisted on having pretty shoes, pretty gloves, and pretty ribbons: the dress in those days was just an accessory.' I would have added that she dressed in quiet colours, discreet shades. The garish element, the 'pistol-shot' effect, in women's clothes today is a victory of foreign taste, of American taste, over old-fashioned French taste.

# 1875

The Flaubert dinners are unlucky. Coming away from the first, I caught pneumonia. Today, Flaubert himself was missing: he is confined to bed. So there were only four of us: Turgenev, Zola, Daudet, and myself.

We talked first of all about Taine. While we were trying to define the deficiencies and imperfections of his talent, Turgenev interrupted us to say with his usual originality of mind and soft, warbling voice: 'The comparison is not a flattering one, gentlemen, but allow me to compare Taine to a pointer I once owned; he quartered, he pointed, he went through all the motions of a hunting dog to perfection; only he had no sense of smell. I was obliged to sell him.'

Zola was tucking into the good food, and when I asked him whether by any chance he was a glutton, he replied: 'Yes, it's my only vice; and at home, when there isn't anything good for dinner, I'm miserable, utterly miserable. That's the only thing that matters; nothing else really exists for me. You know what my life is like?'

And his face clouding over, he launched out on the story of his misfortunes. It is strange what a whiner that fat, pot-bellied young fellow is, and how quickly he falls into a melancholy mood. He had begun painting the gloomiest of pictures of his youth, of the vexations of his everyday life, of the insults that were heaped upon him, of the suspicion with which he was regarded, and of the sort of quarantine established around his work, when Turgenev remarked: 'How peculiarly French! One of my Russian friends, a great thinker, said to me the other day that the Jean-Jacques Rousseau type was a French type and that it was to be found only in France. . . .'

Zola, who had not listened to what Turgenev had said, went on with his jeremiad; and when we pointed out that he had no reason to complain, and that he had come a long way for a man who was not yet thirty-five, he exclaimed: 'Do you want me to be absolutely frank with you? You'll take me for a child, but never mind! I shall never be decorated, I shall never receive any kind of honour in recognition of my talent. For the public I shall always be a pariah, yes, a pariah!'

And he repeated four or five times: 'A pariah!'

We teased the realist about his appetite for bourgeois honours. Turgenev looked at him for a moment with a kind of fatherly irony, and then came out with this charming fable: 'Zola, on the occasion of the emancipation of the serfs, an event in which you know that I played a certain part, Count Orloff, who is a friend of mine and at whose wedding I had been best man, invited me to dinner at the Embassy. I may not be the foremost Russian writer in Russia, but in Paris, seeing that there aren't any others, you'll grant that I must be. Well, that being the case, do you know where I was placed at table? I was given the forty-seventh place; I was placed *after* the pope, and you know how we despise priests in Russia!'

And a little Slavonic smile appeared in Turgenev's eyes by way of conclusion.

Zola was in a talkative mood. The portly young fellow, full of childish naïvety, the greed of a spoilt trollop, and a slightly socialistic envy, went on telling us about his work, about his daily output of a hundred lines, about his cenobitism, his quiet home life, with no other distraction in the evenings but a few games of dominoes with his wife or a visit from a few fellow southerners. In the midst of all this, he forgot himself so far as to confess that at bottom his greatest pleasure, his greatest satisfaction, consisted in feeling the power and influence that he exerted over Paris through the medium of his prose; and he said this in an unpleasant tone of voice, the revengeful tone of voice of a poor devil who had known years of poverty.

During the realist novelist's bitter confession, Daudet, who was slightly tipsy, kept reciting dialect ballads from the south to himself, and seemed to be gargling with the sweet music of that sunny poetry.

*Wednesday, 17 February*

This evening Dumas was dining at the Princess's. The new Academician tried his best to behave like an ordinary mortal and to humiliate his colleagues as little as possible with his triumph.

After dinner, he began to talk very interestingly about the way a theatrical success was organized, and at one point, turning towards Flaubert and myself, he said in a voice in which profound contempt was combined with something akin to pity: 'You fellows, you don't realize the importance, for the success of a play, of the composition of the first-night audience; you have no idea of all that has to be done. . . . For instance you have to make sure that there are friends and admirers sitting around the four or five members every club sends along on those occasions, because they are anything but enthusiastic theatre-goers. And if you don't see about this, and about that . . .' And he taught us a great many things of which we were totally ignorant and which, now that we know them, we shall never be able to put into practice.

*Sunday, 28 February*

At Flaubert's, we were enthusing over the poetry of the Englishman Swinburne when Daudet exclaimed:

'Incidentally, I've heard that he's a homosexual. There are the most extraordinary stories told about his stay at Étretat last year. . . .'

'Further back than that, a few years ago,' said young Maupassant, 'I saw something of him for a little while.'

'Why, yes,' said Flaubert; 'didn't you save his life?'

'Not exactly', replied Maupassant. 'I was walking along the beach when I heard the shouts of a drowning man, and I waded into the water. But a boat had beaten me to it and had already fished him out. He had gone for a bathe dead drunk. But just as I was coming out of the water, soaked to the skin right up to the waist, another Englishman, who lived in the neighbourhood and was Swinburne's friend, came up to me and thanked me warmly.

'The next day I received an invitation to lunch. It was a strange place where they lived, a sort of cottage containing some splendid pictures, with an inscription over the door which I didn't read on that occasion, and a big monkey gambolling around inside. And what a lunch! I don't know what I ate; all I can remember is that when I asked the name of some fish I was eating, my host replied with a peculiar smile that it was meat, and I could not get any more out of him! There was no wine, and we drank nothing but spirits.

'The owner of the place, a certain Powell, was an English lord, according to people at Étretat, who concealed his identity under his mother's maiden name. As for Swinburne, picture a little man with a forked chin, a hydrocephalous forehead, and a narrow chest, who trembled so violently that he gave his glass St. Vitus's dance and talked like a madman.

'One thing annoyed me straight away about that first lunch, and that was that now and then Powell would titillate his monkey, which would escape from him to rub up against the back of my neck when I bent forward to have a drink.

'After lunch the two friends opened some gigantic portfolios and brought out a collection of obscene photographs, taken in Germany, all full-length and all of male subjects. I remember one, among others, of an English soldier masturbating on a pane of glass. Powell was dead drunk by this time, and kept sucking the fingers of a mummified hand which was used, I believe, as a paperweight. While he was showing me the photographs, a young servant came in, and Powell promptly closed the portfolio.

'Swinburne speaks very good French. He has an immense fund of learning. That day he told us a lot of interesting things about snakes, saying that he sometimes watched them for two or three hours at a time. Then he translated some of his poems for us, putting tremendous spirit into the translation. It was very impressive. Powell is no ordinary man either: he has brought back a collection of fascinating old songs from Iceland.

'The whole household, in fact, intrigued me. I accepted a second invitation to lunch. This time the monkey left me in peace; it had been hanged a few days before by the little servant, and Powell had ordered a huge block of granite to put on its tomb, with a basin hollowed out on top in which the birds could find rainwater during periods of drought. At the end of the meal they gave me a liqueur which nearly knocked me out. Taking fright, I escaped to my hotel, where I slept like a log for the rest of the day.

'Finally I went back there for one last visit, to find out the truth, to make certain whether or not I was dealing with perverts or homosexuals. I showed them the inscription over the door, which read: *Dolmancé Cottage*, and asked them whether they were aware that Dolmancé was the name of the hero of Sade's *Philosophie dans le Boudoir*. They answered in the affirmative. "Then that is the sign of the house?" I asked. "If you like", they replied, with terrifying expressions on their faces. I had found out what I wanted to know, and I never saw them again.'

*Wednesday, 3 March*

Nowadays, among literary writers, style has become so affected, so selective, so eccentric as to make writing practically impossible. It is bad style to place fairly close to one another two words beginning with the same syllable; it is bad style to use the word *of* twice in the same expression, and so on and so forth. Poor Cladel, a victim of this modern malady of perfectionism, has just started rewriting for the fifth time a novel in which he has not yet reached page sixty.

Among these exquisites, these dandies of word and syntax, there is a madman madder than the rest, and that is the nebulous Mallarmé, who maintains that one should never begin a sentence with a monosyllable, saying: 'You must realize that those two poor little letters cannot conceivably serve as a foundation for a great sentence, a huge sentence.'

This excessive fastidiousness dulls the minds of the most gifted of writers, and distracts them—busy as they are with the intricate manipulation of every phrase—from all the vital, great, warm things that give life to a book.

*Sunday, 7 March*

Zola, coming into Flaubert's apartment, dropped into an armchair and muttered in tones of despair: 'You can't imagine how much trouble I'm having over Compiègne!'[1]

He went on to ask Flaubert how many chandeliers there were lighting the dining-room table, whether the conversation made much noise, what people talked about, and what the Emperor said. Yes, there he was, trying to discover from a third party, in a disjointed conversation, the *physiognomy of a setting*, which only those whose eyes have actually seen it can possibly describe. And now this novelist, who claims to write history in his novels, is going to depict a great historical figure for us with the information collected

---

[1] Zola was describing the life of the Imperial Court at Compiègne in his novel *Son Excellence Eugène Rougon*, which was published in March 1876.

in ten minutes from a colleague who has kept back the best of what he knows for a novel of his own. . . .

However, Flaubert, half out of pity for Zola's ignorance, half for the satisfaction of showing two or three other people who were there that he had spent a fortnight at Compiègne, put on a classic impersonation of the Emperor in his dressing-gown, dragging his feet, putting one hand behind his bent back, twisting his moustache and uttering idiotic phrases of his own invention.

'Yes,' he said, once he had seen that Zola had got his picture firmly into his head, 'that man was stupidity in person.'

'I agree', I said. 'I am entirely of your opinion. But stupidity is usually garrulous, and his was silent: that was his great strength, because it allowed people to suppose that he was intelligent. . . .'

Then Flaubert recounted a curious episode of the Emperor's affair with Bellanger at Montretout, telling how the Emperor, wearing a paper hat on his head, had papered with his imperial hands the walls of his mistress's morning-room and lavatory. 'And I can tell you this too,' added Flaubert; 'it was a blue wallpaper with little white crosses.'

*Wednesday, 17 March*

This evening the Princess talked about her incurable girls.[1] She spoke of those stunted human wrecks, she spoke of those bodies, on one of which there were fifty-three sores which had to be dressed every day; she spoke of one unfortunate girl whose head kept growing and had to be enclosed and contained in a hoop. And she concluded: 'Well, do you know what the Mother Superior told me? That all of them, all of them, mind you, dreamed of getting married. To which the Mother Superior added with a laugh that that had convinced her that marriage was woman's natural vocation.'

*Tuesday, 30 March*

Paul Lacroix confirmed in conversation with me today what Gavarni had told me about Balzac's thriftiness in the expenditure of

---

[1] The inmates of a home at Neuilly for incurable girls, Notre-Dame-des-Sept-Douleurs, in which Princess Mathilde took a deep interest and to which she bequeathed 100,000 francs.

his sperm. He was perfectly happy playing the love game up to the point of ejaculation, but he was unwilling to go any further. Sperm for him was an emission of cerebral matter and as it were a waste of creative power; and after one unfortunate incident, in the course of which he had forgotten his theories, he arrived at Latouche's exclaiming: 'I lost a book this morning.'

Yet the big fellow could be sensual and depraved enough on occasion. And his favourite pastime was hunting—yes, hunting! He had at that time as a mistress, or as something resembling a mistress, a great lady, a former lady-in-waiting of Marie-Antoinette's, whose name Lacroix would not tell me and whom he described as very well preserved for all that she was seventy years old.[1] Balzac, in a state of nature and on all fours, used to chase the old woman through all the rooms of her apartment, playing both the huntsman and the hound.

*Thursday, 3 June*

Taking me to see the roses in her kitchen-garden, the Princess started talking about the Empress. 'You have no idea how miserly she has become', she said. 'It is quite incredible. . . . She found some old nightdresses of her mother-in-law's at Arenenberg, and she is wearing them out at the moment. . . . Then she has had her son disinherited and taken control of all his money. . . . And finally, do you know how much she gives the Prince every month? She gives him five hundred francs, out of which he is supposed to buy his clothes. Imagine, just imagine!' And after doing a sum under her breath she went on: 'She must have an income of at least five hundred thousand francs a year. And then she goes and gives her son five hundred! And he has to buy his clothes with that! I couldn't refrain from writing to the boy to tell him that although I was no longer a rich woman, if ever he needed ten thousand francs he had only to ask me for them. He replied—he's a sweet boy—that he was very grateful to me but that so far he hadn't become enough of a scapegrace to need the money.'

This evening, her thoughts and her conversation turned on her

---

[1] The lady in question is obviously Laure de Berny, who was a god-daughter of Marie-Antoinette's and whose mother was one of the Queen's ladies-in-waiting. When Balzac fell in love with her, in 1822, he was twenty-three and she was forty-five. She never attained the age of seventy, for she died in 1836.

family, on Napoleon's brothers. She described that mad King of Holland for us, with his greatcoat, his chinchilla cap, the hole in his breeches and underpants, and his beautiful paralysed hands, with which he used to give you taps on the legs which felt as if they were being given with pieces of wood.[1] She described him at Florence, in love with a pretty young thing, and dressed in black with a white cravat and the grand cordon of the Legion of Honour, hanging between two console-tables, his legs giving way beneath him, like a puppet on loose strings.

And finally she told us the amusing rejoinder the King had made, one day when he had told her that she would have done better to marry him.

'You must be joking, uncle: why, you can't even blow your nose.'

'Well, what of it? I should have rung the bell and my valet would have turned me over.'

*Wednesday, 28 July*

A young Japanese who had been asked to translate some poetry stopped in the middle of his work the other day and exclaimed: 'No, it's impossible to make you understand that with the words in your language! You are so coarse!' And in answer to our protests he went on; 'Yes, coarse! You say to a woman: "I love you!" Well, in my country, that would be tantamount to saying: "Madame, I should like to go to bed with you!" All that we dare say to the woman we love, to tell her that we love her, is that we covet the place of the mandarin ducks beside her. Because the mandarin duck, gentlemen, is our love-bird. . . .'

*Monday, 8 November*

'I can tell you what the situation is', said Flaubert, 'in three words: I am ruined! There was a sudden, unprecedented fall in the price of timber. What used to be worth a hundred francs dropped to sixty. First of all I lent some money to my nephew; then, when he was threatened with bankruptcy, I took over some of his debts. Every penny I've got has gone. But if he gets back on his feet—

[1] Louis Bonaparte, husband of Hortense de Beauharnais and father of Napoleon III.

because he's carrying on with his business—I shan't lose anything, seeing that he owes me over a million.'[1]

And Flaubert left me uncertain whether I should pity him or congratulate him on his financial ruin, which he seemed not too displeased to have seen announced in the papers.


*Tuesday, 16 November*

Bishop Dupanloup and Dumas in conversation the other day: 'What do you think of *Madame Bovary?*'

'A delightful book. . . .'

'A masterpiece, Monsieur! . . . Yes, a masterpiece for anyone who has heard confession in the provinces!'


*Saturday, 27 November*

In the midst of the general recognition of our talent, a denial of it, polite, disguised, but absolute, was published in the *Temps* the other day.[2]

The author of this article is young France, the bookseller's son. My brother and I were always charming to the little brat, whose childhood was one long cold in the head. Later on, when he wrote a series of neat little prefaces for Lemerre, I wrote him the most Hugolian of letters. This being so, when I went and asked him for an article in the *Temps*, talking to him frankly and openly of the importance I attached to the Lemerre reprint, not for my sake but for the sake of my brother's memory, I consider that he should have said to me: 'My dear sir, you have come to the wrong person. I have a different ideal in literature from yours and I don't like what you write, so that the article you expect from me will not be at all advantageous to your books. You would do better to approach someone else.'

---

[1] Ernest Commanville, a timber merchant who had married Flaubert's niece Caroline Hamard in 1864, found himself on the verge of bankruptcy in April 1875. Flaubert sacrificed his entire fortune, amounting to some 1,200,000 francs, to save the Commanvilles, condemning himself to financial hardship and worry for the rest of his life.

[2] An article on the Goncourts by Anatole France, on the occasion of the publication by Lemerre of a reprint of *Renée Mauperin* and *Sœur Philomène*, which appeared in the *Temps* of 24 November 1875.

This young man preferred to commit an act of treachery. Was it inspired by Leconte de Lisle, whose protégé he is? I gather that it was not. I am told that he was simply obeying the dictates of his nature, of his jesuitical, republican temperament, and trying to curry favour with his party by attacking us in the name of healthy literary doctrines and revolutionary principles.

# 1876

*Tuesday, 25 January*

The literature inaugurated by Flaubert and the Goncourts might, it seems to me, be defined as follows: a scrupulous study of reality in prose that speaks the language of poetry.

*Monday, 31 January*

'Morny,' said Alphonse Daudet, 'and I wouldn't say this if we weren't the four of us who are here, if there were even two others present, Morny was a bloody fool, an absolute idiot. He used to say: "I have a great gift for poetry; why, at school, when I had a difficult exercise to do, I often used to write it in verse. . . ." Or he would say: "I do believe that I was born to make music: it's astonishing how naturally tunes occur to me!" And he would hum a tune which was a reminiscence of *Au clair de la lune.* . . . But he was no fool when it came to administrative matters. He was always charming to me, and never asked me to do anything except have a haircut. . . . The strangest thing is the way I got into his good graces. Poupart-Davyl, on account of a printing debt, applied for a distraint on my salary: you can imagine the effect this had in my department! But Morny just smiled and poked fun at my creditor. After that, I caught the pox from a lady of high rank, a dreadful pox with chancres and all, and gave it to my mistress. That pox won Morny over completely; and since it was complicated by lung trouble and the medicine I was taking made me spit blood, he told me that he was sending me south and making me the youngest of all the sub-prefects. It is him I have to thank for those journeys to Algeria, Corsica, and Sardinia that put me on my feet again, journeys on which I had nothing to do except write him a little letter of gratitude once a month. . . . As I said before, the man was always kindness itself to me, and never behaved to me as he sometimes did to others.'

'And you mean to say that you aren't using all that!' exclaimed

Zola, who for some time—as always happens when he hears things that are *convertible* into novels—had been wriggling about on his chair, swinging it from side to side. 'But there's a magnificent book there! There's a character. . . . If only I'd known all this when I wrote *Son Excellence Rougon*! . . . Don't you agree with me, Flaubert?'

'Yes, it's all very interesting, but there isn't a book there. . . .'

'But of course there's a book there! What do you say, Goncourt?'

'Oh, I consider that as a rule a novel should be written with the sort of history that doesn't find its way into memoirs.'

'Gentlemen,' Daudet broke in, 'there really isn't enough wine, we just aren't drinking enough! I propose that in future we should be given less meat and more liquid!'

And to make up the deficiency, he promptly poured himself a succession of glasses of liqueur. His hand, of an extraordinary whiteness, kept going up to stroke his Ninevite beard and his long hair, which seemed damp with all that he had drunk and fell in tearful locks over his forehead; and a rakish beauty came to his face, which bent lovingly over his waistcoat as if over a woman's body.

'Be careful, Daudet,' I said to him, 'or you are going to lose your way again in the streets of Les Batignolles. . . .'

At these words he gave a start and, coming out of his reverie, he said:

'Oh, you've no idea how depraved I am. No, you would never guess what a filthy swine I really am.'

'It's true that you make me feel like a bourgeois in comparison', sighed Zola.

'Just imagine,' Daudet went on, 'it was our wedding anniversary a few days ago. . . . Now you know that I love my wife for all sorts of reasons, for fine qualities which I am the only one who knows; and then, I don't need to tell you that I worship my child, and that goes with my affection for my wife. . . . Well, I decided to take home some flowers for her. But there I was, in the Rue d'Argenteuil, in that confounded street with the dark doorways in which dirty women stand hitching up their skirts—the sort of women I like when I'm excited—with the result that I spent half-an-hour pretending to be waiting for the bus and not waiting for it at all, but breathing in the smell of prostitution in that street like a dog on heat. I might still be down one of those alleys now if it weren't for the fact that I'm as superstitious as an Italian, and I started imagining frightful diseases, diseases which would be my punishment if I were unfaithful on that particular day. All of a sudden I took to my heels, rushed into Madame Prévost's, threw all the money I had on to her counter, and said: "Make up a bouquet of white lilac for me with all that!" There were sixteen francs. I hadn't even dared to keep some money for the bus. My wife actually scolded me for arriving home half-an-hour late; but I have never been so pleased with myself in the whole of my life, and you can't imagine how much it had cost me!'

*Monday, 14 February*

The Princess took me this evening to the first night of *L'Étrangère*.

We were in the big stage-box on the left of the theatre. The Princess was sitting on the chair in the middle of the box. Into the opposite box came President MacMahon's wife, who sat down facing the Princess. Her entrance was greeted with a burst of applause. The Princess's back, under the stress of internal upheavals, began to look like a theatrical representation of a sea; then, with the jerk of a body rising all of a piece, she stood up, letting the cloak covering her shoulders fall to the floor, and exclaimed in a choking voice: 'No, I can't stand it! Sitting there in the box the Emperor used to occupy, and greeted as he used to be! All those people applauding. . . . Oh, it's too much! No, I can't stay here any longer!' Into her face, into her tear-filled eyes, there entered all the despair contained in the hearts of fallen dynasties.

And for the rest of the performance, despite all that we could say to her, the Princess, having forcibly installed her niece Bonaparte-Patterson in her place, sat in the shadows at the back of the box, wriggling with indignation on the bench on which she was hiding, turning her angry back on the MacMahonian audience, and revenging herself for the fall of the Empire on Dumas's prose.

*Thursday, 2 March*

There is an old woman going around who says that Delacroix, the Foreign Minister under the Revolution, asked Talleyrand to give his wife a child of genius, that Talleyrand agreed, and that it was as a result of that request and that gracious concession that the painter Eugène Delacroix was born.

*Sunday, 5 March*

Today, Sunday, the last day of the elections, I felt curious to see what the Hugo salon was like.

On the stairs I met, going out, Meurice and Vacquerie, the latter arguing with his daughter, who wanted to take a cab for which he was unwilling to pay.

In the poet's drawing-room, which was practically empty, Mme Drouet, stiff and erect in the dress of a coquettish dowager, was sitting on Hugo's right, in an attitude of religious veneration, on a corner of the sofa. Mme Charles Hugo was lying back lazily in the soft folds of a black lace dress, smiling prettily with a delicate irony in her eyes for this divine service which she had to attend every evening and for the old stories told by the great man, her father-in-law. The men were Flaubert, Turgenev, Gouzien, and a young man I did not know.

Hugo spoke of the fascination of Thiers's eloquence, composed, he said, of things everybody knew better than he did and of a host of grammatical errors, all this delivered in a most unpleasant voice, but which none the less, after an hour or so, took hold of you, aroused interest, forced itself upon you. And going through the other orators of the day, he added: 'Whatever you do, you must never read their speeches! They are just lectures, delightful lectures, whose effect never lasts more than three days. . . . And yet, gentlemen,' he said, getting to his feet, 'shouldn't it be an orator's ambition to speak for longer than that, to speak to the future?'

I gave my arm to Mme Drouet, and we went into the dining-room, where there was fruit, liqueurs, and soft drinks set out on the table. And there, his arms folded across his chest, his body thrown back a little in his buttoned frock-coat, and a white scarf round his neck, Hugo started talking again. He spoke in a soft, slow voice, slightly muffled yet still clear, a voice which played with words and uttered them caressingly; he spoke with his eyes half-closed and with all sorts of feline expressions passing across that face of his which was shamming death, that flesh which had taken on the fine, warm colouring of the flesh of a Rembrandt syndic; and when he grew excited, there was a strange rising and falling of the line formed by his white hair along his forehead.

Hugo aestheticized in this fashion on Michelangelo, Rembrandt, Rubens, and Jordaens, whom he rates, incidentally, more highly than Rubens.

We remained alone all the evening, without a single politician ringing the bell to interrupt this conversation on art and literature. At eleven o'clock everybody got up and went off, Hugo putting on an old hat of Castelar's which the Spaniard had left him in place of a newer one.

*Friday, 1 September*

Flaubert told me that during the two months he had spent confined to his room, the heat had given him a kind of intoxicated urge to work, and he had worked for fifteen hours every day. He went to bed at four o'clock in the morning and was sometimes surprised to find himself back at his writing-table at nine. A grind interrupted only by a swim in the Seine in the evening.

And the result of those nine hundred hours of work is a story thirty pages long.[1]

*Friday, 3 October*

Yesterday I received a novel by M. Huysmans, *L'Histoire d'une fille*, with a letter saying that the book had been seized by the censors.[2] In the evening, at the far end of the Princess's drawing-room, I talked for a good hour with the barrister Doumerc about my dispute with my honest solicitor.

This persecution of a book similar to the one I am writing, and this conversation with a clean-shaven lawyer dressed all in black, resulted in my dreaming last night that I was in prison, a prison with

---

[1] *Un Cœur simple*, written between March and August 1876, and one of the *Trois Contes* published in 1877.

[2] J.-K. Huysmans, who had just published his first novel, *Marthe, histoire d'une fille* in Belgium, had read in the press that Goncourt was also writing a novel about a prostitute. In his letter to Goncourt of 1 October 1876 he apologized for this coincidence and reported that a consignment of copies of his book had been seized at the Belgian frontier.

stone walls looking like a stage-set of the Bastille. And the peculiar thing was this: I had been imprisoned simply for writing *La Fille Élisa*, which had not been published and which was no further advanced than it is now. My fury at this action on the part of the Government may be imagined; and it was exacerbated, in my dream, by the fact that I found myself in a big room in the company of colleagues with their heads shaven as if for the guillotine; colleagues with bloodless hands who talked pretentiously, monocle in eye, about aesthetics; colleagues dressed in correct and sinister fashion, like a Baudelaire or my barrister Doumerc.

*Sunday, 17 December*

It really is unwise to read what one is writing to one's literary friends. I read out to Zola the passage describing the walk of my prostitute Élisa *doing her beat*, and now I find the same walk in his novel, if not entirely cribbed, most certainly inspired by my reading.[1] In another setting he uses exactly the same effects: the darkness, the pitiful shadow she trails behind her. He even uses the phrase: 'But listen to me, Monsieur!'—a phrase used in the Saint-Honoré district but not on the Chaussée-Clignancourt.

*Thursday, 21 December*

Dr. Camus was talking to me today about the anatomy of the Parisienne, of the society woman, saying how little life there was in her body. In this connexion he told me that during a smallpox epidemic in Paris a few years ago he had been called to a great house where a score of young women had decided to have themselves revaccinated. 'You know,' said the doctor, 'pricking those arms of theirs was like sticking a needle into parchment. But after those ladies, it was decided to revaccinate the chambermaids, and that was quite another matter. The steel went into flesh as if into a juicy apple. Yes, a juicy apple. . . .'

*Wednesday, 27 December*

Today, with my book *La Fille Élisa* practically finished, the novel with which I wish to take my leave of imagination has

---

[1] In Zola's novel *L'Assommoir*, which was serialized by the *République des lettres* from July 1876 to January 1877 before being published by Charpentier.

suddenly begun to take shape in my mind. I should like to create two acrobats, two brothers who would love each other as we loved each other, my brother and I. They would put their spinal cords together in a lifelong attempt to perform an impossible feat which would represent for them what the solution of a scientific problem would represent for a scientist. In the meantime I should give a great many details on the childlike character of the younger and the brotherly love, mingled with a little fatherly solicitude, of the elder. The elder would be strength, the younger, grace, with a certain plebeian poetry in his nature which would find its outlet in the sort of imaginative quality that the English artiste brings to an acrobatic feat.

At last the means of performing the trick, which technical difficulties had rendered impossible for a long time, would be discovered. That day, the vengeance of a bare-back rider, whose love had been spurned by the younger brother, would bring about its failure. Naturally this woman would have only an incidental part in the story. The two brothers would have a religion of the muscles which would make them abstain from women and anything else which might reduce their strength.

The younger brother would break both his thigh-bones in the unsuccessful trick; and the day it was realized that he would never perform again, his brother would abandon the profession so as not to break his heart. Here I should introduce all the moral suffering I saw in my brother when he felt that his brain was incapable of further activity.

However, the love of his profession would survive in the elder brother, and when his brother was asleep he would get up to perform his tricks by himself in the attic, by the light of a couple of candles. One night his brother would get up and drag himself along to the attic, and the other, turning round, would see him standing silently there with tears running down his cheeks. Then he would hurl the trapeze out of the window and throw himself into his brother's arms, and the two of them would stay locked in a tender and tearful embrace.

Something very short, built entirely on feeling and picturesque detail.[1]

---

[1] *Les Frères Zemganno*, published by Charpentier in April 1879, would follow the outline given here in every particular.

*Sunday, 30 December*

I finished *La Fille Élisa* this morning. Nothing remains but to re-read it. I had originally intended to develop it much further, to inter-lard the manuscript with a host of little discoveries I should have made in the worlds of prison and prostitution; but perhaps that would have been overdoing it. And then too, the thought that the book may be prosecuted makes me disinclined to do any more to it. I have not the courage to go on working on a book threatened with suppression.

# 1877

An Englishman called to see M. Renan.

'Monsieur Renan?'

'You are speaking to him, Monsieur.'

'Well, Monsieur, do you know whether the Bible says that the hare is a ruminant?'

'I'm afraid I don't, Monsieur. . . . But we can soon find out.'

Renan got out a Hebrew Bible and looked through the Mosaic precepts: 'Thou shalt not eat. . . . Thou shalt not eat the hare, because it ruminates.'[1]

'Yes, it's perfectly true, the Bible says that it is a ruminant.'

'Me very pleased!' said the Englishman, who spoke atrocious French. 'I am not an astronomer, I am not a geologist. The things I do not know are none of my business. I am a naturalist. Now since the Bible says that the hare is a ruminant, and since that is untrue, the Bible is not a book of revelation. . . . Me very pleased!'

And away he went, relieved at one fell swoop of his religiosity. All very English. . . .

*Monday, 12 February*

At Hugo's this evening.

He said that he had never been ill, that he had never caught anything, that he had never suffered from anything except an anthrax, a carbuncle on the back which had kept him indoors for seventeen days. After which, to use his expression, he had been *cauterized* and nothing could affect him, neither heat nor cold nor drenching rain. He had the impression that he was *invulnerable*.

With the stops, pauses, and stresses in his conversation, and with the oracular tone in which he says the simplest things, the great man tires, wearies, taxes the attention of his audience.

[1] Leviticus xi. 6.

*Tuesday, 14 February*

The wife of the presiding judge of a provincial law-court said to Flaubert the other day: 'We are so happy: my husband hasn't had a single acquittal in the whole of this session.'

When one thinks of all that lies behind that remark!

*Sunday, 18 February*

At Popelin's today, Flaubert read his story *Hérodias* to the Princess. This reading made me sad at heart. The fact is, I would like Flaubert to obtain a success, which his morale and his health need so badly. His story certainly contains some good things, some colourful scenes, some delicate epithets; but what a lot of theatrical tricks, and what a lot of modern feelings stuck into that gaudy mosaic of archaic notes! For all the reader's bellowing, the whole thing struck me as a playful exercise in Romantic archaeology.

*Monday, 19 February*

This evening Flaubert, while paying tribute to his colleague's genius, attacked the prefaces, the doctrines, the naturalist professions of faith, in a word all the rather flamboyant humbug with which Zola helps along the sale of his books. Zola replied roughly to this effect: 'You, you had private means which allowed you to remain independent of a good many things. But I had to earn my living with nothing but my pen; I had to go through the mill of journalism and write all sorts of shameful stuff; and it has left me with—how shall I put it?—a certain taste for charlatanism. . . . I consider the word *Naturalism* as ridiculous as you do, but I shall go on repeating it over and over again, because you have to give things new names for the public to think that they are new. . . . You know, I divide what I write into two parts. On the one hand there are my novels, on which I shall be judged and on which I wish to be judged; and on the other hand there are my articles for the *Bien public*, for Russia and for Marseilles, which are just so much charlatanism to puff my books. . . . First of all I took a nail and with a blow of the hammer I drove it one inch into the public's brain; then with a second blow I drove it two inches in. . . . Well, that hammer of mine is the journalism I write myself around my novels.'

*Wednesday, 21 March*

Today *La Fille Élisa* was published. I went to Charpentier's to sign the review copies, with clerks constantly putting their heads round the door and shouting: 'So-and-so, who ordered fifty, wants a hundred. . . . Can you let What's-his-name have fifteen? . . . Marpon wants his stock made up to a thousand.' He wanted to have the books hidden away in case the novel was impounded. And in all the noise and bustle and hurly-burly of this frantic send-off, I wrote my dedications, full of the excitement of a gambler staking his whole fortune on a single throw, and wondering whether this success, taking shape in such an unexpected, unhoped-for fashion, was going to be nipped in the bud by a ministerial prosecution, wondering whether this striking recognition of my talent, coming to me before my death, was not going to be spoilt by yet another stroke of that misfortune which has pursued my brother and myself all our lives. And with every head that came round the door, with every letter that was brought in, I expected the dreadful announcement: 'The book has been impounded!'

On my way to the station to catch the train back to Auteuil, I experienced one of those childish pleasures which sometimes come to an author. I saw a gentleman with my book in his hand who, unable to wait until he got home, was reading it in the street, in the drizzling rain.

*Saturday, 31 March*

A sort of irritated boredom comes from waiting, one's mouth full of gall, for a letter or a ring at the door to bring news of disaster; there are moments when one would like to have done with it and one almost longs for the cruel certainty of catastrophe.

I really am the only one to have successes like that of *Henriette Maréchal* or that of *La Fille Élisa*, successes in which all one's legitimate pleasure in the triumph the work has obtained, or, if you like, the stir it has created, is poisoned by hissing or by the threat of prosecution.

It is exciting and exhilarating all the same, the crude success, the insolent exhibition of one's own book, beside which all the rest might not even exist. I have just seen a big bookshop on a new boulevard which has nothing on show except *La Fille Élisa*, displaying in every one of its windows, to the people who stop outside, my name, my name alone.

Come now, no more of this bourgeois anxiety, this stupid apprehension! I have written a fine book, come what may. . . . Yes, whatever they may say, I believe that my talent has grown through suffering and sorrow. . . . Yes, my brother and I have inaugurated a literary movement which is destined to carry all before it, a movement which will be at least as great as the Romantic movement. . . . And if I live a few more years and can rise from humble subjects and lower-class settings to a distinguished reality to which I can apply my *cruel analysis*, then tradition will be dead and buried, and idiotic conventionality done for.

*Monday, 16 April*

This evening Huysmans, Céard, Hennique, Paul Alexis, Octave Mirbeau, Guy de Maupassant, the young men of realism or naturalism, acclaimed us, Flaubert, Zola, and myself, as the three masters of modern literature, in the course of an exceptionally gay, cordial dinner. This is the new literary army taking shape.[1]

*Tuesday, 17 April*

We were talking this evening about the implacability of the Germans, and the impossibility of touching the hearts of those hard, inaccessible men. Whereupon Cherbuliez told me that this was not so, that there was a quarter-of-an-hour when a German could be induced to make concessions: the quarter-hour between the dessert of a dinner and the tenth puff at a cigar. Saint-Vallier had told him that it was at that moment, and that moment only, that he

---

[1] This dinner, often regarded as marking the foundation of the Naturalist movement, was held at the Restaurant Trapp, on the corner of the Rue Saint-Lazare and the Passage Tivoli. The hosts, with the exception of Mirbeau, were disciples of Zola's who were in the habit of meeting at his house every Thursday. The most devoted of them and the only one to remain faithful to Zola and Naturalism, Alexis, had already publicized the dinner in the *République des lettres* of 13 April 1877, announcing that the menu would consist of: Potage purée Bovary, Truite saumonée à la fille Élisa, Poularde truffée à la Saint-Antoine, Artichaut au cœur simple, Parfait 'naturaliste', Vins de Coupeau, Liqueurs de l'Assommoir. The susceptible Goncourt cannot have failed to notice that this menu contained only one reference to his own work compared with three to Flaubert's and three to Zola's.

had been able to secure what he had secured in the course of his negotiations.[1]

*Saturday, 5 May*

Yesterday, at the dinner given on the occasion of Turgenev's departure for Russia, we talked about love, about the love that is depicted in books.

I said that so far love had not been studied scientifically in the novel and that we had presented only its poetic aspects. Zola, who had brought the conversation round to this subject, in order to pick our brains for his new book,[2] asserted that love was not a special feeling, that it did not affect people as overwhelmingly as it was said to, that the phenomena you found in it were also to be found in friendship, patriotism and so on, and that the greater intensity of love was due simply to the prospect of copulation.

Turgenev replied that this was not true, that love was a feeling with a special *colour* of its own, and that Zola was on the wrong tack if he would not recognize this colour, this difference of quality. He said that love had an effect on a man that no other feeling produced, and that a person who was really in love felt as if he had been born again. He spoke of a heaviness of the heart which had nothing human about it. He spoke of the eyes of the first woman he had ever loved as of something quite intangible and entirely divorced from materiality. . . .

There is one unfortunate thing about all this, and that is that neither Flaubert, for all his bragging about such matters, nor Zola, nor I have ever been seriously in love and that we are all incapable of describing love. Only Turgenev could do it, but he lacks precisely that critical judgement that we could bring to the task if we had been in love as he has.

*Saturday, 4 August*

Set off today for the Château de Jean-d'Heurs, where I have been invited by my cousin Fédora and her husband Léon Rattier.

---

[1] The negotiations on the evacuation of the German forces from France, conducted by Saint-Vallier in July 1871, with General von Manteuffel.

[2] *Une Page d'amour*, which was to be published in June 1878.

As I came in sight of Bar-le-Duc, my mind went back to the time when I came to that town as a youth, full of that tender feeling which follows two or three years after the passionate enthusiasm of First Communion. And I remembered that sweet little solicitor's wife—married, upon my word, less than three months before—who was always late and kept me behind so that I might accompany her to the shooting-lodge in the woods. She complained of suffering from a heart ailment; and as there was a steep slope to be climbed before one got to the woods, she used to get me to put my hand on her uncorseted heart, to show me how fast it was beating. With the result that before setting off on my last visit to the lodge I had sworn to myself that I was going to seduce the solicitor's wife in the woods. But her sister-in-law, who happened to be a cousin of mine, read so clearly in our eyes, when we arrived at the lodge, a determination on my part to try my luck, and perhaps a desire on her part to yield, that she stayed with us all day.

The next morning I left to return to Paris and school; and a fortnight later the solicitor's wife was the not entirely innocent cause of my losing my virginity, one free Sunday, with Mme Charles, a huge woman with a rhomboidal torso fitted with two little arms and two little legs, which, in bed, made her look like a crab on its back.

*Paris, Friday, 31 August*

There is something sad about a man who has reached the summit of the fame a writer can acquire in his lifetime. He is as it were uninterested in his career. He knows that a new book leaves him where he is and takes him no further forward. Out of a certain artistic pride, out of the love of beauty that is in him, he goes on doing his best, but the whiplash of success no longer has the power to drive him on. He is rather like a soldier who has reached the highest rank he can attain in a particular service and who goes on performing brilliant feats of arms without any enthusiasm but simply because he is a gallant fighter.

*Friday, 28 December*

Yesterday at Bing's, the dealer in Japanese curios, I saw a tall, very pale, shapeless woman, wrapped up in an interminable waterproof, turning everything over, moving everything around, and every now and then putting something on the floor, saying: 'That's for my sister.' I did not recognize the woman, but I had a vague feeling that she was a woman known to me and the public. Then her escort came towards me holding out his hand: it was Griffon, the brother-in-law of Courmont, whom people accuse of making him accept a hundred thousand francs a year. It is strange how today, in that grey, rainy light, Sarah Bernhardt reminded me of those gaunt convalescents who, in a hospital, go past you in the gloom of a winter afternoon to join in the prayers at the far end of the ward.

# 1878

Women and love, those are always the subjects of conversation among intelligent men eating and drinking together.

The conversation this evening was filthy and depraved to begin with, and Turgenev listened to Daudet with the fascinated astonishment of a Barbarian who makes love only in the most straightforward manner.

When we asked him what was the keenest amorous sensation he had ever known, he thought for a little while and then said: 'I was very young at the time and a virgin, with all the longings a boy has at fifteen. At my mother's house there was a pretty chambermaid with a stupid face; but as you know, there are some faces to which stupidity lends a certain grandeur. It was a damp, dull, rainy day, one of those erotic days Daudet has just described in *Le Nabab*. Dusk had begun to fall. I was walking round the garden when suddenly that girl came straight up to me and took hold of me—and remember that I was her master and she was just a serf—took hold of me by the hair at the back of my neck and said: "Come!" What followed was a sensation similar to the sensations we have all of us experienced so many times. But that gentle gripping of my hair with that single word sometimes comes back to me, and just thinking about it makes me happy.'

Then we talked about the state of mind that follows on the satisfaction of physical desire. Some spoke of sadness, others of relief. Flaubert declared that he danced in front of his mirror. 'With me something very peculiar happens', said Turgenev. 'After it is all over I enter into communication again with the things around me. . . . Things take on again a reality which they lacked a moment before. I feel myself once more, and the table in the room becomes a table again. . . . Yes, the relations between myself and Nature are restored and re-established.'

Zola, with his coarse hair falling straight down over his forehead, and looking like a brutish Venetian, a Tintoretto turned house-painter, Zola who had said nothing so far, suddenly complained of being haunted by the desire to go to bed with a young girl—not a child, but a girl who was not yet a woman. 'Yes,' he said, 'it frightens me sometimes. . . . I see the Assize Court and all the rest of it.'

*Thursday, 21 February*

The troopers blocking the streets, the illuminated façade, the policemen in leather breeches lined up among the flowers in the anterooms, the guard with his halberd, in a word all the accessories of an official reception under the *ancien régime* were there at a reception being given by the present-day Minister of Education.

There was a crowd, a throng, a mob of bemedalled chests, in the midst of which Bardoux seemed as it were crushed under the weight of his honours and the satisfaction of his pride.

I stayed for a few minutes and came away with a sort of disgust at the whole affair. There, in that atmosphere, the most intelligent people suddenly took on an official quality which seemed to cut them off from mankind; your friends ceased to be your friends, and no longer belonged to you in their stupid pride, their ecstatic vanity.

*Friday, 22 February*

Bardoux, who was dining this evening at Charpentier's, told us about a curious dinner-party he had attended at Axenfeld's house.

All the guests were a little drunk and in their intoxication started talking about the uncertainty of the death that lay in store for each one of them. Axenfeld, who was ailing at the time, remained silent for a while, then suddenly stood up and exclaimed, drowning the babble of conversation: 'I shall die of a haemorrhage of the brain.' And he proceeded to describe his death exactly as it took place. After that, turning to the guest on his right, he said: 'You are going to die of such-and-such a disease and you are going to die like this', giving him a detailed and almost malicious account of his final sufferings. Then, turning to the guest on his left, he furnished him with a horrifying forecast of his death. . . . Everybody sobered up completely.

*Saturday, 30 March*

I have never known a man so hard to please, so dissatisfied with the enormity of his good fortune as Zola. Charpentier was telling me that he had spent a whole dinner complaining, groaning, and grumbling after Charpentier had told him that he was printing 15,000 copies of his *Page d'amour*. In the midst of all this he had been shown the genealogical tree of the Rougon family done by Régamey. The drawing of this tree had given Régamey enormous trouble, it seems, but it did not satisfy Zola, who had complained that one branch was a little higher than another and had said almost tearfully that nobody ever did what he wanted.

*Wednesday, 3 April*

House-warming dinner at Zola's.

A study in which the young master works on a massive Portuguese throne in Brazilian rosewood, a bedroom with a carved four-poster bed and twelfth-century stained-glass in the window, tapestries showing greenish saints on the walls and ceilings, altar frontals over the doors, a whole houseful of ecclesiastical bric-à-brac: all this makes a somewhat eccentric setting for the author of *L'Assommoir*.

He gave us a very choice, very tasty dinner, a real gourmet's dinner, including some grouse whose scented flesh Daudet compared to an old courtesan's flesh marinaded in a bidet.

Flaubert, stimulated by the food and a little drunk, reeled off, to the accompaniment of oaths and obscenities, the whole series of his ferocious, truculent truisms about the *bôrgeois*. And while he was speaking, I saw an expression of melancholy surprise on the face of my neighbour, Mme Daudet, who seemed pained, upset, and at the same time disillusioned by the man's gross, intemperate unbuttoning of his nature.

At a remark by Mme Charpentier, who spoke as a shopkeeper of the benefit to us and our books of introducing politicians into her drawing-room, Zola launched out into a violent attack on them, saying with some truth that they were our natural enemies and that he could see their hatred of us in their wives' eyes. . . . Meanwhile Charpentier, who was suffering from influenza and slumped in an armchair in another room, was murmuring: 'He's an amazing man! He would like to have nobody but himself in the drawing-room!'

In the evening, the band of toadies invaded the little flat; and the archaic knick-knacks in the drawing-room and bedroom soon disappeared in the smoke of the cigars and cigarettes of the Naturalist school.

*Sunday, 14 April*

We were talking of the joy that comes from a mad, exaggerated, childish belief in oneself. In this connexion Zola recalled seeing Courbet planted in front of one of his pictures, stroking his beard, laughing uproariously and saying: 'This is a funny painting. . . .' And the word *funny*, in the mouth of the modern Jordaens, signified *sublime*.

*Tuesday, 23 April*

The critics may say what they like about Zola, they cannot prevent us, my brother and myself, from being the John-the-Baptists of modern neurosis.

*Wednesday, 24 April*

Young Houssaye was present at the first meeting between Renan and Hugo. He told me something which reveals a scurvy fellow in Renan. The author of the *Vie de Jésus*, who had been brought along by Saint-Victor and then deserted by his mahout, found himself alone in the anteroom with the two Houssayes when the time came for him to go. When Hugo held his hand out to Renan to say good-bye, Renan bent down and kissed it. Is there not something there of the seminarist kissing the hand of his bishop?

*Monday, 6 May*

*Le Bouton de rose* was a disaster. The audience, sympathetic to begin with during the first act, got angry during the second and booed the third, which it nearly prevented from finishing. And it was absolutely within its rights. It is a bad play, without originality, without humour, without wit, without even the coarse drollery of a farce. I really cannot understand how a fellow with the ambition to be the leader of a school can—without being impelled by the need for money—allow a theatre to put on something so ordinary, so similar to what the poorest vaudevillist turns out. No, my good friend Zola really has no pride in his work, and he does not understand the importance, for the part which he wants to play in literature, of having a corpus of works in which everything is of quality.

There is nothing quite so pitiful as the failure of a play written by a friend, whom one can neither defend nor support. I did not want to give the impression of deserting Zola and so I allowed him to take me to Véfour's. The poor fellow, completely shattered, let his wife order the meal, and sat with his thoughts elsewhere, oblivious of the conversation going on around him, his pale face bent over his plate and one hand mechanically turning his table-knife round and round with the blade uppermost. Now and then a disconnected sentence would fall from his lips. He said: 'I don't really care, but it alters my whole programme of work. . . . I shall have to write *Nana* next. . . . The fact is, a flop makes you sick of the theatre. . . . *La Curée* will have to wait, I'm going back to the novel. . . .' And he went on twiddling his knife.

His wife, who was not so completely demoralized, ate and drank, revealing the irritation of her nervous system only by some bitter jibe at one of her husband's young disciples, picking for instance on poor Alexis, whom she called her whipping-boy.

It was a dismal supper-party, what with the awkward silences, the comforting remarks made in an unconvincing tone, the wife's recriminations about the cuts Zola should have made, and, in a corner, the shrill yelping of Manet's ugly, cracked voice.

Finally it was decided to let the author go to bed. Coming downstairs, he said to Mme Charpentier, who was walking in front of him with the train of her dress trailing behind her: 'Be careful how you go: I'm not very steady on my legs tonight.' He added: 'Highly-strung people like me . . .' And he left his sentence unfinished.

*Tuesday, 14 May*

Degas, coming out of a house this evening, complained that one no longer saw any sloping shoulders in society. And he was right:

that is a sign of physical breeding which is disappearing from the
new generations of women.

*Monday, 27 May*

I dined today with Daudet and his wife, who is so pregnant that
one almost expected her to give birth at dessert.

He spoke to me about his book *Les Rois en exil*, a book with a
really delightful theme in that it lends itself to a poetic, ironic
realism. He intends to make the tutor of his king a turncoat, the son
of a democrat, whom two Franciscans seek out in a student hotel in
the Latin Quarter with the staircase full of tarts in slippers. If it is
well done, this should have a subtle, magnificent modernity.

But all of a sudden Daudet broke off to say: 'You know, it really
is a shame: you have put me off my stroke. Yes, you, Flaubert, and
my wife. . . . I haven't got a style of my own. No, no, that's certain. . . . People born the other side of the Loire don't know how
to write French prose. . . . What have I got then? Imagination.
You've no idea what there is in my head. . . . Well, but for you, I
shouldn't have worried about that bitch of a language and I should
have just hatched out my stories in blissful peace of mind.'

*Sunday, 8 September*

It is not the length of time, as Flaubert imagines, that makes the
superiority of a work, but the quality of the passion one brings to
the writing of it. What does the repetition of a word or a syntactical
error matter if the theme is new, if the concept is original, and if,
here and there, there is an epithet or a turn of phrase which by itself
is worth a hundred pages of impeccable, commonplace prose?

*Saturday, 21 September*

Flaubert, on condition that one leaves the centre of the stage to
him and resigns oneself to catching cold from all the windows he
keeps throwing open, is a very pleasant companion. He has a jovial
gaiety and a childlike laugh which are contagious; and everyday
contact develops in him a certain gruff affectionateness which is not
without charm.

*Monday, 23 September*

Mlle Abbatucci told me some curious things today about the home-life of the sculptor Triqueti, who owns a very fine château near Montargis. This man, who is steeped in piety and spends all his time in the chapel, has an aged wife with a taste, a positive passion for procuring. She used to invite all the loving couples of the neighbourhood—this at the time when Mme de l'Aubespine-Sully was the sub-prefect's wife—to the château, and instal them in little apartments communicating with one another by a series of little spiral staircases.

Her mania for ruining young women was so well known that her nephew, however much his aunt might insist, never allowed his wife to sleep at the château; and whenever the old lady invited her out for a walk, he promptly put his gloves on to accompany them.

*Sunday, 29 September*

The company at the Princess's is always more or less the same. The women are Mme de Galbois, Mlle Abbatucci, and little Mlle La Tour, who has now been completely accepted. The men are Popelin; Benedetti, who enjoys the influence over the Princess of a man who has occupied a high official position; old General Chauchard, an excellent man but suffering from the disadvantage among the fair sex of being reputed to be a virgin whose greatest amorous exploit was winning a game of badminton in fifteen hundred points; Blanchard the naturalist, who talks with an unbearable stammer and whose charm I cannot for the life of me explain; and the painter Anastasi, whose presence at Saint-Gratien all summer does honour to the Princess's heart and to the kindness of the ladies of the house, who give their arm to the blind man, cut his food up for him, and pour out his wine. And finally there are the two Girauds, who arrive every Saturday morning and go off again on Monday evening.

But the number of guests who are not old acquaintances of the Princess's is constantly diminishing; she has somehow managed to offend a great many of them with blunders like this. The other day Mme Guimet called on her with her husband. The couple were still behind the big screen in the drawing-room when the Princess exclaimed: 'Can anyone tell me why on earth she has brought along her calf's-head?' She was referring to the husband, who is extremely vain of his looks. She will always be the woman who made an irreconcilable foe of the Empress by saying that 'she had no more heart than c . . .'. And then, there is no disguising the fact, the approach of her sixtieth birthday and the death of loving adoration around her result now and then in melancholy moods, sharp remarks, and little fits of anger which alienate those whom affection does not incline to forgiveness.

*Monday, 30 September*

What a mine of pretty details, what a storehouse of rare and unknown human documents Mlle Abbatucci is! If I were a younger man, I should be tempted to marry her, in order to write novels about the girls and women of our time such as do not exist and never will exist.

Here is a scene which occurred a week before the death of Mlle Benedetti, who died at the age of sixteen or seventeen and who, as she puts it, was perversity in person. Mlle Abbatucci had been a close friend of hers, seeing her practically every day during her childhood; but since then a coolness had sprung up between them and she had not seen her for eight years when she suddenly received a letter in which her old childhood friend asked to see her again.

Marie Abbatucci felt a certain reluctance to accept the invitation; but her mother persuaded her to do so, by telling her that she knew for certain that she had only a few days to live. She found Mlle Benedetti in a summerhouse in the garden where a mattress had been laid on the floor on which she was rolling like a worm cut in two, in the grip of agonizing pain. Beside her there was a piece of mouldy cheese in which Marie could see the maggots and which she nibbled at from time to time.

The dying girl looked up as she came in, gazed at her friend for a long time without saying anything, contemplating the life and health that were in her, and finally said:

'We are going to the Théâtre des Italiens.'

'Oh!' said Marie.

'Why, does that surprise you?' asked the dying girl.

They went into the dining-room for dinner. During the meal Mlle Benedetti sat stiff as a ramrod in her place, without eating anything, until she slipped from her chair and fell in a faint on the floor.

She was made to breathe some smelling-salts. Coming to, she returned to her place at table, without eating any more than before.

Straight after dinner, she took Marie to her room and started pacing up and down like a wounded animal, stopping now and then to hurl angry phrases of this sort at her friend:

'You have never been in love. . . . You don't know what it is to be in love. . . . You haven't any senses. . . . Love doesn't mean anything to you. . . .'

And as she uttered these phrases a kind of fury entered into her which made Mlle Abbatucci afraid that she was going to hit her or bite her.

Then, all of a sudden, she plunged her head right into a big basin of water, rang for her maid and quietly allowed herself to be dressed.

And they went off to the Théâtre des Italiens, where she fainted again twice in the course of the evening.

Eight or ten days later she was dead.

*Monday, 14 October*

Today Mlle Abbatucci told me about her childhood and I let her talk, my mind working out the plan of a novel which would describe the life of a girl under the Second Empire.[1]

From the age of five or six, she was allowed to give a dinner every Wednesday, at the Ministry of Justice in the Place Vendôme, to her little friends. She gave me an amusing account of the terror she had felt one day when one of her guests, who had got drunk, suddenly started to undress. The young mistress of the house thought that the ministry was going to collapse.

From that age too, she could take the ministry box any night of the week, in any theatre where children were allowed, and used to fill it with her little playmates of both sexes.

Her grandfather worshipped her and would grant anything to his granddaughter. When he went to attend the Council of Ministers at Saint-Cloud, he would take his granddaughter with him in his carriage, to go through her lessons with her. And on one occasion, when the Empress wanted to appoint Saint-Albin a deputy public prosecutor and the Keeper of the Seals objected in a peremptory

[1] This novel, *Chérie*, published in the spring of 1884, was to include the material given here by Mlle Abbatucci.

manner, the Empress said to him rather peevishly: 'If Marie asked you for the same thing, would you begrudge it to her as you have begrudged it to me?'

*Friday, 25 October*

A profound remark made by a woman to a man talking of the impossibility of arousing love any more once one's hair had turned white: 'Women never look at, or at least never see, the men they love.'

*Wednesday, 20 November*

A sculptor who has spent several years in England was telling one of his friends today that over there he had found the most beautiful women's busts and torsos that he had ever seen, but that the women lacked a flexible spine and that it was impossible to obtain from them what any French model could give you, a twisting, a turning, a gracious movement of the body, the inflexion of a Hebe offering Jupiter his cup.

*Tuesday, 3 December*

At dinner today Francis Magnard recounted the little cause which had brought about the fall of the Vendôme Column.

A tart called Ménier or Magnier who enjoyed a certain notoriety had been abandoned by her rich protector on account of her relations with an engineer. During the Commune, finding herself extremely short of cash, she blamed her poverty on her lover, and he racked his brains to discover some way of making money. He had the idea of applying the system of the bevel-cut to the column, a system without which it would have been virtually impossible to demolish it, and as a reward for his idea he was paid a total of 6,000 francs which he gave his mistress.

*Tuesday, 10 December*

Sad news of poor Flaubert. It seems that he is completely ruined, and that the people for whom he sacrificed his fortune begrudge him

the very cigars he smokes. 'My uncle is a strange man,' his niece is
reported to have said; 'he does not know how to endure adversity.'


*Thursday, 12 December*

Banville told me the other day that Hugo, at the end of a day's
work, had wanted to pay homage to Venus and had found himself
incapable of doing so. This fiasco, happening for the first time to the
man of iron, had plunged him into profound melancholy; he had
seen it as a sign of approaching death.

# 1879

*Wednesday, 8 January*

Labiche told us this evening that at Murger's funeral there was an argument between Thierry and Maquet as to the order of the graveside orations. And as Thierry insisted on speaking first, getting as close as possible to the open grave, Maquet said to him, in the midst of all the mourners who imagined that the two orators were exchanging polite remarks: 'If you keep on, I'll shove you in the hole!' Thierry, without a spark of heroism in his character, gave up the idea of speaking first.

*Saturday, 18 January*

The first night of *L'Assommoir*.

A sympathetic, appreciative audience, in which a hidden current of hostility did not dare come to the surface. How different one generation is from another! Thinking sadly of my brother, I could not refrain from saying to Lafontaine, whom I met in one of the corridors: 'This isn't the audience we had for *Henriette Maréchal*!' Everything was accepted and applauded, and there were only two or three hisses at the final tableau from members of the audience who did their best to remain hidden from sight: this was the only element of protest in the general enthusiasm.

According to his friends, Zola wrote the whole play himself, except for a few comic scenes which he left to Busnach. If this is true, if he really is the author of the play, then Zola has not yet dared to attempt a theatrical revolution. For the play—setting aside the working-class environment which has already been depicted on the stage a good many times—the play is a concoction of all the old tricks, tirades, and sentimental catch-words of the Boulevard du Temple.

As we were coming away, Zola asked us in a plaintive voice, his nose tiptilted inquiringly, whether the play had really been a success.

He had spent the whole performance in Chabrillat's office, reading some novel or other he had found in his bookcase, not daring to show his face to the actors, whom his miserable expression had discouraged the day before at the dress rehearsal.

*Wednesday, 5 February*

In the way of borrowings, my good friend Zola goes rather far with me.

Yesterday, tidying up some books, I opened a copy of *Germinie Lacerteux*, and this reminded me—quite apart from the large-scale plagiarizing from the book—that my Gautruche is called *Gogo-la-Gaîté* and that his undertaker's mute is called *Bibi-la-Gaîté*, and also that my Gautruche finishes one of his tirades with the words: 'Go to bye-bye, children', while his undertaker's mute finishes the famous speech to Gervaise with the words: 'Go to bye-bye.'

*Sunday, 18 May*

This time I had imagined that the theme of my book and my very age would disarm the critics. But no, I am being slated all along the line. Barbey d'Aurevilly, Pontmartin and the rest are all agreed that *Les Frères Zemganno* is a detestable book, with nothing in it.

Not one of these critics seems to have noticed the originality of my attempt in this novel to move the reader with something other than love, of my substitution of a theme different from that used since the beginning of time.

So I am condemned to being attacked and repudiated until the day I die, and perhaps even for some years after that. I must admit that that creates within me a sort of sadness which takes the form of an aching of the arms and legs, a physical weariness for which sleep is both necessary and desirable.

*Tuesday, 20 May*

I feel in myself a strange, peculiar coolness towards other people, and at the same time a sort of pleasure in my isolation. Perhaps this feeling is due to the commonplace nature of the friendships which surround me.

*Wednesday, 21 May*

How many plays are there in which the ending is not brought about by the intercepting of a letter or the overhearing of a conversation behind a curtain? The whole originality of the modern theatre consists in turning the letter into a telegram and replacing the curtain with something like a lavatory door. It does not add up to a great deal, and the theatre seems to me to be the equivalent, for the human mind, of the tiring activity of a squirrel in a cage.

*Wednesday, 28 May*

The steeplechase between Daudet and Zola. There was a time when Zola's portrait alone was to be seen in all the bookshop windows. Recently, however, Daudet's portrait has begun slipping in beside Zola. . . .

Zola has a band of young faithfuls, whose admiration, enthusiasm, and fervour the cunning novelist feeds and nourishes by placing their work abroad, by getting them well-paid jobs on the papers over which he reigns supreme, in a word by rendering them entirely material services.

*Sunday, 8 June*

Lunched with Flaubert today. He told me that his post has been fixed up. He has been appointed supernumerary keeper at the Bibliothèque Mazarine, at a salary of 3,000 francs which is to be raised in a few months' time. He added that it had really hurt him to be forced to accept this money, and that he had already made arrangements for it to be repaid to the State one day. His brother, who is very rich and dying, is going to make him an allowance of 3,000 francs a year: with that and what he makes from his books he will soon be on his feet again.

*Monday, 9 June*

An error of five centimes, in the accounts for a whole year, five or six years ago, cost the seven employees who handle Rothschild's private fortune five days' and five nights' work.

*Friday, 20 June*

I was coming home from the cemetery—it is the anniversary of my brother's death—and walking idly along among people reading newspapers in the streets without paying any attention to them, when, in the Rue Richelieu, a man—it was Camille Doucet—held out a piece of paper to me with a sad gesture. I read the words: *Death of the Prince Imperial.*[1]

The fate of ancient times, the fate which pursued the family of the Atrides, seems to have revived for this family of Napoleon's.

*Tuesday, 8 July*

Today I went to see the Princess, who according to the papers was about to leave to attend the Prince Imperial's funeral.

I found her alone. Anastasi was ill in bed; Mme de Galbois, Mlle Abbatucci, Benedetti, and Popelin were all in Paris.

The Princess was engrossed in a tapestry. Suddenly, looking up from her work, she asked me in a sharp voice:

'Goncourt, I decided not to go over there, but people say I should. What do you think?'

'But Princess, you cannot possibly stay away!'

'You too. . . . Very well, then. . . . But I sent the Empress a telegram as soon as I learnt of the boy's death and she hasn't acknowledged it. . . . I haven't even had a letter inviting me to the funeral. . . . Don't you consider that extraordinary?'

'Yes, but the invitation may . . .'

'After all, she *holds the corpse!*'

And there followed a ferocious account of how the Empress, instead of praying and weeping all night, was said to be going through the Prince's papers with the Duchesse de Mouchy, who was sleeping in her room.

The Princess added: 'If I come face to face with her I shall say to her: "Well, Madame, now that you have nobody left to kill off, it is time you went back to Spain to dance the *cachucha!*" '

And dwelling on the Empress's meanness, she told me that the Prince had so little money that he had been unable to take any expensive weapons out there, that the two horses he had taken with

---

[1] The Prince Imperial had been killed by Zulu warriors on 1 June 1879 while serving in the British Army.

him had died on the way, that he had not had enough money to buy another one, and that the disobedient horse which he had been unable to remount was an English army horse, an ordinary trooper's horse.

At this point the Parisians arrived, including Benedetti with a paper announcing that Princess Clotilde was going to Chislehurst.[1] This threw the Princess into a state of unbelievable exasperation, and she exclaimed: 'I refuse to play second fiddle. . . . This time my mind is made up, I shall definitely not go! . . . I am going upstairs to write to my brother.'

*Tuesday, 15 July*

'Well, it's all over', said the Princess, coming towards me at a bend in the path where I met her. 'It went very well.'

'And did you see the Empress?'

'Oh, yes, but she didn't say anything to me. . . . It was in a pitch-dark room where you couldn't see a thing. . . . Which means that I don't know whether she was crying or whether she just didn't want to speak to me. . . . Incidentally, she has grown enormously fat. . . . No, she didn't say anything to me. . . . All the same, I do think she might have found something to say . . . something pleasant about our relations in the future. . . . Oh, yes, she did say something! She said: "You know, all his wounds are in front." '

She fell silent and, walking more quickly, said in a hissing voice:

'The bitch! . . . Eugène knows all the servants over there. Well, they told him that life was absolutely impossible for the Prince. He hadn't a penny of his own. He couldn't invite a friend along for dinner. . . . If he ordered a carriage to take him to London, she had the horses unharnessed. . . . Every morning she served up to him all the insults in the French papers, carefully cut out. . . . Little Espinasse told me that when he was over there, she didn't even bid him good morning. . . . No, the poor boy's life was sheer hell. . . . They were furious to see us there: it upset all their plans. . . . The Duchesse de Mouchy tried to prevent me from receiving the Queen of England: I had to tell her that I knew, that I didn't need to take

[1] The Kent home of the exiled imperial family, where Napoleon III had died on 9 January 1873.

lessons from her. . . . The Queen of England, now, she was wonderfully correct and dignified. . . . And she said something delightful to me about Canrobert, whom they hadn't allowed to come: "You must admit, Madame, that your government is neither generous nor diplomatic." '

# 1880

Yesterday Turgenev gave Zola, Daudet, and myself a farewell dinner before leaving for Russia.

This time he is setting off for his native land with a strange feeling of vagueness and uncertainty, a feeling which he says he experienced in his early youth during a crossing of the Baltic when the ship was completely enveloped in fog and his only companion was a she-monkey chained to the deck.

Then, while we were still on our own, he started talking about the life he will be leading in six weeks' time, about his country house, about the chicken soup which is the only dish his cook knows how to prepare, and about the conferences he has on a little balcony, almost level with the ground, with the peasants who are his neighbours.

Shrewd observer and clever actor that he is, he gave me an impersonation of the three generations of peasants in Russia today: the old peasants, whose loud, empty talk, full of monosyllables and adverbs, he imitated for my benefit; the sons of those peasants, who chatter endlessly and elegantly; and the grandsons, a silent, diplomatic, secretly destructive generation. And when I said that he must find these conversations boring, he said that this was not the case, and that it was astonishing how much one could learn sometimes from these uneducated people whose minds went on working unceasingly in solitude and peace.

Zola arrived, leaning on a stick: he had a rheumatic pain in the thigh which gave every sign of being sciatica. He told us that when *Nana* began appearing in the *Voltaire*, the style struck him as so detestable that he was seized with an attack of purism and started rewriting the whole novel; so that after working all morning on what still remained to be written, he spent the evening rewriting the instalment which had appeared that day. And this work had killed him, absolutely killed him.

Finally Daudet arrived, with the success of the previous day's performance of *Le Nabab* written all over his face.

And we sat down to dinner, in the midst of this remark by Zola, which kept coming back like a refrain: 'I really think that I shall have to change my method! . . . It strikes me as worn out, utterly worn out.'

The meal began gaily enough, but then Turgenev started talking about a constriction of the heart which had happened to him a few nights before, together with the nightmare vision of a large brown stain which, half-way between sleep and wakefulness, he had recognized as Death. Whereupon Zola began enumerating the morbid phenomena which made him afraid that he would never be able to finish the eleven novels which he still had to write. And Daudet said: 'As for me, there was a week when I felt so full of life that I could almost have hugged the trees. Then, one night, without any warning, without any pain, I felt something sticky and tasteless in my mouth'—and he made a gesture as if taking a slug out of his mouth—'and after that clot, blood came gushing out three times, filling my bed. . . . Yes, it was a torn lung. . . . And since then, I can't spit in my handkerchief without looking to see if there isn't some of that damned blood there!'

And each of us in turn spoke of the fear of death that haunted us.

*Easter Sunday, 28 March*

Today we set off, Daudet, Zola, Charpentier, and I, to dine and stay the night at Flaubert's house at Croisset.

Zola was as gay as an auctioneer's clerk going to make an inventory, Daudet as excited as a henpecked husband out on a spree, and Charpentier as merry as a student who can see a succession of beers coming his way. As for myself, I was happy at the prospect of embracing Flaubert once more.

Zola's happiness was marred by a great preoccupation, the question whether, taking an express train, he would be able to piddle in Paris, at Mantes, and at Vernon. The number of times the author of *Nana* piddles or at least tries to piddle is quite incredible.

Daudet, a little tipsy from the porter he had drunk with his lunch, started talking about *Chien Vert* and his affair with that mad, crazy, demented female, whom he had inherited from Nadar: a mad affair, drenched in absinthe and given a dramatic touch every now and then by a few knife-thrusts, the marks of which he showed us on one of his hands. He gave us a humorous account of his wretched life with that woman, whom he lacked the courage to leave and to whom he remained attached to some extent by the pity he felt for her vanished beauty and the front tooth she had broken on a stick of barley-sugar. When he decided to get married and had to break with her, he was afraid of the scene she would create in a house where other people were living, and took her into the heart of the Meudon woods under the pretext of treating her to a dinner in the country. There, among the bare trees, when he told her that it was all over, the woman rolled at his feet in the mud and snow, bellowing like a young heifer and crying: 'I shan't be nasty to you any more, I'll be your slave. . . .' Then they had supper together, with the woman eating like a workman, in a sort of stupid bewilderment. This story was followed by the account of his liaison with a charming young thing called Rosa, and the description of a night of passion they spent in a room at Orsay shared with seven or eight companions who in the morning cast a slight chill over the poetry and frenzy of their love by piddling at length into their chamberpots and farting noisily. . . . A love that was rather frightening in its unhealthiness and vulgarity.[1]

'Here we are, look, just past the bridge.' It was Zola's voice telling us to look out for his house at Médan. I caught a glimpse of a feudal-looking building which seemed to be standing in a cabbage-patch.

Maupassant came to meet us with a carriage at Rouen station, and soon we were being greeted by Flaubert in a Calabrian hat and a bulky jacket, with his big bottom in a pair of well-creased trousers and his kindly face beaming affectionately.

I had retained only a very sketchy recollection of his property, which is really most attractive. The vast Seine along which the masts of boats which are hidden from sight pass as if at the back of a stage; the tall, splendid trees twisted into tortured forms by the sea breezes; the espalier-shaped park, the long terrace-walk facing due south, the peripatetic path, all make a real writer's home—Flaubert's home —out of what in the eighteenth century was the house of a Bene-dictine community.

---

[1] Nothing else is known about Rosa. *Chien Vert* was Marie Rieu, the model for Daudet's *Sapho*, whom he met soon after his arrival in Paris in 1857 and to whom he remained attached until his marriage ten years later.

The dinner was excellent; there was a cream sauce with the turbot which was something out of this world. We drank a great many wines of all sorts, and spent the whole evening telling each other broad stories which sent Flaubert into peals of childish laughter. He refused to read to us from his novel, saying that he was completely done in. And we went off to sleep in somewhat chilly bedrooms peopled with family busts.

The next morning we got up late and stayed indoors to chat, Flaubert declaring that walking was a useless fag. Then we had lunch and left.

We were at Rouen at two o'clock; we should be in Paris at five: the day was finished. I suggested staying at Rouen, looking round the antique shops, having a good dinner, and returning only in the evening. The others agreed, except for Daudet, who was expected at home for dinner and who had quite possibly espied an interesting young woman in the waiting-room.

We had not gone more than a few yards before we noticed that all the shops were shut; we had forgotten that it was Easter Monday. Finally we saw a curiosity shop with its door ajar: I haggled with the owner over a pair of firedogs which she eventually sold me for 3,000 francs.

Back in the street, we were soon so tired that we went into a café where we played billiards for two-and-a-half hours, sitting in turn on the corners and sighing: 'What a flop!'

At long last it was half-past six, we went to the principal hotel for our good dinner. 'What have you got in the way of fish?' we asked. 'Monsieur, there isn't a single scrap of fish in the whole of Rouen today.' And the solemn head waiter offered us veal cutlets instead.

A pair of firedogs at 3,000 francs by way of a bargain, and a dinner consisting of a poor roast chicken, that was what our day at Rouen brought us; and on top of that the return to the capital of all the Rouen folk living in Paris made the train two hours late. I swear that never again shall I ever go bargain-hunting in the provinces!

*Saturday, 8 May*

'Are you going to Monsieur Flaubert's on Sunday?' Pélagie had just asked me this question when the maid put a telegram on the table containing these two words: *Flaubert dead!*

For some time I was in such a state of agitation that I did not know what I was doing nor in what city I was driving. I felt that a bond, sometimes loosened but always inextricably tied, secretly attached us to one another. And today I recall with a certain emotion the tear trembling at the end of one of his eyelashes when he said good-bye to me on his doorstep six weeks ago.

The fact is, we were the two old champions of the new school, and I feel very lonely today.

*Tuesday, 11 May*

I left for Rouen yesterday with Popelin. At four o'clock we were at Croisset, in that sad house where I did not have the courage to dine.

Mme Commanville spoke to us of dear Flaubert, of his last moments, and of his book, which she believes to be unfinished by ten pages or so.[1] Then, in the middle of our disjointed, disconnected conversation, she told us of a call she had made recently, in order to force Flaubert to take some exercise, a call on a friend living on the other side of the Seine and who that day had had her youngest child installed in a charming pink bassinet on the drawing-room table, a call which had made Flaubert keep on saying all the way home: 'A little thing like that in the house is all that really matters in this world.'

This morning Pouchet took me down a deserted path and said: 'He didn't die from a stroke, he died from an epileptic fit. . . . In his youth, you know, he had had several fits. . . . His travels in the Middle East had so to speak cured him. . . . He didn't have any more for sixteen years. But the worry over his niece's affairs brought the trouble back. . . . And on Saturday he died from an epileptic fit. . . . Yes, with all the symptoms, foam on his lips, and so on. . . . And then his niece wanted to have a cast taken of his hand, but it couldn't be done, the hand was so tightly clenched. . . . Perhaps, if I'd been there to give him half-an-hour's artificial respiration, I could have saved him. . . . I must say it made an impression on me, going into that study of his, with his handkerchief on the table next to his papers, his pipe with the tobacco-ash on the mantelpiece, and

[1] *Bouvard et Pécuchet*, which was to be published in the *Nouvelle Revue* from December 1880 to March 1881 and in book form in May 1881.

the Corneille from which he had read a few passages the day before sticking out from the shelves of the bookcase.'

The funeral procession set off, and we went up a dusty road to a little church—the church where Mme Bovary goes to confession in the spring and where one of the 'little toads' scolded by the Abbé Bournisien was doing acrobatics on the top of the wall of the old cemetery.

What is exasperating about these funerals is the presence of all those journalists with their little scraps of paper in the palm of one hand, on which they jot down the names of people and places, getting them all wrong; and even more exasperating is the presence of that fellow Laffitte of the *Voltaire* who, with 40,000 francs in his pocket, follows the corpse to do business out of it. Among the journalists who arrived this morning I noticed Burty, who had come along to worm his way into this funeral as he worms his way into anything which is likely to yield a profit. He even managed to get hold of one of the tassels of the hearse for a few moments, holding it with one of my black gloves which he had asked me to lend him.

Coming out of the little church, we made our way towards the Rouen cemetery in the bright sunshine, along an interminable road. In the carefree crowd, irritated by the time the funeral was taking, the idea of a little spree began to take root. There was talk of the *barbues à la normande* and the *canetons à l'orange* at Mennechet's, and Burty uttered the word *brothel* with a lecherous wink.

Finally we reached the cemetery, a cemetery full of the scent of hawthorn and dominating the city, hidden in a violet haze which made it look like a city of slate.

Once the holy water had been sprinkled on the coffin, the whole thirsty crowd made off down the hill towards the city, their faces eager and excited. Daudet, Zola, and I refused to join in the feasting which was being planned for this evening, and came home talking reverently about the dead man.


*Friday, 14 May*

Oh, what a sad, heartbreaking funeral Flaubert had on Tuesday —but even sadder is what follows here. . . . The nephew-in-law

who ruined Flaubert is not just a dishonest businessman, but a
crook who took back twenty francs the dead man had asked him
to pay the locksmith, and a cardsharper to boot. As for the
niece, Flaubert's *little darling*, Maupassant says that he cannot make
up his mind about her. She has been, is, and will go on being
an unconscious tool in the hands of her swine of a husband,
who has the power over her that rogues always have over decent
women.

This, then, is what happened after Flaubert's death. Commanville
kept talking all the time about the money to be made out of the
dead man's books, with such peculiar references to our poor friend's
amorous correspondences as to give the impression that he was
quite capable of blackmailing the surviving correspondents. He but-
tered up Maupassant a great deal, at the same time spying on him
and watching his every move like a veritable policeman. This went
on until Monday, when he had to go off to Rouen while Maupassant
and Pouchet put Flaubert's body, which was already decomposing,
in the coffin. On the Tuesday evening, after a dinner at which
Heredia and Maupassant were present and at which, incidentally,
Commanville cut himself seven slices of ham, he took Maupassant
into the little summerhouse in the garden and kept him there for a
good hour, holding his hands in a fake demonstration of affection,
literally keeping him prisoner—with Maupassant, who is no fool,
suspecting that something was up and trying to get away. In the
meantime Mme Commanville had taken Heredia aside and, sitting
beside him on a garden bench, was telling him that Maxime du
Camp had not even sent a telegram, that Osmoy was a harum-
scarum, that Zola and Daudet disliked her, that as for me, she
thought I was a man of honour but she did not know me, and that
in these unhappy circumstances she needed the devotion of a man of
the world who could represent her interests and defend her against
her family; and that woman, whom Maupassant had not seen weeping once, burst into tears in a fit of emotion which brought her head
so curiously close to Heredia's chest that he says he had the impression that if he had made the slightest movement she would have
thrown herself into his arms. And the scene went on, with the
woman taking her glove off and letting her hand rest on the back of
the bench so close to Heredia's mouth that it seemed to be soliciting
a kiss. Was this true love, suddenly invading a woman's torn and

softened heart, for a man whom she had known and desired for some time? Or was it not rather a sort of counterfeit love, which the husband had instructed his wife to simulate in order to capture a young, honest soul, who might be induced by the exciting prospect of possession to get involved in the swindling of the other heirs?

Poor Flaubert! There are machinations and human documents around your corpse out of which you could have made a fine novel of provincial life!

*Tuesday, 7 September*

A sign of the times. Mlle Bourgoin, the day after her wedding, wrote Mlle de La Tour a letter describing her defloration, an extraordinary letter to come from an aristocratic girl. The whole thing is couched in a satirical style, and this is the postscript in which, referring to the seven proofs of his affection which Louis XV gave Marie Leczinska on their wedding night, she has the effrontery to write: 'I can assure you that I have no reason to envy Marie Leczinska. . . . I am not in the least tired; as for him, that is a different matter.'

*Saturday, 11 December*

Daudet has given Heredia the following account of how he was caught out. Thinking that his wife had gone out, and preferring his love-making in the nude, he was completely naked and his companion likewise. The door opened a little way. There was a stifled cry. The door closed again. No mention was made of the incident. Husband and wife spent six months together without a word of explanation. But then the wife started having fainting fits and fell ill. Daudet then ventured an apology. Mme Daudet just replied: 'I felt like throwing myself out of the window, but I thought of our child. . . . But I warn you that if it happens again I shall kill myself.' She is a Bretonne and quite capable of doing that. And Daudet added: 'That's what comes of being caught out, my dear fellow. I have been stripped of all my power; my wife goes through my post every morning, throwing all the letters from women into the fire; and so on and so forth.'

*Wednesday, 14 December*

Zola came to see me today. He came in with that gloomy, haggard air which is characteristic of his way of entering a room. That man of forty really is a pitiful sight; he looks older than I do.

He slumped into an armchair, complaining peevishly, rather like a child, of kidney trouble, of gravel, of palpitations. Then he talked of the death of his mother and the gap it had made in their home life, speaking with intense pathos and at the same time a touch of fear for himself. And when he started talking literature and outlining his plans, he revealed a dread of not having the time to do it all.

Life really is cleverly arranged so that nobody is happy. Here is a man whose name echoes round the world, who sells a hundred thousand copies of every book he writes, who has perhaps caused a greater stir in his lifetime than any other author, and yet, with his sickly constitution and his melancholy state of mind, he is unhappier than the most abject of failures.

# 1881

*Tuesday, 4 January*

There are times when the style of Gautier and Flaubert strikes me as an ornate but heavy pall draped over a work of art.

*Saturday, 29 January*

It was the first night of *Nana*. I dined at the Nittis's, who had invited me to share their box. At dessert, Degas arrived for dinner, with a funereal air about him. He had just come from the sale of his friend Duranty's effects and spoke of the high prices everything had fetched. Then, in the midst of all his expressions of satisfaction as the dead man's executor, he said to Nittis, in a whining voice accompanied by a murderous sidelong glance:

'Your sketch went for two hundred francs.'

'What!'

'Yes, it was sold right at the end of the sale, everybody was tired, and the bidding had fallen off terribly. I had a lot of friends there to support me. Otherwise . . .'

It was fascinating to watch that hypocrite eating his friends' dinner and at the same time, in a doleful, pitying voice, plunging a thousand pins into the heart of the man whose hospitality he was enjoying—all this with the most malevolent skill imaginable.

Then off to the Ambigu. It was Busnach again, despite the sizeable contribution made to the work by Zola. All that the naturalist theatre could produce in this play in the way of naturalism was real water in a zinc gutter and the sound of a nightingale's song coming from a cheap musical box.

The audience was good-natured but in a merry mood. After the third tableau I went to call on Mme Zola who was in floods of tears —something I failed to see in the darkness of the box—and when I ventured to say that the audience did not seem too bad, she hissed at me: 'So you consider this a good audience, do you, Goncourt? Well, you're easy to please, I must say!' I slipped out through the door of the box.

The play went on, to a mixture of ironic laughter and applause. Finally, after a tableau which had been very well received, I went to see Mme Zola again, and this time she was all smiles and apologized gracefully to me. It would be interesting to write a study one day of the nerves of an author and his wife during an opening performance.

There was one very striking effect: the bed in the room in the Grand Hotel, surrounded by the gay music of a ball, and from which, in the solitude of the room, from a body hidden from sight, there came the dying request: 'Water!'[1]

The curtain fell to the sound of applause. We went up the stairs where, a little earlier, we had heard Massin calling out to Delessart: 'Come and stick a smallpox pustule on me!' We went into the manager's office, where Busnach was sitting at a little table looking as if he had gone bankrupt. There was kissing and handshaking all round, while Mme Zola stormed at her husband, who had refused to order supper in advance. And Zola, his shoulders drooping wearily, kept repeating: 'You know how superstitious I am: if I had ordered it, I feel sure the play would have flopped!'

Then the whole company of *naturalist* men and women trooped off to the Café Brébant, where we supped until four in the morning, at one of those first-night suppers which the fatigue of the preceding days, the emotion of the actual performance, and the anxiety about the next day make so dull and grey and poor in life and gaiety.

During the meal there was a typical remark by Zola. Chabrillat, who was supping with the actors, came across to our table for a few moments, to be greeted by Zola with the question: 'Did we cover our costs?'

*Sunday, 13 February*

A curious coincidence. In the novel I am writing I had created a stockbroker to whom I had given the name of Jacqmin, a name taken from an eighteenth-century sale catalogue, the name of a jeweller to Louis XV. Today M. Poisson, a friendly stockbroker

---

[1] This is the final tableau, where Nana, disfigured by smallpox, dies in a deserted room.

whom I had asked to listen to a reading of this passage and to point out any blunders a man as unfamiliar with the Stock Exchange as I am might have committed, said to me when I had finished:

'And you are giving him his real name?'

'What do you mean?'

'But it isn't just the name. . . . He's all there . . . his brutality, his swaggering way of doing business, the character that made him an absolute *bull*. . . .'

It so happened that I had painted a faithful portrait, with the right name as well, of a stockbroker who died eighteen months ago.


*Wednesday, 9 March*

Something quite horrible in the Princess's drawing-rooms is the sentimental promenade of the Taines who, when the husband is not pontificating, go off into a dark corner to look at some picture, which they contemplate bending over one another like an engaged couple on the other side of the Rhine. The stupid walk of that pot-bellied clergyman, with his sly, hypocritical gaze hidden behind his spectacles, and the swarthy, unhealthy ugliness of the horrifying wife, who looks like a diseased silkworm which a schoolboy has daubed with ink, make a truly dreadful sight for the eyes of an aesthete.


*Saturday, 9 April*

Today, after a meeting to organize the erection of a memorial to Flaubert, I went to dinner with Turgenev and Maupassant at the house of an old friend of Flaubert's, Mme Brainne, whose ample charms produced something of the intimidating effect on me of a giant woman in a fairground sideshow.

After dinner we talked about love and the strange tastes women have in love. Turgenev told us that in Russia there was a charming woman, a woman with curly hair of the palest blond imaginable and a slightly *café-au-lait* complexion in which the undissolved coffee grains formed a crowd of little beauty-spots. This woman had been courted by the most intelligent and most famous of men. One day Turgenev asked her why, out of all her suitors, she had made a perfectly inexplicable choice, and the woman replied: 'Perhaps you are

right, but then you have never heard the way he says: "Really? You
don't say!" '

Saturday, 30 April

An anecdote told by Camille Rousset.

After General Sébastiani had repulsed the English attack on
Constantinople, the Sultan Selim said to him: 'What reward would
you like? I will give you anything you ask.'[1]

'In that case, I ask His Highness to allow me to see the harem.'

'Very well, you shall see it.'

And he showed him the harem and all his wives.

When the visit was over, the Sultan asked General Sébastiani:
'Did you notice a woman you liked?'

'Yes', replied the general, and he indicated which one.

'Very well', said the Sultan once more. And that evening
General Sébastiani received the woman's head on a platter, together
with a message to this effect: 'As a Moslem, I could not offer you, a
Christian, a woman of my faith. But like this, you can be sure that
this woman on whom you set your eyes will never belong to any
other man.'

Sunday, 15 May

Degas was ill recently. When Nittis went to see him, the Impressionist painter greeted him with the remark: 'You do look peculiar
to me. I don't know what the doctors are giving me, but it makes
people look as if they had earthenware faces.'

Then he turned to his maid Sabine and said: 'At your age, if a girl
has never made love, if she's still a virgin, she's unbearable. I can't
stand your fussing and fretting any longer. Nittis, go and bed her.'

In came the owner of the house, whom Degas had sent for to
complain about the noise being made by workmen doing repairs.
'As for you,' said the painter, 'when I'm on my feet again, I shall
slap you in the face in front of the concierge.'

Tuesday, 31 May

'Gentlemen,'—it was Bardoux talking—'you doubtless know the
chastity belt in the Musée de Cluny, and you may be aware that

[1] This was in 1806, when General Sébastiani was French Ambassador in Turkey.

these belts are still manufactured. But what you don't know is that there are some made for men. Yes, during my stay at the Ministry, a manufacturer was prosecuted for putting an object of that sort on display. His books were inspected and the names of his customers came to light. Among those names was a well-known figure whose wife, whenever she went away, forced him to wear the belt, taking the key away with her. I know the man in question and I have even twitted him about it.'

*Monday, 20 June*

Today the Daudets, the Charpentiers, and I went to spend the day with Zola at Médan.

He came to meet us at Poissy station. He was very jaunty and pleased with himself, and as soon as he had got into the carriage he exclaimed: 'I've written twelve pages of my novel. . . . Twelve pages, dammit! . . . It's going to be one of the most complicated books I've written so far . . . there are seventy characters.'[1] And while he was saying this, he brandished a horrible little stereotyped volume, which turned out to be a *Paul et Virginie*, which he had brought along to read in the carriage.

It is a mad, absurd, senseless folly, this house which has now cost him over 200,000 francs and which suffers from the limitations of the original property that cost 7,000 francs. You go up to the first floor by a staircase which is a mill ladder, and you have to do something like the horizontal leap in a Deburau pantomime to get into the lavatory, which has a buffet-type door.

The study is a very handsome room. It is tall and spacious, but spoilt by a collection of appalling knick-knacks. There are suits of armour, a whole set of Romantic bric-à-brac, Balzac's motto, *Nulla dies sine linea*, over the fireplace, and in one corner a harmonium with a *vox angelica* which the author of *L'Assommoir* plays at nightfall.

As for the garden, it consists of two narrow strips of ground, one ten feet higher than the other, which extend across fields cut by the railway line, across bits of waste land which apparently belong to him, and finally across a fifty-acre island to the other side of the river.

[1] *Pot-Bouille*, published in April 1882.

We had a gay lunch and afterwards went over to the island, where he is building a chalet on which the painters were still at work. It contains a single big room, all in pine-wood, with a huge porcelain stove of great simplicity and excellent taste.

We came back for dinner, and as the sun went down, there rose from that treeless garden and that childless house a melancholy which affected Daudet as it did me.

*Thursday, 30 June*

The real connoisseurs in art are those who make people accept as beautiful something everybody used to consider ugly, by revealing and resuscitating the beauty in it. Those are the only true connoisseurs: the rest are the blind slaves of taste of the prevailing fashion.

*Wednesday, 31 August*

According to a lecherous Englishman, the best place to pick up a woman in Paris is in the omnibus offices, and the remark is that of a foreigner who knows his Paris.

It was Theodore Child who told me that, and he went on to draw an amusing picture for me of evenings in England, where at dusk, along the twilit roads, groups of young men and girls, dressed in the faded colours of the old clothes which the Pre-Raphaelite painters have brought back into fashion, indulge in flirtations constantly interrupted by the swift, silent passing of athletic youths mounted on velocipedes.

*Thursday, 13 October*

A call from the director of the *Voltaire*, who told me that he was going to cover Paris with posters, and that on the day the first instalment appeared he was going to have a hundred thousand chromolithographs of La Faustin distributed in the streets of the capital. Then he started complaining that the police prohibited sandwich-men, who were one of the principal publicity methods used in London. But he had something up his sleeve. Going downstairs, unable to keep his secret to himself any longer, he turned round, leaned on the banisters, and said: 'Well, this is my idea. . . .

You know those big posts along the Boulevard. I'm thinking of having streamers tied to them bearing the words: *"La Faustin, 1 November in the Voltaire."* Of course the police are certain to intervene and have them taken down, but it will have lasted a whole day.' I listened to this, ashamed but, I must admit, not sufficiently disgusted at the prospect of shortly being dishonoured by this Sarah Bernhardt-type publicity.

*Monday, 31 October*

There are posters in every conceivable colour and of every conceivable size covering the walls of Paris and announcing everywhere in colossal letters: *La Faustin.* At the station there is a painted advertisement thirty yards high and two hundred yards across. This morning 120,000 copies of the *Voltaire* were given to passers-by. This morning too, 10,000 copies of a chromolithograph showing a scene from the novel were distributed on the boulevards, and the distribution is to go on for a week.

*Thursday, 10 November*

Of the reading of my novel, of that reading imposed by publicity, not a single sign has reached me, not a single letter, not a single word, not even a mention in a newspaper.

*Sunday, 27 November*

Daudet, who had drunk two glasses of Vouvray, taking me by the lapels of my coat and pushing me back against a door of Charpentier's morning-room, said: 'I'm not at all well. . . . I've got a stricture that hurts like the devil there', and he touched the back of his neck. 'You know, the day we spent at Zola's I couldn't manage to pass water all day. . . . And here in my pocket I've got a letter of recommendation for a surgeon. . . . But I dread the idea of going to see him and I keep putting it off from one day to the next.'

We went and sat down at the far end of one of the drawing-rooms.

'Well,' I said, 'how about your novel on the south of France?'

'My novel on the south of France? But my dear chap, it's just a cover!' And his eyes swept round the room. 'With the thieves in our profession,' he said, 'with people like Zola, you have to hide what you are doing. And when people ask me later on what has happened to my novel on the south of France, I shall say that I wasn't in a laughing mood. . . . And then, life is so short. . . . A fellow mustn't repeat himself. . . . I want to produce something very powerful, the story of a liaison. I have read my notes for the book to my wife as the story of a close friend.'

And he told me again about his affair with *Chien Vert*.[1]

[1] The novel in question, *Sapho*, was to be published in 1884. On *Chien Vert*, cf. the entry for 28 March 1880.

# 1882

*Thursday, 5 January*

Bing's head clerk gave his employer notice today . . . by telephone. Yes, by telephone! The very latest thing, this leave-taking which cuts out all possibility of argument.

*Thursday, 19 January*

Everywhere *La Faustin* is prominently displayed. At Marpon's I saw copies of the fifth thousand and at Lefilleul's I was surprised to find my book enjoying the supreme honour of the 'throne'. . . . Suddenly, in the midst of my contemplation, I heard the boulevard resound with shouts of: 'Gambetta resigns!' Am I condemned to remain all my life the man who published his first book on the day of the *Coup d'État* ?

*Monday, 23 January*

When I looked at the bookshop windows today, it seemed to me that the numbers of the impressions were not changing and that the covers of the copies on display were growing sadly grubby.

*Sunday, 29 January*

I have had a letter from Mme Daudet containing a curious paragraph.

At her son Léon's school the pupils were told to write a composition in French on the death of some person whose name I do not know. Three pupils in succession read out compositions into which they had introduced the sardonic death-agony from *La Faustin*.[1]

---

[1] At the end of the novel, the actress La Faustin, watching by the bedside of her dying lover, Lord Annandale, is impelled by her theatrical instincts to imitate the sardonic laugh into which his face is contorted. She is grimacing at herself in the mirror when Annandale comes to, realizes what she is doing, and rings for the servants to throw her out of the house.

The master, who knows nothing of contemporary literature, was utterly nonplussed, while little Léon laughed up his sleeve.

After reading this, I came across a newspaper in which a woman accuses me of unhinging women's minds with my book.

*Tuesday, 7 February*

Vallès, jealous of any sensation that he has not created himself, and quite prepared to allow me to make a stir in the past but not in the present, is almost prudishly indignant about me, describes me as a cross between the Marquis de Sade and Scudéry, compares the book to the buzzing of a cantharide in a hospital cap, and makes fun of my sardonic death-agony.

All right, I agree that that sardonic death-agony is an invention . . . but possible and even probable. And I would not have risked it without a certain piece of information. This is what happened to Rachel. She had an old maid to whom she was very attached and whom I have portrayed under the name of Guénégaud. This old maid fell seriously ill in her mistress's house; and one night the actress was woken up and told that the sick woman was dying. Rachel went downstairs in tears and genuinely upset; but before a quarter of an hour had passed, the artiste was completely absorbed in studying the death-agony of the unfortunate woman, who had become a stranger for her, a *sub·ect*. I was given this detail by Dinah Félix.[1]

*Wednesday, 8 February*

My colleagues do not seem to have noticed that *La Faustin* is different from my previous books. They do not appear to realize that in this book I have introduced a new poetry and fantasy into the study of reality, and that I have tried to help realism to take a step forward by endowing it with certain chiaroscuro qualities it did not possess before. For after all, things are surely just as real seen in moonlight as in the rays of the noonday sun.

[1] In 1894 Dinah Félix denied that she had furnished Goncourt with this anecdote, maintaining that her sister's maid had died in 1882 at the age of eighty-one, after twenty years in Rachel's service and twenty-four in hers. The article by Vallès mentioned here appeared in the *Gil Blas* of 7 February.

Yes, there is something new in my latest book, and it is not impossible that in twenty years' time a school should have formed around *La Faustin* just as one has grown up around *Germinie Lacerteux*.

*Thursday, 9 February*

One could say of Zola that the eroticism which my books administer in homoeopathic doses, in infinitesimal quantities, his novels dole out to the public in bucketfuls, in tubfuls.

*Monday, 6 March*

Our old dinner of the five was revived today, with Flaubert missing but Turgenev, Zola, Daudet, and myself still here.

The moral difficulties of some of us and the physical sufferings of the others brought the conversation round to death—and we went on talking about death until eleven o'clock, trying now and then to turn to something else but always coming back to that gloomy subject.

Daudet said that it was an obsession with him which poisoned his whole life, and that he had never moved into a new flat without looking for the place where his coffin would stand.

Zola for his part said that when his mother had died at Médan, the staircase had turned out to be too narrow for the coffin, so that she had had to be lowered out of the window, and that since then he had never looked at that window without wondering which of the two of them, his wife or himself, would be the next to go through it.

'Yes,' he went on, 'death has been in our minds ever since, and often—we keep a night-light burning in our bedroom now—often at night, looking at my wife, who is lying there awake, I can tell that she is thinking of death too; and we stay like that without ever saying what we are both thinking about . . . out of tact, yes, out of a certain tact. . . . Oh, it's a terrifying thought!' And fear came into his eyes. 'There are nights when I suddenly jump out of bed and stand there for a second in a state of indescribable terror.'

*Tuesday, 28 March*

Daudet told me this evening that one day during the serialization of *Nana*, he had met Zola coming out of Charpentier's and had taken him to a café on the Boulevard Saint-Michel where most of the customers were women. They had scarcely sat down before one of the local cocottes came in with a copy of the *Voltaire* that she had just bought. She sat down beside them, spread the paper out on the table at the serial page, and turning towards them without knowing who they were, exclaimed: '*Merde*, if this isn't a smutty one, I'm not going to read it.' This rather upset Zola, who decided that it was too hot in the café and suggested going somewhere else.

*Thursday, 6 April*

I looked into Charpentier's bookshop for a moment today, and saw copies of *Pot-Bouille*, which is due to be put on sale next week, being stacked in piles reaching up to the ceiling.

This evening, at Zola's, I found him morose and despondent, tormented by the desire to leave Paris and saying that he was 'sick and tired of the place'.

Céard and Huysmans arrived soon afterwards and the rest of the evening was one long argument between the master and his disciples, whom I saw rebelling against him for the first time.

'Real life,' exclaimed Zola, who puts so little of it in his books, 'do you think it's as necessary as all that? . . . I know that it's all the rage just now, and that we are partly responsible, but writers in other times managed perfectly well without it. . . . No, no, it isn't as indispensable as people say.'

On the subject of mixing with other people, which his disciples with all possible respect and humility advised him to do, he flew into something of a temper, one of those superficial tempers which consist simply in the raising of the voice: 'Society . . . now I ask you what a drawing-room can teach you about life. . . . Not a thing. . . . I've got twenty-five workmen at Médan who teach me a hundred times more.'

There was talk of *Les Liaisons dangereuses*, which he had never read and which I urged him to read. 'Read it?' he repeated. 'But there isn't time. . . . I haven't the time!' And he said this in a tone which seemed to say: 'What's the use? It's a waste of time!' And so it is with everything he does not possess, everything he does not do, everything he does not know.

And with his jacket unbuttoned at the neck, his chin in his hands and his elbows on the little table among the big tankards of beer which forced him to restrict his gestures, he went on grousing and grumbling all evening, with something of the sulky ill-humour of a fat boy in a little school smock who had been given a wigging.

*Tuesday, 25 April*

Today, at the sale of Mme de Balzac's property, I pushed the price of the manuscript of *Eugénie Grandet* up to eleven hundred francs. For a moment I thought that the manuscript was mine; I was its owner for five minutes.

*Tuesday, 23 May*

'Hugo has ideas about everything', somebody said at our table today.

'Ideas, no! Just pictures', said Berthelot.

*Saturday, 27 May*

At Nittis's this evening, Bourget told us about a Jesuit, a certain Abbé Milleriot, who was mad about confession and used to spend his evenings scouring the streets confessing any more or less Catholic coachmen whom he found waiting in their carriages outside houses—climbing up on to their seats beside them to confess them.

Richepin, who had heard about him, thought that he would astonish him and asked him to hear his confession. But at the end of this confession, which Richepin in his innocence considered utterly revolting, the rogues' confessor came out of his confessional, embraced him and said: 'I'll give you a wipe with the dishcloth—absolution—on Saturday, and we'll go and eat God together on Sunday.'

This priest is said to have had a horrible, delirious death-agony, during which he confessed imaginary criminals far worse than Richepin.

*Sunday, 28 May*

A call this morning from Tissot, who came to see me about illustrating *Renée Mauperin*. He is an inconsequential, garrulous character, with a flood of tiring words among which an occasional painterly phrase attracts your attention and puts you back in contact with what he is saying.

He told me that he loved England, London, even the smell of coal in the air because it smelt of the battle of life. 'Oh, they aren't sentimental people, those islanders', he said. 'I remember a rainy day, in one of those downpours you get in London, when the road was a lake—it was the evening—a lake reflecting the gaslight of the shops. In that water there was a poor epileptic who had fallen face-down in the roadway and who was drowning in the midst of people who were looking at him without doing anything to help him. I was on my way to a play or a concert. My cabby, as we shot past, shouted to the onlookers: "Turn him over!" Those three words meant: "Put him on his back; otherwise he will drown." And that "Turn him over!" is all the pity one Englishman will ever show for another.'

*Wednesday, 14 June*

He found the design of his carpet dreary in its immobility. He wanted a moving colour, a moving light on it. He went to the Palais-Royal and there he bought a very expensive tortoise. And he was delighted with the perambulations across his carpet of that living, shining thing.

But after a few days he began to find the animal's sheen a trifle dull. He accordingly took it to a gilder's and had it gilded. The mobile, gilded knick-knack kept him amused until one day, all of a sudden, the idea occurred to him of having it set with jewels by a jeweller. He had its shell encrusted with topazes. And he was still congratulating himself on the result when the tortoise died from its encrusting.[1]

The eccentric who had this idea was brought to see me today by Heredia. It was young Montesquiou-Fezensac, who had put on a pair of trousers made in the tartan of a Scottish clan to see me and had prepared 'an *ad hoc* state of mind' for the occasion: a crank, a literary lunatic, but endowed with the supreme refinement of an aristocratic race on the verge of extinction.

[1] The jewelled tortoise was one of several of Robert de Montesquiou's eccentricities with which Huysmans credited Des Esseintes, the hero of his novel *A Rebours*, published in 1884.

*Thursday, 20 July*

Rattier asked Lortic the other day why binders lived in such dirty houses. He replied: 'It is because we destroy stone houses and the owners of such houses won't have us. Only wooden houses can stand up to our presses, and it is only in wooden houses that you will find us.'

*Saturday, 26 August*

'I had a friend. He fell ill: I nursed him. He died: I dissected him.' Du Camp might well have taken this remark by an eighteenth-century doctor as an epigraph for his memoirs about his friend's epilepsy.[1]

*Saturday, 9 September*

This morning at Saint-Gratien, Popelin gave me an account of the Princess's departure from France in 1870. Quite easy in his mind and not expecting anything untoward to happen, he had left the Princess in her hotel at Dieppe and was in a tobacconist's shop choosing a cigar when an old woman came in and announced that Princess Mathilde had just been arrested. With Giraud, he rushed back to the hotel through streets already thronged with noisy crowds, and urged the Princess to leave. She scoffed at his fears and practically called him a coward, but then Eugène came in, terrified by the menacing shouts he had heard outside. At the sight of her major-domo's pale face, the woman's courage failed her; she decided to leave, and to leave straight away.

Popelin was on his way to get a cab when he noticed Alexandre Dumas walking past the hotel. He caught up with him, and Dumas put his carriage, which was waiting nearby, at his disposal. And off they went, saying that they were going for a drive. But scarcely had they got safely out of the town when the Princess exclaimed: 'My diamonds! I hid them in my bed and forgot to tell Julie!' Popelin had to return to the town in a fast cab which took him back to the hotel and then caught up with the Princess a few minutes later.

[1] A reference to Du Camp's account in his *Souvenirs littéraires* (1882–83) of the attacks of what was presumed to be epilepsy from which Flaubert had suffered as a young man.

Finally the fugitives reached the little station, a station right out in the fields. The train which they thought was due only at six o'clock was not due until nine. They had to wait. The Princess had two dogs with her, one of which had a cough, and she was absorbed in the coughing of her dog, worried and on edge. The other members of the party, however, were beginning to feel hungry. Popelin asked the stationmaster where they could get a meal. He told them of a waggoners' inn a good half-hour away, a disgusting inn with hunks of meat hanging from the ceiling, black with flies. The innkeeper grudgingly cooked one of these hunks of meat and the trio dined on that and an omelette of rotten eggs, by the light of a candle stuck in a bottle. Giraud played the fool all the way through this wretched meal, while the Princess kept dabbing her dog's head with her sodden handkerchief, a treatment which did nothing to cure its cold.

At last, at nine o'clock, the train arrived and took them to Rouen, where the Princess took a room in a hotel where she was not known, while Popelin, going out for a moment, saw people reading something on the walls by the light of matches they kept striking. It was the proclamation of the Republic. On being told that the Republic had been proclaimed, the Princess raised no objections to the idea of leaving France, and the little party set off for Mons. Near the frontier there was an alarming delay of nearly three hours, in a district swarming with fierce-looking gunners, overwhelmed by defeat.

They crossed the frontier and reached Mons, but there was not a room to be had in any hotel. At the last moment, the fugitive Princess was given the little bedroom of a traveller who had just left and whose bed, which he had dirtied in every possible way, had not been changed. The coverlet was pulled over the bed and the Princess sat down on it. And Giraud and Popelin propped her up with blankets and travelling-bags so that she could have a few hours' rest.

The Princess took us to Puteaux today to see the house of the famous dressmaker Worth.

It is impossible to imagine the lunatic knick-knackery in that house. The walls are covered with plates of every age and every country. Mme Worth said that there were twenty-five thousand of them. And everywhere, even on the backs of the chairs, there are crystal drops. The place is a nightmare of broken china and carafe stoppers. It is as if somebody were turning a kaleidoscope of glittering pieces of glass in front of your eyes all the time, and you come away from that house, with its crystal salad-bowls set in the window-panes, as dazed as if you had been in a monstrous fairyland palace.

The owner returns there every evening, incapable of eating, incapable of enjoying his astonishing home, his head aching from all the scents and perfumes of the great ladies he has been dressing during the day.

*Thursday, 14 September*

Today the Khedive, Mehemet Ali's grandson, came to Saint-Gratien.

He is a red-bearded Oriental, looking rather like a Théophile Gautier with a squint. He speaks French with a perfect command of the Parisian idiom and a certain humour that smacks of the gutter. One sometimes forgets that this is an 'old Turk' who murdered his ministers, he is so skilful at disguising his thoughts in the urbane euphony of a civilized language. But in the middle of a peroration in which he is painting a bucolic picture of himself as a simple peasant, he will give a curious intonation to a phrase such as this: 'Yes, when my uncle was burnt alive!' And then, willy-nilly, the Europeanized man speaks all of a sudden with the accent of the Nile.

*Wednesday, 27 September*

'I found something to amuse her every day; I read her interesting books for three hours at a time, until her eyes closed; I rubbed her body wherever she felt aches and pains; I cut her corns. . . . Yes, my dear fellow, I cut her corns. . . . I was her reader, her masseur, her chiropodist, her steward, her lover, her husband. If I hadn't been there to make her stay in one place, heaven knows what would have become of her. She would have let herself be dragged off to the ends of Europe, where with her unstable character she would soon have grown tired of places and people.'

Popelin said all this to me in the park, and what he said was true. A few minutes later he added: 'I hate that fellow Du Camp. You know what he has been saying about the Princess? That he left her because she was wearing him out with her sexual demands! Well, the truth is that there isn't a woman in the world who is more reserved or shows less imagination in her love-making. In a word, I don't know a woman with a temperament more like that of a middle-class housewife. And if her husband hadn't behaved like a brute to her, hadn't torn her ear-rings from her ears, hadn't thought it amusing to pinch the bottoms of the gentlemen he invited to get into her carriage beside her, I feel sure that she would never have taken a lover. . . . What she likes most of all, you know, is to feel surrounded by friendships into which there enters an element of love.'

*Saturday, 30 September*

The Princess, who was talking to me as we were strolling round the park, began walking quickly, very quickly, so that we left the others behind. Then, looking at me with a piercing gaze, she spoke to me about Popelin, about his moodiness, and asked me, knowing me for a shrewd observer, whether I could explain it. She spoke of the man's affection in doubting terms and worried phrases, and after all manner of vague circumlocutions she said: 'Does he love me? Does he love me? . . . No, Goncourt, I can tell that nowadays it's as if he were doing his duty.'

At this I replied that she was being unfair and that Popelin's moodiness was not due to any diminution of his love for her but to his poor health and his anxiety about his son's accident. The Princess did not listen. She went on: 'It's strange: when his son was small, just a child, he wasn't like this at all. Now that his son's a man, he does nothing but fuss and worry about him. Just look at him nowadays when he has to go to Paris, with his gloves put on in advance and his overcoat over his arm, consulting his watch every few minutes and worrying whether the carriage is going to be late. . . . Don't you think he looks as if he's going to a rendezvous?'

'Oh, come now, Princess, you know that all he cares about is his son and his translation of Colonna.'

'Six years ago, he was quite a rake. And lately he has been to see some of those dreadful women again, Madame Feydeau and Madame Dardenne de la Grangerie. . . . One just can't tell, one can never tell. . . .'

'Princess, he's absolutely devoted to you.'

'Oh, Goncourt!' exclaimed the Princess in a tone which spoke volumes. She went on: 'He does so little for me now. He doesn't talk to me any more, he doesn't tell me anything. Oh, he's very peculiar.' And tears came into her eyes. 'There was a time', she continued, 'when I came to certain conclusions, and my conclusions go a long way. . . .'

'Imagination, nothing but imagination!'

'But let him go and settle in Italy with his son if he wants to, I shan't do anything to stop him. . . . I know what men are like when their love grows cold. . . . I got used to having my heart broken a long time ago. . . . But I refuse to let it get me down.'

Here the tears came in floods, and the Princess went on walking round the park, breaking off convolvulus blossoms from the shrubs, chewing them nervously, and spitting them out on to the path.

*Sunday, 5 November*

It is strange that the beauty of the female body should never have been represented by the artists of the East, who have always confined themselves to depicting the grace of its veils and garments—and I cite the miniatures of Persia as an example—and that it should be only in the lands of bodices and panniers, hoops and corsets that the charms of the female nude have been rendered by a Rubens and a Boucher.

*Wednesday, 27 December*

Henri Renaud came to see me today to ask me to join a committee to set up a statue to Balzac. He has had two noteworthy replies to date. A deputy from Touraine exclaimed: 'Balzac? But he wasn't a politician!' And Hugo said to him: 'Ah, Balzac! . . . I've an objection to raise against him: he was a royalist!' That comes oddly from the man who wrote the *Ode on the Birth of His Royal Highness the Duc de Bordeaux*.

*Saturday, 30 December*

Yesterday or the day before yesterday, Dumas told Mme de Nittis how tired he was of having to go and dine at Mme Aubernon's, saying: 'There are days when a man is out of sorts and other days when he is not in form. . . . But there a fellow must always do his stint, always be witty and gay. . . .'

In that house Dumas is a god, it is true, but it seems that it is a tiring business, being God every day.

# 1883

*Monday, 1 January*

This morning little Blanche could not find a single *Figaro* at the station. At three o'clock Daudet, coming with his wife and children to wish me a happy new year, told me that Gambetta was dead. If the Prince Imperial were still alive, it would be all up with the Republic within a fortnight. Popelin, who came to see me about five o'clock, told me that it was strange how excited Prince Napoleon was about the death of Gambetta . . . unnecessarily, I believe.

*Wednesday, 3 January*

Yesterday, in the Princess's smoking-room, Dieulafoy told us about Trousseau's heroic death. One day Trousseau asked Dieulafoy to feel a swelling on his leg, saying: 'Now tell me what that is. . . . And I want a serious diagnosis!'

'But it's a . . .'

'Yes, it's a . . .'—and he used the scientific term—'and on top of that I've got cancer. . . . Yes, I've got cancer. . . . And now, keep that to yourself, and thank you.'

And he went on living as if he did not know that he was condemned to die within a short time, seeing his patients and inviting friends to musical evenings at his home, serene and impenetrable. But he found himself growing weaker. He accordingly got rid of his carriage but went on seeing his patients at home.

However, for all his courage and determination, the change taking place in him was obvious to everyone and the rumour spread that he had cancer. Mothers promptly came rushing to see him, saying brutally: 'Is it true what they are saying, that you are going to die? But what about my child? What's to become of my daughter when she reaches puberty?' Trousseau smiled, asked them to sit down, and dictated copious advice to them.

Apart from all this, the last months of his life were poisoned by dreadful worries. He had a scamp of a son who, after getting involved in some shady business, announced that he was going to commit suicide and failed to do so—with the result that there were some dreadful financial tangles to sort out.

Finally he could no longer stay on his feet and had to take to his bed. There he received his friends, carefully shaved and exquisitely groomed, like a man who was suffering from a slight indisposition. Soon he began to suffer appalling pain. It was only then that he asked for injections of morphine, but in infinitesimal doses which gave him peace and calm for no more than a few minutes. Then he would come back to his painful life, pull himself together and say to the doctor friend beside him: 'Let's do some intellectual gymnastics and talk about . . .' And he would mention some medical thesis, determined to keep his mental faculties intact to the very end.

One day he blurted out: 'I had hoped for a perforation or a haemorrhage; but no, it's going to be longer than I expected.' And he endured the full range of sufferings of a long-drawn death-agony. It went on like this for seven months, during which he never gave any sign that he knew he was going to die on a certain day.

Towards the end, Nélaton came to see him. 'Your last visit, eh?' he said. Nélaton nodded. Whereupon Trousseau said to him, referring to some colleague in the provinces, Charvet I believe: 'I should have liked to see him decorated. . . . You ought to do something about it.'

Nélaton came back a few days later and said: 'This really is my last visit . . . but the decree has been signed.'

When he was on the point of dying, he asked his daughter to come closer, took her hand and sighed: 'As long as I hold your hand I shall still be alive. . . . After that, I don't know where I shall be.'

*Tuesday, 9 January*

The *Temps* dinner.

The conversation was all about Gambetta. Robin said that there were two perforations in the caecal appendix. He maintained that the shooting accident had not had any effect, that it had been purely concomitant, that the man was doomed to die within a few days or a few months as the result of tiredness or indigestion or some such minor cause.[1]

'What a blow!' exclaimed Spuller as he came in, his fat face as pale as if he were truly grief-stricken. There was talk of the dead man's brain, which was with one doctor, his arm, which was with another, and his caecum, which was with a third. There is something horrible about the way they split up an illustrious corpse these days.

Somebody mentioned the possibility of an operation. 'An operation!' exclaimed Liouville. 'But haven't you heard what Verneuil said at the post-mortem? "What a mercy that we didn't operate!"'

'Our good friend was a gluttonous eater', said Hébrard, who never takes life seriously. 'You remember those partridges, and how he wolfed them down . . . he may have swallowed some shot: that's enough to produce a perforation isn't it? . . . Lannelongue, who has written a hundred pages on his illness—yes, a day-to-day account—thinks it was a piece of truffle at lunch that brought on an attack of indigestion. . . . He's trying to track it down in his diary.'

Spuller said sadly. 'He was as great as he was good, for he was the best of men.' He added: 'People don't know it, but he loved science and philosophy. . . . When Robin was made a senator, it pleased him as much as the elections of '76. He said: "Now Robin's a senator; that's a beginning: one day we'll be in control of the Academy of Medicine, and then", he went on in that triumphant, jovial tone he adopted at moments like that, "we'll show them what's what!"'

There followed a discussion about his brain, which definitely weighs less than Morny's. This annoyed the present company, annoyed them dreadfully, and they maintained that weight was unimportant, that what mattered was the beauty of the convolutions, and that he had the most beautiful convolutions in the world.

*Saturday, 17 February*

Looking at the Jews I know growing old around me, I am sometimes astonished at the peculiar ugliness which the years bring

[1] Gambetta had wounded himself in the hand and forearm while handling a revolver in his garden on 27 November 1882.

them. It is not our decrepitude but a moral ugliness. What is the explanation? I believe that it is to be found in purely material appetites and desires, in a life with no other object than money.

*Tuesday, 10 April*

The dinner which Zola, Daudet, and I used to hold with Flaubert and Turgenev was revived today with Huysmans and Céard.

We talked about Veuillot, whom Zola refused to recognize as a great writer because . . . because . . . because he had not left a disciple, a Paul Alexis! Zola really is too personal and limited in his arguments. Daudet, with no enthusiasm for Veuillot's talent, said all there is to be said about him: 'The press has lost its writer.'

Then the conversation turned to Maupassant, whose new book, *Une Vie*, I had just seen displayed in the Galeries de l'Odéon, and which was dedicated to Mme Brainne. When they heard about the dedication, Huysmans and Céard told us about a terrible slanging Mme Brainne had given the author at Zola's. He had arrived that day in evening dress, boasting that he had dropped one society woman whom he had been supposed to take to the Opéra that evening, in order to take another. The door opened and in came Mme Brainne, who had never been to Zola's before and has never come back since. As soon as she had sat down, speaking in a hissing voice and whipping one gloved hand with the long glove she had taken off the other, she started chaffing the sheepish Maupassant with a cruelty which embarrassed all those who were there. 'It was just like Madame Plessy in *Henriette Maréchal*', said Zola. Then the woman went out after motioning to Maupassant, who disappeared a few minutes later, furious with all the witnesses of that moral thrashing, whom he has avoided seeing again after that scene.

*Saturday, 21 April*

The English poet Wilde told me this evening that the only living Englishman who had read Balzac was Swinburne. And he described this fellow Swinburne to me as a braggart in the matter of vice, who had done everything he could to convince his fellow citizens of his homosexuality and bestiality, without being in the slightest degree a homosexual or a bestializer.

*Wednesday, 25 April*

Our old friend Turgenev is a real man of letters. He has just had a cyst removed from his stomach, and he told Daudet, who went to see him a few days ago: 'During the operation I thought of our dinners and I searched for the words with which I could give you an exact impression of the steel cutting through my skin and entering my flesh . . . something like a knife cutting a banana.'

*Saturday, 5 May*

Dined at Nittis's with the English poet Oscar Wilde. This individual of doubtful sex, with his barnstormer's language and his tall stories, gave us an amusing description of a town in Texas with its criminal population, its constant shooting-matches, and its places of amusement where there are notices reading: 'Please don't shoot the pianist: he is doing his best.' He told us of the theatre which, as the biggest building in the town, is used as a courtroom and where condemned men are hanged on the stage after the play is over. He said that he had seen one man who was being hanged clinging to the uprights in the wings while the audience fired at him from their seats.

It appears too that in that part of the world theatre managers look for real criminals to play criminal parts; and when *Macbeth* is being put on, a contract is offered to a poisoner who has just come out of prison, and the posters read: 'The part of Lady Macbeth will be taken by Mrs. —— (Ten years' hard labour).'

*Thursday, 31 May*

Today at the Sichels', somebody who had lived for many years in Japan said that the kiss did not exist, as it were, in Japanese love-making, and that love there was purely animal, without any of the tenderness of human caresses. He added that the kiss was also very rare in displays of simple affection. He had been present at the parting of a mother and child, in which the mother had expressed her grief by hunching her shoulders and sobbing quietly, without taking the child in her arms or kissing it.

*Saturday, 7 July*

I find that I am obsessed by the idea of continuing after my death, of outliving myself, of leaving behind pictures of my house and my person. But what is the use?

*Friday, 7 September*

Today the religious service around Turgenev's coffin brought out of the houses of Paris a swarm of creatures with huge bodies, flat faces and God-the-Father beards: a little Russia whose existence in the capital one had never suspected.

There were also a great many Russian women, German women, and English women, pious, faithful readers who had come to pay homage to the great and subtle novelist.

Despair at growing old fills the Princess with a fury which every now and then needs to rush, like a bull in the arena, at somebody or something.

This evening, hearing somebody mention Degas, whom she does not know personally, she exclaimed: 'Can you understand anybody having the impudence to paint a nose or a mouth as he does? . . . Oh, I should like to smash his head against his pictures!'

*Saturday, 15 September*

Princess Mathilde has a peculiar sort of religion, or rather fetishism. She has a little crucifix and a little religious picture, given to her I believe by her Aunt Julie, which she puts on a chair and before which she says her prayers. But as she finds it inconvenient to say her prayers last thing at night, when she wants to go to sleep, she says them before dinner, breaking off now and then to give orders or to remind those who are there of something that has to be done.

*Thursday, 27 December*

This evening Daudet was talking about his rebellious youth and told this anecdote. He had left home at the age of sixteen and went back when he was twenty-four; but, sharp-eyed to begin with, he had grown still more observant and extremely quizzical over the years, and he found certain things in his family so funny that he begged leave to go away again. His father, a typical southerner, a violent, tender-hearted creature with a passionate affection for Alphonse, was cut to the quick, and began heaping his beloved son with insults, insults of every conceivable variety, insults which Daudet compared to the sewage from all the drains of Rome pouring into the Tiber, and which he brought to a close with this sententious peroration: 'For you love neither concierges nor bailiffs nor police-men.'

Zola shows a curious lack of decency in matters of the heart. In *La Joie de vivre* he has made copy out of his mother's death. I can understand the recording of such intimate sorrows in memoirs, in posthumous publications; but using them for copy paid for by a newspaper at so much a line is something beyond my compre-hension.

# 1884

Bonvin, who had agreed to illustrate the new edition of *Sœur Philomène*, came to see me today and told me that he was terribly sorry, that he was perfectly prepared to do the illustrations, but that his doctor had warned him that if he did any engraving in the present state of his eyes, he would lose his sight.

He told me that he had gone all the same to La Charité and that he had met a Sœur Philomène there, a Sœur Philomène so beloved by her patients that every day she found a bunch of violets in her cell.

He told me too the most curious and amusing things that he had noticed during the long periods he had spent in hospital with various protracted illnesses, including hydrarthrosis. He gave me some delightful details about love in hospital and how affairs were conducted in Saint-Louis. It was all arranged during Mass. There, the patients of an amorous nature, the women dressed up to the best of their ability in their grey coats, the men wearing their cotton caps with a conquering air, used to sit in the seats nearest the aisle, along which a nurse walked up and down. They would pick the side which would allow them to display an undamaged profile, for many of them were suffering from scrofula in an advanced state, and each person would hold his missal in such a way as to show the number of his bed, which was marked on it. Seats along the aisle cost five sous each.

If I were in Popelin's place and had the honour of being the Princess's lover, I should feel humiliated in my vanity as a lover by the food served to the Princess's friends and mine, and I feel sure that this would eventually part us. What is absolutely certain is that I should never agree to dine at her table every day: I should ask for every other day off in order to *depoison* myself at my own house or somewhere else.

*Wednesday, 16 January*

Zola came to see me today. He looks and behaves like a whole-sale dealer in copy. He kept grumbling that the lines in the *Gil Blas* contained four letters more than the lines in all the other papers. That is why he has sold the novel to Dumont for 20,000 francs, because with those four letters his copy would have come to only 18,000 lines. Now he does not care how many cuts the paper makes . . . it will still have to pay him 20,000 francs.

He is worried about the novel he has to do next, *Les Paysans*. He wants to spend a month on a farm in Beauce, with a letter of recommendation from a rich landlord to his farmer, a letter announc-ing the arrival, with her husband, of a sick woman in need of country air.[1] 'You see,' he said, 'all we need is a couple of beds in a white-washed room. . . . And of course our meals at the farmer's table. . . . Otherwise I shouldn't learn anything. . . .'

As for *Les Chemins de fer*, his novel about the noise and bustle of a railway station and a man living in all that noise and bustle, with some sort of dramatic plot, he does not see his way to writing that yet. . . .

He would rather make a start on something about a strike in a mining district, beginning with a bourgeois having his throat slit on the first page. . . . Then the sentence, with some of the men con-demned to death and others sent to prison. . . . The trial serving as a pretext for a serious, thoroughgoing study of the social question.[2]

*Tuesday, 5 February*

Today, at the Brébant dinner, we talked about the crushing of the minds of children and young men under the huge volume of things taught them. We agreed that an experiment was being carried out on the present generation of which it was impossible to predict the consequences. And in the course of the discussion somebody advanced the ironical idea that our present-day system of universal education might well deprive society of the educated man and

---

[1] This novel, under the title of *La Terre*, was published in 1887. Zola's documenta-tion, carried out at Cloyes in Beauce, lasted less than a week: from 6 to 10 May 1886.

[2] The two novels mentioned here eventually appeared as *La Bête humaine* (1890) and *Germinal* (1885).

endow it with the educated woman: not a reassuring prospect for the husbands of the future.

*Sunday, 10 February*

Viaud, the author of *Le Mariage de Loti*, a thin, slight, skinny man with the big sensual nose of Caragueus, the punchinello of the East, and the far-away voice of a sick man. A silent fellow, who admits to being terribly shy. Words have to be dragged out of him. He gave us this horrifying information about Calmann-Lévy's usurious contracts: that for six years the author is bound to share with the publisher all the fees he is paid for his contributions to newspapers and periodicals, so that Calmann-Lévy got half the fee for Viaud's articles on Tonking published in the *Figaro*. Is this not absolutely monstrous, and should not that legal robber be put beyond the pale and deprived of the handshakes of decent people?

A little later, Viaud told us in a few words, as if it were the most ordinary thing in the world, of a sailor he had seen washed overboard in heavy weather and of the chaplain who had given absolution from the deck to the poor wretch abandoned on his lifebuoy. And when Daudet asked him if he came from a family of sailors, he replied with the utmost simplicity in his soft little voice: 'Yes, I had an uncle who was eaten on the raft of the *Méduse!*'[1]

*Monday, 10 March*

It is strange how an old man of letters still feels a stupid satisfaction at seeing his work printed in a newspaper. This morning, before seven o'clock, I went downstairs two or three times in my nightshirt to see if the *Gil Blas* was in my letterbox and if it contained the first instalment of *Chérie*.

Then I roamed round Paris, looking for my posters on the walls, and after that, sacrificing a good quarter of my fee for the novel, I finished the day with a visit to Bing's, where apart from a box by Ritzono costing 500 francs, I paid 2,000 francs for a masterpiece by Korin, a writing-desk in gold lacquer decorated on top and inside

[1] Jean-Louis-Adolphe Viaud was a cabin-boy on the *Méduse* in 1816. Though not 'eaten on the raft', he died shortly afterwards at the age of thirteen.

with chrysanthemums with golden blossoms and mother-of-pearl leaves, a thing in the most wonderfully barbaric taste.

*Saturday, 15 March*

'I'm sorry, but I haven't been reading your novel. A book in serial form is such a horrible thing, especially a book like those you write.' That is what all your friends and relations tell you. An excuse invented by idiots which has been adopted by intelligent men. Well, for my part, I read my friends in serial form, and I am grateful to those who read me as I read my friends. For it is good for an author, and almost as necessary as food and drink, to hear people talk about what he publishes; and if it became the general practice to stop reading the serial in a newspaper, then the best part of what now goes into the press would be doomed.

*Tuesday, 25 March*

Nowadays, in the sexual act, I am somewhat distracted from the physical pleasure of the thing by a continual preoccupation. 'You know, old fellow,' my dizzy brain says to the sensualist in me, 'it is quite possible that today the little convulsion will be accompanied by the last and the *little death* will bring on the great.'

*Wednesday, 2 April*

*Zézé* Daudet came here today with his father. He wanted to cut the goldfish with the pruning-shears, he tried to pull off all the rhododendron buds without being seen, and he did his best to wreak havoc wherever his little hand could reach; and when he had broken or destroyed something, his face shone with happiness. I had already met this instinct for destruction, in perhaps an even fiercer, more inhuman, more frenzied form, in a child as beautiful and intelligent as *Zézé*, the little Béhaine, who died from meningitis. . . . In that child jubilation over the breaking up of things had something diabolical about it. I had observed the same weird appetite for the annihilation of objects in another child, Pierre Gavarni's little boy. But the latter, having a quiet, gentle, orderly nature, always asked politely for permission to destroy. He would say in his sweetest voice to Pélagie: 'Tell me, Madame, it is all right to break this? . . . And that?'

While *Zézé* was laying waste the kitchen and the garden, his father, talking about *Sapho*, spoke to me of the difficulty of putting certain amoroso-intellectual phenomena into words. He recalled a certain evening in his life when he had been in love, an evening when Paris had seemed a different city to him, a *white* city, with no prostitution on the street-corners. . . . And he had felt the need to go and communicate this impression to the elder Coquelin, whom he had found in his dressing-room taking off the costume in which he had been playing Mascarille, and who had said to him: 'Are you drunk?'

And then the lovable rascal started describing the ineffable pleasure he had derived, in a crowded omnibus in the south of France, from touching the hand of an innocent little girl, who had said to him in the Provençal idiom: 'You are making me shiver', and who finally, giving in to him, had let him slip his fingers against hers inside her poor little filoselle glove. And he said that the slipping of his fingers into that glove had given him more pleasure than if he himself had slipped completely into the girl.

*Wednesday, 23 April*

A stir, a great stir. . . . All this arouses unreasonable hopes in you, but those intoxicating hopes vanish in the face of disappointing reality.

'You know,' Charpentier's secretary said to me, all puffed up with the success of the book, 'we are reprinting. . . . Yes, another four thousand! . . .'

Well, that makes twelve thousand in all. It is a respectable figure, but it is not a surprise, that surprise which I have never had in the whole of my life.

This evening, in a corner of the drawing-room at Jourdain the architect's, Daudet, his features drawn, his eyes dull, his fine hair curling in a sickly way, told me in a melancholy voice: 'Yes, yes. . . . The trouble is that I have had everything . . . yes, everything, my dear fellow. . . . And I am paying for it now. . . . I have the strangest sensations. . . .' And he stopped, gazing vaguely into space, like a man afraid of mysterious, inexplicable, painful things going on inside him.

*Saturday, 26 April*

Melancholy this morning. The attacks of literary critics do not take effect immediately, but they poison the individual attacked after a given number of hours, a given number of days, and I am beginning to feel the effect.

This evening, I dined at the Nittis's with the Princess. That false creature, Mme de Galbois, came over to me in a corner of the room, with her hypocritical airs and graces, and in a whining voice commiserated with me at length on the attacks which were being made on me. Truth to tell, I felt a certain apprehension about meeting Mlle Abbatucci at this dinner, knowing that she had just read my book; I was afraid that she might complain to me of certain indiscretions in it, and the thought frightened me. It seemed to me that my heart would grow cold if this friendship of ours, for all that it is nothing more than friendship, were to come to an end. . . . But she was perfectly charming; and with would-be reproachful eyes and laughing lips she said to me straight away: 'You know, this evening, you will have to be especially nice to me!'

*Wednesday, 30 April*

Today, before going to Dr. Fournier's, Daudet came to see me. We spent several hours alone together. He was in a mood for confidences—confidences about his sensual ego, his corrupt ego. He told me that he had lost his virginity at the age of twelve. He had stayed for a week in a brothel where, for fear of the police, he had been kept out of sight. He had spent nearly the whole week in bed with a woman from Lorraine whose skin was covered with freckles but was so soft to the touch that it had driven him mad.

*Sunday, 4 May*

Today I received a letter informing me of the death in her seventy-sixth year of Fanny Curt, a cousin of mine whom I had completely lost sight of a good many years ago.

It is strange, the memory this black-edged letter brings back to me. I was still a child, but a child already preoccupied with the enigma of sex and the mysteries of love. I was spending a few days' holiday at Bar-le-Duc, and my cousin Fanny, who had been married only a short time, was a pretty young woman. Neither she nor her husband ever stood on ceremony with me, and I used to go into their rooms whenever I liked, whether they were in bed or not. One morning when I wanted to ask the husband to fasten some hooks to a line for me, I went into their bedroom without knocking. And I went in just as my cousin, her head thrown back, her knees up, her legs apart and her bottom raised on a pillow, was on the point of being impaled by her husband. There was a swift movement of the two bodies, in which my cousin's pink bottom disappeared so quickly beneath the sheets that I might have thought it had been a hallucination. . . . But the vision remained with me. And until the day I met Mme Charles, that pink bottom on a pillow with a scalloped border was the sweet, exciting image that appeared to me every night, before I went to sleep, beneath my closed eyelids.

*Friday, 16 May*

Huysmans's *A Rebours* is like a book written by a favourite son of mine about the future husband of Chérie. The hero is a wonderful neurotic. They may say what they like against the book, it brings a little fever to the brain, and books that do that are the work of men of talent. And it is written in an artistic style to boot. . . . Yes, literature—our literature—is making progress.

*Thursday, 23 May*

This evening Mistral informed us, with a curious pride, that the next number of the *Chat noir* is to be entirely devoted to his works and his person. Salis, the red-haired tavern-keeper, has done him the honour of asking him for something on the black cats of Provence, and he has written down a local legend for him. . . . As I have said before, he is a real windbag, that secessionist troubadour, and must owe a great deal of his fame to the gibberish in which he writes.

I left Daudet's feeling very tired, and fell asleep in the open cab taking me back to the station. When I awoke in the Place de la Concorde, where six or eight electric lights were burning like mortuary tapers in lofty lamp-standards under a blue-black, starless sky, I thought for a second that I was no longer alive but travelling along

a Road of Souls of which I had read a description in Poe. But a moment later we were driving up the Avenue de l'Opéra and along the
boulevards, in the midst of the tangle of thousands of carriages, the
jostling crowds on the pavements, the crush of people on the tops
of the trams and omnibuses, the procession on foot or awheel of a
multitude of human beings silhouetted against the golden letters of
the shopfronts, with, in the darkness, the agitated, hurried awakening, the movement, the life of a Babylon.

*Saturday, 31 May*

My good friend Daudet is too much of a spoilt child. The whole
press is singing *Sapho*'s praises, he is going to sell 100,000 copies,
his book is killing every other book and mine in particular—and
yet a few scratches make him angry, irritated, bitter. Today, finding
myself in a window recess with Mme Daudet, I gently criticized this
extreme susceptibility of her husband's and reminded her of the
fierce attacks that had just been made on me. She interrupted me to
say: 'But you have had some enthusiastic reviews too!' To which I
replied: 'Yes, from a few unknown young men with a dozen
readers. . . .' I must say that my good friend Daudet's nerves are in
a bad way.

*Wednesday, 4 June*

Daudet and his wife dropped in on me today. They began by
finding Hennequin, whom Daudet knows to be no admirer of his
prose. Then in came Joseph Gayda, who had just published an
article saying that *Sapho* showed the influence of Zola and myself.
There was a dreadful chill, then an explanation—from Daudet first,
who was very huffy to begin with, but then thawed and said that he
was not as angry as he looked and that he had simply written to his
editor to say that Gayda was 'a little greenhorn'. The tone in which
he said this took the sting out of it, and the two men parted on good
terms.

At this point the Daudets left and I showed them out. When I
had shut the door, Daudet knocked on it and came back by himself
to whisper in my ear: 'It's tomorrow that I go to bed for my operation.'

*Saturday, 7 June*

A surgeon leaves something strange and disturbing in an apartment he has visited; the apartment takes on the character of a house
a few days before a move. Something of the everyday life of the
place has already gone. . . .

I waited for a few minutes in Daudet's study, and was then shown
into his bedroom. I found him in his bed, bending over a little table
heaped with books, letters, and telegrams, including one from La
Rounat proposing a new revival of *L'Arlésienne*. The dear fellow,
so sweet in his bed-linen as Lagier would say, smiled broadly and
talked almost gaily about the pretty little steel instruments which
had sliced through his skin. It turned out to have been Delpit's
brother-in-law who had operated on him. 'So you are returning the
sword-cut I gave your sister's husband!' Daudet had said to him.
He added with a burst of laughter: 'And then, you know that Léon
has an alarm-clock, an alarm-clock that makes the devil of a
din? Well, just at the very moment that the surgeon started work,
the bell went off, and the damned machine carried on ringing all
the time!'

*Sunday, 8 June*

In order to depict Nature, Gautier used only his eyes. Since then,
all the senses of writers have been called into play in the rendering
of landscape in prose. Fromentin used his ears and produced a fine
passage on the silence of the desert. Now it is the nose's turn, and
we have the smells and perfumes of a place, whether it is the Central
Market or a corner of Africa, with Zola and Loti. Both men, when
one comes to think of it, have curious olfactory organs, Loti with
his sensual punchinello nose, and Zola with his pointer's nose,
aimed inquiringly at things and quivering like a mucous membrane
twitching at the touch of a fly.

*Wednesday, 18 June*

Daudet is a queer fellow! He confided to me that yesterday, after
his surgeon had told him that he would probably have to have
another operation, he had had a *venereal fainting fit*. . . . Yes, he had
been to see a tart who had, he assured me, the sweetest little face.

This had been his way of cocking a snook at the impending operation . . . and also, he added, of finding out what sort of condition he
was in. And dammit all, he had practically fainted away in the middle
of his experiment.

Daudet was just going when, followed by Heredia, in came
Montesquiou-Fezensac, the model for the hero of the novel *A
Rebours*. Looking at him and listening to him today with a certain
deliberate curiosity, I found him altogether more human than Des
Esseintes, who is nothing but a caricature of the man. For there is
no denying that Montesquiou is a most distinguished, fastidious
person, who might well have real literary talent.

*Monday, 23 June*

Today, eating and drinking mean nothing to me. I have completely given up smoking. As for physical love, when I indulge in it
I dread its sweet convulsion. Only that which contributes to the
survival of my personality can afford me a little pleasure: the
engraving of a portrait, the republishing of a book.

*Saturday, 12 July*

Daudet, who is staying at Champrosay, had an appointment with
Potain this morning, and invited me to lunch with himself and his
wife at the Café d'Orsay afterwards.

When he arrived, he told me that Potain had found him a lot
weaker. Lunch was a gloomy meal; we talked about our health and
the cholera epidemic. Then, while his wife went shopping at the Bon
Marché, Daudet asked me to accompany him to the house of the
surgeon who had operated on him, and whom he needed to see
again.

In the cab, he told me in short, staccato phrases that he was eaten
up with syphilis, that he had all the symptoms of softening of the
brain, but that he hoped that iodine might help him.

Finally we came to an old house in the Rue de la Ville-l'Évêque,
where he was shown into the surgeon's drawing-room under the
name of Dr. Daudet. It was a drawing-room full of knick-knacks
which looked as if they had been won in a lottery at a charity bazaar:
Venuses de Milo by Barbedienne, tapestries printed by the Berville

process, *foukousas* bought at the 'Mikado's Empire', all sorts of gaudy rubbish which, in the half-light filtering through the closed shutters, seemed to be wrapped in the grey of a spider's web; and in this silent, bleak, twilit setting, a clock slowly ticked away the seconds.

Daudet told me about life at Champrosay, with himself playing endless games of chess with his mother-in-law; his father-in-law painting water-colours from morning to night in his study, breaking off only to give himself an injection of morphine; and Mme Daudet helping *Zézé* with his lessons and writing an occasional paragraph full of original impressions.

We waited for an hour, an hour-and-a-half, talking a little now and then to make a noise in that fearful silence and to reduce the strain of waiting. Finally somebody came for Dr. Daudet, who returned a little later saying: 'I have to lie down, yes, lie down for a week. . . . And that's the devil of a nuisance, because lying in bed wakes up all my other pains!'

*Monday, 25 August*

Coming back from Saint-Germain to Paris in the train last Friday, Dumas talked to me a lot about Mme Sand, whom he described to me as a monster unconscious of her depravity, her egoism, her good-natured cruelty.

Summoned to Nohant when Manceau had died, he had asked her, with the dead man still awaiting burial, how she felt. 'I feel', she answered, 'like having a bath, going for a walk in the woods, and going to the theatre this evening.' To which he replied: 'For the theatre, you will have to wait until you go to Paris!' Going to stay in Paris for a while, the old woman started going out to supper, drinking champagne and making love, in fact living the life of a girl student in her fortieth year, a life which eventually laid her low and forced her to send for Dr. Favre. The doctor told her bluntly that she was suffering from senile anaemia; and after warning her that she would *peg out* if she went on leading this life for a few more months, he prescribed a quiet family life in a recommendation revealing sublime scepticism about the woman writer's heart: 'What you must do now is try to persuade yourself that you love your grandchildren!'

*Monday, 20 October*

Today, at the Cassin exhibition, I met Daudet, whom I accompanied as far as Dentu's. Walking slowly beside me, he confessed to me that he was not working on the novel he was supposed to be writing after *Sapho*. Without telling anybody, he is doing a sort of *Tartarin in Switzerland* for an international company which is paying him *two hundred and seventy-five thousand francs* for it![1] Did you hear that, shades of Gautier, Flaubert, and Murger, whom Lévy used to pay 400 francs for the complete rights of a book? Daudet was a little shamefaced about his confession and seemed to be waiting for a few reassuring words. 'Good heavens,' I said, 'the sum is so considerable as to excuse *a little commercialism* in a lifetime of literature. And then, you aren't alone in the world as I am. . . . Dammit all, you've got children to think of!'

*Saturday, 8 November*

These last few days, I have found real pleasure of heart and mind in reading a bundle of letters from my brother found in Louis Passy's house, a bundle of letters written in his youth which light up parts of our life that had grown dim in my memory, bringing them out of the mist which the years spread over the past.

These old letters have even sent my mind back, I cannot tell why, to a past more distant than that which they recount. They have conjured up for me, alive and real, the memory of my little fair-haired sister, Lili. I can see her again in 1832, coming with her nanny to fetch me from the Pension Goubaux so that we could all flee from the cholera epidemic. I can see her still, the dear little thing, with her blue eyes and her pretty fair hair, not wanting to sit beside me in the cab but perching on the ledge at the bottom of the door, the better to see me, the better to devour me with her eyes, with that adoring, almost religious attention which children give to those they love.

Poor child! The next night, in the stage-coach taking us towards the Haute-Marne, the cholera took hold of her. And I remember that journey with that dying child on our knees, and my mother and father not daring to stop in any of the villages or little towns along our route for fear of not being able to find a doctor capable of

[1] *Tartarin sur les Alpes*, published in 1885.

treating her, and arriving at Chaumont only when she was already as good as dead.

*Friday, 21 November*

I keep hearing people say that nobody is capable of self-abnegation and self-sacrifice any longer. Yet I have sacrificed to literature, if not a grand passion, a very serious and tender affection.[1] I certainly would not have gone on living in my present isolation but would have married instead if I had not believed that by depriving myself of that happiness I would be able to do something great and useful for literature after my death.

*Wednesday, 24 December*

Today Maupassant, coming to see me about the bust of Flaubert, told me two things which are typical of the present day.

Smart young people nowadays are learning from *ad hoc* writing-masters how to write the fashionable script, the script of the moment, a script devoid of all personality and looking like a string of m's.

Another smart innovation at the Rothschilds'. As they have exhausted the possibilities of every sort of hunting, and as there is not a single animal left on earth which can arouse their hunting instincts, they have a deerskin dragged through the woods in the morning and spend the afternoon following the scent of this non-existent animal with a pack of specially trained hounds, in a kind of shadow-hunt. Then, as Mme Alphonse Rothschild is very good at jumping, obstacles are set up in advance and the grass is watered so that if the Jewish huntress takes a tumble she will not be hurt.

Guy de Maupassant told me that Cannes is a wonderful source of information for him. There the Luynes, the Orléans and the Princesse de Sagan spend the winter; and there life is much more easy-going and people talk more freely and more readily than in Paris. And he gave me to understand that, understandably and intelligently, he goes there to find his male and female characters for the novels he is planning to write about life and love in Parisian society.

This evening, in a corner of the Princess's drawing-room, the

---

[1] By rejecting the advances of Mlle Pauline Zeller, who had hoped that he would marry her.

Japanese Hayashi, whom I had brought along, told me about a *hara-kiri* at which his father had acted as registrar and which he had witnessed as a child. After the preliminary formalities had been concluded, the condemned man read a poem in which he declared that he had begun the task of ridding the people of the scourge of his existence. Then he took a little sword, wrapped it in paper to within an inch of the top of the blade, and, after really opening his own stomach, said to his fencing-master, whom he had chosen to be his executioner: 'Now go to it!'

# 1885

Today Daudet and his wife came for a preview of my Grenier. They stayed a long time, until dusk fell; and in the half-light we talked together freely and affectionately.

Daudet spoke of the first years of his married life. He told me that his wife did not know that there was such a thing as a pawnshop; and once she had been enlightened, she would never refer to it by name but would ask him: 'Have you been *there?*' The delightful thing about it all is that this girl who had been brought up in such a middle-class way of life was not at all dismayed by this new existence among people scrounging dinners, cadging twenty-franc pieces, and borrowing pairs of trousers.

'You know,' said Daudet, 'the dear little thing spent nothing, absolutely nothing on herself. We have still got the little account books we kept at that time, in which, beside twenty francs taken by myself or someone else, the only entry for her, occurring here and there, now and then, is: *Omnibus, 30 centimes.*' Mme Daudet interrupted him to say ingenuously: 'I don't think that I was really mature at that time: I didn't understand. . . .' My own opinion is rather that she had the trustfulness of people who are happy and in love, the certainty that everything will turn out all right in the end.

Daudet went on to say that during all those years he had done nothing at all, that all he had felt had been a need to live, to live actively, violently, noisily, a need to sing, to make music, to roam the woods, to drink a little too much and get involved in a brawl. He admitted that at that time he had had no literary ambition, but just an instinctive delight in noting everything down, in recording everything, even his dreams. It was the war, he declared, which had changed him, by awakening in him the idea that he might die without having achieved anything, without leaving anything durable behind him. . . . Only then had he set to work, and with work had come literary ambition.

*Sunday, 1 February*

Today saw the inauguration of my Grenier. I had sent out only wenty-two invitations and fifteen or sixteen people came along. Gayda, who had asked if he might write an article for the *Figaro* on this first gathering, arrived at five o'clock to say that he had been forced to write the article before coming: Blavet, the chief writer of the *Parisis* column, had to dine out, in the suburbs I believe, and had asked for the article to reach him before three o'clock.

There was talk of Vallès, who is seriously ill, and from Vallès the conversation turned to Séverine. She would appear to be a victim of the University in her way, just like Vallès. She is the daughter of a schoolmaster who was such a pedant that he used to talk Latin to her at mealtimes. And hatred for her family reached such a degree in Séverine that during the last days of the Commune, watching Paris burning from Passy as a little girl, she sighed: 'Oh, if only the fire would burn down Papa's house!'[1]

Then Montesquiou was mentioned, and somebody described his first love-affair, a Baudelairean love-affair with a female ventriloquist who, while Montesquiou was straining to achieve his climax, would imitate the drunken voice of a pimp, threatening the aristocratic client.

Daudet produced an original comparison. He said that Renan's brain was like a deconsecrated cathedral, full of piles of wood, bales of straw, and heaps of assorted lumber, but retaining its religious architecture.

*Tuesday, 3 March*

It was five o'clock. I had intended to go and have dinner in a Right Bank restaurant, where I should be sure to meet nobody I knew, and then roam the deserted streets around the Odéon until nine o'clock. But it was pouring with rain, my conversation with myself was becoming unbearably tedious, and I felt the need to spend the hours until the play began in the company of people who were fond of me.

So there I was, a moment later, bowling along in a cab in driving rain, with a limping horse and a cabby who did not know his way,

[1] Séverine's father, Onésime Rémy, was a pedant but no pedagogue: he was a civil servant employed at the Prefecture of Police.

through desolate streets in which, as if through the dirty water of a neglected aquarium and by the flickering light of a gaslamp, I caught sight of a shop-sign reading: *Maison Dieu: all sorts of trusses repaired.* . . . 'Will you give me a bowl of soup?' I asked, going into Daudet's study. The comfort and affectionate warmth of a friendly house enveloped me, and soon we were dining at the end of a table already laid for the supper in honour of the revival of *Henriette Maréchal.*

I let the Daudets go into the Odéon by themselves. For my part, I wandered round the brilliantly lighted building without daring to go in, waiting for the end of that first act which I dreaded. Thinking about the Princess, who, behaving like a true princess, had refused to be satisfied with a first-tier box and had insisted on having a stage-box, I imagined her being insulted and abused with every one of those gusts of noise which escape now and then through the closed doors and windows of a theatre.

Finally I could stand it no longer, and after walking round the Odéon ten times I pushed open the stage door, climbed the stairs, and asked Émile: 'Is it a good house?' To which he replied: 'Excellent.'

This answer only half reassured me and I went panting down into the wings, where the muffled noise of the applause in the auditorium sounded at first like hissing. But this impression lasted for no more than a second: it really was applause that I could hear, frantic applause to which the curtain fell on the first act.

The rest of the play went splendidly, with perhaps a slight coolness at the end of the second act, which had been the high spot of the dress rehearsal, but with an enthusiastic ovation at the end of the third.

The Princess, who had asked for me but whom I had refused to go and see in the auditorium, came to the green-room with her suite to congratulate me. Slightly intoxicated by the cheering and clapping, she said to me: 'It's superb, it's superb. . . . Shall we kiss?'

After everyone had embraced, we went off to Daudet's, where I was given the place of the master of the house. And we supped in the midst of general gaiety and the hope that my success would throw open the doors to the realist theatre.

When I reached home at four o'clock in the morning, Pélagie, who got up again to let me in, confirmed the success of the evening, telling me that for a moment she and her daughter had been afraid that the gallery, crowded with students and young people, was going to collapse on their heads, the stamping had been so delirious.

*Thursday, 5 March*

This evening at the Odéon, at the third performance of *Henriette Maréchal*, there were great gaps in the auditorium, the audience was icy cold, and Léonide Leblanc was so hoarse that one could scarcely hear what she was saying. Porel, in his stage-box, where I was listening to the play, exclaimed: 'She sounds as if she's got bronchitis. . . . The play's done for if we have to suspend it for four or five days.' And an announcement had to be made asking for the audience's indulgence.

I looked into Léonide's dressing-room for a moment. She said that she had been overworked during the last few days of rehearsal and had caught cold; but that in spite of everything she would go on playing.

After such a triumphant first night, is this revival of our play going to be a flop?

*Friday, 6 March*

I really am out of luck. Favart, who could not come to the first two performances, was present at yesterday's. The tour she was thinking of doing round France with *Henriette Maréchal* can be written off.

All that effort, all that upheaval in my life, all that trouble, all that expenditure of care, interest, and nervous energy, for such a paltry result: no, it simply was not worth it.

*Saturday, 7 March*

Somebody or other called me the victor yesterday. A funny sort of victory I have won, I must say! All day long I kept saying to myself: 'You must go to the Odéon tonight, you must be there to encourage the actors with your presence. . . .' But faced with the prospect of finding a house like the one the day before yesterday, I could not summon up the courage to go to the theatre.

*Sunday, 8 March*

This evening there was a full house and the applause was deafening. Léonide, delighted to have partly recovered her voice, proudly showed me her back, where the skin has all been taken off by the *taxia*. Chelles promised me a hundred performances. And the pessimist that I was when I arrived departed an optimist once more. These ups and downs, without any transition between them, are the worst thing about the theatre.

*Tuesday, 17 March*

Pélagie brought me a letter today which had been given her by a gentleman who was waiting downstairs for my reply. This letter was signed Léon Bloy, the star writer of the *Chat noir*, who, less than six months ago, concluded an article on my brother and myself with these words: 'the survivor of the two blackguards'. In his letter he told me that seeing *Henriette Maréchal* had brought about a change in his attitude to me, which had hitherto been extremely hostile, and he ended up by asking me, after a series of dramatic statements, for fifty francs, 'which he would pay back, if he could, or which he would not pay back'. Upon my word, I feel perfectly capable of giving these fifty francs to a literary enemy, however virulent he may be. But if I gave them to an insulter of that ilk, who showed no mercy to my dead brother, I would consider myself a coward—and it seems to me that you must have tremendous cheek to come in person to ask for money from a man with every reason to slap you in the face.

*Tuesday, 12 May*

Dined at Daudet's with Barbey d'Aurevilly, whom I met today for the first time at close quarters.

He was dressed in a frock-coat, with a skirt which made his hips look as if he were wearing a crinoline, and a pair of white woollen trousers which looked like underpants with under-straps. Under this ridiculous, homosexual outfit, a gentleman with excellent manners and the soft voice of a man accustomed to talking to women, a voice which, on account of his lack of teeth, recalled the guttural intonation, but in a minor key, of Frédérick Lemaître.

He spoke of *Le Bague d'Annibal,* which he called his first *vagitus,* adding with a touch of irony that it had been published under Montépin's auspices, that it was thanks to Montépin that he had found his first publisher: 'Yes, Cadot, the famous Cadot. Montépin told me that he was prepared to publish me in these words: "He will take you, but he won't pay you!"'

Then he went on to *Les Diaboliques,* asserting that the prosecution of the book had been instigated by the Duchesse de MacMahon, at the suggestion of one of her young friends in her pious little circle whose work he had attacked.

He ate scarcely anything, drank a great deal, and held his half-empty cup of coffee out to Daudet, who had a bottle of brandy in his hand, saying: 'Fill this up, will you, like the cup of a Breton parish priest!'

Then he spoke of his ability to go without sleep and of his delight in staying up at night, which allowed him to work and released him from horrible, terrifying dreams. 'An alcoholic's dreams', said Daudet. 'Oh, come now,' retorted Barbey, 'I drink only with my friends.' And Daudet and Barbey recalled times when they had swilled champagne in broad daylight, in the middle of the street, to the astonishment of the passers-by.

*Sunday, 24 May*

Just as somebody in my Grenier was saying that Hugo was the apotheosis of the word, Zola came in and said in a theatrical whisper: 'I thought that he was going to bury us all, yes, I really thought so!' And having said this, he walked round the room as if relieved by this death and as if convinced that he was going to inherit the literary papacy.[1]

*Tuesday, 2 June*

It seems that the night before Hugo's funeral, that night of a nation's sorrowful wake, was celebrated by a wholesale copulation, a priapic orgy, with all the prostitutes of Paris, on holiday from their brothels, coupling with all and sundry on the lawns of the Champs-Élysées—Republican marriages which the good-natured police treated with becoming respect.

[1] Hugo had died on 22 May.

Somebody remarked today that the Élysée had made it such an enormous celebration in order to diminish and efface in the minds of the people the memory of Gambetta's funeral. Then Spuller declared with a triumphant air that the Republic now had at its disposal for its great occasions a public of a million spectators, roughly the number of pilgrims which the Catholic festivals in Rome used to draw in the fifteenth century. And maintaining that the Church no longer had anything or anybody at its disposal—which comes close to the truth—he called for a halt to be called to the construction of the church of Sacré-Cœur, which he described as a monument to civil war.

Renan, after suggesting that the church should be turned into a Temple of Oblivion, with a chapel for Marat, another for Marie-Antoinette, and so on, went on to attack Lamartine as compared with Hugo, speaking of his unwillingness to accept new ideas, his stubborn adherence to his principles, and his clumsy behaviour, which had brought him a miserable, lonely old age, whereas Hugo's behaviour had won him the funeral we had witnessed. This was just the sort of sermon one expected to hear from Renan, the toadying, servile adulator of any sort of success.

*Sunday, 15 November*

A lot of people today in my Grenier: Daudet, Maupassant, Bonnières, Céard, Bonnetain, Robert Caze, Jules Vidal, Paul Alexis, Toudouze, Charpentier. At the end of these purely masculine gatherings, a slight feminine element is introduced by wives calling for their husbands; and today the spouse-collectors were Mme Daudet, Mme de Bonnières, and Mme Charpentier. The women look very well against the background of the scene and harmonize wonderfully with the furniture. . . . But the majority of my guests prefer them to come late, late, late.

*Tuesday, 17 November*

The last words of Robin, who expected to die of a heart ailment and was surprised to find himself being carried off by a different malady: 'Apoplexy? . . . Curious!' The remark of a true scientist.

*Tuesday, 1 December*

Today, coming out of the bookshop, I met Charpentier, who got into my brougham for a moment. He promptly started joking about Mme Daudet's pregnancy, that secret which is now an open secret, and laughing at the comical fury of the poor woman, who regards this Martinmas summer pregnancy as a curse of the south of France, which she already detested.

Then he told me in confidence that a painter called Delort, the man whom Daudet had portrayed under the name of Potter in his novel, prevented from picking a quarrel with Daudet by Scholl, who had told him that it would be a despicable action to fight a man in such a poor state of health that he could scarcely stand upright, had been bitten once more with the itch to fight at the prospect of seeing the character modelled on himself represented on the stage. At the first night of *Les Jacobites* he had accordingly announced his intention to slap Daudet in the face, so that when Daudet had come into the foyer Charpentier had had to draw Delort into a corner, plead with him and practically lay hands on him to prevent him from hurling himself at the author of *Sapho*. However, Delort, a violent-tempered, courageous man who complains that Daudet has used intimate confidences of his, declared there and then that he would slap him at the dress rehearsal or the first night of the play at the Gymnase, and that he was ready to fight him with pistols or any other weapon he pleased, if he was unable to hold a sword. I thought of the wife expecting a child: I thought of the poor fellow himself, who, though better than he was, is in no state to fight a duel of any sort. . . . And the sad thing about all this is that there is nothing one can do. If Daudet were warned, he would go and meet the slap half-way! One can only hope that the two men do not come together that day . . . and that somebody can persuade the painter that a challenge on his part, after such a long interval, might appear untimely and even ridiculous.

*Thursday, 3 December*

My constant preoccupation is to save the name of Goncourt from oblivion in the future by every sort of survival: survival through works of literature, survival through foundations, survival through the application of my monogram to all the *objets d'art* which have belonged to my brother and myself.

*Sunday, 20 December*

'Well, here comes the new theatre, your new theatre!' Thus Daudet, coming into my Grenier on legs as shaky as they were in the bad months last year. 'Yes,' he went on, 'the *Matin* has published an article on the new theatre, and Duret is going to interview you, Zola, and me about it.'

The conversation promptly turned to *Sapho*, and Daudet admitted in front of everybody that Déchelette's speech had been rewritten on the basis of suggestions I had made. This led to a discussion of the tact needed to represent reality on the stage and of the care which had to be taken in calculating the doses to be administered to the theatre-going public.

'In this connexion,' said Daudet, 'there's a story of a woman in a bus which I sometimes tell and which strikes me as perfectly applicable to the theatre. It's about a woman in black who boards a bus and whose dress, bearing, and expression impel her neighbour to ask her for the story of her misfortunes. So with the passengers murmuring sympathetically and the conductor blowing his nose to hide his tears, she describes the death of a first child and then a second. But at the death of her third child, interest slackens in the bus; and when she comes to the death of her fourth child, eaten by a crocodile on the banks of the Nile, despite the fact that it must have suffered more than the other three, everybody bursts out laughing. ... The story of my woman in a bus is one which every author should keep in mind when he writes a play.'

We all laughed and then started analysing the audience's reactions on the first night. Lorrain, who had been in Mme de Poilly's stage-box next to Mme de Galliffet, described the impressions of the 'old society hens'. They had been shocked most of all by the passionate dialogue in the scene of the break, having always subordinated their feelings to the conventions, and some of them admitted that their partings were much calmer, much more genteel than that.

Thereupon Daudet remarked very soundly: 'My play, like my book, will appeal to the men, who will all find part of their lives in it, but it will never appeal to the women; and the reason is that the tart has a lewd side to her which excites us men, and the decent woman can't understand that excitement, and is even jealous of it, knowing that she can't give it to us, for all her decency and virtue. ... Yes, it's all very strange. . . . Last night, for instance, in the carriage taking them home from the theatre, Madame Charcot gave her husband a scolding for crying over Déchelette's account of little Doré's death, telling him: "I can't understand why you should get so upset about that *trollop*." '


*Thursday, 24 December*

All Leconte de Lisle's rancorous, cannibal malice is to be found in this macabre remark of his. After being received with great kindness by the Duc d'Aumale when he called on him to ask for his vote in the Academy election, he met some acquaintance or other and expatiated on the politeness, graciousness, charm, and dignity of the Prince d'Orléans, pausing at the end of this tirade and adding: 'But to know what he is really like, one would have to see him on the scaffold!'

# 1886

*Wednesday, 20 January*

The only sincere lover, the only real lover of our times, is probably Octave Mirbeau—a sort of Othello in miniature! One evening when he arrived to spend the night with the woman for the love of whom he had become a stockbroker and found that she was sleeping out, he went into her dressing-room and tore into shreds, with his murderous hands, his mistress's little dog, the only creature on earth that she really loved.

*Tuesday, 16 February*

I went to see Robert Caze, who was wounded in a duel yesterday. It was right at the end of the Rue Condorcet, where the street begins to take on a suburban look. A fourth-floor flat on the far side of a courtyard: the home of a little clerk. A pale, thin woman glimpsed in the half-light of a corridor.

He was in bed, his fine features revealing the anxiety of a wounded man with no private means and dependent on his pen for his living. 'I was much better than he was!' he told me. 'But sword-fighting always intoxicates me . . . even in the fencing-school. . . . I threw myself on to his sword. . . . The liver has been punctured. If I haven't got peritonitis . . .' He did not finish his sentence.

Weak as he was from loss of blood, and although he had fought a nonentity to avoid fighting Champsaur, one could see in his eyes the secret determination to fight Champsaur one day.[1]

---

[1] The young journalist and novelist Robert Caze had refused to fight a duel with Félicien Champsaur, whom he accused of having libelled him in a newspaper article, and had taken legal action against Champsaur instead. Taunted with cowardice by Charles Vignier, he had fought a duel with the latter on 15 February and had spitted himself on Vignier's sword. He was to die on 23 March 1886.

*Sunday, 28 February*

The Princess came today to my Sunday to treat herself to the sight of my naturalists. She was extremely amusing in her curiosity and at the same time in a sort of moral dread of these creatures whom she calls 'the dirty little beasts'.

*Wednesday, 3 March*

At dinner, referring to the young men of letters whom she had seen in my Grenier, the Princess said with an air of surprise: 'Yes, they really are quite sweet . . . and Huysmans has a distinguished look. . . . What they need is the chance to mix with people of good position . . . to see something of society.' To which I replied: 'But you have only to ask them: they would be delighted.'

*Tuesday, 23 March*

I had set off to go and call on Robert Caze, who Daudet had told me was getting better, and I had practically got to the station when a young man came up to me, raised his hat and asked me if I was M. de Goncourt. When I answered that I was, he said: 'Here is *Grand'mère*, the book by Robert Caze which he has dedicated to you. . . . He has asked me to apologize to you for not having written anything in the book, but he is too weak to write.' And he told me that the poor fellow was regarded as done for.

Filled with gloom, I continued on my way, trying like a coward to put off my visit, dawdling in the streets, dropping into La Narde's and Bing's, and hesitating in the Rue Condorcet as to whether I should not just leave my card with the concierge, I finally decided to go upstairs, where poor Mme Caze told me that her husband was desperately ill and that he had had a dreadful fever for a good five hours.

I sat down in the little study, where Huysmans, Vidal, and an Impressionist painter were waiting. Through the open door I could hear the *glug-glug* of all sorts of drinks the wounded man kept tossing down, one after the other, in his unquenchable thirst; I could hear the incessant coughing of his consumptive wife; I could hear the scolding voice of the maid, as she told one of the children: 'You're taking advantage of your father's illness to do no work.'

The surgeon was expected, but he didn't come. After waiting

for half-an-hour, Huysmans and I got up and left, talking about the dying man and his preoccupation with his book and with the dispatch of the copies printed on superior paper. Huysmans saw him today for a moment, and the only thing he had to say was: 'Have you read my book?'

We sat down for a little while in a café on the Boulevard, and Huysmans told me about the beginning of his literary career. Hearing somebody near us mention the name of Hetzel, he told me that after his *Drageoir à épices* had been turned down by a whole succession of publishers, his mother, who on account of her bindery had business relations with Hetzel, had suggested that he should take his manuscript to Hetzel. A few days later, Hetzel asked him to go and see him and, in a fierce interview, informed him that he had no talent whatever, that he never would have any talent, that he wrote in an execrable style, and that he was starting a revolutionary Commune of Paris in the French language . . . and the half-witted author, the imbecile bourgeois and the commercial crook that was Hetzel told him that he was mad to think that one word was better than another, to believe in the existence of superior epithets. . . . And Huysmans described the anxiety this scene had caused his mother, who had complete confidence in the publisher's judgement, as well as the painful doubts it had given him about his talent.

*Saturday, 27 March*

Dinner at Zola's. Over coffee, Zola and Daudet talked about the hard times they had had in their youth. Zola recalled a period when his trousers and his overcoat were generally at the pawnshop and he stayed in his room in a nightshirt. The mistress he was living with at that time used to call those days 'the days he went Arab'. Yet he scarcely noticed the poverty in which he was living, his mind was so absorbed in a huge poem in three parts—*Genesis, Mankind, The Future*—which was the epic and cyclic story of our planet, before the appearance of mankind, during the long centuries of its existence, and after its disappearance. He had never been happier than at that time, poor as he was. This, he explained, was because he had never for a moment had any doubts about his future success, not that he had had any clear notion of what was going to happen to him, but he had been convinced that he would succeed. He added that it was difficult to express that feeling of confidence which, out of consideration for our susceptibilities, he defined as follows: 'that if he didn't have much confidence in his talent, he had great faith in his capacity for work'.

Then he spoke of an icy room, a sort of lantern-tower on the seventh floor of a house, which he had occupied for several years, and of his excursions on to the roof of the eighth storey in the company of his friend Pajot. From that eighth storey one could see the whole of Paris, and while the future police-superintendent Pajot amused himself by piddling into the tenants' chimney-pots, he, Zola, admired the view. And at the sight of that panorama of the capital spread out beneath him, the thought of conquering Paris insinuated itself into the mind of the literary débutant.

Daudet in his turn talked about his appalling poverty and about days when he had literally starved . . . but he added that he had found that poverty sweet because he had felt free to go where he pleased and do what he liked, because he had stopped being a school usher. He listed all the sordid hotels he had lived in, and told us that when L'épine had come to see him on Morny's behalf at the Hôtel du Sénat, there had been so little to sit on in his bedroom that his mistress, a really good-natured girl, had gone to the lavatory and had stayed there during the three-quarters of an hour the call had lasted.

*Sunday, 4 April*

Today Huysmans recounted the death of Verlaine's mother to us. Mother and son lived in a wine-dealer's house: the son downstairs, unable to leave his bed on account of something wrong with his legs, the mother upstairs, watched over after her death by friends of Verlaine's who were dead-drunk all the time. Friends and undertaker's mutes, each as tight as the other, had enormous difficulty in manœuvring the coffin down the narrow staircase: a descent in the course of which the son's door was opened for a moment and an aspergillum handed to him so that he could sprinkle holy water on the coffin from his bed.

*Saturday, 10 April*

At four o'clock, dropping into Charpentier's, I found Zola there, and I spoke to him about *L'Œuvre*, intending to let him know what

I honestly thought about the book, but speaking with all the tact and consideration that colleagues of the same literary faith owe to one another.

I told him, then, that I considered the exposition of Christine's love in a series of chaste calls very charming and delicate, but that the beginning and end of that love-affair struck me as improbable. . . . He interrupted me to say that he for his part believed that anything could happen in life, absolutely anything. . . . To which I replied that I was not convinced of this . . . and that in any case we, and above all he, Zola, the self-styled leader of the naturalist movement, had an obligation to make things truer to life and less improbable than the most fervent idealist. As a second criticism, I added that in my opinion he had made a mistake in introducing himself into the novel in the characters of both Sandoz and Claude, after which I repeated my praise of the beginning of the novel. Zola fell silent, his face turning slightly grey, and we parted.

At seven o'clock we met again, the Zolas and I, at Daudet's, where there was a big dinner. Right at the beginning, with regard to the delicate pastel drawing of his daughter which Raffaelli has put on show and which I praised, Zola declared that Raffaelli had a laborious talent and lacked 'sincerity'. . . . We sat down at table. Daudet called out to me: 'Goncourt, I've been to Joret's to get some morels for you.' At this Mme Zola's shrill voice could be heard saying: 'Oh, morels are quite common now; they only cost three francs. . . .' And she went on making amiable remarks of that kind all the way through dinner. Poor Mme Charpentier, who did her best to calm her down and who, in connexion with a bouillabaisse which the Daudets had had sent from Marseilles, spoke to her of her skill at cooking that particular dish, was rewarded with the sharp retort: 'Really, Madame, you are going to make people think that I spend the whole of my life in the kitchen!'

Lockroy, who arrived in the middle of an argument between Zola and myself, coming from a quiet lecture on agriculture and believing in the good fellowship of the naturalist family, listened to us in amazement with his eyes lowered, dumbfounded by the sharp tone of the conversation and by the latent hostility which he could sense between all the men and women there. The atmosphere was very bitter and quarrelsome, so quarrelsome, it seems, that during the jousting Mme Zola kept saying to herself: 'If this goes on, I shall cry. . . . If this goes on, I shall leave.'

The fact is that that man, living in isolation with no contact with anybody but the servants of his fame, is beginning to suffer from delusions of grandeur: the author can no longer take the slightest observation, the smallest criticism. It would appear that all the violent remarks made by the Zolas were the result of my conversation with him at Charpentier's in the afternoon and the reservations I expressed about *L'Œuvre*.

*Thursday, 15 April*

Daudet, to whom Zola made a cruel remark about his illness, a reference to the case of Manet, when leaving my house last Sunday, decided to return to Paris on foot, with the pot-bellied Zola panting along in his wake, for the sole purpose of showing him that he was not completely dead yet.

He confided to me that during this walk Zola had suddenly unbosomed himself, admitting his envy of me and giving vent to his feeling of spite against Bourget for putting me in his *Psychologie moderne* instead of Zola. It should be noted that Bourget has not included a single writer of Zola's generation in his book.

This outburst against me was combined with scurvy compliments to Daudet, who told me that this walk had left him with a sorry opinion of Zola, that the veil which had hidden the man's worst side from him had suddenly been torn aside, and that he had found himself in the presence of a false, shifty, hypocritical creature, 'an Italian, yes, an Italian', he kept saying.

*Saturday, 17 April*

This afternoon Bracquemond took me to see the sculptor Rodin. He is a man with common features, a fleshy nose, bright eyes flashing beneath unhealthily red lids, a long yellow beard, hair cut short and brushed back, and a round head, a head suggesting gentle, stubborn obstinacy—a man such as I imagine Christ's disciples looked like.

We found him in his studio on the Boulevard Vaugirard, an ordinary sculptor's studio with its walls splashed with plaster, its

wretched little cast-iron stove, the damp chill emanating from all the
big compositions in wet clay wrapped in rags, and a litter of heads,
arms, and legs in the midst of which two emaciated cats were posing
like fantastic griffins. There was a model there, stripped to the waist,
who looked like a stevedore. Rodin made the turn-tables revolve
carrying the life-size clay figures of his six *Burghers of Calais*,
modelled with powerful realism and with those splendid hollows in
the human flesh that Barye used to put in the sides of his animals.
He also showed us a robust sketch of a naked woman, an Italian, a
short, springy creature, a panther as he put it, which he said regret-
fully that he would never be able to finish since one of his pupils, a
Russian, had fallen in love with her and married her. He is a real
artist in flesh, introducing into the most beautiful and accurate
anatomy a detail of extraordinary disproportion—nearly always his
women's feet.

One of his finest works is a bust of Dalou done in wax, a trans-
parent green wax which looks like jade. It is impossible to imagine
anything more sensitive than his rendering of the shape of the eyelids and the delicate texture of the nose. . . . The poor devil really
has had bad luck with his *Burghers of Calais*! The banker who was
entrusted with the funds has absconded, and Rodin does not know
if he can be paid; yet the work is so far advanced that he will have to
finish it, and this will cost him 4,500 francs for the models, rent, etc.,
etc.

From his Boulevard de Vaugirard studio Rodin took us to his
studio near the École Militaire to see his famous door destined for
the future Palace of the Decorative Arts.[1] It has two panels covered
with a jumble, a mix-up, a tangle, something like the concretion of a
shoal of madrepores. Then after a few seconds the eye distinguishes
in these apparent madrepores the protrusions and hollows, the pro-
jections and cavities of a whole world of delightful little figures,
moving so to speak in an animation, in a mobility which Rodin has
tried to borrow from Michelangelo's *Last Judgement* and from certain tumultuous crowd scenes in Delacroix's pictures—all this with
an unexampled relief which only Dalou and he have ever attempted.

---

[1] This door was commissioned by the Government in 1880 and Rodin worked on
it for over twenty years. In 1904 the Government cancelled its order and Rodin re-
funded the advances he had already received, keeping the door, which can be seen
today in the garden of the Musée Rodin.

The Boulevard de Vaugirard studio contains a wholly realistic humanity; the studio of the Ile des Cygnes is as it were the home of a poetic humanity. Making a random choice among the plaster casts lying on the floor, Rodin showed us at close quarters a detail of his door. It consisted of some admirable little female torsos in which he had represented to perfection the slope of the back and so to speak the beating of wings of the shoulders. He also possesses in the highest degree an intuitive knowledge of the embraces and inter-twinings of two loving bodies, knotted together like the leeches one can see rolling on top of one another in a bowl. One group of the highest originality represents the idea of physical love, but without the translation of that idea being at all obscene. It shows a male hold-ing clasped against the top of his chest the tense body of a female faun with her knees drawn up in an astonishing contraction like that of a frog about to jump.

The man seems to me to have a hand of genius but to lack a per-sonal view of life, to have in his mind a hotch-potch of Dante, Michelangelo, Hugo, and Delacroix. He also strikes me as a man of plans and sketches, dissipating himself in a thousand ideas, a thou-sand creations, a thousand dreams, but never bringing anything to a final realization.

*Thursday, 22 April*

I dined this evening with Drumont, who is going to fight Meyer of the *Gaulois* on Saturday, with Daudet and M. Albert Duruy as his seconds.[1] Drumont arrived in a nervous, excited, gay mood. 'Today', he exclaimed, 'I had fifty-five callers . . . the bell never stops ringing. Crowds have started collecting in the street at the sight of all the people coming in . . . people who come to say to me: "How grateful we are to you for saying what we think!" There are some Carmelites who sent word to me that they would pray for me on Saturday . . . and somebody told my new housekeeper, who's a pious old thing, that I was a sort of lay priest. . . . She doesn't know what to believe. . . . Yes, there isn't a single copy left, the whole

---

[1] This duel was fought because Drumont, in his anti-semitic work *La France juive*, had reprinted an old article describing Meyer as a cardsharper. The encounter itself brought no credit to the director of the *Gaulois*, for Meyer grasped Drumont's sword while wounding him in the groin.

two thousand have gone. . . . Marpon wants to reprint . . . they are going to put eight presses on the job. . . . It's an exhausting business, though. I've talked for eight hours today and I've no voice left.'

And when I told him that he ought to have given a picture of the newspapers, showing how the Jews control them all, he said: 'Yes, that would have been interesting. . . . Take *L'Autorité* for instance, Cassagnac's paper. I've got a friend on that paper, not just an acquaintance but a friend who knew poverty with me in the bad old days, and who admires my book tremendously. . . . Well, he has written to tell me that he doubts whether he will be able to do an article on it, even in the form of an attack. . . . Because the money behind *L'Autorité*, that conservative paper, is supplied by a Jew, by a certain Fould, and there's a clause in his agreement by which Cassagnac undertakes not to attack the Jews.'

*Sunday, 25 April*

Little Lavedan, who never misses anything, was present at Meyer's return from his duel. The whole boulevard outside the *Gaulois* offices was full of Jews, and every few minutes a brougham such as you see outside the church of Saint-Augustin when there is a society wedding discharged a *sheeny* on to the road. All the Dollfuses and Dreyfuses in creation were there, and Halévy and Koning and Ollendorff dragging Ohnet in his wake.

Finally Meyer arrived and all the *sheenies* rushed up to him to congratulate him. 'I don't deserve your compliments, gentlemen', he said. 'I acquitted myself very badly in this affair. . . . That man is a lion!'

At this point Daudet came in and told us that it had been a fierce fight, that he himself had been on the point of fighting Meyer, and that he would have fought him to give him a chance to redeem himself, but he had seen 'a nasty look' in his eyes.

He described the duelling-ground to us: an old estate belonging to Baron Hirsch, with an open stretch of country in which there were horses roaming at liberty and stupidly coming up to the two duellists.

Then he came back to the details. There had been a first encounter in which Meyer had parried with his left hand and Drumont had called him a scoundrel, saying that he ought to have his hand tied behind his back. A second encounter had followed, and this time Meyer had grasped Drumont's sword and wounded him. And Daudet described how Drumont, from the doorway of the barn where he had been carried, with his trousers already removed and slapping his bloodstained shirt, had shouted angrily at Meyer and his seconds: 'To the ghetto with you, you filthy Jews! You murderers! . . . It was you who chose this house belonging to Hirsch which was bound to bring me bad luck!' And Daudet added: 'You know, that ill-bred individual, that guttersnipe shouting abuse at his opponent, was absolutely superb, while Meyer, that correct little Semite, looked like a haberdasher's assistant.'

Then, lost for a moment in the memory of the beauty of the day, the grandeur of the landscape, the serenity of the scene, Daudet said that in the midst of all that, those two little creatures, jerking their limbs about in an attempt to kill each other, had seemed utterly ridiculous.

*Saturday, 14 August*

Strauss has made a very good impression here at the Princess's. I find him a shrewd, intelligent, observant man, with a kindly nature, the humility of a Jew and something of the volubility of a lawyer; but he has a mephistophelian air about him which rather puts me off.

He spoke to me of the profound sorrow which Mme Bizet still felt at the loss of her husband, and he gave me this delicate proof of it. If she starts humming a tune from *Carmen* or any other tune composed by her husband, she always comes to a stop after a few notes, as if to say that she had begun humming the tune unconsciously and that almost immediately it had reminded her of her bereavement and brought back the painful emotion of her recent loss.

*Sunday, 12 September*

In *L'Éducation sentimentale*, what a wonderful scene Mme Arnoux's last call on Frédéric is, and what a sublime scene it would be if, instead of being written in very prettily turned phrases, but bookish phrases like: 'My heart lifted like dust after your foot-steps', it were all written in ordinary speech, in the true language of love used in real life.

All the same, it must be admitted that there is a delicacy in this scene which is a surprise to anyone who knew the author.

*Saturday, 25 September*

This morning in the garden we talked about copulation, the insipidity of it with a woman who is dressed, and the glorious frenzy of it with a woman who is naked, a woman one rolls on top of and covers with kisses: copulation as practised by artists, men of passion, men who really love women. And Daudet mentioned Morny, that peculiar ladies' man, who never slept with a woman but who, every morning, on a corner of one of the official divans on the first floor of the Parliament buildings, did homage to Venus with a caller dressed in all her petticoats and pantaloons, delighted and satisfied with this one and only indulgence in sensual pleasure.

This conversation led us on to a recognition of the strange and unique beauty of the face of any woman—even the commonest whore—who reaches her climax: the indefinable look which comes into her eyes, the delicate character which her features take on, the angelic, almost sacred expression which one sees on the faces of the dying and which suddenly appears on hers at the moment of the *little death*. And Daudet confided to me that in his fits of pure animality in the old days, he used to be irritated, yes, irritated by this spirituality, this divinity, so to speak, which transfigured the face of some filthy trollop and made him wish that he could make love to her in some other fashion.

*Thursday, 18 November*

This evening found me with the Daudets in Porel's box at the first night of the play adapted by Céard from *Renée Mauperin*. The audience, cold to begin with, thawed as soon as Cerny and Dumény came on, and after that took an obvious pleasure in the wit of the play. Applause and curtain-calls: all the signs of a big success.

The Daudets, as the godparents of my play, gave a supper-party in their apartment, with four tables in the dining-room and a table in the ante-room for the young people. Porel and I exchanged affectionate congratulations. I was delighted to have given him a successful play, and he for his part said to me: 'You know, from now on you can consider yourself at home in the Odéon!'

*Friday, 19 November*

A terrible press this morning. The fact is, the question at issue is not just the play. Writers are simply not wanted in the theatre, and those journalists who are connected with people in the theatre are furious to see novelists taking over the Odéon. . . . As for poor Renée, I very much fear that she has been done to death.

This evening I found Porel in his office, all by himself, sitting in his curule chair with his arms hanging limply by his sides. He greeted me with these words: 'What a dreadful press! The *Petit Journal*, the *Gil Blas*. . . . It's iniquitous! They just refuse to admit that last night was a success. . . . It has killed bookings!'

I went off to wait for him in his box, where he promised to join me but did not come.

An interesting audience to watch. An audience which did not dare to laugh or applaud, an audience which did not talk or move or even breathe in the intervals, an audience which seemed like a class in disgrace, afraid of showing the slightest sign of life for fear of being scolded. There is something impressive about the lack of personal judgement of the enlightened Parisian, who is a slave to the judgement of the newspaper he reads.

All the same, it is terrible to have this disappointment the day after that enthusiasm, that success, that triumph. And a manager, who yesterday put his theatre and himself at your disposal, cold and embarrassed today, his mind occupied with the play which is going to take the place of yours tomorrow. Yet it is only natural, dammit, and I remain grateful to him in spite of it all.

But what a succession of flops, failures, and fiascos over nearly forty years! As I have said before, we really are under a curse!

Zola is a wily fellow. He took good care not to choose one of his young men of Médan as a collaborator. He picked Busnach instead, who contributes nothing to his plays but who, as a professional dramatist, serves as a lightning conductor to divert the thunderbolts of the press from the novelist's head.

*Wednesday, 24 November*

Today, as I went into the Princess's drawing-room, before bidding me good day she called out to me from the table at which she was sitting: 'Goncourt, I'm furious about your *Journal*!'

'Why?'

'The expressions you use! ... Saying that Gautier called an artist like Gounod *an absolute donkey*!'

White with anger which had accumulated in me as a result of the coolness I had noticed in the Princess's drawing-room for some time past, I went right up to her, looked her in the eyes, and said to her in a furious voice, to the stupefaction of the people who had already arrived:

'Yes, you would like me to serve up nothing but plaster saints, wouldn't you! ... Oh, I know full well that people here don't like the truth. ... But you can rest assured that if Gautier came back to life, he would find my prose less demeaning than certain pages I could mention. . . .[1] I want to show people as they really are, in dressing-gown and slippers. I want to make them talk as they really talk when they are among friends. . . . And the essence, the beauty of Gautier's conversation was exaggeration . . . and anybody with half a mind should be able to understand that *an absolute donkey* isn't a serious judgement of the musician by the critic.'

As I was beginning to run out of breath and indignation, I stopped at this point and looked at the Princess, expecting an angry outburst which would make me collect my hat and go. To my astonishment, the Princess, her head bowed and her arms dangling, merely remarked in a tone of gentle reproof that her comment had been inspired by her friendly regard for me and the fear that I was going to make too many enemies.

That violent-tempered woman makes one forgive her incivilities and even love her again with her strange and charming demonstrations of affection.

[1] A reference to an appreciation of Gautier which Princess Mathilde had written after his death.

# 1887

Dinner at the Charpentiers'.

Macé, the former head of the Sûreté, a man with the same shifty yet searching gaze as Taine behind his spectacles, told some amusing stories about thieves—thieves in high society, of which he said there were so many in the streets of Paris that he lived in the country so as not to meet them. He spoke too of the financiers who were always in and out of prison, citing one, without giving his name, whom he had consigned to Mazas only to meet him again shortly afterwards at a ministry dinner, sitting on the Minister's right hand, from which place of honour he had given him a kindly, patronizing wave; and citing another who, in the course of his stays in two or three prisons, had had foreign decorations bestowed on all the governors and warders.

*Monday, 14 February*

This morning I found Daudet furious with Zola, whose treacherous tricks he has noticed on several occasions; and he both recounted and mimed for my benefit a little scene which took place yesterday at Charpentier's, an interesting scene in that it marked the meeting and mutual recognition of two evil minds.

He was talking to Zola in a corner when he saw Degas come in, circle round him, inspect him at length, pretend to be uncertain as to his identity, make as if to go, and then come back and stare at him at close quarters. 'Yes, it's me, Daudet!' said Daudet, more than a little irritated by the act put on by that unpleasant character to suggest that he had changed beyond recognition. An act which Zola understood at once, for he gave Degas his cue by saying: 'Yes, the years change us all!' To which Degas replied: 'No, time hasn't had any effect on you.' And Daudet went into ecstasies over the spontaneous understanding between those two evil minds, and the wonderful quickness of Zola's, which needs no preparation and is always on the alert. Then he expatiated on the cunning air of stupidity which Zola can assume on occasion, on the diplomatic turn which he can give his phrases when he wants them to say something, on the Italian perfidiousness which he claims to recognize in him, and what is more the Italian perfidiousness of the fifteenth century: Machiavellism!

*Sunday, 27 February*

Today, in the Grenier, we talked about the fine bearing, the stylistic gait of refuse-collectors and, as a general rule, of all those who carry heavy loads, the lifting of those loads producing an impressive thrust of the shoulders and throwing out of the chest. And Raffaelli remarked that no movement was ever isolated and that in his paintings he tried to indicate in every gesture the centre, the pivotal point of a movement.

*Wednesday, 2 March*

It is nearly a year since poor Caze died. Today I received an invitation to his wife's funeral. A single year has seen the disappearance of this couple of which one partner was thirty-four and the other thirty-one. For certain human beings Fate can be cruel indeed.

*Thursday, 3 March*

Today saw the publication of our book, the *Journal des Goncourt*.

*Sunday, 6 March*

Zola really has nothing in him that he can call his own, and any reader who makes a thorough study of his work will be astonished at all he has taken from other writers in the way of types, characters, situations, scenes, endings, and even images and comparisons. That huge, awe-inspiring animal that he makes out of a factory, a barracks, or a shop, is a comparison taken from *Notre-Dame de Paris* which he uses again and again in all his lyrical works.

*Thursday, 10 March*

The few women I have really loved, loved with the whole of my heart and part of my brain, I have not possessed—and yet I believe that if I had wanted them badly enough they would have given themselves to me. But I have always derived indescribable pleasure from leading a decent woman to the edge of sin and leaving her there to live between the temptation and the fear of that sin.

*Saturday, 12 March*

Oh, what a rabbit, what a coward, what a poltroon that fellow Taine is! Having read that in the second volume of my *Journal* I was going to reproduce conversations from the Magny dinners, he has written to remind me that he is 'still alive' and to beg me not to quote any of his opinions or observations on anything whatever, 'earnestly requesting silence on his score' as he does not wish to be compromised by anything that he may have said in the frank expression of his ideas.

Oh, yes, it annoys these Academicians to have their humanity exposed to the public gaze. One day it is Halévy forbidding me to paint his portrait; another day it is Taine forbidding me to reproduce his words. Dammit all, they would like to go on being little tin gods, but they are not going to have their way.

*Sunday, 27 March*

It is extraordinary that in spite of my quiet life, my reputation for hard work, and the publication of forty books, the *de* in front of my surname and perhaps a certain distinction in my appearance should go on leading the fools in the press, who work a hundred times less than I do, to take me for an amateur. Bauër, in an extremely kind article on my *Journal*, expresses a certain surprise that the book should have been written by a man he had always considered an ordinary gentleman of leisure. Why, I wonder, in the eyes of certain people, is Edmond de Goncourt a gentleman of leisure, an amateur, an aristocrat toying with literature, and why is Guy de Maupassant a real man of letters? Why, I should like to know, why?

*Monday, 11 April*

In spite of everything, it stirs the heart of an old man like myself to receive from a young, fair-haired girl letters like this:

Easter Day

I am sure that I have upset you. I know you so well, and the very idea has spoilt my day.

The children are scattered all over the place rehearsing fables and plays for this evening. The house has been full of flowers since this morning, and I want you to have an Easter too, so I have gathered a few sprigs for you: here they are. But please, I beg you, *not a word of this to a soul.*

Your friend asks you to be mute, but not deaf. Till Wednesday.

Looking at this scrawl, with the little stains on the paper made by the flowers, I tell myself that it would indeed be good to have one's last years surrounded by the affection of the girl who wrote this to me. But then I think of our whole lives devoted, dedicated, sacrificed to literature, and I say to myself: I must carry on to the bitter end, I must not marry, I must keep the promise I made to my brother, I must found that Academy we thought of together.

*Wednesday, 11 May*

This evening at the Princess's she said to me:

'You would not sacrifice anything for me!'

'And what would you sacrifice for me?' I retorted.

'Everything!' she said, looking me straight in the eye.

I very nearly said: 'Everything, everything. . . . A man I knew once said of the woman he loved: "For that woman I would sacrifice my future, my life, my honour." Would you sacrifice to me what he put last?' But I was afraid of receiving a favourable reply.

She was charming this evening, with her sad eyes, her curly fair hair, and the two beauty-spots on her white breast.

I really must have a strong will not to send my Academy packing!

*Tuesday, 7 June*

Those three beauty-spots on the upper part of one arm and where her breasts begin, that little tuft of hair of the most Titian red adorning the back of her neck, why do I see them before me, day and night, whenever my mind is not occupied by thoughts of literature?

... Yes, her attraction for me is purely sensual, purely physical. For her mind strikes me as rather babyish, and her character, which is languid and melancholy, is not the character a sad person like myself needs beside him. And the other day, when she was wearing a tight collar under her rather plump chin, I noticed a momentary resemblance to Louis XVI in her that made my blood run cold. .... Then there are times when the sceptic, the doubter in me thinks that he can distinguish in the sleepy blue eyes of that blonde the iron determination of a German woman hunting for a husband. But although I had decided not to go and see her as she had asked me to, I went in the end, and she said to me: 'Do you know what I did on Wednesday?' Her father had been away and so had not been able to take her to the Princess's. 'I took one of your books, *La Faustin*, and I read it in bed all evening. I put out my candle only when I thought that you would have left the Rue de Berri. That was one way of spending the evening with you. ...' At that point her mother came in. Oh, parents. ...

*Tuesday, 14 June*

This morning I had a note from her saying: 'I shall come on the stroke of noon to ask you for a drop of your Tokay wine.' The devil of it was that I did not feel capable today of not giving her that kiss on the lips which a woman who has some feeling for you does not resist; and a kiss, together with what follows if you are not made of bronze, leads a man of my age, sooner or later, to marriage. ... So I said to Pélagie: 'You will tell Mademoiselle —— that Daudet collected me yesterday at Madame Charpentier's funeral and took me off to Champrosay.'

And I shut myself up in my bedroom, where I went to bed after closing the shutters. ... I heard a carriage rolling up, the bell ringing, the door opening, and then Pélagie calling to her daughter who was in her room: 'Blanche, come down and lay a place for Mademoiselle ——.' So she had come to invite herself to lunch! She sat down and lunched in leisurely fashion, and after that I heard her little shoes tip-tapping over the pebbles in my garden for half-an-hour while I lay low in my bed, not daring to cough in case she heard me, and dying of hunger. A comical situation. ... What an adventure for a man of sixty-five! But upon my word, I long for a life devoid of adventure.

*Monday, 20 June*

The first anniversary of my brother's death that I have forgotten.

*Wednesday, 22 June*

The end of the story. . . . Today I received this little note from her:

' "*Amen!*" said a drummer-boy, and burst out laughing (Coppée). Read it again. Regards.'[1]

She had asked me to go and see her on her name-day at the country house where she is living now, and this was the reply she sent me when I refused on the pretext of having an appointment with Porel at Champrosay.

All day long that little note haunted me, and this evening after dinner, in the twilight, I fell into a profound melancholy. . . . After all, she is probably the only decent young woman who has ever really loved me. I remember how she pressed my arm against her heart, one Wednesday when I gave her my arm to take her in to dinner at the Princess's, in a movement which cannot have been meant in jest. . . . I have been cruel, very cruel to her, but with the undertakings I have given with regard to my Academy, I really cannot marry. . . .

And then, in all sincerity, among the reasons which have led me to repulse this love there is a question of decency; I consider it indelicate for an ailing old man, with at the most two or three years of sickly life in front of him, to take a young wife, even with her consent, in order to make her the sick-nurse of those sad years. . . . Where I went wrong, after first of all spurning all her advances, was in suddenly taking pleasure in that flirtation and encouraging it. . . . But now flirtation is not enough for either of us . . . and the only decent, honourable thing to do is to break it off.

*Thursday, 18 August*

To my surprise, when I opened the *Figaro* this morning, I found an attack on Zola on the front page signed with the following five

---

[1] A quotation from the scene in *La Bénédiction* by Coppée in which, during the war in Spain, a rebel priest is shot by French soldiers while saying Mass.

names: Paul Bonnetain, Rosny, Descaves, Margueritte, Guiches.[1] And the devil of it is that four of the five form part of my Grenier!

Léon Daudet came to take me to see Potain, with whom he had made an appointment for me. Afterwards we took the train to Champrosay, where I stayed to dinner. Daudet had known no more than I had about the *Manifesto of the Five*, who had done their wicked work in the utmost secrecy. At this time when the press does nothing but truckle to Zola, we agreed that the thing showed courage, but considered the manifesto badly written, containing too many scientific terms and concentrating too scurrilously on the author's physical characteristics.

At one point in the evening, Daudet exclaimed that he had conceived a positive loathing for his colleague's work one evening at Charpentier's, at the time when *Pot-Bouille* was being printed, when Mme Zola had turned to her husband after dinner and said: '*Mimile*, your book's dirty, really dirty!' Zola had said nothing, but Mme Charpentier, beaming happily, had murmured: 'Oh, come now, surely it isn't as bad as all that?' And Charpentier, in hilarious mood, had patted his cheeks and chortled: 'It will sell all the better if it is!'

*Sunday, 21 August*

Rosny, who came to see me today, told me that in an article in the *Réveil-Matin* Bauër, no doubt drunk with the honour of having been placed on Mme Zola's right at the supper to celebrate *Renée*, had described me, though without naming me, as an old fakir who had planned the *Manifesto of the Five* behind a Japanese screen, impelled by the diabolical envy of a writer whose books were not appreciated by the public.

[1] In this so-called *Manifesto of the Five* the signatories, who claimed without much justification to be erstwhile disciples of Zola's, denounced his latest novel, *La Terre*, attacked 'the indecency and filthy terminology of *Les Rougon-Macquart*'—which they attributed to 'a malady of the author's lower organs'—and repudiated Zola's works 'in the name of our sane and virile ambitions, in the name of our cult, our profound love, our supreme respect for Art'. It is still impossible to say with certainty whether—as Zola not unreasonably assumed—this attack was inspired by Goncourt and Daudet, or whether—as Goncourt would have us believe—it was made without their knowledge.

And at ten o'clock this evening, just as I was going to bed, along came Geffroy who, pained and angered by the attacks being made on me, had come to read me an article he had written which cleared us, me and Daudet, of any participation in the manifesto. But I asked him not to publish it, saying that I did not want to make any reply, that I considered the accusation beneath my notice, that I had known absolutely nothing about the manifesto, that if I had felt the need to express my opinion of Zola's works I should have done so myself, with my signature at the bottom, and that it was not in my nature to hide behind other people.

*Wednesday, 7 September*

The Comtesse de Beaulaincourt, the former Marquise de Contades, said today at Saint-Gratien that on the two occasions in her life when she had dined next to Talleyrand, on each occasion Talleyrand had spoken of the malconformation of Mme de Staël, for whom M. and Mme Necker had been obliged to have thigh-twisters made, to turn her legs and feet outwards.

*Saturday, 1 October*

The mania for fighting which has taken hold of Drumont is turning him into a figure of fun. Nature is nothing for him now but a setting for affairs of honour. When he took the lease on his house at Soisy, he exclaimed: 'Ah, now there's a real garden for a pistol-duel!' A certain walk in Daudet's park called forth the comment: 'Oh, what a splendid spot for a sword-fight!' And when, recently, his friends were discussing a marriage they wanted to arrange for him, he suddenly said: 'Yes, everything you say about the girl is perfect. . . . But do you think she is likely to get upset when two gentlemen call for me of a morning?'

*Tuesday, 11 October*

This evening the Théâtre-Libre put on *Sœur Philomène*, a play adapted from our novel by Jules Vidal and Arthur Byl.

I went along with Geffroy and Descaves. A strange theatre. Lost among streets which look like streets in provincial suburbs where one expects to find a brothel, a middle-class house, and in that house a stage trodden by actors reeking more strongly of garlic than any Vaugirard omnibus. A strange audience too, not at all like that to be found in the big theatres, with the women the wives, mistresses, or models of writers and artists: what Porel called 'a studio audience'. To my surprise, the play was well acted, and acted with the charm of excellent society actors. Antoine, in the part of Barnier, was wonderfully natural. Instead of uttering his *'Nom de Dieu!'* standing, he said it lying back on the table, and this *'Nom de Dieu!'* accentuating his defence of the sisters was extremely effective. . . . It was a tremendous success. The scene of the evening prayers with the sick women making their responses, interrupted by the singing of the dying Romaine, was greeted with thunderous applause and the tears of an audience stirred to the depths. . . . The effectiveness of this play, an effectiveness which I had not appreciated on reading it, comes from the combination of delicate feelings, style, and action with theatrical realism.

Zola, with whom I came face to face on the stage, and to whom I must admit I gave the cold shoulder, made two remarks which were absolutely typical of the man. He said to Raffaelli, referring to my play: 'Oh, at the moment, anything they put on at this theatre would be a success!' And he said to somebody or other in my presence: 'Personally, I'm convinced that if a theatre manager took this play, the censors would prohibit its performance!'

*Sunday, 30 October*

Young Descaves confided to me that Zola spends every evening at the Théâtre-Libre, that he has taken two subscriptions, that he pays the most extravagant compliments to Antoine, that he bestows fatherly kisses on the actresses, in fact that with the aid of his disciple Céard he is trying to get hold of the theatre for himself. He also told me that Antoine was rather hurt that I had not written to compliment him, and that the actresses themselves bore me something of a grudge for not having kissed them.

*Sunday, 25 December*

Today Huysmans told me this story about Bourget. Wyzewa went to see him to ask him to do something for Laforgue, who was dying of consumption in the most abject poverty. 'Yes,' said Bourget, 'it is true that Laforgue was a close friend of mine. . . . Let me think what I can do for him. . . .' And a few days later Laforgue received from his sometime close friend four bottles of claret.

# 1888

*Monday, 9 January*

In the preface to his new novel, Maupassant, criticizing the *artistic style*, has attacked me without naming me.[1] This attack reaches me at the same time as a letter in which he assures me through the post of his admiration and affection. He thus puts me under the necessity of considering him a typical Norman. Zola, indeed, once told me that he was the king of liars.

Now he may be a very clever Norman *novelliere* of the Monnier type, but he is not a true writer, and he has every reason to denigrate the *artistic style*. The true writer, from La Bruyère, Bossuet, and Saint-Simon, going by way of Chateaubriand and finishing up with Flaubert, puts his hallmark on every sentence he writes, so that the cultured reader can recognize it even if it is not signed, and one cannot be a great writer without fulfilling that condition: well, Maupassant's work bears no hallmark, it is simply good, commonplace copy such as anyone might have written.

Guiches, last Sunday, made the best criticism I have ever heard of that undeniable but second-rate talent when he said that Maupassant's books were readable but not re-readable.

*Saturday, 4 February*

Among all the writers that have ever lived, there has not been a single one brave enough to declare that he did not care a damn about morality or immorality, that all he wanted to do was produce something great and beautiful and human, and that if immorality made the slightest artistic contribution to his work, then he would

[1] In the preface to *Pierre et Jean*, published separately in the literary supplement to the *Figaro* on 7 January and with the novel in book form on 9 January, Maupassant wrote: 'There is no need of the weird, complicated, intricate, exotic vocabulary which is imposed upon us nowadays under the name of the *artistic style* to represent every shade of thought.'

serve immorality up to the public, openly and honestly, without stating hypocritically that he was being immoral with a moral purpose, however much indignation this might arouse among conservative or republican journalists, those virtuous souls who keep several mistresses and live on the profits of a gambling club.

*Friday, 17 February*

Today a dinner was given in Rodin's honour by his friends and admirers, a dinner at which I presided, with a draught in my back.

I found myself sitting next to Clemenceau with his round Kalmuck head, and he told me some curious anecdotes about the peasants in his province and how they would stop him out in the open during his tours of the department to consult him about their illnesses. He described one huge woman who, just as the horses of his brake were about to gallop away from some place or other, leaned on their cruppers and called out: 'Oh, Monsieur, I suffer from wind something awful!' To which the Radical deputy, giving his horses a crack of the whip which sent them on their way, replied: 'Then fart, my good woman, fart!'

*Wednesday, 11 April*

Somebody told me today that when the younger Menier chartered a yacht a few years ago to go on a sort of trip round the world in the company of some friends and their mistresses, the young men's mothers expressed such anxiety about this journey, and such regret that if any of them died they would have no grave at Père-Lachaise or Montmartre to weep over, that room was found in the hold, in the middle of the cargo of *pâtés de foie gras* and champagne, for some lead coffins. Then, considering the fact that soldering is a difficult operation, a solderer was taken on who took his meals with the crew. And it seems that it was an odd experience, constantly bumping into that *Memento mori* on deck in the course of that pleasure-trip round the world.

*Saturday, 14 July*

Today I wrote to Zola: 'My sincere congratulations on a tardy reparation.' Tardy is true. But if I had been Zola, I'd be hanged if I would have accepted the decoration at this late date. Does he not understand that he is demeaning himself by becoming a Chevalier? But the literary revolutionary will one day be a Commander of the Legion of Honour and perpetual secretary to the Academy and will end up writing books so drearily virtuous that people will hesitate to give them as prizes at speech-days in young ladies' boarding-schools.

*Tuesday, 21 August*

My cousin Fédora, talking to me today about a branch of her family which is almost poor, said: 'Just imagine: they are people who for five generations have married for love!'

*Friday, 7 September*

The present success of the Russian novel is due to the annoyance which devout, respectable folk felt at the success of the naturalistic French novel: they searched for something which they could use to counter that success. For there can be no doubt about it, it is the same kind of literature: the realities of life seen in their sad, human, unpoetic aspects.

And neither Tolstoy nor Dostoevsky nor any of the other Russian writers invented this kind of literature! They took it from Flaubert, from me, from Zola, and added a strong dose of Poe. Oh, if one of Dostoevsky's novels, whose black melancholy is regarded with such indulgent admiration, were signed with the name of Goncourt, what a slating it would get all along the line! And the man who discovered this clever distraction, who so unpatriotically diverted to a foreign literature the sympathy and—yes!—the admiration which should have come to us, is M. de Vogüé. So he has deserved well of the Academy, which will summon him before long to join its company.

*Sunday, 21 October*

Huysmans came today. He has just spent eighteen days in Hamburg, in an atmosphere of prostitution. And there are brothels there such as can be found nowhere else in Europe: brothels for seamen, far superior to those in the Latin Quarter, and brothels for bankers, where the girls are young Hungarians of fifteen or sixteen and the bedrooms are full of orchids. It is amusing to hear him describe that city with the lilac-coloured sea and the blotting-paper sky; that city which, every evening, turns from a busy trading centre into a fairground where the money earned by day is scattered and spent by night in opulent *riddecks*.

*Sunday, 4 November*

At Charpentier's this evening a gentleman came up to me whom I did not recognize at first. It was Zola, but so changed that in the street I should really and truly have passed him without greeting him. He no longer has that resemblance to the portrait by Manet, which he had recovered for a little while; with the hollows under his cheekbones, his hair brushed up from his high forehead, the squaloid yellow of his complexion, the nervous contraction of his mouth, and a certain fixity in his gaze, he looks like a ghost with a sickly spitefulness spread all over its face.

Seeing our surprise and alarm at the change which had occurred in his appearance, Zola told us how he had come to grow so thin. At the performance of *Esther Brandès* at the Théâtre-Libre,[1] he met Raffaelli in a corridor and, try as he might to flatten himself against the wall, he found it difficult to give him room to pass. 'It's such a nuisance having a pot-belly like this!' he said. 'You know,' remarked Raffaelli, squeezing by, 'there's a very simple way of losing weight, and that is to stop drinking with meals.' At lunch the next day Zola remembered what Raffaelli had said and murmured: 'Now what if I didn't have anything to drink?' To which Mme Zola retorted that it was a ridiculous idea and that in any case she was sure that he would never be able to do it. There followed an argument between husband and wife, with the result that Zola drank nothing with this first lunch and kept up the diet for three months.

*Wednesday, 19 December*

At half-past six today, which is Mme Daudet's day, I found Mme de Bonnières, who had already called to see me on Sunday, at the Daudets'. It was obvious that she wanted to come to the supper-party which the Daudets were giving tonight in honour of my

---

[1] *Esther Brandès*, a play by Léon Hennique, was performed at the Théâtre-Libre on 13 November 1887.

*Germinie Lacerteux.* But she was not invited, because we should have had to invite Magnard too, and Daudet and I felt that we ought not to give the impression of trying to get a good press by inviting journalists to this supper-party.

Straight after dinner, there I was in Porel's stage-box with the Daudets, sitting right at the back so that Scholl, coming across to speak to Daudet and leaning on the edge of the box, did not even notice that I was there.

'A first-night audience such as I have never seen at the Odéon', Porel said to me.

The play began. There were two phrases in the first scene on which I was counting to enlighten me as to the state of mind of the audience: 'An old hag like me' and 'Kids whose bottoms you've wiped'. Both phrases passed muster, and I concluded that the audience was in a good mood.

During the second scene there were a few hisses as the audience began to feel its modesty being offended. 'I can smell gunpowder in the air. I like that', said Porel, in a tone of voice which suggested that he was not as fond of gunpowder as all that.

Daudet went out to restrain his son, whom he had seen in the stalls on the point of creating a scene, and he came back soon scowling with anger and accompanied by Léon, who said that his father had looked so angry in the corridors that he had been afraid he was going to get involved in a fight. I was deeply touched at the sight of father and son mutually preaching moderation to one another when each was really as furious as the other.

The battle between the hissers and the applauders, among whom I noticed the ministers and their wives, went on during the scene in the Boule Noire dance-hall and the scene in Jupillon's glove workshop. Then came the scene of the little girls' dinner. There I thought everything would be all right, but the hissing grew louder, Mme Crosnier's speech was shouted down, and there were cries of 'Go to bed, children!' For a moment I was afraid that they would not allow the play to finish. That was a fearful thought! For as I had told my friends, I did not know how my play was going to fare, but all I asked was to be allowed to fight the battle, and now I was afraid that I would not be able to fight it out to the end. . . . But at last Réjane obtained silence with the scene in which Jupillon borrows Germinie's forty francs.

I went backstage for a moment and saw two of my little actresses, cruelly shaken by that pitiless audience, weeping against the framework of a flat.

Réjane, whom I probably have to thank for having seen the whole of my play, despite the audience's noisy determination not to listen, managed to make herself heard and applauded in the scene where Germinie brings her lover his conscription money.

During the following scenes the thing became a regular battle, in the midst of which, at Mlle de Varandeuil's exclamation: 'Oh, if I'd only known, I'd have given you a dish-cloth to be buried in, you filthy trollop!' a woman's voice was raised in protest, calling forth a general storm of indignation. And that voice was the voice of Marie Colombier, a notorious whore.

For that matter, the indignation of the men in the audience was of much the same kind. It was the indignation of Vitu, who was sitting in his box with his mistress and his son. It was the indignation of Fouquier, who is generally understood to be the lover of his wife's daughter. It was the indignation of Koning, who began his career by being the Jupillon of the sexagenarian Déjazet, of Page, and of heaven only knows how many other old women. And it was the indignation of Blavet, Blavet the most contemptible of men.

At the end, when Dumény stepped forward to name the author, the audience flatly refused to allow my name to be uttered, as a name bringing dishonour upon French literature, and Dumény had to wait a long time, a very long time, and then take advantage of a pause in the hissing, to shout that name, which he did, I must say, defiantly, throwing it in the audience's face as you throw your card at a man who has insulted you.

I stayed there to the very end, at the back of the box, without giving any sign of weakness, but thinking sadly that my brother and I were born under an unlucky star—and surprised and touched, when the curtain came down, to receive a handshake from a man who had always been hostile to me, a strong, comforting handshake from Bauër.

*Thursday, 20 December*
This is what Vitu says about my play in the *Figaro*: '. . . There is not a single melodrama of former times or recent times in which

the lower classes of Paris are not depicted with more life, more colour, more relief, and more realism.'

Perhaps, Monsieur Vitu, that statement contains a slight element of exaggeration.

This evening I found Mme Daudet utterly appalled by this morning's notices, which all more or less repeat Vitu's comments. As for Daudet, fuming at the injustice of it all, he said that he would like to do somebody an injury.

*Friday, 21 December*

A delightful visit from Réjane, all smiles and gaiety, who said how sorry she was that I had not been to yesterday's performance, to that second performance at which the play had made a complete recovery, adding sweetly that if she had scored a hit it was thanks to the prose behind her acting and speaking.

She told me that Derenbourg, the manager of the Menus-Plaisirs, had confided to her that on the eve of the first night he had dined in a house he had refused to identify where somebody had said: 'That play mustn't be allowed to finish tomorrow!'

And returning to the subject of yesterday's applause and curtain-calls, she confessed that in their feverish delight she and Porel had gone out to supper together like a couple of schoolboys, and that in the cab taking them to the restaurant Porel had kept on saying over and over again: 'Two thousand five hundred francs of bookings to-day . . . after this morning's press. . . . So I wasn't wrong after all. . . . I'm not a silly old fool!'

*Wednesday, 26 December*

I have just read in an evening paper a report of a sitting of the Senate at which the Right, the whole of the Right, demanded the banning of my play.

*Saturday, 29 December*

This evening, thinking of *Germinie* being performed while I was lazily installed beside a cosy log fire, I thought how good it was of all those people to leave their homes and brave the cold and the fog to go and see—instead of just imagining it—my play.

I also reflected this evening that I had had everything there was to be had in life, except thoroughbred horses and thoroughbred women.

# 1889

Today Gibert, the drawing-room singer, told us that there was a doctor in Paris who specialized in massaging women's faces, and that he obtained some astonishing results, completely refashioning a face deformed by puffiness or fat and giving it back its original oval form. What is more, this benefactor of the woman of forty can apparently eradicate wrinkles and even triumph over crow's-feet, and the once very beautiful Mme de Pourtalès is an assiduous client of his.

On the subject of wrinkles, I remarked that the face was like a diary of our sorrows, our excesses, our pleasures, and that each of these left its mark upon it, like a written record.

I chatted for a while with Zola about our lives which we had sacrificed to literature as perhaps nobody had ever sacrificed his life before, and we admitted to each other that we had been real 'martyrs to literature' and also perhaps 'damn fools'. Zola confessed to me that this year, on the eve of his fifties, he felt a new surge of life within him, a longing for physical satisfaction. And breaking off suddenly, he went on: 'My wife isn't here. . . . Well, I can't see a girl like that go by without saying to myself: "Isn't that worth more than a book?" '

*Sunday, 27 January*

Daudet told me today about his hanging before dinner: a new treatment for ataxia imported from Russia by Charcot. For this mysterious operation, they wait at the baths until everyone has gone and then go furtively to a poorly lighted room full of shadows. There, in the presence of Keller and another doctor, the hanging takes place, a hanging which lasts a minute, a long, long minute, a minute made up of sixty seconds. Then they unhook you and you find yourself back on the ground with a dreadful pain in the neck.

'That hanging in the half-light is something quite indescribable', said Daudet.

'A real Goya!' I said.

'Yes, that's it, a Goya! . . . And while I'm dangling in the air like that, if Keller happens to be on his own, I remember that last year he was out of his mind for three months, and I think that if he went mad again and forgot me . . . Don't tell anybody, will you? . . . If Bloy heard about it, you can imagine the macabre article he would write about me in *L'Événement*!'

*Tuesday, 5 February*

This evening I went to the Odéon for the last performance of *Germinie*.

I found Réjane intoxicated with her part. She took me into her little dressing-room behind the stage and while she was changing her dress, revealing her breasts and armpits with an actress's unconcern about such exhibitions, she thanked me warmly, very warmly, for having given her the part.

Then I looked into the green-room, where my little actresses were lamenting the end of the run and the end of their nightly shindies up in the attics of the theatre.

Porel, whom I found jingling five-franc pieces in his trouser-pocket the way little shopkeepers jingle the money they have taken during the day, told me that the play had brought in over 82,000 francs and assured me that he was making money.

A good house, full of people in white ties and people in the cheaper seats too, who found the play interesting and amusing. Not a single hiss, not a single boo, not a single hostile comment. Applause all the time and for everybody, even for Mme Jupillon, and curtain-calls after every scene. It was all quite astounding.

*Thursday, 28 February*

This evening, in the *Temps*, I read these words addressed to the workers by President Carnot during his visit to the state tobacco factory:

'I thank you most sincerely for the welcome you have just given me, my dear friends, for you are my friends, since you are workers. . . .'

I wonder if in any age, in any part of the world, any courtier of a king or emperor has uttered words of such despicable servility as these words from a courtier of the masses.

*Monday, 1 April*

There is no doubt about it, and I must accept it as a fact: at the revival of *Henriette Maréchal* I had the whole younger generation on my side, but now only part of it is with me. The Decadents, although they owe something to my style, have turned against me. And then, in the present younger generation, there is a curious attitude which marks it out from the younger generations of other periods: it refuses to recognize the existence of ancestors and progenitors and considers itself, at the age of twenty and in the infancy of its talent, as the originator of everything. It is a generation in the image of the Republic: it wipes out the past.

*Tuesday, 16 April*

Minarets, domes, moucharabies, a whole pasteboard Orient, with not a single monument recalling our French architecture. One can tell that this Exhibition is going to be an Exhibition for dagoes. In any case, in present-day Paris, the Parisian and the Parisienne are beginning to be rare birds in this Semitic or Auvergnat or Marseillais society, as a result of the conquest of Paris by Jewry and the South. Paris, in fact, is no longer the Paris of old, but an open city to which all the robbers in the world, after making their fortune in business, come to eat poor food and rub against flesh which calls itself Parisian.

*Wednesday, 17 April*

The Princess's drawing-room is now completely under the thumb of the Dumas family, and Dumas dined there this evening with his two daughters. He talked amusingly about Sarah Bernhardt, who fell into his arms yesterday at the Variétés. He expatiated on the masculine build of her body, which has no breasts but a plump stomach, and on the amazing stamina of the woman, who is never tired, never weary, and who spits blood with no more effect on her constitution than if she were spitting gobs.

The society women of today are really rather astonishing. They behave just like madwomen from La Salpêtrière turned loose by Charcot. The ill-bred eccentricities of these lunatics are beyond belief: this evening, for instance, after we had dined on a bouillabaisse which the Princess had had sent from Marseilles, the Lippmann woman went round with all manner of mad, childish gestures which were not without charm, breathing the garlic in the bouillabaisse into the faces of the people she knew.

*Sunday, 28 April*

Daudet took Fleury to task in the Grenier today for saying that Barbey had only ten francs to his name when he died, when in fact Mlle Read had 1,500 francs belonging to Barbey.[1] Fleury put up an unconvincing defence, saying that it was Mlle Read who had given him that detail. And he described poor Mlle Read as absolutely distraught with grief, calling the corpse *darling*, kissing its hands, and licking the tears of the death-agony from its eyelids. . . . And with her to watch over her beloved, she had had Buet, the accredited homosexual, and Bloy, the mendicant pamphleteer, who had taken the opportunity to lunch off the funeral expenses and to borrow five francs from Barbey's concierge.

Daudet then proceeded to entertain us with Barbey's hyperbolic stories of his noble ancestry and aristocratic childhood, depicting him with the priest in charge of his education, to whom he used to shout, before fencing with him: 'Come along, Abbé, hitch up your cassock!' Then there was his riding-lesson, when his father used to put a five-franc piece on the saddle which Barbey was allowed to keep if he cleared the saddle without displacing it. But he was so nimble that this practice had to be abandoned, for otherwise, as he used to explain in his guttural voice, 'he would have ruined his father'.

The trouble with all these stories was that at the elder Barbey's home there was neither a priest nor a horse nor a saddle nor even a five-franc piece. . . . One day, when he was drunk with champagne, Barbey confessed to Daudet that in the whole of his life he had got no more than forty francs out of his father, and that only at the cost of enormous effort.

[1] Barbey d'Aurevilly had died at his home in the Rue Rousselet on 23 April 1889.

*Monday, 6 May*

While the guns were firing to celebrate the anniversary of 1789,[1] I thought about the fine article there would have been to write on the greatness of present-day France, if only there had not been that revolution in '89 and Napoleon I's victories and Napoleon III's revolutionary policy. True, France would probably be under the rule of an imbecile Bourbon, a scion of an effete old monarchical dynasty, but would that rule be very different from that of a Carnot, chosen as everyone knows for his non-existent personality?

Returned on foot from the Rue d'Amsterdam to Auteuil through the crowds.

A mauve sky, which the illuminations filled with something like the glow of an enormous fire—the sound of countless footsteps creating the effect of the rushing of great waters—the crowds all black, that reddish, burnt-paper black of present-day crowds—a sort of intoxication on the faces of the women, many of whom were queuing up outside the lavatories, their bladders bursting with excitement—the Place de la Concorde an apotheosis of white light, in the middle of which the obelisk shone with the rosy colour of a champagne ice—the Eiffel Tower looking like a beacon left behind on earth by a vanished generation, a generation of men ten cubits tall.

*Tuesday, 2 July*

This evening I dined on the platform of the Eiffel Tower with the Charpentiers, the Hermants, the Dayots, the Zolas, etc. Going up in the lift, I had a feeling in the pit of my stomach as if I were on a ship at sea, but no dizziness. Up there, we were afforded a realization, beyond anything imaginable on ground level, of the greatness, the extent, the Babylonian immensity of Paris, with odd buildings glowing in the light of the setting sun with the colour of Roman stone, and among the calm, sweeping lines of the horizon the steep, jagged silhouette of Montmartre looking in the dusky sky like an illuminated ruin.

We talked about the Javanese women, and when I mentioned their rather repulsive yellow flesh, Zola said: 'It has a softness you

[1] The guns were fired to celebrate the anniversary of the opening of the States General in 1789 and to mark the inauguration of the Universal Exhibition.

don't find in European flesh.' And he finished his sentence by squeezing his nose, which in the grip of his sensual fingers took on the appearance of a piece of indiarubber.

A peculiar sensation, rather like that of taking a header into space, the sensation of coming down those open-work steps in the darkness, plunging every now and then into an infinite void, and one feels like an ant coming down the rigging of a man-of-war, rigging which has turned to iron.

And there we were in the Rue du Caire,[1] where every evening all the erotic curiosity of Paris is concentrated, in the Rue du Caire, with its obscene-looking ass-drivers, with its big Africans in lascivious postures, gazing lecherously at the women who go by, with its excited crowds reminding one of cats pissing on hot coals— the Rue du Caire, a street which could be called Rutting Street.

*Sunday, 14 July*

The anniversary, noisily proclaimed by all the guns of the good city of Paris, of the Revolution of '89, that revolution which turned the great France of old into the ridiculous little France of today and endowed it with the present-day Government, in which, out of the seven ministers composing it, three at least deserve to be sent to prison.

*Sunday, 21 July, and Monday, 22 July*

Opposite that great iron door with the words *Académie de Médecine* above it, on the other side of the Rue des Saints-Pères, at No. 38, there is a tall, narrow building in which a blue-painted fruitshop intersects an eighteenth-century bay surmounted by a sculptured head in the midst of rococo foliage, and on the left of the shop there is a narrow door beneath a big lantern labelled: *Hôtel de l'Étoile*. I never pass that door without a memory of love stirring within me; and on the eve of my departure from Paris, a crush of people and carriages, delaying me outside the door, brought back to my mind that old story of my youth.

[1] Between the various industrial exhibitions on the Champ-de-Mars and the Avenue de Suffren, a replica of an Egyptian village had been set up and named the Rue du Caire.

I was twenty-four, I think, and at that time I often went to Mabille, where one evening I met a girl of sixteen or seventeen, accompanied by her mother, a woman with the head of a procuress. The girl had big, sky-blue eyes, set close to a long, aquiline nose, and she was tall, thin, flat-chested, and dressed in the humble clothes of a grisette.

I danced with her that evening—people danced in those days. Then I met her again the following nights, and after seven or eight evenings spent almost entirely dancing quadrilles and polkas with her, she readily granted me the rendezvous I asked her for.

I took her to a little apartment occupied by one of my young cousins at the bottom of the Rue d'Amsterdam. And there, intimidated by her silence and the angelic look in her eyes and impeded by what I took to be a physical malformation, I *muffed* her twice. Finally the second time, as she was getting ready to go, I threw her on to a sofa in the ante-room; and while I was on my knees, taking my pleasure with her, I heard something like the sound of a toy drum bursting, and I saw tears come into her eyes, though she did not utter a single cry, a single groan, a single sigh. And when she got up, her thin summer dress was stained with blood. . . . That *habituée* of Mabille was a virgin. I would never have thought it possible.

She was a strange creature, that girl, with the ecstatic pallor of her face when we made love together, the inert passivity of her body, in which nothing was alive but the pounding of her heart, and the expression in her big blue eyes, which occasionally gleamed with the perversity of an angel cast out of Heaven. Ah, those eyes! I have seen them since at Florence, in that snake-eyed angel in Simon Memmi's *Annunciation*.

I cannot say that I was in love with her; but I felt a sort of curiosity, an affectionate curiosity about the secretive, enigmatic creature that was inside her, together with a little of that proud gratitude that any man feels towards a woman who has given him her virginity.

Oh, that story! There are gaps in my memory, and I cannot remember the years and the months. . . . But it seems to me that I met Marie in the spring; and this is what happened in the autumn. A school friend of mine and I arranged to go for an outing in the country, this outing to be preceded by a good lunch at Véfour's, where we were going to treat ourselves to *suprême de volaille aux truffes*, the speciality of the house at that time.

My friend, who had bad teeth but charming eyes and the handsomest face in the world, arrived late, his mistress having let him down, and this had put him in such a bad mood that he got completely drunk. The result was that when we got to the Gare Saint-Lazare, we had to go into that café which has just been demolished on the corner of the old station and ask for a room—a room in which an acquaintance of mine later blew his brains out—a room where my friend was violently sick, so sick that he looked as if he were having a stroke. And Marie and I were forced to spend the whole day melting two or three pounds of ice over his head, until he was in a fit state to go home to the house where he lived with his grandfather, an old man who was not indulgent to the peccadilloes of youth.

Winter came, and carnival time, and my friend and I arranged to go in a party with some young people he knew to the ball at the Opéra. All of us, men and women alike, were to change into fancy-dress at the little Hôtel de l'Étoile and come back there for supper. Only two or three of us had brought women along; my friend was still alone. Marie had brought a Pierrot costume in white silk, and I had never seen that frail girl look more delightful than she did in that light, floating material, nor her eyes look more strangely seductive. We went to the ball, and we came back for supper; and that evening, to my passionate attempts to possess her, before we left and on our return, she put up an incomprehensible resistance, gently but firmly repulsing my kisses and caresses with evasive movements of the body, little pouts, solemn rebuffs, and finally, when pressed too hard, with a dumb show which seemed to imply that she was afraid of being seen in that hotel bedroom.

Some time later, I had a definite intuition that my friend had become Marie's lover, and that my mistress's affection for him dated back to the day we had lunched together at the Palais-Royal; and I was seized with a cold contempt for that girl, for that love born in the midst of a fit of drunken vomiting. At that time there were a lot of things I did not know about women, such as the hold which illness has over them, the secret ties which caring for the sick creates within them, and, one ought to add, their lack of disgust for the filthy side of suffering. And as contempt for the woman took hold of me, the indignation I had felt about my friend, to whom I had been devoted since childhood, disappeared so completely that I never spoke to him of his treachery.

The years went by. My mother died. My brother had left school and was painting and writing with me when I met Marie again. She asked me up to a little room in a house behind the Stock Exchange, where she worked during the day, and told me how she had broken with my friend, who had left the Military Academy and entered the Department of Civil Engineering. And she gave herself to me again with the same willingness as a German girl whom you simply throw on to a bed.

My brother had not yet got a mistress of his own, and a few days before my meeting with Marie he had spoken to me of the disgust aroused in him by a streetwalker whom he had accompanied to her room and who had removed half her hair and teeth. Was what I did intended simply to give him a pretty mistress whom I no longer loved? Was it not also inspired by the desire to test the poor girl's frailty? Did not the wish to degrade her in my eyes enter into it to some extent? I honestly cannot say. All I remember is that I invited her to dinner at the Café d'Orsay, and that after dinner I told her that I had an appointment and that she was to give herself to my brother as she had given herself to me.

My brother, after making frenzied love to her for several weeks, decided that she was too melancholy, and even rather frightening, with the sort of lethargy into which love-making plunged her, and with the far-away look which came into her great blue eyes; and he dropped her.

I heard no more of her until, one morning after a night in which my brother and I had worked until three o'clock, Rose put a letter on my bedside table which had come by the first post. I glanced at the address and, not recognizing the writing, went back to sleep. When I awoke, I opened the envelope with the unfamiliar hand-writing and found inside a black-edged funeral invitation and a note from a friend of Marie's whom I had met two or three times, saying that Marie had just died of consumption and that on the eve of her death she had asked her to tell me, saying three times that she desperately wanted me to be at her funeral.

The invitation, stating that the funeral was to be held that same day, gave Marie's age as twenty-one.

I jumped out of bed: it was after half-past twelve.

*Wednesday, 14 August*

The newspapers, which reported the Shah of Persia's call on Princess Mathilde, did not give any details of what happened on that occasion. Before the visit of the Persian sovereign, the Princess received a message asking her to have ready: 'A glass of iced water, some cakes, and a night-commode.' The night-commode was placed in a corner of the library downstairs, and Primoli had made arrangements to take a snapshot of the Shah in position; unfortunately the Shah wanted the night-commode placed like a throne in the middle of the room, and Primoli was foiled of his photograph. . . . 'A filthy old man!' exclaimed the Princess. 'A filthy old man!'

Tholozan, the Shah's doctor for the past thirty years, coming back to Paris with us this evening and not having heard about this before, told us that he, knowing the Shah's constitution, could assure us that the Shah was never in a hurry over such matters and that he regarded this incident as a demonstration on the part of the King of Kings of his contempt for the sovereigns of Europe. And he told us how, at a dinner at St. Petersburg at which the Shah had given his arm to the Tsarina, on getting up from table he had walked off by himself for a little way, pretending to have forgotten the Tsarina, who had followed him with an ironic look on her face.

And all the way to Paris, Tholozan went on retailing curious anecdotes about the eccentric sovereign. Among other stories, he told us that a few years ago, having found his Minister of Police guilty of certain malpractices, the Shah had decided to have him flogged in front of him; and considering that the man was screaming too much and too loudly, he had sent for a pretty little cord and had had him strangled as quietly as could be.

*Wednesday, 9 October*

Today Poictevin brought me his book entitled *Double*, informing me in the course of our conversation that if I were to say in my *Journal* that he was a mystic—which I now do—he would be the happiest of men. He has just spent ten days in Brittany with Huysmans, who seems to me to have been making cruel fun of him, looking in the latrines of some castle or other for the bones of children killed by Gilles de Rais, carrying off, for want of better booty, a priest's *caecum* found in a monastery graveyard, to put in his ossuary of souvenirs, heaping extravagant praise on the character of Selwyn in my work and nothing else, speaking with almost religious eloquence of the spiritual aspects of physical love, and trying in fact to trouble poor Poictevin's feeble wits with his Mephistophelianism.[1]

*Monday, 19 December*

While Voltaire and the rest were still rhyming away, stubbornly turning out doggerel with nothing poetic about it, Diderot used nothing but prose as the language of his thought, his imagination, his anger; and he made a powerful contribution to its victory, its supremacy in this present century, in which, except for Hugo, poetry is little more than a pastime for young men of letters starting on their career, and, so to speak, the loss of their intellectual virginity.

[1] The castle in question was the Château de Tiffauges, where Huysmans was collecting material on Gilles de Rais for his novel *Là-Bas* (1891).

At last Wednesday's dinner, the Princess, talking literature and turning to me, asked me ingenuously: 'But why do you always want to break new ground?' To which I replied: 'Because literature renews itself like everything in this world and it is only the people who are at the head of those renovations that survive. . . . Because, without suspecting it, you yourself admire only the literary revolutionaries of the past. . . . Because—let's take an example—Racine, the great, illustrious Racine, was hissed and booed by Pradon's admirers, by the supporters of the old-fashioned theatre, and because that Racine whom critics use to attack modern dramatists was just as much a revolutionary in his own time as certain authors are today.'

*Wednesday, 15 January*

'Renan,' I asked, 'which candidate is the Academy going to elect?'

'The stupidest', the Academician replied imperturbably.

Then, bursting into satanico-priestly laughter, he said:

'Probably Thureau-Dangin, who, in his history of the Orléans dynasty, doesn't mention the 1830 Revolution, nor the 1848 Revolution, nor the insurrections of 1832. It strikes me, though, that in modern politics the common people are a factor which has to be taken into account. But it seems that he is very sound on foreign policy. . . .'

'And after him, who has the best chance?'

'Ferdinand Fabre.'

'Ah. . . . And Loti?'

He gave a twist of the lips and a roll of the eyes which summed up the prospects of the author of *Mon Frère Yves*, adding:

'The fellow's a child, a child!'

'And Zola?'

'He'll have one vote.'

'Oh, I know that he won't get in this time, but the third or fourth time he'll manage it. . . . Academic bodies are so cowardly!'

'I agree with you there', said Renan. 'But Zola in the Academy?'

And he looked at me in a way which said that he would never get in, adding: 'In any case, all of us over there are convinced that he just wants to create a stir.'

*Wednesday, 12 February*

Delzant told me today that Mme Sandeau had left him all her husband's papers, and that among those papers there was a letter which Mme Sandeau always carried next to her heart and which she showed her husband from time to time, as a reproach and a vengeance for his past love-affairs. It was a letter written by Mme Sand to a medical student while she was living with Sandeau, a letter in which the mother combined with the mistress and the phrase 'my dear boy' occurred in the middle of the most passionate, frank, and explicit references to their happy copulation.

*Friday, 21 February*

It is a strange thing, Stendhal's perpetual preoccupation with women. There are days when I need a woman to go to bed with, and other days when I need friendship and not love from women I do not go to bed with, and that too in a somewhat intermittent fashion. But as for making woman the object of my thoughts every day, from morning till night, no, no, no!

*Saturday, 1 March*

Took round to the *Écho de Paris* the beginning of my copy of the *Journal des Goncourt* (Second Series, 1870–90).

I find it difficult to understand why a man with the brutish appearance of Valentin Simond should publish in his rag material as unlike what is usually to be found in newspapers as Stendhal's autobiography and the Goncourts' autobiography.

*Wednesday, 12 March*

'What are you writing now, Zola?' I asked the author of *La Bête humaine*, who came and sat beside me this evening at the Charpentiers'.

'Nothing. . . . I just can't settle down to work. . . . And then, *L'Argent* is such a huge book that I don't know where to start; and I'm having more trouble collecting material than I've ever had before. I don't know where to look for it, whom to ask. . . . Oh, I should like to have done with those three last books. . . . After *L'Argent* there's *La Guerre*, but that won't be a novel, just an account of an individual's observations during the Siege and the Commune, without any plot. . . . But at bottom, the book which really tempts me is the last of the lot, a book in which I intend to portray a scientist. . . . I should like to model him on Claude Bernard, if I could obtain communication of his papers and letters. It will be an amusing thing to do. . . . I shall make him a scientist married to a narrow-minded bigot, who will destroy his work as fast as he writes it.'

'And after that, what are you going to do?'

'After that, the sensible thing to do would be to stop writing books, to abandon literature, to start a new life, regarding the old one as over.'

'But one never has the courage to do that.'

'You may be right.'[1]

*Saturday, 12 April*

The new Emperor of Germany would seem to have a sadistic side to his mystico-religious character. A well-known Parisian cocotte, La Lowe, with whom a friend of Jollivet's used to sleep, apparently became the Prince's mistress while he was doing his military service at Strasbourg. She became his mistress without knowing who he was, until one day when he was still so drunk in the morning that even with her help he was unable to put his boots on and had to send for his batman. Meeting this friend of Jollivet's in the train from the east, when he got in at Saverne station, she told him how the future emperor made love. She had orders to wait for him naked, stark naked except for a pair of long black gloves coming up above her elbows; he came to her similarly naked, with his arms tied together, no doubt because of his withered arm, and after looking at her for a

---

[1] Zola was to publish *L'Argent* in 1891. *La Guerre* was to become *La Débâcle*, published in 1892. The last of the Rougon-Macquart novels, *Le Docteur Pascal*, would appear in 1893, followed in 1894 by *Lourdes*, the first of the *Trois Villes* cycle.

moment, hurled himself upon her, throwing her on to the floor and
taking his pleasure with her in a bestial frenzy. Those black gloves,
of course, are a characteristic of sadism. . . . And they recall the
black stockings in Rops's obscene etchings.


*Thursday, 17 April*

A novel like *La Bête humaine*, a novel such as those which Zola
manufactures nowadays, in which everything is invention, imagination, fabrication, in which the characters are pure or filthy secretions
of his brain, a novel without a scrap of real humanity in it, holds no
interest for me now. I am interested only in novels in which I can
feel the transcription in print, so to speak, of creatures in flesh and
blood, in which I can read a little or a great deal of the memoirs of a
life that has been lived.


*Monday, 5 May*

Léon was saying yesterday that most of the women of the Faubourg Saint-Germain were alcoholics, not through their own fault
but through the fault of their ancestors, and that Potain prescribed
chicory for them, a prescription which they did not understand but
which was intended to make them drink a lot of water.


*Friday, 24 October*

Today I find a report in *La France* in which Renan speaks rather
harshly about me in connexion with my record of the Siege and the
Commune in my *Journal*.

He declares, with profound indignation, that he has never, never
given voice to a single unpatriotic opinion. Not a single unpatriotic
opinion? Oh, come now! I have heard him say that it was a matter
of complete indifference to him whether he was ruled over by a
William or a Napoleon, and I had the kindness not to reproduce
that entry in my *Journal*. He also calls me an 'indiscreet individual'.


*Tuesday, 28 October*

It is surprising how I have devoted the whole of my life to a
special sort of literature: the sort that brings one trouble. First there

were the naturalistic novels I wrote; then the revolutionary plays I put on; and now the *Journal*.

Today, at my request, the *Écho de Paris* sent me an *interviewer* whom I asked to reply on my behalf to Renan's attack, giving him the rough draft of the reply. But I made the mistake of chatting with him for a little while and of giving him my book when he left, and I am terribly afraid that I may have cause to regret my politeness.

'I have no intention', I told him, 'of entering into a discussion about the conversations recorded in the latest volume, which in any case Monsieur Renan says that he has not read, any more than he has read the earlier ones. But I assure you on my honour—and those who know me can testify that they have never heard me tell a lie— that the conversations I have quoted in the four volumes which have so far appeared are as it were shorthand transcripts, reproducing not only the speakers' ideas but more often than not their actual expressions. And I feel certain that every disinterested and perceptive reader will recognize that my desire and ambition have been to depict exactly the men I was portraying, and that not for anything in the world would I have wished to attribute remarks to them which they did not make.

'Monsieur Renan calls me an "indiscreet individual". I accept the reproach and I am not ashamed of it—especially as my indiscretions are not disclosures of people's private life, but simply disclosures of the thoughts and ideas of my contemporaries, documents for the intellectual history of the age. . . . Yes, I repeat that I am not ashamed of what he calls me. For ever since the world began, the only memoirs of any interest have been written by "indiscreet individuals", and my only crime is to be still alive twenty years after these were written—something for which, humanly speaking, I cannot feel any remorse.

'And then, frankly, Monsieur Renan has been so "indiscreet" about Christ that he really ought to allow a little indiscreetness about himself.'

*Thursday, 30 October*

Daudet remarked this evening, with perfect justice, that the success of Maeterlinck's books was due to the fact that they were forty years behind their time.

*Sunday, 9 November*

In the drawing-room, as we were talking about the unveiling of the bust of Flaubert, Bauër told us this story.[1] One evening the younger Brainne took him home and invited him to examine Flaubert's letters to his mother. Bauër was not alone: he was accompanied by a sweet little actress, with whom I believe he was living, and who started reading the letters out to him. She read one, two, three, then at the fourth suddenly stopped short, complained of feeling unwell, and asked Bauër to take her home.

Outside, Bauër asked her what was the meaning of this sudden indisposition, and she replied: 'Did you want me to read the letters of a woman's lover in front of her son?' Young Brainne had apparently read only the first few letters.

This correspondence would seem to kill the legend that Mme Brainne had refused to marry Flaubert; but it appears that the old rascal did not have just Mme Brainne but Mme Pasca too, of whom he said to Charpentier one day: 'My dear fellow, you can't imagine anything more delightful than La Pasca's little marble buttocks!'

*Sunday, 23 November*

Did not sleep all night, for fear of not being awake at the early hour fixed for our departure. At three o'clock, looked at my watch by the light of a match. At five o'clock, out of bed.

Finally, in the filthiest weather imaginable, there I was in the train for Rouen, with Zola, Maupassant, etc.

I was struck this morning by Maupassant's unhealthy appearance, by the thinness of his face, by his brick-coloured complexion, by the *marked* character, as they say in the theatre, which he had taken on, and even by his sickly stare. It seemed to me that he was not destined to make old bones. As we were crossing the Seine just before Rouen, he pointed to the river shrouded in fog and exclaimed: 'It's rowing in that every morning that I have to thank for what I've got today!'

On our arrival at Rouen, we called on Lapierre to settle the accounts. His niece asked us to wait a moment because he was being given an injection of morphine; and a few minutes later the doctor

---

[1] It was not a bust but a bas-relief by Chapu which was to be unveiled at Rouen on 23 November 1890.

asked us to be as brief as possible, because the sick man was very tired. We found poor Lapierre looking just like Don Quixote on his deathbed.

After that, lunch—an extremely good lunch—with the mayor, a very charming, fat, common man, with an ugly, simple, good-natured wife who recommended the champagne to me, a champagne made by her family: Goulet champagne.

Outside, the same mist, rain, and wind, the usual weather for un-veilings at Rouen; and a population completely indifferent about the impending ceremony and taking all the streets that did not lead to it. Altogether, a score of distinguished Parisians from the worlds of literature and journalism, and a fête with a tent for the authorities and fairground music just like the agricultural show in *Madame Bovary*.

I read out my speech in a voice which made itself heard right to the end, in a stormy squall which flattened my fur-coat against my body and blew my notes about in my hand. For the speaker on this occasion had to be an open-air orator. But my emotion today, in-stead of affecting my throat, showed itself in my legs, which started trembling so badly that I was afraid I was going to collapse and had to keep shifting my weight from one foot to the other.

Then, after me, a very tactful speech by the fat, red-haired mayor. And after the mayor, a speech by an academician of Rouen Academy, roughly twenty-five times as long as mine and containing all the clichés, all the commonplaces, all the hackneyed phrases, all the *Homaiseries* one could possibly imagine: a speech for which Flaubert will give him a thrashing on the day of the Resurrection.

As for Chapu's monument, to be perfectly frank, it is a pretty bas-relief in sugar, in which Truth looks as if she were relieving herself in a well.

At the end of the mayor's lunch, Zola, stroking my arm caress-ingly, had sounded me on the possibility of a reconciliation with Céard; and reflecting how embarrassing our quarrel was for the elder and younger Daudets, and how bothersome it was for us to give each other the cold shoulder when we were among friends, I had replied that I was quite prepared to make it up with him. So after the ceremony, when he came across to compliment me on my speech, we embraced in front of the medallion of Flaubert, reunited as if by the intercession of his shade.

It was half-past three when the ceremony came to an end, the rain was coming down more heavily than ever, and the wind had become a hurricane. There was no longer any question of the lunch which Maupassant had talked about offering us all the way from Paris, as the Norman author had gone off to call on a relation. We had to settle down in a café with Mirbeau and drink hot toddies during the two-and-a-half hours until dinner. And Bauër, who had come the day before for the performance of the opera *Salammbô*, told us that the manager of the local theatre had been thoughtful enough to give all the visiting critics an envelope containing a key to the stage-door, after urging his chorus-singers to be kind to the gentlemen of the Paris press, with the result that at dinner-time Bauër left us to go and dine on the sly with one of those little ladies whom he had invited the day before.

# 1891

*Sunday, 4 January*

Huysmans was talking today, with a rather childish satisfaction, about his close acquaintance with the thieves and fences of the Château-Rouge and his relations with Gamahut's mistress.[1]

It is interesting, all the same, this house of Gabrielle d'Estrées which has become a filthy hotel where the very bedroom of Henri IV's mistress has been turned into the 'Mortuary': the room where several layers of drunkards are piled one on top of another until the time comes for them to be swept out into the gutter. A hotel whose proprietor is a giant in a blood-red jersey with a couple of black-jacks and an armoury of revolvers always within reach. And in this hotel, strange down-and-outs of both sexes, including an old society woman, an *absintheuse* who 'puts away' twenty-two glasses of absinthe a day—that dreadful absinthe tinted with sulphate of zinc —a sexagenarian whose son, a barrister at the Court of Appeal, was unable to get her away from it all and, according to the local legend, committed suicide out of shame and despair.

*Sunday, 22 February*

A typical trick of the *Figaro*'s! By way of thanks for my preface which it printed yesterday, it published today, under Bonnières's signature, the fiercest of attacks on the writer and the gentleman in me.

It is an interesting article, though, for the intensity of hatred it displays: for twenty years now, I have been on my last legs; *La Faustin* and *Chérie* are worthless; *Les Frères Zemganno* is spoilt by

---

[1] Gamahut was a murderer who had been executed in 1885. It was not his mistress but the mistress of an accomplice of his called Midi whom Huysmans knew: a certain Louise Hellouin, *alias* Tache-de-Vin. Huysmans was to describe the Château-Rouge —a house at No. 57, Rue Galande, which has since been demolished to make room for the Rue Dante—in *La Bièvre et Saint-Séverin* (1898).

lack of tact; *La Fille Élisa* would have been forgotten if Ajalbert had not had the idea of adapting it for the stage and writing a second act of a warmth and eloquence of which I am incapable; Zola and Daudet have done nothing but increase their stature by means of their works, whereas all I can do is invent an academy which Vallès considers ridiculous and from which Vallès has just escaped; my *Journal*'s only value lies in its malice, and my portraits of the people of my time are nothing but caricatures. . . .

Finally his exasperation goes to the length of describing me as 'a gentleman from the provinces', when in fact my father and mother were people who lived in Paris, who were married in Paris, and who only after their marriage tried living in the provinces.

*Thursday, 5 March*

At dinner at the Daudets' there was talk about symbolism and about Mallarmé, whom somebody described as an artful fox. Mme Rodenbach, who was sitting next to me, whispered to me that his wife had confided in her that he had had a stroke a few years ago—which suggests that he may be sincere in his logogriphic language. She told me a few minutes later that her husband had written a big, admiring article on my *Journal* which had been forestalled by the Bonnières article; that he had then offered it to the *Gaulois*, where Meyer had rejected it, giving him to understand that he did not want to contradict the *Figaro* for fear that the *Figaro* might attack him for the support he had given Boulanger in the past. Journalism really is a peculiar business!

This evening saw the first visit to the Daudets' of Jules Renard, the ironic creator of *Poil de Carotte*, a fellow with a head just like Rochefort's, but without his clown-like stubble of hair, a young fellow, but cold, serious, phlegmatic, not laughing as a young man would at the jokes told in his presence.

*Sunday, 15 March*

In the Grenier, there was talk of Huysmans, who says that he is ill, troubled by the feel of something cold moving across his face, and rather alarmed at the thought that he might be surrounded by an invisible force. Could it be that he has fallen a victim to the

succubus he is describing just now in his novel?[1] He is secretly terrified too by the fact that his cat, which used to sleep on his bed, now
refuses to do so and seems to be avoiding its master. The Lyons
canon, who he says gave him information about the Black Mass,
has written to tell him that these things were bound to happen
to him, and every day he warns him of what is going to follow the
next day, enclosing anti-satanic prescriptions to be used in his
defence.

Lorrain, who gave us these details about Huysmans, says that the
author of *Là-Bas* now wears a scapulary containing a bloodstained
host sent to him by the aforementioned canon.

During the day, Lorrain had told me that he had met Zola at
Charpentier's and that he had shown signs of irritation on the subject of my *Journal*, complaining that I had represented him to the
public as a fool. This evening, this irritation was confirmed by Mme
Daudet, who had had an argument about the *Journal* with Mme
Zola in which the latter had declared that I had been unpleasant about
everybody, repeating two or three times, in that fishwife's voice that
she has when she gets angry: ' . . . and about you too!'


*Sunday, 10 May*

Poor Daudet, how he suffers! I saw him today, in the Grenier,
breaking off in the middle of a conversation, twisting his body
about, painfully stretching his legs—and all the time looking so
terribly ill! And during the three hours he spent here, the poor fellow gave himself three injections of morphine.

Daudet and I both spoke almost angrily today against the corro-
sion of the French mind by the foreign mind, against the irony in
French literature which is no longer the irony of a Chamfort but
that of a Swift, against criticism in France which has become Swiss,
German, and Scottish, and against the present-day mania for Russian novels and Danish plays.[2] Daudet remarked that if Corneille
borrowed from Spain, he put a French stamp on his borrowings,
whereas today the borrowings we make in our servile admiration are
nothing less than a denationalization of our literature.

---

[1] *Là-Bas*, then being serialized in the *Écho de Paris*. The 'Lyons canon' mentioned
later was the Abbé Joseph Boullan, portrayed in *Là-Bas* as Dr. Johannès.

[2] Read 'Norwegian' for 'Danish': Goncourt is clearly referring to Ibsen.

*Saturday, 23 May*

Zola, asked a few days ago to say which books had had the most influence on him, gave this list: Musset's poetry, *Madame Bovary*, Taine's writings.

Dammit all, I feel sure that *Germinie Lacerteux* made a greater impression on the brain of the author of *L'Assommoir* than the books quoted above.

*Monday, 1 June*

In my interview with Huret, I could have said: 'I gave the complete formula of naturalism in *Germinie Lacerteux*, and *L'Assommoir* was written from beginning to end on the lines laid down in that book. Later I was the first to abandon naturalism—not, like Zola, for a sordid reason, inspired by the success of *L'Abbé Constantin* which made him write *Le Rêve*—but because I considered that the genre, in its original form, was worn out. . . . Yes, I was the first to abandon naturalism for what the young writers are now using to fill its place—dreams, symbolism, satanism, etc., etc.— when I wrote *Les Frères Zemganno* and *La Faustin*, for in those books I, the inventor of naturalism, tried to dematerialize it long before anyone else thought of doing so.'

*Saturday, 27 June*

What with the weakness of present-day governments in the face of the working-class scum whenever there is a strike, the cost of living is going to become impossible, unless one fine day the middle classes stage a counter-strike; unless, at a time such as this, when the bakers' apprentices are making impossible demands, the middle classes agree not to eat any bread for a week or a fortnight and to eat rice and potatoes instead. Yes, we are approaching the time when the remuneration of the unskilled work which keeps a society alive will become so costly that that society will be unable to survive.

*Tuesday, 7 July*

Called on Montesquiou-Fezensac, the Des Esseintes of *A Rebours*.

A ground-floor apartment in the Rue Franklin, with tall windows fitted with little seventeenth-century panes of glass which give the house an old-world look. A place full of a medley of heterogeneous objects, old family portraits, horrible pieces of Empire furniture, Japanese *kakemos*, Whistler etchings.

One original room: the dressing-room, with a *tub* consisting of a huge enamel Persian tray next to a gigantic kettle in beaten copper from the Far East, all enclosed within screens of coloured glass rods; a room in which the hortensia—no doubt a token of the family's pious remembrance of Queen Hortense[1]—is represented in every sort of material and in every form of painting and drawing. And in the middle of this dressing-room, a little glass show-case revealing the delicate colours of a hundred or so ties, underneath a somewhat homosexual photograph of Larochefoucauld, the gymnast at the Mollier circus, taken in tights displaying to advantage his handsome ephebian figure.

When I stopped in front of a Whistler etching, Montesquiou told me that Whistler was doing two portraits of him at the moment: one in evening dress with a fur-coat over his arm, and the other in a long grey coat with the collar turned up and, at the neck, a tie of a colour, a colour . . . which he did not specify but which the expression in his eyes indicated was the ideal hue.

Montesquiou was very interesting on the subject of the painting technique used by Whistler, to whom he gave seventeen sittings during a month's stay in London. The preliminary sketch, with Whistler, is apparently 'a mad rush at the canvas', one or two hours of feverish frenzy, from which the thing emerges all wrapped up in its covering. Then there are long, long sittings during which, most of the time, the painter brings his brush up to the canvas, does not touch it, throws the brush away, and takes another—with the result that in three hours he will add about fifty touches to the painting, each touch, in his words, removing one veil from the sketch's covering. Sittings in which it seemed to Montesquiou that Whistler, with his fixed attention, was emptying him of life, was 'pumping away' something of his individuality; and afterwards he used to feel so exhausted that his whole body was unutterably tense, and he felt thankful to have discovered a certain *coca* wine which restored his energy after those dreadful sittings.

[1] Reproducing this passage in his autobiography *Les Pas effacés*, Montesquiou added a note here: 'Nothing of the sort.'

*Wednesday, 15 July*

Today there was a big dinner at the Daudets', to which the Zolas, the Charpentiers, and Coppée were invited.

Zola came in. He is no longer the moaner and whiner of the old days. Today, in his words and in his walk, there is something energetic, tough, almost truculent. And he is forever mentioning the name of Bourgeois or the name of Constans, to whom he has written or whom he has seen, something which suggests that he has become strangely infected with *officialism* and perhaps also with political ambition. As for his wife, beside whom I walked a little way and who is suffering from appalling headaches, she told me that she was convinced that she was going mad, and when I poked fun at the idea, she kept coming back to it with a curious insistence, as to a rooted obsession.

Soon Coppée arrived from Combs-la-Ville, a little village on the other side of the forest of Sénart where he has taken a house this year. In the poet's sun-tanned face, the brightness of his sea-green eyes gave him the appearance of an old salt.

Sitting out on the little terrace, we talked about the malice shown to us by the young critics of the day. This gave Zola a chance to come out with his question: 'Why bother about attacks? They don't matter a damn.' And he asserted that for his part he rather enjoyed being attacked, and that it was a pleasure for him in the evening to linger over a ferocious article he had noticed in the morning. Liar that he is, this man who is so sensitive to criticism that his face falls at the slightest observation, he went on to declare a positive affection for his critics, defending the Symbolists and Decadents against us, generously trying to find some merit in them, and finally calling forth this delightful query from Coppée: 'Come now, Zola, do you mean to say that you are interested now in the colour of vowels?'

*Friday, 17 July*

Out walking this morning, Daudet asked me whether my brother had been tormented by the thought of an after-life. I replied that he had not and that not once during the whole of his illness had he mentioned an after-life in his conversations with me.

Then Daudet asked me what my own opinions on the subject were, and I answered that in spite of my longing to see my brother again I believed that the individual was totally annihilated at death, that we were utterly insignificant beings, ephemeral creatures lasting a few days longer than those which lived for a single day, and that if God existed it was expecting too much of Him in the way of accounting to imagine that each one of us would have a second life in another world. Daudet told me that he shared my opinions; somewhere in his notes, he said, he had a record of a dream in which he was crossing a field of broom to the sound of the crackling of the bursting pods, and he compared our lives to those little explosions.

*Monday, 20 July*

A few days ago I replied to a letter mentioning the hope of marriage to me with a brutal letter which must have killed that illusion stone-dead in the unfortunate woman's heart. Today I received a note from her containing these words: 'Poor me!'—a note which has made me feel sad all day. After all, it may well be that the poor girl is the only woman who has ever really loved me!

*Thursday, 15 October*

A young Rumanian woman knocked at my door today and asked to see me. When she was told that I was out, tears came into her eyes, since she was unable to come again next Wednesday. She returned a few minutes later and said to Pélagie: 'Couldn't you give me something belonging to Monsieur de Goncourt?' And Pélagie, not wanting to disturb me, gave her the pencil she uses to keep her shopping accounts.

*Saturday, 5 December*

Borelli dropped in on me this morning to thank me for recommending his play to Antoine.

When I said to him: 'You ought to write novels about high society, because people like Maupassant and Bourget don't live in that world and only very rarely put on a red coat.' To which Borelli replied: 'Yes, but unfortunately, to write novels or plays about that world, you mustn't belong to it.'

After telling me all sorts of stories, he ended up by saying that the only women he liked were tarts. He praised them to the skies, declaring that these creatures, born in the humblest circumstances, managed to become the arbiters of taste and fashion in Paris, thanks to their wonderful diplomacy and *savoir-vivre*, for they knew that they would lose their position if they were seen with a pimp on their arm or a vulgar dress on their back. And comparing them with society women, who start with so many advantages, he observed that the latter only lowered themselves if they tried to be at all striking, citing the Morny girl and the Pillet-Will woman as examples.

He remarked that every year about 80,000 tarts started work and that of those 80,000 only about forty got to the top in Paris. And he pointed out that these were not women born and bred in Paris, because the latter have a mocking, ironical side to them which irritates the customer, who is usually an official of some sort. 'Yes,' said Borelli, 'the great cocottes are all women born in the provinces, who have something of the servant about them and are quite prepared to say *Monsieur le Comte* to the man they are sleeping with.'

*Tuesday, 8 December*

Dined at the Charpentiers' with the Zolas. When I went in, Mme Zola greeted me with quite remarkable chilliness. 'All right,' I said to myself, 'that means that I am going to have a scene with Zola during dinner.'

But no! All that he said to me, as we got up from table, was: 'You know, your memoirs are our memoirs!'

Then he spoke about his superstitions, saying that he added up the figures of the carriages he noticed, that 7 was his favourite number, and that he tapped the doors and windows a given number of times before going to bed.

On the way home the Daudets said to me: 'You've had a narrow escape! Madame Zola is furious about your reference to Médan as a "childless house". We had all the trouble in the world keeping her calm, and as you saw, she vented her anger on Madame Charpentier, pulling her house at Royan to pieces.'

*Wednesday, 9 December*

Maupassant is apparently suffering from delusions of grandeur, thinks that he has been made a count, and insists on people calling him *Monsieur le Comte*. Popelin, warned that Maupassant was developing a stammer, did not notice any stammer at Saint-Gratien this summer, but was struck by the improbable exaggeration of his stories.

He spoke of a visit he had paid Duperré in the Mediterranean squadron and of the salutes fired in his honour and for his amusement, salutes costing hundreds of thousands of francs; until finally Popelin could not refrain from commenting on the enormity of the sum involved. The extraordinary thing about this story is that Duperré, some time later, told Popelin that he had not seen Maupassant at all.

# 1892

*Sunday, 10 January*

Conversation on the fuss being made about Maupassant, which everyone thought excessive in view of the writer's real value. . . . Somebody made the sad observation that Maupassant had not a single close friend: the only person one might describe as a close friend of his is his publisher, Ollendorff.[1]

*Wednesday, 13 January*

Bonnetain, coming to see me today after a long absence, told me that at a lunch at Maupassant's with Bauër and Lepelletier, Maupassant had said something trivial over the hors-d'œuvre which had offended Lepelletier, who had whispered in Bonnetain's ear: 'I'm going to get him now.' And as he said this he assumed the concentrated expression of a man bent on revenge, just as Maupassant started cutting his steak. Then he launched out on a long dissertation on eye trouble as a symptom of diseases of the spine. And Bonnetain noticed that from the moment Lepelletier opened his mouth Maupassant left his steak and did not eat another morsel.

*Tuesday, 2 February*

Dr. Martin told me yesterday that he had often seen Musset taking his absinthe at the Café de la Régence, an absinthe that looked like a thick soup. After which the waiter gave him his arm and led him, or rather half-carried him, to the carriage waiting for him at the door.

*Wednesday, 3 February*

A visit from Guiches and Huysmans, the latter complaining bitterly that he cannot get hold of the material he needs for his book,

[1] At Cannes, during the night of 1–2 January 1892, Maupassant had attempted to commit suicide. A few days later he had been taken in a strait-jacket to Dr. Blanche's clinic in Paris, where he was to die on 6 July 1893.

for all that he spends every Sunday in church. But he intends to go to a Trappist monastery this summer, under an assumed name, with a letter of recommendation from a priest he has in his pocket, and then he will have to . . . And the interrupted sentence finishes with a Mephistophelian smile.[1]

This evening at the Princess's, bad news of Maupassant. He imagines himself to be full of salt, and is alternately depressed and irritated. He thinks that he is being persecuted by doctors who lie in wait for him in order to inject him with morphine, the drops of which make holes in his brain. And he is obsessed by the idea that he is being robbed, that his manservant has stolen 6,000 francs from him, 6,000 francs which after a few days become 60,000 francs.

*Sunday, 6 March*

Dinner at the Charpentiers' with a crowd of musicians, all old, all ugly, all pot-bellied, all bad-tempered.

Zola, who was sitting next to me, as soon as he heard that there was going to be a revival of *Germinie Lacerteux*, started declaring that Réjane was incapable of creating a part . . . that she had neither spirit nor passion nor soul . . . that she would never, never be a *focus*. . . . 'Yes, yes,' he said, 'she was not bad in a few scenes of your play'; and without listening to the objections raised by his neighbours he exclaimed: 'But she has no talent, no talent whatever!' And he went on repeating this several times, just like a deaf man who cannot hear other people and is rude without knowing.

How typical of Zola this dinner-table attack was! Every newspaper article must be about him, and every actor and actress must play only for him. And critics and actors become targets for his wrath if they dare to praise or play anybody other than the master of Médan. Oh, what a greedy ego the man has!

He went on to say that he had taken the post of President of the Society of Authors to . . .

'Learn the art of oratory', I said.

'No . . . but to learn how to speak in front of people without

[1] The priest in question was the Abbé Mugnier and the monastery Notre-Dame d'Igny, where Huysmans made a retreat in the summer of 1892 which marked his return to the Catholic faith. He was to publish the story of his conversion in *En Route* (1895).

feeling embarrassed, without getting confused, as I used to do in the old days, when I had five or six people in front of me, but as I no longer do now.'

'Zola,' I said, 'you are going to end up by becoming a politician.'

'Yes,' exclaimed Mme Charpentier enthusiastically, 'one day he will speak as a deputy, as a senator!'

And Zola gave a solemn, earnest nod of the head, from which one could tell that his mind was calculating how much politics had helped and profited Lamartine and Hugo.

A few minutes later Zola was telling me of the fatigue involved in finishing *La Débâcle* and of the huge size of the book, which is to have 600 pages, saying that the manuscript had already come to nearly a thousand pages of 35 lines—his usual little pages, consisting of a sheet of foolscap cut in four.

And when somebody asked him what he was going to do after the Rougon-Macquarts, after *Le Docteur Pascal*, he hesitated for a moment and then said that the theatre, which had greatly tempted him, appealed to him less now that he was approaching the time when he would be able to write for it, adding that every time he had been into a theatre where one of his plays was being performed, he had been disgusted with the thing as presented on the stage.

Here he broke off to tell us that he had been to Lourdes, where he had been impressed and amazed by that world of hallucinated believers, and that there was something worthwhile to be written about that revival of faith which in his opinion was responsible for the mysticism to be found at the moment in literature and elsewhere. Listening to him, I thought what a cunning rogue he was, realizing that naturalism was on the decline and deciding that here he had found an opportunity of going mystic with a big sale, just as from being an opponent of the Academy he had become a candidate for election.

*Sunday, 13 March*

This evening at the Charpentiers', Aristide Bruant came along to sing: the *chansonnier-cabaretier* whom I had never been to hear, put off in advance by reports of the vulgar abuse with which he greets you.

He appeared wearing a blood-red silk shirt, with a velvet jacket and long polished leather gaiters. Beneath a centre parting, fine, regular features, dark, velvety eyes in the shadows of deep brows, a

short, straight nose, a dark, matt complexion, and on this face something half feminine, half cynical male, which produces an overall
impression of an enigmatic androgyne.

What he sang before the society women who were there was
quite indescribable. This ignoble lyricism consisted of foul adjectives, dirty words, purulent slang, the vocabulary of sordid brothels
and clinics for venereal diseases.

You had to see Bruant belching this out in his brassy voice, see
him as I saw him, in profile, the look in the sinister shadow of his
perfidiously gentle eye, the coal-black nostril of the tip-tilted nose,
and the movements of the facial muscles, reminiscent of the jaw
movements of a wild beast eating carrion.

Meanwhile I, for all that I am no prude, had the impression that I
was attending a prison concert. . . . And to think that those society
women, without the protection of a fan, without even a blush on
their cheeks, listening to the man from close to, smiled and clapped
their pretty aristocratic hands at words no different from the
obscene scribblings on walls from which they avert their eyes.

Oh, Bruant's songs in society drawing-rooms and dynamite in
carriage entrances! These are two warning signs of the approaching
end of the bourgeois age.

*Thursday, 17 March*

Conversation with old Stevens, who is a real storehouse of anecdotes about the world of art, and better still, an extraordinary word-
museum of all the typical phrases of the painters of his acquaintance,
in the past and the present, phrases which give a better definition than
twenty pages of criticism of a character, a temperament, a talent.

Stevens expressed surprise at the complete absence of any feeling
for art in most great writers, saying that this was not the case with
regard to literature in painters of talent, even those who had not had
a classical education, and that one would never find a good painter
reading a book by a mediocre writer.

*Monday, 9 May*

Barrès, recently married though he is, has a mistress, an old chain
which he has not broken; and in order to keep her, he has convinced
his wife that every time he writes something for the *Figaro* he has to

pay 500 francs, so that one day the innocent creature told a friend: 'It's so annoying. . . . This month there were two articles by my husband in the *Figaro*, and that cost us a thousand francs. . . . Still, the publicity value of the *Figaro*. . . .' The 500 francs taken from the couple's funds together with the 150 or 200 francs paid for the article make up the mistress's keep for the month.

*Tuesday, 17 May*

Received a card from the Baronne de Galbois to tell me that Popelin died this morning.

He behaved very badly to me in recent years, and yet the news of his death has given me a sad evening, recalling as it does the memory of our close acquaintance in the past.

*Wednesday, 18 May*

I went to see the Princess this morning. In the courtyard I ran into old Sauzet and with her I found Benedetti and Bapst.

Looking utterly grief-stricken she was sitting on the sofa at the far end of the morning-room next to her bedroom. Her words, spoken in a far-away voice, were interrupted by long pauses. She said: 'It was Easter Sunday, when we lunched at Ollivier's. . . . In the Bois de Boulogne he wanted to get out . . . it was cool. . . . I stopped him and brought him back here. . . . He said: "I have never felt better!" He said the same to his son. . . . It was during the night that he had his attack. . . . Yes, it was the 17th, just a month ago.'

After a few moments of silence she went on: 'I don't know where I want to be. . . . I want to be at his house and here too . . . and I can't stay anywhere more than a minute or so. . . . He looks very beautiful . . . there is a peace, a tranquillity in his features. . . . I should have liked his son to do a portrait of him, but he didn't want to and wouldn't let anybody else. . . . It's true that it's a sad business!'

After I had taken leave of her and was just going out, she called out to me: 'Goncourt, they are a long way off now, our good years!'

*Friday, 27 May*

Yesterday Mme Daudet confessed that she listened at the keyhole when she heard a woman's voice that she did not know in her husband's study, and that yesterday she had cocked her ears at the sound of a Spanish woman's voice which had begun with the words: 'I have nine children . . .' At this she had gone back to her dressing-room, completely reassured.

*Sunday, 12 June*

Lorrain told us today that the table wine drunk at home by the great cocottes, whose throats were scorched by their champagne suppers with *écrevisses à la bordelaise*, was a drink made from centaury, liquorice, and something else refreshing and cleansing.

*Monday, 13 June*

Durand-Ruel's home is a strange habitation for a nineteenth-century picture-dealer. A huge flat in the Rue de Rome, full of pictures by Renoir, Monet, Degas, etc., with a bedroom with a crucifix at the head of the bed, and a dining-room where a table is laid for eighteen people and where each guest has before him a Pandean pipe of six wine-glasses. Geffroy tells me that the table of Impressionist art is laid like that every day.

*Saturday, 18 June*

This month my life has been poisoned by the unbearably sentential letter which my solicitor wrote to me a fortnight ago, informing me that my plan of founding an Academy after my death was impracticable, and treating the whole project as a madman's whim . . . a whim to which I have sacrificed the chance of happiness in marriage with a woman who loves me!

*Monday, 4 July*

Zola's novel *La Débâcle*. Here and there an episode from a crude boulevard drama; but in the whole book, not a single page of great prose, not even a single detail with the emotional quality of something seen or suffered, nothing but commonplace literature put together from other people's stories.

As I have said before, I think that if Zola and I had seen something of the fighting—and seen it with the intention of describing it later—we could each of us have written a new book, an original book. But without having seen anything of the war, all one can write is a book which may be interesting but is bound to resemble all the others which have been turned out on the same subject.

*Friday, 8 July*

At present the nape of a woman's neck, both the round nape and the thin nape, with its indiscreet tuft of curly hair on the glowing flesh, produces an aphrodisiac effect on me. I find myself following the nape of a neck—for the pleasure of looking at it—as other men follow a pair of legs.

*Tuesday, 26 July*

Dinner with the Charpentiers and the Zolas.

When I spoke to Zola about the book which he had said he was writing on Lourdes, he said:

'I arrived at Lourdes in pouring rain and stopped at a hotel where all the good rooms were already taken. And I was in such a bad mood that I felt like leaving the next morning. . . . But I went out for a while, and the sight of all those sick people, those poor wretches, those dying children carried up to the statue, those men and women lying prostrate in prayer . . . the sight of that city of faith, born of the hallucinations of that little girl of fourteen, the sight of that grotto, those processions, those stampeding crowds of peasants from Brittany and Anjou . . .'

'Yes,' said Mme Zola, 'it was ever so colourful!'

Zola snapped at her: 'It isn't a question of colour. This time it's a spiritual upheaval that I have to paint. . . . Well, as I was saying, that sight made such an impression on me that when I got to Tarbes I spent two whole nights writing about Lourdes.'

*Wednesday, 17 August*

In the train to Saint-Gratien, just as the newspapers were announcing an improvement in Maupassant's condition, Yriarte told me about a conversation he had recently with Dr. Blanche.

Maupassant apparently spends the whole day talking to imaginary people, who are all without exception bankers, stockbrokers, and financiers; and one can hear him suddenly say: 'Are you trying to make fun of me? What about the twelve million you were due to bring me today?'

Dr. Blanche added: 'He doesn't recognize me any more: he calls me *Doctor*, but for him I am Doctor What's-his-name, not Doctor Blanche.' And he gave a pitiful description of his appearance, saying that he now had the face of a real madman, with his haggard eyes and slack mouth.

*Wednesday, 5 October*

All this humbug about the great Renan is nauseating.[1] Surely Flaubert merited the honours being paid to Renan more than the latter; and surely the novelist's literary legacy has enriched France more than that of the pettifogging philosopher, whose fame twenty years from now strikes me as highly problematical.

*Saturday, 12 November*

First night of *Sapho* at the Grand-Théâtre.

Poor Zola, here more than anywhere else, found it impossible to hide the spiteful envy which a colleague's success always inspires in him. You had to hear the tone in which he paid Daudet this compliment this evening: 'My dear fellow, I do congratulate you on having your play staged so artistically. . . . Yes, it's very artistic . . . very artistic. . . . But in an auditorium as unfinished as this, don't you think there's always something likely to go wrong? The electricity works properly, does it? . . . And then, I wouldn't be surprised to see people rushing to get their overcoats back from the cloakroom.'

*Friday, 9 December*

When I want to write a stylistic passage I have to wash my hands beforehand. I cannot write with my hands dirty.

*Monday, 19 December*

On my arrival, at two o'clock, at the theatre, where there was a final rehearsal of *Charles Demailly*, Koning told me that he had heard that there was going to be a terrible rumpus in the theatre

[1] Renan had died during the night of 1–2 October.

during the fourth act and that he had immediately informed the police. First shock.

He added that he would be happy to have Bauër, who was organizing the protest, thrown into jail, and that he was ready to offer five hundred francs to a policeman to perform this arrest, an arrest which would gratify an old personal spite on the part of the manager of the Gymnase. Second shock. Bauër was on the paper I wrote for, and whatever sort of attack he might make on the play, I was and always would be grateful to him for having been the only critic to support *Germinie Lacerteux*.

Finally Méténier and Alexis arrived, and we took a glass of madeira together at the Café Riche. All of a sudden Méténier started slanging Alexis because the latter had said that he thought the sum of 600 francs, which Méténier had spent during the day on flowers for our actresses, was a little excessive. I said nothing, but I thought to myself that except for Sisos it was madness to spend so much money beflowering the untalented prostitutes who acted in a play and that instead of looking like a man of letters one gave the impression of being a foppish amateur whose play had been accepted by accident.

Méténier said to me what a bore it was to have to dine with somebody, then added after a silence: 'The fact is, I'm dining with my mistress, and I daren't invite you . . . but really I should be delighted. . . .' To which I replied: 'Oh, come now! I'm not as prudish as all that!'

So we agreed to meet at Marguery's at seven o'clock. I was punctual. There was such a thick fog that you could not see the other side of the boulevard. A quarter-past seven, half-past seven, no Méténier. Finally I saw the Zolas getting out of a carriage, accompanied by the Charpentiers. I asked if I might sit at their table while I was waiting for my amphitryon. Eight o'clock struck, and still no sign of Méténier. Alexis and I decided to order a dozen oysters, and we had just eaten them when I saw Méténier and his mistress coming along. Oh, a charming creature! A pretty girl born in Seville, with a supple figure and a sweet, distinguished face. An intelligent forehead, bright, voluptuous eyes, a straight little nose, and a beauty-spot in the middle of one of her pink cheeks.

During this impromptu dinner, Méténier, as if intoxicated in advance by the coming performance and overflowing with words, started telling us his life-story, in staccato phrases: 'La Fleury, the *Marie-Coup-de-Sabre* in your play . . . I had her virginity. . . . And the second time I slept with her, a child. . . . Oh, we were poor then . . . so poor that I gave up smoking so that she could eat. . . . And to think that when I was twelve I had a valet and a horse. . . . And that at fifteen I hadn't a sou and had to support a mother and a brother. . . . All on the eighteen hundred francs I earned as a police-station clerk. . . . But I was determined to get ahead. . . . I earned forty thousand francs this year, and I shall earn sixty thousand francs next year. . . . I even won eighteen thousand francs gambling last month. . . . Yes, I'm a gambler . . . a gambler who doesn't like gambling: I do it to put butter on my bread!'

The theatre bell cut short my collaborator's spoken monograph.

First act, chilly, very chilly, Duflos suffering from a heavy cold.

Second act. The scene of conjugal love which takes up the whole act, a rather artificial scene played by that artificial actress Sisos, had no effect on the audience.

Third act. With this act, which is really the first act of the play, the audience caught fire and began to applaud.

The fourth act, the act which takes place in the offices of the newspaper *Le Scandale*, the act in which the play was going to be sabotaged, was a triumph.

I was in Koning's little stage-box. He could not help shouting: 'To hell with them!' and he grasped my hands as one grasps the hands of a mistress.

Finally, in the last tableau, the actors were enthusiastically applauded, especially Duflos, who acted his mad scene superbly, who acted the whole play, according to Havet, as he had never acted in a play before.

I left the theatre after Koning had given me the box-office report: 'The journalists are furious, and Kerst refuses to write an article.'

I was looking for a cab when someone took me by the arm. It was Mme Charpentier, who took me to have a cup of chocolate at Prévost's with the Fasquelles and the Zolas, who both congratulated me on the play.

It will really be amusing to see the attacks by the press after this evening's success!

*Tuesday, 20 December*

In the theatre, only a Russian or a Norwegian is allowed to write something fine, something which makes no bourgeois concessions. If a Frenchman wants to succeed, he has to fill his play with vulgar things which a Sarcey is capable of understanding and appreciating.

*Thursday, 22 December*

Oh, the theatre! In the joy of victory, in the certainty of a hundred performances, I met Alexis and Méténier today, who told me that the play was not making any money, that during these first few days it had averaged 1,800 francs a day, something which had never happened before after a success.

There has obviously been a combination of unfortunate circumstances: the bad press, the political situation, the hoodoo on the theatre, and perhaps, for me, the hoodoo of this month of December, in which my brother and I were hauled before the courts, in which *Henriette Maréchal* was staged, and in which these last few years I have had attacks of pneumonia which have left me bronchitic.

# 1893

All day today, hope and despair succeeded each other in my brain, volatilizing like medicinal drops in a glass of water.

The fact of the matter is that I am sick of the theatre. It turns your life upside down, it distracts you from your real work, and it upsets you to no useful purpose.

At eight o'clock, in the midst of a snowstorm so heavy that I did not know whether I should not be obliged to spend the night in a hotel in Paris—and only out of a feeling of respect and duty towards my actors—I ventured out, caught the train, and eventually arrived at the Gare Saint-Lazare, where the cabby I told to take me to the Café Riche asked a friend the best way to go in this weather, to which the friend replied that he would never get there by way of the Boulevard.

At the Café Riche I found Scholl, who was having dinner and told me that he did not dare venture as far as the Place du Châtelet, where he had a ticket for the opening performance of *Werther* at the Opéra-Comique.

A cabby agreed to take me to the Menus-Plaisirs, where at Antoine's request I gave him permission to put on *A bas le progrès* at the end of the evening.

While waiting to see my play, I hid at the back of Daudet's box and watched Strindberg's Danish[1] play, *Mademoiselle Julie*, in which poor Nau, in an impossible part, was given a rough reception.

At the end of my own play, my name was pronounced to the sound of feeble applause, and I had the impression that the thing had not had the effect I had expected. . . . But for the moment, like the audience, I was more preoccupied with the problem of getting home than anything else.

[1] For 'Danish', read 'Swedish'.

*Tuesday, 17 January*

At last, thank heavens, I have finished with rehearsals and performances! ... What a journey home yesterday! No cab from the Théâtre-Libre to the Gare Saint-Lazare, so that I had to walk through a whirlwind of snow without my umbrella, which I had left at the Café Riche. Then, at the Gare Saint-Lazare, I slipped on some ice near a public urinal and found myself flat on my back. I finally got up with nothing strained, nothing broken, and cured, I do believe, of incipient lumbago.

*Thursday, 19 January*

A press such as I have never had before. According to the *Figaro* it is 'a collection of old-fashioned paradoxes, so boring that everybody walked out'. According to the *Liberté*, 'a buffoonery full of elephantine wit'. According to the *Libre Parole*, 'the pitiful ramblings of an old man'. And according to the grim, talented Stoullig of the *National*, 'it is pretentious in its ineptitude, futile in its incoherence, and completely devoid of all imagination'.

*Thursday, 23 February*

Mallarmé, whom Alphonse Daudet asked with every circumspection whether he was not trying at the moment to be more obscure and abstruse than in his first works, in that slightly wheedling voice which someone once said occasionally goes flat with irony, after a great many strange phrases such as: 'One cannot write in white', finished his nebulous amplification by confessing that at present he regarded a poem as a mystery to which the reader had to find the key.

*Monday, 20 March*

These last few days I have been haunted by the idea of death combined with anxiety as to the fate of my will, which may be annulled like my Academy, and anxiety as to the preservation of the manuscript of my *Journal*. I shall die not knowing what is to become of the two great projects of my life intended to ensure my survival.

*Tuesday, 25 April*

Today, as the result of my outing to Paris yesterday, I am suffering from a headache and stiffness of the joints. I asked the doctor to have a look at a varix the size of an egg which Pélagie told me she had on her thigh, and now she is condemned to wearing an elastic stocking which comes almost up to the pelvis.

This varix, developed by constant climbing of the stairs during my illness and left, the doctor told me, rather a long time, might one day produce a sore which would take six or eight months to cure. This has plunged me into gloom, particularly as my Grenier and my knick-knacks have taken up the whole house and I could not give her a room if she had to be replaced; and with an aching heart I foresee a separation if she becomes incapable of working.

*Sunday, 30 April*

Hearing somebody in the Grenier mention the name of Oscar Wilde, Henri de Régnier started smiling. I asked him why. 'Oh, don't you know?' he said. 'He makes no secret of it. Yes, he admits that he's a homosexual. . . . It was he who said one day: "I've been married three times in my life, once to a woman and twice to men." After the success of a play of his in London he left his wife and three children and installed himself in a London hotel where he is living with a young English lord. A friend of mine who went to see him told me afterwards that there was only one bed in the room, with two pillows, and that while he was there Wilde's wife, who brings him his post every morning, arrived in tears.'

And when I said that in a man so given to plagiarizing his fellow authors, homosexuality must be a plagiarism from Verlaine, Régnier agreed with me, saying that the English author was always praising Verlaine.

*Sunday, 14 May*

This evening at Daudet's we were talking about poor Mme Zola, sadly wandering around with the two children her husband has had by her chambermaid.[1]

[1] Jeanne Rozerot. The two children were Denise, born in September 1889, and Jacques, born in September 1891.

She apparently had a previous chambermaid whom the good Zola started pawing about. She dismissed her and stupidly filled her place with another very beautiful girl, whom she kept for some time in spite of Mme Charpentier's warnings that she was being foolish: this was the girl whom Zola has made the hetaira of his second home.

Daudet then spoke of the coolness which had arisen between Céard and Zola on account of this mistress. Whenever Zola was at Médan, the mother of his two children was installed in the vicinity, and Céard acted as postman for the letters he wrote to the young woman: letters in which, for some reason or other, Zola, with his Italian duplicity, poked cruel fun at his postman. And one day, Mme Zola, irritated at the part Céard was playing in the affair, ridiculed the trust he placed in Zola's friendship, quoting the jokes her husband had made about him in certain letters which, somehow or other, she had seen.

Then there was a scene between the two friends which nearly turned them into two enemies. One evening at Médan, after a violent quarrel between husband and wife, Mme Zola started packing her bags and Zola went to his room, just letting her go. Céard, who was at Médan at the time, abandoned his tactful reserve and with praiseworthy indignation told Zola that he was a cad and a swine, if he let the woman go who had shared the poverty of his bad years and whom he was heartlessly throwing out now that he had got to the top.

*Thursday, 18 May*

Talking about Mallarmé, Leconte de Lisle declared that there was a mad side to the symbolist, and that he had met him one day carrying a letter from his daughter addressed to Prince Azure, which he was taking in all seriousness to the post.

When someone mentioned Vigny's noble character, Daudet, referring to his poem *La Mort du loup*, remarked that he had died rather after the fashion of his wolf, maintaining a frightening silence in the most appalling pain. Someone else added, as an illustration of the man's love of ornament, that he had had an officer's great-coat spread over the foot of his bed, burying himself in advance under his old uniform.

This talk of Vigny's death led Leconte de Lisle to say that Holmès was his daughter, and he quoted the musician's cruel comment when her father asked to see her during his last days: 'He wanted to live by himself, let him die by himself!'[1]

*Wednesday, 28 June*

Poor Lorrain is due to have an operation on Friday for a tumour or a fistula or something in his intestines, and these last few days he has been lunching and dining at friends' houses or entertaining friends to lunch and dinner in order to forget about Friday as far as possible.

Today he invited me to dinner and served up as a curiosity Yvette Guilbert.

No, she is not beautiful. A flat face, a turned-up nose, pale blue eyes, eyebrows with a rather devilish twist to them, tow-like, colourless hair wound round her head, and very low breasts: that is what she looks like.

But combined with a feverish animation of the body, this woman has a vivacious eloquence which is really very amusing. She came in talking about the famous Rougon-Macquart lunch in the Bois de Boulogne,[2] describing the various types of *stunning* women who had been present, the caricatural figures of the men who had delivered speeches, and the stammering of the embarrassed Zola, in a comical report which would have been a great success in a newspaper. What is so original about her lively wit is that her modern style is studded with adjectives borrowed from the Symbolist and Decadent poets, archaic expressions and old verbs like *ambulate* brought back into use: a mish-mash, a hotch-potch of the present-day Parisian idiom with the facetious language of Rabelais.

At bottom, however, this woman, rescued from the shoe department of the Printemps by a poor Italian prince to whom she has remained absolutely faithful, has not the fire of a great artiste but simply the ambition to make a pile of money—she earns more than a

[1] Vigny was a close friend of the Holmès family and godfather to Augusta Holmès, who used to draw attention to her resemblance to the poet but frequently denied that she was his daughter.

[2] On 21 June 1893 a great banquet was held at the Châlet des Îles in the Bois de Boulogne to celebrate the completion of Zola's Rougon-Macquart cycle of novels.

hundred thousand francs a year—and to retire in two years' time in order, as she puts it, 'to sing sad songs to herself'.

*Saturday, 8 July*

Maupassant's funeral in that church at Chaillot where I attended the wedding of Louise Lerch, whom I once thought of marrying. Mme Commanville, with whom I rubbed shoulders, told me that she was leaving tomorrow for Nice with the kindly intention of seeing and comforting Maupassant's mother, who is in an alarming state of grief.

*Sunday, 9 July*

Maupassant's success with loose society women is an indication of their vulgarity, for never have I seen a man of the world with such a red face, such common features, or such a peasant build—and what is more, clothes which looked as if they came from the Belle Jardinière and hats crammed down on the back of the head as far as the ears. Society women definitely like men who are crudely attractive; cocottes are more particular, they like men who are delicately attractive.

*Thursday, 20 July*

Before dinner Céard gave us some curious details of the executions he had witnessed. He spoke of the condemned man's head wobbling on his shoulders as if it were no longer firmly attached, of the slackness of his jaw making his face seem longer, of the pallor of his complexion turning a sort of chocolate colour. He spoke of the long drop of the knife, a drop which lasted a good second, and described the knife travelling up again splashed with blood and showing clearly the mark of the two carotids. These were things he noticed at the execution of Allorto and his accomplices, the murderers of the Auteuil gardener.

Over dinner he talked about Maupassant, saying that with him writing was purely instinctive and spontaneous, and declaring that he had never known anyone more indifferent to everything and that when he seemed most excited about something he had already lost interest in it.

*Friday, 4 August*

Every six months Zola feels the need to feel our pulses, Daudet's and mine, to find out how we are, physically and mentally. Today then, he was to dine here. And we waited for him with a certain apprehension, in view of the nervous condition we were both in. Mme Daudet advised us not to be so tense and urged me to take a really restful siesta before he arrived.

Zola spoke of the theatre, saying that he was tired of it but that it was a field in which he thought he might be able to break new ground, and that he was tempted to write a play between his novels *Lourdes* and *Rome*. Then, jumping from one subject to another, he admitted to a passion for cakes, confessing that he ate a whole plateful with his four o'clock tea; and then he launched into a eulogy of insomnia, saying that it was while he was lying awake in bed that he made his decisions, which he started executing as soon as he had put on his boots, an action which he performed while thinking aloud: 'Here I am on my feet again!'

Then came the sweetly hypocritical compliments, the questions which are traps, the declarations which, if you follow him, he will suddenly interrupt with an: 'Oh, my dear fellow, I wouldn't go as far as you!' followed by a virtual recantation of his previous arguments. In fact that art of talking without saying anything of which the man of Médan is the unrivalled master.

Meanwhile Mme Zola, aged, wrinkled, influenza-ridden, and in Mme Daudet's words looking like an old doll in the window of a bankrupt toy-shop, was sitting in a corner with Mme Daudet, describing her sad life at Médan, and saying of her husband: 'I only see him at lunch. . . . After lunch he takes a few turns round the garden, waiting for the papers to arrive and until then throwing me a few words . . . telling me to look after the cow. But I don't know anything about that sort of thing, and it seems to me that it's more a job for the gardener. . . . Then he goes back upstairs to read the papers and take his siesta. . . . I had a cousin of mine to stay the last few years; this year I miss her; she's at the seaside.' And I could see Zola anxiously following the conversation from a distance.

We sat down to dinner, and a black cloud which seemed to foreshadow a storm led Mme Zola to tell us once more of Zola's fear of thunder, both as a child, when he had to be taken down to the cellar, wrapped in blankets, and now, when, in the billiard-room at Médan, with the windows shut and all the lamps lit, he still covered his eyes with a handkerchief.

*Thursday, 10 August*

The young English writer Sheppard told us today of a conversation he had had with Zola about his coming visit to England. Zola had declared that London did not interest him at all, but that this visit might destroy the idea that he was unpopular abroad, might help his election to the Academy. And the malicious Englishman finished his account of the conversation with this sentence: 'For a whole hour in fact we circled round the word *publicity* without pronouncing it once.'

*Sunday, 1 October*

Paul Alexis, just back from the south of France, told me that he had paid a call on Mme de Maupassant which had left him convinced that Maupassant was Flaubert's son.

In a long conversation which he had with her and which lasted from one o'clock till six o'clock, first of all Mme de Maupassant brought a certain passion to the task of proving to him that physically and morally Maupassant had nothing of his father in him. Then, in the course of the conversation, she said to him about the funeral: 'I should have liked to go to Paris. . . . But I sent specific instructions that he was not to be buried in a lead coffin. Guy wanted his body to be reunited after death with the Great All, with Mother Earth, and a lead coffin delays that reunion. He was always preoccupied with that thought and when, at Rouen, he supervised the funeral of his dear father . . .' Here Mme de Maupassant corrected herself, but very quickly, without stopping: 'Of poor Flaubert . . .' And later on, never suspecting what proofs she was giving against herself, she returned to the beginning of her conversation: 'No, his illness can't be traced to any of us. . . . His father died of rheumatic fever. . . . I suffer from heart disease. . . . His brother, who was said to have died mad, really died of sunstroke, because of his habit of inspecting his plantations wearing a hat too light to protect him.' And Paul Alexis wondered whether it was not quite likely that a person suffering from epilepsy should be followed in the next generation by a madman.

*Wednesday, 6 December*

Alidor Delzant has been amusing himself these last few months sorting and classifying Alice Ozy's papers. Among the autograph letters of the contemporaries who were the woman's admirers or lovers there is a whole volume of letters from Charles Hugo, very interesting, very beautiful letters, written at the time when Ozy was being courted by old Hugo and about to succumb to him, and when the son wrote to her that he refused to take part in this incestuous relationship and that he was retiring broken-hearted from the lists.

# 1894

*Thursday, 22 February*

This evening, at Daudet's, news came of Zola's failure and of Heredia's election to the Academy. Hervieu, who had just seen Heredia, told us that he had manœuvred very well and shown himself a very skilful strategist as a candidate.

All the same, I do not think that since the Academy was founded any writer has joined the Immortals with so little work to his credit. Come now, an Officer of the Legion of Honour and an Academician, with a prize of 6,000 francs into the bargain: he has not done too badly.

*Sunday, 25 February*

Ernest Daudet dined this evening at his brother's. What he knows about the private lives of actors, people in society, politicians, and business men is quite incredible. He told us for instance of the autocratic way in which Clemenceau, in this country ostensibly under the rule of law, had managed to organize, speed up, and finally obtain his divorce. He had his wife followed, but without success; then one of his daughters, yes, one of his daughters, told him: 'You'll never do it that way; it's her lover you ought to have followed.' Finally, thanks to this filial advice, the loving couple were caught in the act. The wife was taken to the Prefecture of Police, where the Prefect—who was Lozé, I believe—told her that unless she agreed to a divorce he would have her taken to Saint-Lazare. She had no option but to give her consent. She was put on board a ship for the United States, and allowed to take along her lover, who turned out to be a young man at the École Normale. And by the time she reached New York our French judges had already put through the divorce.[1]

[1] Mme Clemenceau was American-born. As Miss Mary Plummer she had been a pupil of Clemenceau's when the latter, a French master at Greenwich (Connecticut), had married her on 23 June 1869.

A piquant detail. She had no money of her own. What did she do to earn a living? She gave lectures on the Panama scandal, advertised by big posters on which one could read her maiden name followed by the words: *Ex-wife of M. Clemenceau.*

*Saturday, 21 April*

That little wife of Forain's has undoubtedly got her husband's malicious sense of humour, but her wit has a more delicate eighteenth-century flavour than his. Dining recently with Séverine and her lover Labruyère, throughout dinner she kept calling Labruyère *Séverin.* But her best remark these last few days was this. Kissed on the shoulder by Lorrain, who has the reputation of being a homosexual, she asked him: 'Are you looking for an alibi?'

Today, when I asked Pélagie what was the matter with her daughter, whom I had seen this morning looking very peculiar, she replied: 'She didn't want any lunch and she's crying in her room. . . . She says it's because of you.'

'Because of me?'

'Yes . . . because of what you wrote about her!'

I went to Blanche's room to speak to her. She was misery in person! And when I said that I could not understand why she should be upset, and that I had always spoken of her affectionately, she sobbed: 'You've made me out to be so poor and unhappy . . . people will feel like giving me bread in the street!'

*Sunday, 29 April*

Today Duret and Raffaelli spoke enthusiasticallyabout Whistler's portrait of Montesquiou-Fezensac. And when someone mentioned the painter's reputation for eccentricity, Duret told us that a distress had been levied on him in London one day when he was giving a lunch at which the guests were the Duchess of Westminster and some Englishman or other, both of them among the richest people in England, and that he had thought it amusing to place the bailiffs next to these guests at table. And Whistler, after this lunch which marked his farewell to London, used to say of these two millionaires who had allowed a distress to be levied on him that they had not done so out of spite, nor out of complete indifference, but because it had simply not occurred to them that there might be something in his studio which they could buy to enable him to pay his debts.

This evening Mme Daudet told me that *Mémé*, playing in the Tuileries Gardens with the little Fasquelle girl, had seen Zola pass so close that she had felt obliged to say: 'Good day, Monsieur Zola!' Now Zola was not alone; he had a young woman on his arm and was followed by two children escorted by a maid. Yes, he was walking his second family round the most public place in Paris!

*Thursday, 3 May*

Feeling too tired and weak to go to Daudet's, I sent him a telegram; and five minutes later I received a letter from his brother describing the indignation he had felt on reading my pen-portrait of his mother. This literary portraiture of one's contemporaries really is disastrous for the author; thus in return for all the pleasant things I have said about people, I have received a solitary card from Scholl, while for the rest, which is mild enough, I have had three almost abusive letters. The result is that at the moment I cannot open a single letter without expecting to be insulted.

*Sunday, 6 May*

I waited today for Daudet with a certain apprehension. What sort of attitude was he going to adopt? He arrived on Hennique's arm and spoke to me very affectionately, taking my side and condemning his brother's letter, of which he had been completely ignorant. He was, I repeat, very friendly; but I could tell that there was something in him which had not come out, but which would come out before long.

Sure enough, as soon as we had got into his carriage, he began by describing the indignation of his fellow southerner Bonnet at my physical portrait of Mistral, told me of hostile articles in the *Débats* and the *Courrier français*, gave me the opinions of our friends, of Geffroy saying that it was 'too topical as literature', and mentioned two or three little references to himself which had not hurt him but which he would have preferred not to see in print.

I confessed that I had been led by my love of the truth and my desire for sincerity to be perhaps unconsciously indiscreet and to portray others as I portrayed myself and I added: 'Yes, I was wrong not to let you see the volume and ask you to cut out anything that shocked you in it. Because you must realize that my friendship for you is such that I would not want any expression of that friendship to be distasteful to you. . . . So I shall let you see the whole of the next volume and you shall read it before publication.'

*Friday, 11 May*

Lorrain told me this morning that Montesquiou was going to give a big party at his Versailles house and that Sarah Bernhardt was to send out the invitations; and he added that Sarah had asked him not to attack Montesquiou any more, saying that every one of his aggressive articles about Montesquiou was 'like a slap in her face'.

Then he talked about Liane de Pougy, whose fine, delicate beauty he compared to the slender, shapely grace of a heraldic figure, repeating a story going round Paris to the effect that Meilhac had paid 80,000 francs simply to look at her naked body.

Mme de Bonnières spends nearly all her time in the company of the young Symbolist, Decadent, Altruist poets. When somebody asked her the other day whether they did not pay court to her, she answered with a wit with which I would not have credited her: 'Oh, there's no danger! They have all been found unfit for military service!'

*Sunday, 10 June*

Rodenbach today denied that Maupassant had had any talent, declaring that he had never written a single quotable phrase in any of his books, and speaking eloquently of the hatred which the true artist aroused in his colleagues, because they felt, he said, that they were writing the literature of today while he was writing the literature of tomorrow.

Rodenbach having expressed surprise at the enormous success of *La Maison Tellier*, Toudouze told us that at Maupassant's funeral he had found himself in the same carriage as Hector Malot, who had informed him that it was he who had given the story to Maupassant, but that he had spoilt what Malot had told him by finishing his tale with a party, when in fact the madam had said to her girls: 'Tonight, my dears, it's bye-byes alone.'

*Friday, 29 June*

Today, forwarded to me by the *Écho de Paris*, and still in connexion with the serialization of my *Journal*, I received an envelope full of soiled rags, anonymous excrement.

*Wednesday, 11 July*

Today, the second day of my stay with the Daudets, I had an attack, and what promised to be a severe attack. At three o'clock I went downstairs to find Daudet, to whom I said: 'You must give me an injection, old fellow.' He got out his needles and sterilized them, and there we were, as he put it, the paralytic hanging on to the hepatic, tottering up the narrow staircase to my bedroom. And his trembling hands gave me the first injection I have ever had, so skilfully that I did not feel anything. He went a little pale with the emotion caused by this injection, for all that he gives himself injections all day long, and I saw him looking anxiously around for his stick which he had mislaid and without which he could not go downstairs again. . . . A quarter-of-an-hour later I felt the pain slipping away in a sort of drowsiness.

*Thursday, 11 October*

The Daudets spoke of the dinner they had given Zola after my departure, the chilliest, most embarrassed dinner imaginable. Told that Daudet was about to publish *La Petite Paroisse*, Zola could not refrain from saying: 'But jealousy is a subject that has been treated so often! . . . Isn't Anatole France's *Lys rouge* about jealousy?' To which Daudet replied: 'There's *Othello* too. . . .' Whereupon Zola went into a cold fury, caused by his envious annoyance that anyone but him should publish a book. Then Coppée had the misfortune to refer to Dumas's extra-marital activities, and this led Mme Zola to make allusions to the behaviour of her husband, who was reduced to nervously tapping the handle of his knife on the table and who, in his hurry to leave, did not even wait for his landau to be got ready to take him to the station, but rushed headlong out of the baneful house.

*Monday, 10 December*

The Seine at five o'clock.

A violet stretch of water, along which boats go by with a fringe of white foam at their bows, beneath a pink sky in which on one side there rises the Eiffel Tower and on the other the minarets of the Trocadéro, in the shadowy blue of fantastic fairy-tale buildings.

Never has Paris, in the shrill voices of the newspaper boys this evening, in the tangle of the carriages, in the busy bustle of the people, in the brutal jostling of the passers-by, struck me so forcibly as the capital of a land of madness, inhabited by lunatics.

And never has the Paris of my youth or the Paris of my maturity seemed as poverty-stricken as the Paris of this evening: never have so many women's pleading eyes asked me for a meal, never have so many men's weary voices asked me for a sou.

*Wednesday, 19 December*

The doorbell rang before ten o'clock this morning. It was the Zolas in the most affectionate mood, both husband and wife, but especially the wife, who had been treated in Rome with the politeness accorded to society women, something to which she is not accustomed. The couple had come to thank me for the charming welcome which Béhaine had given them on receiving my letter of recommendation, and both were effusive in their praises of the ambassador's kindness and courtesy.

This evening at the Princess's I found Anatole France. Extremely talkative, he speaks with the eloquence of an academician—which he has yet to become—appreciated by society, but with an admixture of paradoxical, anti-bourgeois ideas, somewhat reminiscent of Renan, which make his conversation amusing. And then he no longer has the foolish face he had when he was young: somewhat thickened features give him a thoroughly masculine head, which has shed the silly fatuity of his adolescence. Moreover he was very pleasant to me, devoted most of his time to me, and made some complimentary references to my description of Florence in *L'Italie d'hier*.

At one point he gave a witty account of the search made by the politicians for the stupidest soldier in the Army in order to make him Minister of War, because the politicians know that there always comes a day when that Minister is tempted to get rid of his civilian colleagues, a temptation which each successive Minister of War has felt at some time or other, but more timidly than General Boulanger, not having his physique, his popularity, or his black horse.

# 1895

Carrière, who, lost in the crowd, was present yesterday at the cere-mony of Dreyfus's reduction to the ranks, told me that I, who in *La Patrie en danger* had so skilfully rendered the movement of the streets during the Revolution, should have been there, for I could certainly have made something out of the mood of that crowd.[1]

He could see nothing of what was happening in the courtyard of the École Militaire and had just the echo of the crowd's emotion provided by some little boys up in the trees who, when Dreyfus arrived holding himself erect, shouted: 'The swine!' and a few moments later, when he bowed his head: 'The coward!'

And this provided me with the opportunity to say, with regard to that poor wretch, that I was not convinced of his guilt, that the judgements of journalists were the judgements of little boys up in the trees, and that in a case like that it was really very difficult to establish the innocence or guilt of the accused from an examination of his bearing.

This morning's *Figaro* contains a ferocious article on me under the title of 'The Goncourt Banquet'. And it is not the writer who is attacked but the man. The author insinuates that I have exploited brotherly love in my books, casts doubt on the sincerity of that love which I buried so speedily and merrily, and, God forgive me, accuses me of keeping silent about my brother's collaboration.

And this article, signed Maurice Talmeyr, ends with a reference to a Funeral Committee constituted on my behalf by the author of the article, who is probably also the author of all those paragraphs in *La Plume* in which he says how sorry he is, whenever a hearse

---

[1] Dreyfus had been sentenced on 22 December 1894 to deportation for life and reduction to the ranks.

passes him in the street, not to see Alphonse Daudet in it. What would you? That is the tone of the homicidal, anthropophagous, Caribbean criticism of the present day.

This very evening, copying the *Figaro* in *Le Jour*, the dull-witted Formentin waxes indignant that I use the personal pronoun *I* to talk of myself in my memoirs—do you know a way for an author to write his memoirs without using the word *I?*—and expresses astonishment at the sort of notoriety I have acquired with 'the little I have produced'. Heavens above, what does the good man want? Are forty volumes on unexplored subjects nothing to him?

*Sunday, 27 January*

I was thinking, last night, that one of the reasons for the implacable literary enmities that I encounter was the decency of my life. Yes, there is no doubt about it, this is an age which has a liking for unsavoury conduct. Who, after all, are the idols of the youth of today? They are Baudelaire, Villiers de l'Isle-Adam, and Verlaine: three men of talent admittedly, but a sadistic Bohemian, an alcoholic, and a murderous homosexual.

*Thursday, 7 February*

Mallarmé told us this evening that as a boy he was sent to a boarding-school at Auteuil—a boarding-school run by a priest on Baron Gros's forty-acre estate—by a snobbish grandmother who wanted to see little aristocrats in her house on Sundays. There, on account of his plebeian name, he was kicked and beaten by his noble schoolmates, and this gave him the idea of declaring that Mallarmé was not his real name and that he was the Comte de Boulainvilliers. And when his grandmother had him called for, he stayed for a long time in the far reaches of the park before responding to the call, letting his real name fade away and evaporate in his delay in answering to it.

*Sunday, 10 February*

At the very end of the evening Daudet asked me from his armchair, where he was sitting writing: 'At Fasquelle's dinner-party last Friday, did the Charpentiers say anything to you?'

'No.'

'You are sure? They didn't say anything?'

'No, on my word of honour!'

Then Daudet came and sat down beside me and, practically whispering in my ear, said:

'I shouldn't be telling you this. . . . But since Zola has let Madame Charpentier into the secret, in spite of the undertaking we gave not to say anything to anybody, I might as well tell you. . . . Well, here goes! The President of the Republic, in exchange for two Chevalier's crosses, has obtained an Officer's cross for you, and Poincaré has asked to preside over the banquet in order to bestow it on you. . . . I must admit that Zola behaved very well and worked very hard to get the cross for you. He suggested going to see the Minister by himself, but I wouldn't agree to that, and we went together.'

There followed a comical account of the visit of Zola and Daudet to the Ministry, with Zola taking Daudet's hat so that he could lean on his stick and his colleague's arm, and making his speech carrying both hats in his hand.

Daudet went on: 'And do you know what happened afterwards because of you? When I shook hands with Zola, feeling that I was touched by what he had done for you, he was affected by a renewal of friendship and told me of the unhappiness of his life, confessing that for two years he had gone in fear of seeing himself splashed with the blood of his children and his mistress, murdered by his wife, in fear of seeing himself disfigured by that fury whose shrieks forced him to shut himself up at night in his bedroom so as not to hear her.' And Zola had said all this in a sort of hysterical outburst, with tears pouring down his cheeks.

*Friday, 1 March*

A charming tribute from Mme Rodenbach. This morning she sent me a big bunch of roses carried by her fair-haired baby in its nanny's arms, together with a note from the child's father: 'Constantin Rodenbach sends M. de Goncourt the respect and admiration of the next century, to which they will both belong.'

The baby having departed, I opened the *Libre Parole* and was pleasantly surprised to find in it an article similar to those which Drumont used to write when we were on friendly terms, an article in which he associated himself with those who were giving me the banquet. I thanked him in a note in which, referring to Daudet's memories of him and to the memories which he must have of Daudet after so many years of friendship and collaboration, I told him that they could not end their lives in an atmosphere of hatred unworthy of two noble souls.

Then came the long hours of a day due to end with a moving occasion, the impossibility of staying at home, and the need to go out for a walk with unseeing eyes and aimless legs.

An endless queue and admittance so badly organized that after waiting for forty minutes on the staircase of the Grand-Hôtel, Scholl lost patience and went home. Finally, in spite of a waiter who refused to let me in, I managed to slip into the drawing-room upstairs, while Daudet went and sat down straight away at the banqueting-table downstairs.

Warm, nervous handshakes greeted me; and one of these handshakes came from Lafontaine, who gave me a little bunch of violets with a card from his wife on which was written: *Henriette Maréchal* —the part she had played in 1865.

We went down to dinner; and coming down one of the last, from the top of the sweeping staircase, I was struck by the splendid, grandiose appearance of the dining-room, two storeys high, brilliantly lighted, and filled with the happy, good-humoured conversation of the guests taking their places at tables cleverly arranged to seat 310 people.

I had Daudet on my left and the Minister on my right. Poincaré was still suffering from influenza and told me that he had refused to dine with the President of the Republic yesterday, wishing to keep his strength for my banquet.

When we came to the dessert, Frantz Jourdain stood up and read out telegrams from Belgium, from Holland, from the Italian Goncourtists, Cameroni and Vittorio Pica, and from Germany, among which were these two lines from Georg Brandes: 'All Scandinavian writers will be with me today when I cry: "*Hail* the master initiator!"'

And in the midst of these telegrams, the homage of a Haarlem flower-grower, asking for permission to give my name to a new hyacinth.

And there were letters and telegrams from literary friends in

France who had been unable to attend the banquet: letters and tele-grams from Sully-Prudhomme, Claretie, Philippe Gille, Déroulède, Margueritte, Henri Lavedan, Theuriet, Larroumet, Marcel Prévost, Laurent Tailhade, Curel, Puvis de Chavannes, Alfred Stevens, Helleu, Alfred Bruneau, Gallé of Nancy, Colombey, and Mévisto.

Then the Minister began to speak, and made a speech such as no minister has ever made before when decorating a man of letters, denying that he was there as a minister and asking me almost humbly on the Government's behalf to allow myself to be de-corated.

The emotion which I felt at that moment was shared by the com-pany, who burst into frenzied applause. 'Never,' said some people who had attended a good many banquets, 'never have we witnessed such complete adherence on the part of those present!'

Then there was a toast from Heredia to my golden wedding with literature.

Then the expected speech by Clemenceau, saying that I, the knight-at-arms of Marie-Antoinette, had become, through my love of beauty and truth, the apologist of a Germinie Lacerteux and an Élisa, the women of the mob who had accompanied her to the scaffold. A somewhat fanciful argument in a speech so long that it made Daudet, who was beginning to suffer behind me, murmur: 'What a lecture!'

Then a completely reconciled Céard, speaking affectionately of our literary relations in the past.

Then, from Henri de Régnier, a delicate tribute.

Henri de Régnier was followed by Zola, who frankly admitted that his work owed something to me: and he who was now about to start writing *Rome* was kind enough to recall *Madame Gervaisais*.

After Zola, Daudet made the speech of a close friend, a speech full of tender affection.

Then I got to my feet and said these few words:

'Gentlemen and colleagues in art and literature. . . . I am in-capable of saying a dozen words before a dozen people. . . . And there are more than a dozen of you, gentlemen. . . . I can therefore only thank you in a few brief words for your affectionate sympathy and say that this evening which you have given me compensates me for many difficulties and sufferings in my literary career. . . . Thank you once more!'

We went upstairs for coffee and liqueurs; and there were embraces and reminders of the identity of people whose names and faces I had forgotten, introductions of Italians, Russians, and Japanese, grumbles from the sculptor Rodin, who complained of tiredness and spoke of his need of rest, a request from Albert Carré for an appointment to talk about *Manette Salomon*, thanks from Gung'l, Lagier's son, for the few lines in my *Journal* about his mother, and whispered anecdotes about the Vaudeville and the Gymnase from Antoine. And my hand was kissed by that madman Darzens, who has dedicated a book to me of which he has never given me a copy.

In the midst of all this I caught sight of myself in a mirror with a gentle stupefaction on my face, something of a Buddhist beatitude.

Eleven o'clock struck. I was dying of hunger, having eaten absolutely nothing. I knew that the Daudet brothers were going to have supper with the Barrès and the young Hugo couple; but I was afraid of casting the chill of old age over that gathering of turbulent youth. And then I hoped to find some chocolate at home, since I had told my women to make some while they were waiting for me; but when I arrived there was no chocolate left, and no cakes: everything had been eaten.

I came home with a magnificent basket of flowers in my hand, a basket placed before me during the meal and which, in my emotion, I had not looked at closely, simply reading the card from Mme Mirbeau who had sent it to me. Now, here at home, examining it more carefully, I see that it is a pile of little bunches of flowers intended for the buttonholes of the members of the committee. . . . How silly of me, how very silly of me!

*Thursday, 11 April*

At the end of the evening, just as I was going into the Daudets' ante-room to get my overcoat, Sherard, who was drunk but ice-cold, told me that he had written to Rodays to ask who the bounder was who had written the article on Oscar Wilde in the *Figaro*, so that he could give him a thrashing, waxing indignant that anyone should treat a man who had not been convicted in that way. And he started talking movingly about Wilde's mother, who was at the point of death, about his wife, who worshipped him, and about his two children. When I asked him whether he did not believe the accusation made against Wilde, he replied that he did not busy himself with what his friends did in public lavatories. And speaking of the profound distress this trial was causing him, making him ill and preventing him from eating and smoking—puffing at a fat cigar all the while—the strange, likeable lunatic helped me on with my coat, asking me to send a message of sympathy to Oscar Wilde.

*Monday, 3 June*

This evening Mme Sichel told me about her relations at Honfleur with Mme Aupick, Baudelaire's mother.

She portrayed for my benefit that tiny, delicate, charming woman, very slightly hunchbacked, with clumsy, gnarled hands big enough to hold half-a-dozen dominoes, and so short-sighted that she had to hold her sewing next to her nose.

Then she described her house, on a cliff-top at the foot of the Côte de Grâce, a site chosen by the General, a former ambassador a Constantinople, because it reminded him of the entrance of the Golden Horn: a house in which the General's room was hung with sailcloth and looked like a tent, while the other bedrooms were hung with *toile de Jouy*. The stables contained two state coaches whose horses Mme Aupick had been obliged to sell when she had been reduced to living on her widow's pension, and the maids used to take these coaches out into the courtyard for an airing every Saturday.

It seemed to the girl Mme Sichel was at that time that the old woman had a high opinion of her son's intelligence, but that she did not dare to express it because of the influence on her mind exerted by a certain M. Hémon, who regarded her son as a scoundrel who always talked of coming to see his mother, never came, and wrote to her only to ask for money.

A curious piece of information arising from this conversation is that Baudelaire's mother, who died after her son, died of the same disease, aphasia. This disposes of the legend which attributed to a life of excess this disease which he had simply inherited.

On several occasions the old woman said in her romantic language to Mme Sichel, whose Christian name is Laure: 'I am so sorry that my son does not want to marry, because I should very much like him to be your Petrarch.'

*Sunday, 10 November*

Someone or other has met fat little Zola bicycling in the Bois de Boulogne with his mistress, while his wife is travelling I do not know where by herself.

*Wednesday, 27 November*

Mme Zola, gay and young again, with a bunch of violets in her belt, called today to bring me news of Béhaine and to thank me very warmly indeed for the welcome the ambassador had given her. She told me that in the course of this quite extraordinary fortnight's escapade she had written a letter every day to her husband and he had written every day to her—doubtless after his bicycle ride with his mistress.

This evening at the Princess's, when I told Primoli about Mme Zola's visit, he burst out laughing, gave some knowing exclamations, and finished up by telling me that she had had a flirtation with an Italian journalist—a flirtation which he believed to have been platonic.

Throughout dinner the conversation was about Dumas's recovery or resurrection, and about the witty and brutal remarks he made on his return to life. Apparently when he recovered consciousness he exclaimed: 'Oh, all these women attached to my buttocks!'

After dinner Coppée, Porto-Riche, and I were chatting in the hall about Bornier's pitiful play when Primoli came up to us and said: 'Dumas is dead. . . . The Princess has just had a telegram giving her the news.'

*Thursday, 28 November*

Dumas's death has upset me. He died, I believe, as my brother died, from a disintegration of the brain at the base of the skull.

Heavens, what tyranny the theatre exerts over minds in France! To think that on receiving the news of Dumas's death, the President of the Republic, the King of France of the day, attending a first night at the Comédie-Française, walked out of the theatre with his wife and daughter and left his box empty all evening.

In this connexion, Daudet recalled that the news of Flaubert's death, like that of Dumas's, had reached his friends and the authorities of the Republic at the Théâtre-Français during a first night, and that authorities and friends alike had remained in their seats, had applauded the play being performed before them, had done their duty, some of them with heavy hearts, as a well-mannered audience.

*Monday, 2 December*

Colette Dumas is reported to have told her friends: 'People say that father had a fortune amounting to three million francs. . . . He hadn't as much as that, but he can't possibly have had less than eleven hundred thousand, seeing that the sale of his house and pictures produced a hundred thousand francs. . . .' And she hinted that he must have handed over a large sum of money direct to Mme Escalier.[1]

It was apparently this same Colette who, expressing her regret that Dumas had not asked to be buried at Villers-Cotterêts, where his father and his grandfather lay and where she would have liked to join him after death, was given this crumb of hope by Mme Escalier: 'I will keep a little place for you.'

*Monday, 30 December*

I have to admit it. At the present moment, in spite of my reputation and the literary interest presented by my *Journal*, I cannot find a home for it in any newspaper. Although I have not offered it to anyone but Simond, every newspaper editor in Paris knows that it is available for anyone who wants it, and nobody has asked for it.

[1] Mme Félix Escalier had married Dumas *fils* in June 1895, three months after the death of his first wife, the former Princess Naryschkine.

# 1896

'*A child! The eyes of a child!* . . . No, it's too much!' exclaimed
Daudet in connexion with the graveside speeches and newspaper
articles about Verlaine's funeral. 'A man who used to stab his lovers,
who, in a fit of bestial lust, once tore off his clothes and ran stark
naked after an Ardennes shepherd! . . . And that article by Barrès,
who has never written a line of verse and who acted as one of the
pall-bearers, Barrès who is fundamentally a champion of stylish
dressing and decent living. . . . The joker wrote that article just to
proclaim that he is the intellectual prince of the younger generation!'

*Sunday, 19 April*

Lorrain came to the Grenier today, and told me of a dinner at
Paillard's with Liane de Pougy and her protector at which a man
walking through the restaurant made a deep bow to Liane de Pougy,
who returned his greeting. It was the Tom Levis of Daudet's *Rois
en exil*.

'What's that?' exclaimed the lady's protector. 'You greet a
usurer?'

'Of course,' replied Liane, 'because I can't tell whether I shan't be
forced to borrow money from him tomorrow.'

'One pays one's bills . . . one doesn't greet a man who sells
money.'

'But everybody sells something', said Liane de Pougy. 'I sell my
body. . . . You are the only one who doesn't sell anything, and
that's because you're a fool.'

Then the conversation turned to Verlaine's alcoholism and the
softening effect it had had on his flesh, and Rodenbach told us that
Mallarmé had said that he would never forget the wet, soggy sound
made by the removal of the death-mask from his face, an operation
in which part of his beard and mouth had come away too.

This evening I dined at the Daudets'. Léon, suffering from a terrible headache, had gone to bed and did not have dinner with us. Mme Daudet, in a dreadfully irritable mood, made a scene because I had accepted two invitations to dinner on Thursday and Sunday next week at Zola's and Rodenbach's, invitations accepted at a time when I had thought she would be away and before this unexpected return from Italy. The fact of the matter is that she is upset about the publication of my *Journal* in the *Écho de Paris*, which she told me would refuse to print anything complimentary which I had written about her son.

*Tuesday, 26 May*

My birthday and the day of publication of the last volume of my *Journal*, in the midst of trouble which began with its appearance in the *Écho de Paris* and which will go on.

*Wednesday, 3 June*

Acknowledging receipt of his book *Rome*, I wrote today to Zola, paying him the usual compliments, but adding that his three books, *Lourdes, Rome, Paris*, were historical works rather than novels, that he should have made these books frankly historical and omitted the element of love, which in a serious work always appeared contemptible, and that for him, wishing as he did to leave the Rougon-Macquart series behind, this would have been a means of making a fresh start.

*Sunday, 7 June*

Lorrain described Liane de Pougy to me today as a whore who was subject to fits of cerebral passion. The story goes that she had fallen in love with Dr. Robin, who one day dined with an old mistress of his under the pretext of attending a scientific banquet. Liane heard about this and gave herself out of pique to the painter Béraud, a real ladies' man. Whereupon Robin told her that he was finished with her. There followed the scene one night beneath Mme Robin's windows, with Liane calling out to her and asking for her husband, then the poisoning, and finally the reconciliation. Lorrain, who was present at this last scene, said that she was charming in her invalid pallor, and that in a lake of tears she promised Robin that henceforth she would take only lovers whom she did not love.

*Sunday, 14 June*

Bonnet brought me a worried note from Daudet, telling me that there was an attack on my *Journal* in the *Figaro* by his brother Ernest, and asking me with a certain anxiety whether this attack would prevent me from coming to dinner this evening.

An attack signed Daudet, just when there are rumours of an quarrel between myself and the Daudets, is a dirty trick typical of that fellow Ernest, who is out to be as unpleasant to his brother as to me.

*Friday, 19 June*

Went to the cemetery, then to the dinner given by Fasquelle at Cubat's, in that house of La Païva's where I used to dine before the war with Gautier and Saint-Victor.

Zola, who ceded the place of honour to me, told me—not that I believed him—that he wanted to talk about my *Journal* in one of his articles in the *Figaro*, but that Ernest Daudet's article prevented him from doing so.

Claretie was very friendly and offered to put on *La Faustin* at the Théâtre-Français. At the end of the evening Antoine came and sat beside me, and told me that he was meaning to come and ask me for *La Faustin* for the Odéon, where he would engage a star to play the part.

Coming home, I found a solicitor's letter informing me that the Lauths were bringing an action for libel against me in connexion with an anecdote in my *Journal*.

Really, this ninth volume is causing me too much trouble, and I shall be lucky if I escape a recurrence of my liver complaint.

*Friday, 3 July*

A day spent with Mirbeau at the Clos-Saint-Blaise. The Robins were expected, but at the moment Robin belongs to Liane de Pougy. Montesquiou was due to leave with me at 2.25, but he arrived only in time for dinner. On the train afterwards, talking about the book in prose which he intends to write and which only he can write, a book of memories of old personalities of the Faubourg Saint-Germain, he told me countless anecdotes, including this one about a woman he knows who is very proud of her wealth. She engaged a little maid in a neat bonnet. After all the terms of service had been settled, just as the maid was going out she stopped at the door and said: 'I must ask Madame whether Madame *plays the dog*, because if so I can't accept those terms.' To *play the dog* is to go shopping with one's maid.

*Here ends the* Journal *of Edmond de Goncourt,
who died twelve days later at Champrosay*

# INDEX

OXFORD

## MORE OXFORD PAPERBACKS

Details of a selection of other books follow. A complete list of Oxford Paperbacks, including The World's Classics, Twentieth-Century Classics, OPUS, Past Masters, Oxford Authors, Oxford Shakespeare, and Oxford Paperback Reference, is available in the UK from the General Publicity Department, Oxford University Press (JN), Walton Street, Oxford OX2 6DP.

In the USA, complete lists are available from the Paperbacks Marketing Manager, Oxford University Press, 200 Madison Avenue, New York, NY 10016.

Oxford Paperbacks are available from all good bookshops. In case of difficulty, customers in the UK can order direct from Oxford University Press Bookshop, 116 High Street, Oxford, Freepost, OX1 4BR, enclosing full payment. Please add 10 per cent of published price for postage and packing.

# CONCEPTS AND CATEGORIES

*Isaiah Berlin*

## With an introduction by Bernard Williams

This second volume of Isaiah Berlin's four-volume *Selected Writings* contains most of his philosophical essays, apart from those already reissued in *Four Essays on Liberty*. It includes his early arguments against logical positivism, and later essays which more evidently reflect his lifelong interest in political theory, the history of ideas, and the philosophy of history. And in two related pieces he gives his view of the nature of philosophy's task, best summed up in his own words: 'The goal of philosophy is always the same, to assist men to understand themselves and thus operate in the open, and not wildly, in the dark.'

'No one writes about large and abstract matters in a more richly nutritive and idiosyncratic way.' Anthony Quinton

'Isaiah Berlin's many admirers and readers will be glad to have this book; and those too young to have had the chance to listen to his lectures might well begin their acquaintance by reading it.' *British Book News*

# NINETEENTH CENTURY PLAYS

## Second Edition

### *Edited by George Rowell*

This volume contains *Black-Ey'd Susan*, Douglas Jerrold's nautical melodrama; Bulwer-Lytton's skilful comedy *Money*; Tom Taylor's play that tackles a theme of some social importance, *The Ticket-of-Leave Man*; T. W. Robertson's *Caste*, the one Victorian comedy that has had a place in the repertory for over a century; and James Albery's light-hearted *Two Roses*. Half the plays included here are, typically of the period, collaborations or adaptations: Charles Reade and Tom Taylor's theatrical comedy *Masks and Faces*; Dion Boucicault's Irish 'spectacular' *The Colleen Bawn*; C. H. Hazlewood's 'Society melodrama' based on Miss Braddon's novel *Lady Audley's Secret*; *The Bells* by Leopold Lewis, with the role that Henry Irving made melodramatically his own; and Sydney Grundy's sentimental comedy *A Pair of Spectacles*.


# BECKETT/BECKETT

## *Vivian Mercier*

Vivian Mercier is, like his subject the playwright and Nobel Prize winner Samuel Beckett, a displaced Anglo-Irishman. Out of this shared background and a deep understanding of Beckett's writings, he has woven an account of the playwright and his work that is often humorous, admiring yet critical, and sensitive to that subtle strain of contradictoriness which provides a structure for his study as it does, he believes, for Beckett's work.

'Vivian Mercier's qualifications for writing a book about Beckett are numerous and impressive . . . *Beckett/Beckett* provides a valuable addition to the published material on Beckett.' *Times Literary Supplement*

# FOUR ESSAYS ON LIBERTY

## Isaiah Berlin

The four essays are 'Political Ideas in the Twentieth Century'; 'Historical Inevitability'; 'Two Concepts of Liberty', a ringing manifesto for pluralism and individual freedom; and 'John Stuart Mill and the Ends of Life'. There is also a long and masterly Introduction written specially for this collection, in which the author replies to his critics.

'The densely-written, richly allusive style perfectly matches the contents; practically every paragraph introduces us to half a dozen new ideas and as many thinkers—the landscape flashes past, peopled with familiar and unfamiliar people, all arguing incessantly.' *New Society*

# MONTESQUIEU

## Judith N. Shklar

Charles Louis de Secondat, Baron de Montesquieu (1689–1755) was perhaps the most authentic of the political thinkers of the Enlightenment. He believed passionately in toleration and in the moral benefits of science, and constructed a naturalistic system of political science based on a study of history, comparitive government, and psychology. His *magnum opus* is undoubtably *The Spirit of the Laws* (1748), which examines the concept of law as both cause and effect of the structure of political systems.

Inspiring everything he wrote was a profound hatred for, and fear of, despotism, which he regarded as the supreme evil, and which served him as a moral standard for judging regimes. Of those, he considered England the best modern example, and his account of its constitution which was to provide a model for the American constitution of 1787, inspired many of the French liberals of his day.

*Past Masters*

# THE AGE OF ENLIGHTENMENT

## The Eighteenth-Century Philosophers

### *Isaiah Berlin*

'The intellectual power, honesty, lucidity, courage and disinterested love of the truth of the most gifted thinkers of the eighteenth century remain to this day without parallel. Their age is one of the best and most hopeful episodes in the life of mankind.'

These are the closing words of Isaiah Berlin's introduction to his selection, with running commentary, from the major works of Locke, Berkeley, Hume and other leading eighteenth-century philosophers. This book provides an excellent starting-point for the study of the Enlightenment, letting the leading lights of the period speak in their own (readable) words, and providing background information and elucidation where necessary.

# MAX ERNST: BEYOND SURREALISM

## A Retrospective of the Artist's Books and Prints

### *Introduction by Vartan Gregorian*

During the latter part of 1986 a major retrospective of the graphic work of surrealist artist Max Ernst was held in New York. This book is the catalogue of that major exhibition, which contained more than 150 original etchings, lithographs, collages, and books from the artist's private collection, and sculptures lent by galleries throughout the world. Extensively illustrated throughout, it contains essays by three major American critics, *Robert Rainwater, Evan Maurer,* and *Anne Hyde Greet,* on Ernst's development as a graphic artist.

The book includes 24 colour plates and 165 halftones.

## STRINDBERG: A BIOGRAPHY

*Michael Meyer*

This outstanding biography of Strindberg reveals previously unknown details about his three tempestuous marriages, his dabblings in the occult, his recurrent bouts of madness, and his friendships with Gauguin, Munch, and Delius, that were the touchstones of his tormented life.

'This will remain the standard life in English for many years.' Anthony Storr in the *Spectator*

Oxford Lives


## SELECTED LETTERS

Marcel Proust

### Edited by Philip Kolb
### Translated by Ralph Mannheim

These are the letters of Proust's formative years as a writer: in his relationships with his parents, with schoolfriends, with the literary figures whose approval he courted, Proust displays all the emotional sensitivity and penetrating social analysis that were to become the hallmarks of his famous masterpiece.

'will be of special interest to those who have already read Proust's novel in English and found themselves wanting to know more about the emotional and stylistic workshop from which this supremely complex artefact emerged . . . [an] extraordinarily revealing volume' *Times Literary Supplement*

# DIDEROT

## Peter France

Denis Diderot was one of the most brilliant minds of the French Enlightenment, on which his editorship of the *Encyclopedia* gave him a unique vantage-point. In no man were the currents of eighteenth-century thought more intensely present.

This book takes account of the full range of Diderot's writing, from politics to the theatre, from physiology to painting. It stresses the critical impulse which lies at the heart of his work, and pays particular attention to the complexity of his writing, with its manifold and often contradictory voices, and to the nature of his demands on his readers.

'*Diderot* is a provocative study which makes a genuine attempt to give a rapid appraisal of Diderot's breadth. The book never fails to interest.' *Journal of European Studies*

*Past Masters*


# MONTAIGNE

## Peter Burke

Montaigne created a new literary genre—the essay—and his own essays have had a widespread influence on thought and literature since the Renaissance. In them he put forward ideas on a wide variety of subjects viewed as highly unconventional by his contemporaries, and because of this he has often been treated as a 'modern' born out of his time. Peter Burke replaces him in his cultural context, and shows what he had in common with his Renaissance contemporaries.

'this brisk and lively introduction . . . provides, in a tiny compass, a balanced view and a clear and eminently readable account of the issues Montaigne tried to grapple with' *British Book News*

'a handbook for students of unique wisdom and tolerance' *Tablet*

*Past Masters*

# JAMES JOYCE
## *Richard Ellmann*

### Winner of the James Tait Black and the Duff Cooper Memorial Prizes

Professor Ellmann has thoroughly revised and expanded his classic biography to incorporate the considerable amount of new information tht has come to light in the twenty-two years since it was first published. The new material deals with most aspects of Joyce's life: his literary aims, a failed love affair, domestic problems, and his political views.

'The greatest literary biography of the century.' Anthony Burgess

'Richard Ellmann's superb biography . . . [is] a great feat of twentieth-century literary scholarship.' Christopher Ricks

'A superlatively good biography of Joyce.' Frank Kermode, *Spectator*


# THE CONCISE OXFORD DICTIONARY OF FRENCH LITERATURE
## *Edited by Joyce M. H. Reid*

This abridgement of the classic *Oxford Companion to French Literature* preserves the unique quality of the original work and at the same time extends its scope with the addition of some 150 new entries to bring it up to date. The *Dictionary* retains the distinctive features of the *Companion,* including its coverage of a great variety of major and minor writers, genres, and movements in French literature. Like its parent volume, the *Dictionary* contains entries on other relevant aspects of French history, philosophy, and culture.

# PROUST

## Derwent May

Marcel Proust's great novel, *Remembrance of Things Past,* is not only an epic work of lyrical reminiscence, it is also a dazzling and witty portrait of French character and society. Derwent May explores the historical and social aspects of Proust's novel, and examines the relationship between Proust's ideas and those of the narrator of the book, Marcel, particularly emphasising the way in which the book's style reflects its content.

'A delightful little introduction and celebration of one of the great books of our century.' *The Times*

Past Masters

# SELECTED LETTERS OF OSCAR WILDE

## Edited by Rupert Hart-Davis

When Sir Rupert Hart-Davis's magnificent edition was first published in 1962 Cyril Connolly called it 'a must for everyone who is seriously interested in the history of English literature—or European morals.' That edition of more than 1,000 letters is now out of print; from it Sir Rupert has culled a representative sample from each period of Wilde's life, 'giving preference', as he says in his Introduction to this selection, 'to those of literary interest, to the most amusing, and to those that throw light on his life and work.' The long letter to Lord Alfred Douglas, usually known as *De Profundis,* is again printed in its entirety.

'In Mr. Hart-Davis's *The Letters of Oscar Wilde,* the true Wilde emerges again for us, elegant, witty, paradoxical and touchingly kind . . . I urge all those who are interested in the contrasts between pride and humiliation, between agony and laughter, to acquire this truly remarkable book.' Harold Nicolson, *Observer*

# BERKELEY

## *J. O. Urmson*

Unlike Dr Johnson in his famous jibe, J. O. Urmson achieves an unusually sympathetic assessment of Berkeley's philosophy by viewing it against a wider intellectual background than is customary. He sees Berkeley's work as a serious critical analysis of the scientific thought of Newton and his predecessors, and of its metaphysical basis; and he gives a clear account of the relationship between Berkeley's metaphysics and his analysis of the concepts of science and common sense.

'Professor Urmson's *Berkeley* is welcome, not just because he makes Berkeley's view that there is no such thing as matter perfectly intelligible and rather persuasive . . . but because he devotes some time to explaining the moral and political positions which Berkeley thought materialism threatened.' *Listener*

Past Masters

# PASCAL

## *Alban Krailsheimer*

Alban Krailsheimer opens his study of Pascal's life and work with a description of Pascal's religious conversion, and then discusses his literary, mathematical and scientific achievements, which culminated in the acute analysis of human character and the powerful reasoning of the *Pensées*. He argues that after his conversion Pascal put his previous work in a different perspective and saw his, and in general all, human activity in religious terms.

'Mr Krailsheimer's enthusiasm is eloquent and infectious.' *Observer*

Past Masters